'Everyone concerned with innovation will want this book. Giving equal weight to products and services, the authors' lively and authoritative approach builds a host of "real" examples onto a comprehensive foundation of principles. . . . Teachers will welcome its structure and rigour, students will welcome its accessibility and examples but, perhaps most important of all, practitioners will find practical tools and techniques to help them make a difference!'

Professor Mike Gregory, CBE
Head of the Manufacturing and Management Division of the University Engineering Department and of the Institute for Manufacturing
Cambridge University
Cambridge, UK

'A clearly written and practical handbook for companies and teams charged with developing new businesses. Goffin and Mitchell present a simple, yet compelling, framework that will help both manufacturing and services companies identify and nurture new growth opportunities.'

Mike Northcott
Director, PPO (Product Processes Organization) Transformation Services
Hewlett-Packard Corporation, USA

'Until now there has been the lack of an overall strategic framework through which practitioners in business can fully understand the innovation process. The authors are to be congratulated on the way they have used case studies to illuminate this complex area and have linked to academic research in a number of disciplines. This book should be an invaluable and essential tool to those seeking to innovate successfully.'

Walter Herriot, OBE
Managing Director
St John's Innovation Centre
Cambridge, UK

'This new book provides managers with detailed insights into the challenge of managing innovation. The selection of practical management tools and techniques covered is excellent, as are the extensive case studies on how companies are taking steps to become more innovative. Innovation management is a constantly changing field and it is good to see an up-to-date book with a prag   '   fresh approach.'

Bob Weedon
Director, World Wide Chipset
Texas Instruments, USA

Innovation Management

Strategy and Implementation Using the Pentathlon Framework

Keith Goffin and Rick Mitchell

First published 2005 by
PALGRAVE MACMILLAN
Houndmills, Basingstoke, Hampshire RG21 6XS and
175 Fifth Avenue, New York, N.Y. 10010
Companies and representatives throughout the world

PALGRAVE MACMILLAN is the global academic imprint of the Palgrave Macmillan division of St. Martin's Press, LLC and of Palgrave Macmillan Ltd. Macmillan® is a registered trademark in the United States, United Kingdom and other countries. Palgrave is a registered trademark in the European Union and other countries.

ISBN-13: 978–1–4039–1260–2
ISBN 10: 1–4039–1260–2

This book is printed on paper suitable for recycling and made from fully managed and sustained forest sources.

A catalogue record for this book is available from the British Library.

A catalog record for this book is available from the Library of Congress
Library of Congress Catalog Card Number: 2005049756

10   9   8   7   6   5   4   3   2
14   13   12   11   10   09   08   07   06   05

Printed and bound in Great Britain by
Creative Print & Design (Wales), Ebbw Vale

Brief Contents

Contents

List of Case Studies

Each chapter includes four or more short 'box case studies' and one main case study. The main chapter case studies look at themes raised in the chapter and include a set of assignment questions. These are designed to help the reader generalize some of the ideas from the case study. The majority of the cases are new and based on interviews with the managers involved. A deliberate international mix of examples from both the service and manufacturing sectors has been selected.

# Preface

This book is based on a framework of innovation management – the Innovation Pentathlon – which was developed from our research and has been used extensively in our work with companies. Our research showed that senior managers felt the need for an overall framework to help them understand the innovation performance of their companies, as well as tools and techniques to improve it. For example, the director of one company in the engineering sector said he needed a 'systematic way to encourage and manage innovation'. At a meeting in 2000, where over 20 European universities presented the results of their research to industrialists, a senior manager from the Glaxo-SmithKline pharmaceutical company commented forcibly. He said that, as a manager, he needed integrative tools for innovation management, not the *ad hoc* collection of 'snippets of best practice', which he felt he was given by university researchers. In discussions with other managers, it emerged that they recognized that there were many facets to managing innovation: it involves strategy (for example, whether to be first-to-market, or to be a fast-follower); people management (for example, organizing and motivating teams); and good project management (for example, in striving to meet challenging time-to-market goals). Integrating the many facets of innovation management is the challenge, if the needs of the real world are to be matched with academic rigour.

Researchers have looked at innovation in many ways. Economists have studied how innovations affect industries and also the contribution innovation makes to economic performance. Organizational theorists have looked at how a company culture supports creativity and innovation and at the role of teamwork in this. Similarly, operations management researchers have investigated which practices can be used to speed new product development (NPD) and drawn parallels with theories of production management. Each type of research gives pointers on specific aspects of innovation, but practitioners must also deal with the 'bigger picture' – how to choose the combination of individual approaches which will increase the overall performance of an organization.

This book was primarily written to meet the needs of MBA students following courses on the strategic management of innovation, or conducting in-company projects related to innovation management. However, the contents will also be very relevant to managers in either the service or manufacturing sectors, who want to boost the innovation performance of their organizations. Specifically, the book addresses how to develop and successfully implement an innovation strategy and it borrows ideas and concepts from a range of disciplines, from economics, to organizational behaviour, and change management. Throughout the book we have tried to provide pertinent examples of innovation management and there are four or more half-page 'box cases' and one multi-page case study per chapter. In writing these cases we have deliberately sought to achieve parity between the manufacturing and service sectors – too often the service sector is not done justice in writings about innovation management. In addition, we have tried to provide a truly international mix of cases.

There are no 'quick fixes' in a complex field such as innovation management. Therefore, the challenge for managers is not just to adopt the ideas in this book but to adapt and blend them to fit the context their organizations face. We wish them every success in meeting that challenge.

KEITH GOFFIN
RICK MITCHELL

Acknowledgements

To write a book aimed at MBA students and practising managers requires a high level of contact with both of these groups, in order to try and understand their needs. In our teaching and research we are fortunate to come into constant contact with excellent students, and managers who are not only very good at what they do but are also reflective on the issues they face. We have benefited enormously from interacting with both these groups, and from their ideas, probing questions and the experiences they have shared with us.

A number of our MBA students have directly helped us with preparing material for the book and in providing comments on drafts: many thanks to Danu Chotikapanich, Micha Dannenhauer, Rodrigo Gamarci, Synthiea Kaldi, Helmut Kraft, Hector Martinez, Alejo Ribalta and David Watsham. Several of our doctoral students, particularly Ursula Koners and Bertram Lohmüller, helped us by identifying the key literature on specific aspects of innovation management and through generating new ideas from their own research.

The Pentathlon framework that provides the backbone for this book was developed from research generously supported by the Anglo-German Foundation. Thanks also to the many managers who were interviewed as part of this research and contributed many of the ideas about how a framework for innovation management could be used.

A large number of managers in industry have given up precious time to help us in with the case studies, or have provided material and ideas through being regular guest speakers at our lectures. Thanks to the following: Patty Arellano (Texas Instruments), Stefanie Bartle (Mondial), Seth Bishop (Leapfrog), Simon Bradley (Domino Printing Sciences), Gary Calverley (Unilever), Mark Chizlett (Britannia), Vorapant Chotikapanich (Cobra International), John Clayton (Unilever), Malcolm Colbeck (Unilever), Dave Cope (Domino Printing Sciences), Martin Cserba (21Torr Agency); Massimo Fumarola (Fiat-Iveco), Klaus Fischer (Fischer GmbH), John Fisher (PA Consultancy), Torsten Herzberg (Vodafone), Dr Christiane Hipp (Vodafone), Erik Hoppenbrouwer (Organon), David Humphries (PDD), Dr Amin Khan (Malaysia Airlines), John Lagerling (NTT–DoCoMo), Mr T. Linganatham, (Texas Instruments Malaysia), Dr Michael Mallon (Fruit of the Loom), Steve Marriott (Domino Printing Sciences), Bob McKune (Texas Instruments), Liam Mifsud (Equant), Dr Edwin Moses (Oxford Asymmetry), Sachin Mulay (Wipro Technologies), Wim Obouter (Micro-mobility), John O'Neill (AXA), Dr Mario Polywka (EvotecOAI), Dr Helmut Rapp (Sidler GmbH & Co.), Klaus Stemig (Mondial Assistance GmbH); Dr Magnus Schoeman (UK Passport Office), Daniel Scuka (Wireless Watch Japan), Nigel Spencer (Unilever), Chris Towns (Clarks), Mr A. Vasudevan (Wipro Technologies), Eva Weber (Vodafone), Bob Weedon (Texas Instruments), Catherine Whelan (AXA),

Howard Whitesmith (Domino), Werner Widmann (Agilent Technologies), David Williams (Richardsons, Sheffield) and Michael Yonker (Texas Instruments).

To help keep a practical focus to our work, three managers assisted in reviewing early drafts, providing contacts in industry, and in helping with the preparation of case study material. Their help was invaluable and so many thanks to: Trudy Lloyd (Synectics), Mike Northcott (Hewlett-Packard) and William Pipkin (Pipkin Associates).

Matching pragmatism with academic rigour is essential and we are fortunate to have supportive colleagues who looked at many drafts and helped us to get our ideas straight. Professor Dr Harald Hagemann (Hohenheim University), Professor Dr Cornelius Herstatt (Hamburg-Harburg), and David Probert, Dr Rob Phaal, Pete Fraser, Clare Farrukh and Dr Francis Hunt (all of Cambridge University), and Dr Adegoke Oke (Cranfield), all contributed material and gave us useful ideas. Thanks to Professor Dr Rolf Pfeiffer (Reutlingen) who jointly conducted the original research from which the Pentathlon framework originated. Dr Ralph Levene (Cranfield), Professor Paul Millier (EMLyon), and Chris van der Hoven (Cranfield) also contributed ideas on how best to present the Pentathlon. Particular thanks to Dr Fred Lemke (Germany); Professor Dr Udo Staber (Germany), Dr Marek Szwejczewski (Cranfield) and David Walker (Giraffe Consultants, UK) for reviewing drafts and giving us their insights. Anna Faherty of Palgrave Macmillan read and commented on our work and provided many useful ideas on how to develop the style of this book. Our anonymous academic reviewer also took the time and effort to make many useful and concrete suggestions. Copyright issues were managed largely by Carole Hutchings. And 'last but not least', many thanks to Susanne Jochum for doing the bulk of the checking of the manuscript, the preparation of the associated teaching material and having an ever-alert eye for detail.

The authors and publishers are grateful to the following organizations for permission to reproduce copyright material:

Figure 1.1 is used by permission of John Wiley & Sons Inc., from *Bringing Innovation to Market: How to Break Corporate and Customer Barriers*, by Sheth, J.N. and Ram, R. Copyright © (1987, Sheth and Ram).

Figure 2.1 is used with permission from the European Commission Copyright © 2000.

Figure 3.2 is used by permission of Pearson Education Limited, from *Operations Management*, by Slack *et al*. Copyright © 1998, Pearson Education.

Figure 3.3 is used by permission of Word Scientific Publishing Co. Pte Ltd, 'The Incidence and Effects of Innovation in Services; Evidence from Germany', from *International Journal of Innovation Management*, vol. 4, no. 4 (December 2000), fig. 3, p. 425. www.worldscinet.com/ijim/ijim.shtml.

Figure 4.2 is used by permission of Pearson Education Limited, from *Exploring Corporate Strategy*, by Gerry Johnson. Copyright © 1997, Pearson Education.

Figure 4.6 is reprinted (with modifications) by permission of Industrial Research Institute, Inc. from *Research-Technology Management*.

Figure 4.7 is used by permission of McKinsey & Company, from *Innovation: The Attacker's Advantage*, by Richard N. Foster. Copyright © 1986, McKinsey & Co. Inc.

Figure 4.12 is adapted and reprinted by permission from *Mastering the Dynamics of Innovation*, by J.M. Utterback. Copyright © 1996 by the Harvard Business School Publishing Corporation; all rights reserved.

Figure 4.13 is adapted and reprinted by permission from *The Innovator's Dilemma*, by C.M. Christensen. Copyright © 1997 by the Harvard Business School Publishing Corporation; all rights reserved.

Figure 5.1 is reprinted (with modifications) by permission of PFD on behalf of © Hutchinson, 1964.

Figure 5.3 is reprinted (with modifications) by permission of Sage Publications Ltd from Goffin, K., 'Repertory Grid Technique' in Partington, D. (ed.), *Essential Skills for Management Research*, Sage, London, 2002. Copyright © Keith Goffin 2002.

Figure 5.5 is adapted and reprinted by permission of *Harvard Business Review*, from 'Creating Breakthroughs at 3M', by von Hippel, E., Thomke, S. and Sonnack, M., vol. 77, no. 5 (September–October 1999), pp. 47–57. Copyright © 1999 by the Harvard Business School Publishing Corporation; all rights reserved.

Figure 8.2 is used by permission of Pearson Education Limited, from *Exploring Strategic Change*, by Balogun *et al.* Copyright © 1999, Pearson Education.

The case studies Richardsons Sheffield, UK, and Sidler GmbH & Co., were modified from Goffin, K., Lee-Mortimer, A. and New, C., *Managing Product Innovation for Competitive Advantage*, Haymarket Business Publications Ltd: London, 1999. Used with permission.

The case study Lever Faberge – Unilever was modified from Szwejczewski, M., Wheatley, M., and Goffin, K., *Process Innovation in UK Manufacturing: Best Practice Makes Perfect* (London: Department of Trade and Industry, dti/pub 5468/15k/06/01/np, June 2001). Used with permission of the DTI.

The case study Equant was reprinted (with modifications) by permission of Sage Publications Ltd from Goffin, K., 'Repertory Grid Technique' in Partington, D. (ed.), *Essential Skills for Management Research*, Sage, London, 2002. Copyright © Keith Goffin 2002.

Every effort has been made to trace all the copyright-holders, but if any have been inadvertently overlooked the publishers will be pleased to make the necessary arrangements at the first opportunity.

Cranfield, Bedford, UK   KEITH GOFFIN
                                                            RICK MITCHELL

1 The Role of Innovation

'innovation – n., introducing something new.'

(*Oxford English Dictionary*)

Introduction

Innovation, innovation . . . innovation. There have been countless management books and articles published in recent years on the need for companies to become more innovative. It is also widely recognized that, without innovation, companies will quickly lose their competitive edge. Peter Drucker has stated that although the importance of innovation is clear, how to achieve it remains a largely unanswered question.[1] In practice, recognizing the need to become more innovative and achieving it are two vastly different things, as many managers have realized. Increasing the capacity of an organization to be innovative – whether it is in the manufacturing or the service sector – is a real challenge. Consequently this book concentrates on presenting leading-edge techniques and examples of how to meet the challenge of developing and implementing an innovation strategy.

This book was written to meet the needs of MBA students following courses on the strategic management of innovation, or conducting in-company projects related to innovation management. The content of the book will also be very relevant to managers in either the service or manufacturing sectors. Specifically, it addresses how to develop and successfully implement an innovation strategy. It provides both MBA students and managers with selected tools and techniques and examples of managing innovation, which are based on the findings of the latest management research. The choice of which tools and techniques to present was based not only on an extensive review of the literature but also on the authors' own experience in industry, teaching and research. In making these choices we have focused on the approaches that really can improve the process of innovation management.

Managing innovation is complex and so there are no 'quick fixes'. The challenges with managing innovation are also compounded by the fact that many ideas that are effective in one organization cannot be easily transferred; managers must adapt them to the situation their company faces. This book describes the results of management research and it does not try to oversimplify the issues. Where the results of research are ambiguous, or solutions to innovation problems are difficult to manage, these are clearly identified.

Companies aiming to increase their innovation levels need to improve the management of a number of areas, including the generation of ideas and their quick implementation. In this sense, innovation management is like competing in an event like the Olympic pentathlon; excellent performance in one discipline alone will not guarantee a gold medal. Too many companies have focused on just one area of innovation management – for example on improving new product development – when there are other aspects that are equally important. Leading companies take a broad view of innovation management, considering a range of issues from idea generation, to implementation, to business culture. We have categorized the main issues into five different areas, which we will refer to as the Innovation Pentathlon Framework. This framework, which is presented in this chapter, forms the structure of the book.

This chapter introduces the role and characteristics of innovation, and the 'art' of managing innovation. It covers issues that are equally important to companies in both the service and manufacturing sectors, including:

▸ The drivers of the need for innovation.
▸ Characteristics of innovation.
▸ An overview of the management research on innovation.
▸ The Innovation Pentathlon Framework.
▸ The structure of this book.
▸ A detailed case study on NTT-DoCoMo, a Japanese company in the service sector, which shows how a broad approach to innovation can lead to successful market segmentation.

Innovation Drivers

Four main factors drive market change and, in combination, create the need for innovation. Figure 1.1 shows these to be: technological advances, changing customers, intensified competition and the changing business environment.

Technological Advances

The rate at which knowledge is being created has accelerated and there are numerous examples of where new technologies are having a major influence on markets. For instance, logistics will be revolutionized by RFID technology – radio frequency identification labels – which automatically transmit information about the nature and location of articles. New technologies can also create new industries and both biotechnology and multi-media have created significant employment over the last decade.[3] Companies need to constantly monitor new technology, as it may influence or potentially transform their markets. Existing technologies must also be considered, as today these are being more widely applied. For instance, sophisticated electronics are now an important aspect of car design. With such a vast array of technological developments taking place, even multinational companies that used to conduct all their own basic research are finding that they cannot keep abreast of developments, using internal resources alone. This means organizations need to become good at tracking the

Figure 1.1   Drivers of the need for innovation

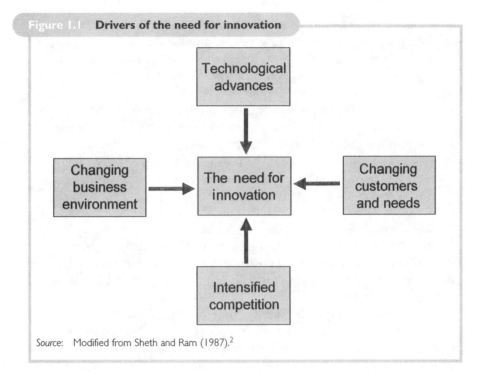

Source: Modified from Sheth and Ram (1987).[2]

progress of a wide range of technologies. This includes monitoring both the performance of the technologies they currently use and those which may replace existing technologies.

Technology is equally important for service companies and R&D is increasingly having a major impact on how service companies do business. For example, banks are developing technologies that will allow them to have customized services for specific customer segments. Fedex, the leading courier services company, has long recognized the importance of investing in technology and was at the leading edge of the development of hand-held bar-coding devices, which enabled them to provide the first parcel tracking capability. Bank of America and some other service organizations have created innovation departments to monitor new technology and test it with actual customers (see box case: 'Metro's Future Store').

> **Box case 1.1   Metro AG's 'Future Store' – prototyping a supermarket**
>
> Technology can help companies in the service sector make it much easier for their customers to receive a service and reduce costs. Take the retail trade, where RFID 'smart-tag' technology is poised to make a big impact. Chip manufacturer Intel and supply-chain software giant SAP have joined forces with the world's fifth largest retailer, the German company Metro AG, to create a fully running prototype of the supermarket of the future, in the small town of Rheinberg, Germany.[4]

Products in the supermarket are all labelled with RFID in order to automate stock-keeping and make shopping easier for customers. Each shopping trolley has a touch screen computer with a scanner and, as the customer selects each item, it is scanned in. The computer displays a range of useful information for the customer. This includes detailed product information on the item scanned, the total amount spent, special offers, the customer's 'standard' shopping list, and a map with the customer's position in the store. One big advantage is that the items in the trolley do not need to be unloaded at the cashier's desk and this saves time for the customer. The trolley's computer automatically indicates the total amount to be paid and, having paid the cashier, the customer can simply push their trolley to their car. Queuing is virtually eliminated.

Metro has named the project the 'Future Store Initiative' and through the extensive use of technology is looking for major improvements in supply-chain efficiency. The main limitation at the moment is that smart tags cost 0.5 euros each and are therefore too expensive to be used for every individual item in every supermarket. The cost of tags is expected to fall quickly, though, as they are more widely used.

Manufacturing companies often use prototypes to gain detailed customer feedback on new products. Extending the idea to the testing of a new service concept is a bold approach that few service companies have yet contemplated. Metro's prototype is helping the company to identify: 'real advantages for both the retail industry and consumers'.[5] And the rollout of the concept across other locations in Germany is expected soon.

Changing Customers and Needs

The second driver of innovation is the changing characteristics and requirements of customers. The demographics for the next 50 years show that many markets will evolve. For instance the aging population in many countries will have different requirements, and the size and nature of many consumer markets will change. In contrast, other markets (for example Southeast Asia) are largely made up of young consumers with different aspirations. The earnings in many newly industrialized countries will soar (as short-term economic difficulties are weathered) and demand for particular products and services will consequently develop. The Whirlpool Corporation has recently launched the 'Ideale', the world's cheapest automatic washing machine, which retails at around $150 in countries such as Brazil and China.[6]

Changing customers also means that traditional market segments are disappearing or fragmenting and companies will need to adjust their product ranges accordingly – for example, car manufacturers now target over 15 key segments in the USA, as opposed to only five in the late 1960s. Contrast this to the type of market faced by Henry Ford! At the same time, there are additional pressures such as customer demand for more environmentally acceptable products and services. As basic needs are met, there is an additional challenge to innovation – determining customers' hidden needs.

Intensified Competition

The third driver shown in Figure 1.1 is the evolving nature and sources of competition. Logistics costs have plummeted and, consequently, 'safe, home markets' are being threatened by foreign competition. Companies may also face competition from sources normally outside their industries. An example of this is the bicycle industry in Japan where a new entrant, Nippon Bicycle, has taken a significant share of the market by offering made-to-order, highly customized mountain bikes with a fast delivery time. Interestingly, Nippon is owned by the consumer electronics company Panasonic, which has made use of its expertise in logistics to become successful in a new market.

Changing Business Environments

Finally, business environments are changing. Worldwide, markets are becoming more open as the market economy is embraced by most governments and through the efforts to reduce tariffs by trade groupings such as the European Union and North American Free Trade Association. Additionally, the regulations affecting specific markets are being relaxed in many Western countries (for example, the deregulation of transport, post and telecommunications). An example of changing regulations that could drastically change one market is the US Food and Drug Administration's (FDA) planned faster approval of generic drugs.

In the last decade, an additional factor in the business environment has emerged which also influences the need for innovation. Management has largely focused on cost-cutting through a reduction of the resources required for key business processes. Many companies have redesigned their business processes and significant efficiency gains have been achieved. A continued focus on efficiency gains will only bring diminishing returns and cost-reduction myopia needs to be replaced by a focus on increasing revenues and profits. For many companies the most promising approach is to develop more new products and services.

A clear symptom of the amount of market change is the short product life-cycles and high levels of new product failures reported in many markets. Therefore, companies in both service and manufacturing are becoming more dependent on constant innovation. A recent survey of manufacturing managers showed that the ability to introduce new products was perceived as one of the key challenges facing European companies.[7] Survey evidence from the service sector in Europe also shows that innovation is becoming more important and is perceived by managers as the most important way to improve the quality of services to customers.[8]

Responding to the Need

Although the need for innovation is clear to see, responding to this need is challenging. The *Financial Times* suggested that 'there is no doubt that properly managed innovation can bring industry the solutions which it needs and help it to achieve a competitive edge'.[9] However, is 'properly managed innovation' easy to achieve and how are companies attempting to manage innovation?

To be innovative, companies can choose to invest in research and development (R&D). Different industries make very different levels of investment. Increasing R&D spending can lead to more innovation but it should be recognized that such investments are inputs to the innovation process. They do not guarantee outputs or commercial success, as innovation performance is also very dependent on the people in an organization. Therefore, many companies are taking other steps to stimulate innovation.

Companies' Innovation Management – Examples

Companies are taking steps to improve their innovation performance and of the management initiatives, the 3M Company's highly publicized initiatives have become icons of innovation management. In order to start to understand the scope of innovation, it is useful to review some of these service and manufacturing companies' initiatives, starting with 3M:

▸ If your company's portfolio already has over 60,000 products, where do you start if you want to increase innovative levels rapidly? The 3M Company has launched a host of initiatives to drive innovation. The cornerstone of 3M's management of innovation has been a focus on a clear measure of innovation performance – the percentage of revenues generated by new products. For example in 1995 the company aimed (and succeeded) in generating 30 per cent of revenues from products less than four years old. In 1997 tougher goals were set including 10 per cent of revenues from products less than one year old. The use of tough, financially based measures is only one aspect of 3M's initiatives. Their approach to stimulating creativity is legendary – employees are allowed 10 per cent of their time to work on ideas and projects that they have themselves devised. Ideas developed during this 'free' time can be nominated for special funding.

▸ Service firms and organizations are becoming more focused on process innovation and are looking at how technology and new approaches can both speed and improve customer service. Companies such as American Express and Mastercard are looking at how new 'contactless' technology can avoid credit cards having to be swiped through a reader and thus speed up the process of payment. Hospitals are increasingly applying process management concepts, which were originally developed in the manufacturing sector, such as just-in-time management.

▸ Consultants Arthur D. Little recently organized a convention of research-intensive companies including Philips, Renault, Nestlé, ABB, Audi, 3M, Nokia, BASF & BMW. These manufacturers identified three common aims in their innovation management.[10] Firstly, they wanted to develop 'seamless innovation processes', which break down 'barriers' between departments such as R&D, manufacturing and marketing. Secondly, these firms are pushing to make their R&D departments more commercially aware. Thirdly, each company is making more use of external sources of technology.

❑ Budget airlines such as Ryanair and Easyjet can be said to have rewritten the rules of the air travel business. Prices for air travel have been slashed through a focus on 'no-frills' service, flying to airports with lower or subsidized handling fees, and also improved business processes (for example maximizing aircraft utilization).

❑ Some companies are announcing that they are focusing more on increasing new product output. For example, Vorwerk, a household products company decided that it needed to renew its entire product portfolio within two years.[11] The automotive manufacturer DaimlerChrysler also has a strategy to develop more new products.[12]

❑ Some major financial service providers, such as HSBC and Bank of America, have chosen innovation as an area on which to focus. For example, HSBC management have strongly communicated to staff the importance of innovation, and workshops are used to create ideas for new or improved customer services. In addition, HSBC have developed fast processes for implementing innovative ideas.

❑ Johnson & Johnson, the healthcare products company, has recently chosen to make innovation one of their core values. To support a coherent view of innovation throughout the company, the company has identified three ways in which innovation supports the business: it forges a vision of the future; fuels business growth; and promotes continuous learning. Regular articles in the company magazine give examples of successful innovation within the company, with process innovation being given as much attention as new products.

The above examples demonstrate the multifacetted nature of innovation management. Innovation management includes ways to motivate employees, selecting clear performance measures and creating a positive business culture. It also includes an emphasis on R&D, new products, technology and process innovation. Overall, this shows the wide range of approaches to stimulating and managing innovation that we need to consider. The main theme of this chapter is to introduce *how* innovation can be managed. Before we can discuss *managing innovation*, we need to establish what is actually meant by *innovation* itself and the terminology that we will be using in this book.

Characteristics of Innovation

Although the need for more innovation is widely recognized, there is no commonly accepted view of what innovation means in a business context. Many employees think of it primarily as radically new products delivered by R&D departments; this is a narrow view, as we will see.

The dictionary definition of *innovation* – introducing something new – is clear, but this does not help managers or employees understand the nature of innovation sufficiently. It focuses on newness and can lead us to overlook the fact that innovation can be based on modifying existing ideas. The dictionary definition also fails to give insights into the following questions. What are the most important types of innovation? How can innovation lead to sustainable competitive advantage? What is the most effective way to improve the innovation performance of a company? This book suggests answers to these questions and this section looks in detail at:

- Definitions of innovation.
- The different *dimensions* of innovation.
- The different *degrees* of innovation.
- The *phases* of an innovation.
- The functional areas involved.

Definitions of Innovation

Various definitions of innovation have been developed and these will be reviewed, in order to develop our terminology. Managers have different views on the nature of innovation.[13] Therefore, establishing a clear understanding of the characteristics of innovation is not only essential for this book but also in organizations, where diffuse views on innovation arising from different functional perspectives, may hinder the implementation of innovation strategy.

The Austrian economist Joseph Schumpeter has strongly influenced the understanding of innovation and this will be discussed in Chapter 2. Schumpeter considered five different aspects of innovation and, although developed over 70 years ago, his definition is comprehensive:[14]

1 The introduction of a good (product), which is new to consumers, or one of higher quality than was available in the past;
2 Methods of production, which are new to a particular branch of industry. These are not necessarily based on new scientific discoveries and may have, for example, already been used in other industrial sectors;
3 The opening of new markets;
4 The use of new sources of supply;
5 New forms of competition, that leads to the restructuring of an industry.

Michael Porter defined innovation:

to include both improvements in technology and better methods or ways of doing things. It can be manifested in product changes, process changes, new approaches to marketing, new forms of distribution, and new concepts of scope . . . [innovation] results as much from organizational learning as from formal R&D.[15]

This definition covers very similar points to Schumpeter's but indicates that innovation can stem from an organization's learning and not just the R&D department.

Both Porter and Schumpeter use the word 'new' in their definitions. It should not be forgotten that many commercial innovations are not totally original and Everett Rogers, an expert on how innovations spread through markets, reminds us that innovation '. . . is an idea, practice, or object that is perceived as new by the individual or other unit of adoption'. The perception of newness is important rather than the originality.

Innovation is a term that can lead to confusion in the service sector.[16] A useful definition for the service sector is,

> innovations in the service sector comprises [sic] new services and new ways of producing or delivering services as well as significant changes in services or their production or delivery. An innovation has been implemented if it has been introduced to the market (product innovation) or used in producing services (process innovation).[17]

The definition from the Organization for Economic Cooperation and Development (OECD)[18] is:

> innovation consists of all those scientific, technical, commercial and financial steps necessary for the successful development and marketing of new or improved manufactured products, the commercial use of new or improved processes or equipment or the introduction of a new approach to a social service. R&D is only one of these steps.

Similar to Porter's definition, this points out that R&D is not the only element to innovation. In addition, the OECD definition adds understanding of the different steps involved and points out that innovations can be important in sectors other than the private economy.

Psychologists view innovation as a social process, 'the intentional introduction and application within a role, group, or organization of ideas, processes, products or procedures, new to the relevant unit of adoption, designed to significantly benefit the individual, the group, organization or wider society'.[19] This indicates that the emergence of innovative ideas depends on the culture of an organization.

Comparing the various definitions of innovation given above, it can be seen that they have many common attributes covering: *what* is changed (such as product or process changes); *how much* is changed (whether it is completely new or only perceived as such); the *source* of the change (sometimes technology); the *influence* of the change (for its example social or commercial value).

Dimensions of Innovation

Based on the broad understanding collated from the definitions of innovation, Figure 1.2 shows what we will refer to as the *dimensions of innovation*. These can be applied to the service sector but we will first discuss how they apply to manufacturing. *Product innovation* is important and can be thought of as the first dimension of innovation. However, opportunities for sustainable competitive advantage can be missed if an organization focuses solely on product innovation

Figure 1.2 The dimensions of innovation in the manufacturing sector

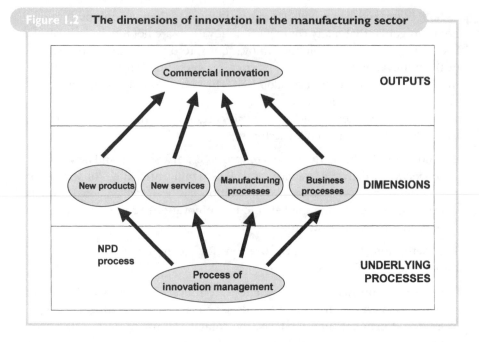

(see box case: Gillette). Companies in the manufacturing sector can also create services to help differentiate their products – *service innovation* is the second dimension. Improvements can also be made to the manufacturing and delivery process (normally referred to as *process innovation*). Finally, companies can use *business process innovation*; optimizing processes to make it easier for customers to do business with the company (for example order fulfilment), or to cut costs. The term business process innovation covers a wide range of possibilities and we need to differentiate it from process innovation. Process innovation refers to enhancements in the actual manufacturing process (or service delivery process in the service sector). Business process innovation can be improvements to any business process other than the actual manufacturing: ranging from supply chain improvements, to faster transactions with customers. Improving business processes often requires innovative approaches to the formal organization of companies.

Box case 1.2   Gillette – first-to-market risks

Some managers perceive innovation as being intimately linked to a first-to-market strategy. Breakthrough products such as the Sony Walkman have captured the imagination of many people so that they see innovation as only consisting of radically new products. Unfortunately, this view can lead managers to forget the biggest downside of being first-to-market – competitors may copy your innovation if you do not think of ways to protect it. What is worst, competitors may learn from the limitations of the first-to-market product and the 'copy' is likely to be better than the original.

The Gillette 'Mach 3' razor is a first-to-market product. Gillette developed this advanced razor, with its characteristic three blades set at different very precise angles, at a very high cost. A UK supermarket chain was quickly able to introduce a good copy of the product at a fraction of the development costs. This has meant that Gillette is more dependent on expensive television advertising to try and protect sales of their product. When products are easy to copy, competitors can even 'leapfrog' the original features and the Wilkinson Sword Company has now introduced a four-blade razor.

It is not only for academic clarity that it is important to consider how innovation should be defined. Promoting a clear understanding of the nature of innovation throughout a company is one of the key roles of top management because innovating in a number of dimensions can enable sustainable competitive advantage. Most products are relatively easy to copy and patents seldom give sufficient protection. For example, Cannon worked round several hundred patents owned by the Xerox Company in the development of their first and very successful photocopier. Leading companies have recognized the risk of their products being copied, and actively to combat this are focusing on other dimensions of innovation, such as manufacturing processes, to gain a sustainable competitive advantage[20] (see box case: Tetley's Teabags and contrast this to the earlier one on Gillette). Taking what we will call a *multi-dimensional* view of innovation leads companies to look for ways to complement product innovation through service, process and business process innovation.

Box case 1.3   Tetley's Teabags – sustainable competitive advantage[21]

Tetley is a market leader in the world teabag market and the company was the originator of the round teabag. On the face of it, the round teabag is only an incremental innovation over the traditional square version. However, through the process innovation required to support the production of the new product, Tetley found a way of gaining a sustainable competitive advantage. When the company developed the round teabag, it knew that with suitable marketing this new product could capture significant market share. Advertising copy was based around the better cup of tea that would result from bags where the tea could circulate better. However, Tetley also knew that competitors would quickly try to copy this product innovation. Therefore, the company decided not to talk to its normal supplier of manufacturing equipment about the new requirements. Instead, it hired Cambridge Consultants Ltd to develop a new manufacturing line for round teabags. When the new product was introduced the competition was unable to obtain similar manufacturing equipment quickly and Tetley maintained its lead. Even ten years later, the company is still enjoying a strong market position.

Management are the guardians of the underlying process that stimulates innovation within a company – the *process of innovation management* shown in Figure 1.2. Some parts of this overall process will be formally defined and documented, such as the new product development (NPD) process. Others will be less tangible, such as the management of company culture to ensure bright new ideas are constantly being generated. Therefore, managers need to look for ways to improve the fundamental way by which innovation occurs in their organizations.

Consider the following analogy: in a modern manufacturing company, the line operators are not simply responsible for manufacturing products. They are also given full responsibility for constantly improving the manufacturing processes (through continuous improvement and other means). Some companies even talk about their operators being 'process owners'. Therefore, senior managers need to see themselves as the process owners for innovation management and not simply as managing the outputs of new products and services. With this different perspective, managers view the processes in their organizations as one of their biggest assets.

Dimensions of Innovation in Services

Service-sector managers also perceive the need for innovation to be high though the dimensions of innovation differ in services. An insurance and financial services company was concerned that its output of new products was low and decided to examine its overall innovation performance. A group of senior and product managers took part in a workshop to identify all of the dimensions of innovation relevant to their markets. To stimulate the team to come-up with ideas, the discussion was based on the parallels to innovation in manufacturing companies (Figure 1.2).

The workshop results are summarized on Figure 1.3. New products – in this

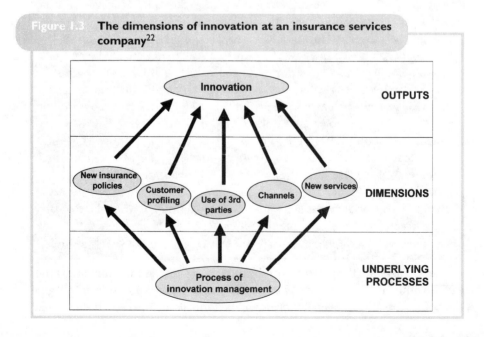

Figure 1.3 **The dimensions of innovation at an insurance services company**[22]

case new insurance policies – are important for competitive advantage. However, a range of other dimensions was identified. This included customer profiling to identify and contact customers with a unique value proposition; closer contact with third parties to help them contribute more to innovation (as most of the insurance policies were underwritten by suppliers); use of different sales channels (including banks, the Internet and brokers); and the creation of innovative new services – typically better ways for customers' enquiries to be handled – in order to increase customer loyalty.

Through the review of the role of innovation in their markets, this company recognized that they had more possibilities to innovate than they had previously thought. Now, as each new product is developed, the company looks for ways to innovate in all of the dimensions shown in Figure 1.3, with the goal of making their new insurance products 'hard to copy'. It is becoming crucial for service companies to examine the different dimensions of innovation and how these can complement one another.

Box case 1.4   Les Concierges – serving Indian professionals[23]

The 'cash-rich, time-poor' market segment consists of professional people who are top earners, but because of their demanding jobs and family commitments have very little spare time. Providing services for this segment in India has allowed founder and CEO of Les Concierges, Dipali Sikand, to build a business of over $1M with over 350 staff. The company was started in the Bangalore area, which is the centre of India's software industry, but is now active in half a dozen Indian cities.

The idea behind Les Concierges is simple and extends the concept of the 'travel desk' operated by travel companies for large employers. Sikand's business targets large employers (rather than individuals) and offers to make their employees' life easier by taking on some of their personal tasks and family organization. This means that a company can help its employees focus more on their work and Les Concierges has posted one or two of its staff to 70 companies, mainly in the information technology industry. The host company provides a desk and an intranet connection for Les Concierges and then the 'help desk' can go live, offering four categories of service: shopping, everyday tasks, entertainment and travel. The host company pays a retainer each year based on its number of employees (but it sees the return through increased employee productivity) and a transaction fee is normally paid by the employee (who saves precious time in a busy schedule).

The interaction with customers is highly important and Sikand refers to this as 'high touch'. She has hired almost exclusively women, as she feels that they are more sympathetic to customers' needs. With such empathy, Les Concierges can often delight its end-customers by coming up with original ideas for birthday presents and the like. The importance of the behind the scenes organization is also recognized and Sikand has concentrated on making this high-tech – including proprietary software to track each customer transaction and coordinate the many tasks passed daily to outside suppliers. The idea behind Les Concierges may be simple, but recognizing the need and developing a 'high-touch, high-tech' solution are Sikand's real innovations.

The above discussions on both the service and manufacturing sector demonstrated the multi-dimensional nature of innovation. In 2002, the R&D manager from an industrial safety equipment company told the authors 'if I ask five different people at our company what innovation is, I will get at least five different answers'. This illustrates the need for a common understanding of the goals of innovation and this manager has focused strongly on communications as part of his innovation strategy. AXA Insurance made a similar experience and their 'definition' of innovation will be discussed in the main case study at the end of Chapter 3 on managing innovation in services.

Degrees of Innovation

Innovation can be dramatic. Breakthroughs such as penicillin, the Walkman personal stereo, and the ubiquitous Post-It are often examples that people name when they talk about innovation. However, it is important to recognize that there are different *degrees of innovation*. There can be breakthroughs, which are normally referred to as *radical* innovations. They may be based on new technology and can create new markets or completely change existing ones. In addition, though, there are *incremental* innovations, small changes to existing products, services or processes that can also be important.

Although radical innovations such as breakthrough products often capture the imagination of the public, a lower degree of innovation is more common. Research at INSEAD business school in France investigating over 100 companies showed that 84 per cent of product innovations were 'line extensions' (that is incremental innovation) and that on average 62 per cent of revenues came from such products.[24] As might be expected, though, 38 per cent of revenues (and 61 per cent of profits) came from the radical product innovations.

The degrees of innovation – from no change, to incremental, to radical – is an important concept. Consultants Booz-Allen and Hamilton proposed that there are six degrees of product innovation (Table 1.1). The first degree is the improvement of existing products to provide improved performance or greater perceived value to customers. Developing new products that provide similar performance at lower cost is the second degree, followed by existing products that are targeted to new markets. New products that supplement a company's established product lines is the fourth degree. Another form of product innovation is the creation of new product lines. The last degree is defined as 'new-to-the-world' products that create entirely new markets. Table 1.1 shows that three categories are related to 'old product development' and three to 'new product development'. The degree of innovation is a somewhat controversial subject, as some observers will view certain innovations as radical, whereas others may perceive them to be incremental. This discourse often heard in academia. However, the search for an

Table 1.1   Degrees of product innovation[25]

	Degree of product innovation	Old–New product development
1.	Improvement and revisions of existing products	Old
2.	New products that provide similar performance at lower cost	Old
3.	Existing products that are targeted to new markets	Old
4.	Addition of products to an existing product line	New
5.	Creation of new product lines	New
6.	New-to-the-world products	New

unambiguous definition of, for example, radical innovation is probably not a very productive one – since the degree of innovation is context-dependent.

Evaluating Dimensions and Degrees

The concepts of the dimensions and degrees of innovation can be used to analyse the competitiveness of individual innovation projects and also a company's portfolio of innovation projects. We refer to this as a *dimensions and degrees analysis*. Consider the example of an innovation project to develop an incremental product. This product might not be very competitive, as it is based on previous products. Table 1.2 shows a typology and the tick in the column 'product' indicates that it is an incremental product innovation ('improvements'). Although the degree of product innovation is low, the new product could be supported by related services, which can be provided at lower cost (see tick under column 'service'). In the manufacturing process, radical innovation is

Table 1.2   Example of a dimensions and degrees analysis

	Degrees of innovation	Dimensions of innovation			
		Product	Service	Process	Business process
1.	No innovation				✓
2.	Improvements	✓			
3.	Similar performance at lower cost		✓		
4.	Targeting to new markets				
5.	Addition to an existing product line				
6.	Creation of new product line(s)				
7.	New-to-the-world			✓	

planned in the way the product will be produced, as this will lead to a sustainable advantage in terms of lower costs. The utility of Table 1.2, in analysing individual projects, is that it forces organizations to think how they can innovate in the various dimensions to become and remain competitive. For example, the Mars Group, manufacturers of confectionary and other products, always consider where their prowess in manufacturing can be utilized for each new product.

Table 1.2 can also be used as the basis for reviewing the range of innovation projects that a company is in the process of implementing. Each individual project can be analyzed and then the overall balance in the portfolio, for instance the mix between incremental and radical products, can be determined and compared to the goals of the innovation strategy.

Continuous improvements can improve manufacturing processes or service operations, leading to higher-quality output at lower cost. Incremental improvements add up over time to significant increases in performance. Many manufacturers have and continue to reap rewards from continuous improvement – *kaizen* in Japanese. The challenge is for management to communicate to employees the potential contribution of continuous improvement to innovation.

The service sector has been relatively slow to adopt continuous improvement and other techniques to improve processes. This is partly because an intimate part of the service delivery process is the interaction between a company's employees and the client or customer. Although the service delivery process is dependent on people, this does not prevent constant improvements being possible. On the contrary, continuous improvement is essential in the service sector because even small improvements to operations are quickly recognized by customers and can increase satisfaction levels significantly.

Phases of Innovation

Any innovation must progress through a number of *phases* before it is commercially viable. This is true, irrespective of the type of innovation – whether it is a new product, a new service, a new process, an improved business process, or any combination of these. All innovations begin with the generation of ideas and the road to implementation and commercial success can be a long one. Additionally, many ideas fall by the wayside. For example, in the pharmaceutical industry, ideas for new drugs are based on novel chemical structures called 'new chemical entities' (NCEs). These take years to develop, test and to introduce to the market. The majority of NCEs are rejected along the way for one reason or another (for example undesirable side effects) and typically only one NCE in a thousand will be commercially successful. Within any organization, ideas in every dimension of innovation need to be generated because as researchers have recognized, 'too much of the focus of new product development is on product features. Successful NPD should focus on not only product features but on the entire product/service/financial offering . . .'.[26]

Irrespective of the dimensions and degrees of innovation involved, ideas are generated, some are selected and developed into *concepts*, and the best of these concepts are chosen for implementation. Figure 1.4 shows the typical phases of

Figure 1.4   **The typical phases of an innovation ('the development funnel')**[27]

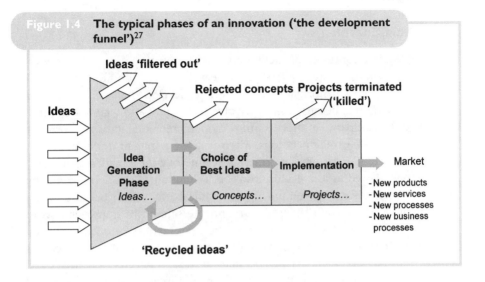

innovation, with a funnel of ideas being generated and collected by an organization. Some ideas are filtered out quickly whereas others progress further and are developed into what are normally called concepts. An initial idea might be developed into a concept by a small team of people from different functional areas of the business working together part-time over a few weeks or, for more complex ideas, the process of developing the concept may take longer. At the concept stage, an idea for a new product or new service will have been formalized to the extent that some questions such as the size of the potential market and the best way the product or service can be designed will have been considered (although these questions will not have been answered to a high level of detail). Similarly, at the concept stage, ideas for new processes will have been analysed as to the investments required and the returns these can bring. Normally, management takes the decision on which concepts will be chosen to become *projects* (the implementation phase), although the way in which an organization chooses the particular concepts for development may not be transparent to many of the employees. Certain concepts may be rejected as currently uninteresting, to emerge later as 'recycled ideas'.

Obviously, the innovations developed will have varying levels of success. The analogy to a funnel used in Figure 1.4 is not new; Simon Majaro of the Cranfield School of Management has used it for many years. Kim Clark and Steven Wheelwright from Harvard Business School have also used it as a basis for discussions with managers on the typical phases of innovation.[28] They asked managers to draw their own versions of the how their organizations manage ideas through to implementation. From this it was found that managers perceived that the different phases often overlap, problems are common and so iterations are necessary. Therefore, it must be recognized that Figure 1.4 is a simplification and the efficient and linear flow from idea, to concept, to implementation is desirable but not necessarily easy to achieve.

Innovation Complexity

The time required for the implementation of an innovation depends on several factors, as shown by Figure 1.5. Firstly, the degree of innovation influences it. A radical innovation will normally take longer to develop than an incremental improvement. This is because it may involve techniques and technologies that are new to the company. In process innovation, incremental ideas are normally improvements to existing operations, whereas new equipment (for example, for a manufacturing line, or new information technology for a bank's operations) can often be viewed as a radical innovation. (The Fruit of the Loom company views new manufacturing equipment as a radical innovation because of the investment required, the risks involved, and the significant improvements in performance levels that are expected from the equipment. Wipro Technologies, the Indian R&D off-shoring company has helped its financial services clients achieve radical improvements in customer service levels through better IT.) Secondly, the number of dimensions of innovation involved can add complexity. For example, a new insurance policy which is dependent on new information technology and establishing a new set of distribution channels, will take longer to develop than an incremental product innovation, which uses existing systems and channels. Overall, the complexity and risk of an innovation project depends on the dimensions of innovation involved, the degree of innovation in each dimension, whether new technologies are required, and the market being targeted. In Figure 1.5, the '+' signs indicate that the factors increase complexity, which in turn normally increases both the implementation time and the risk. However, management can take steps to prevent complexity increasing both the risk and the time required for innovation projects.

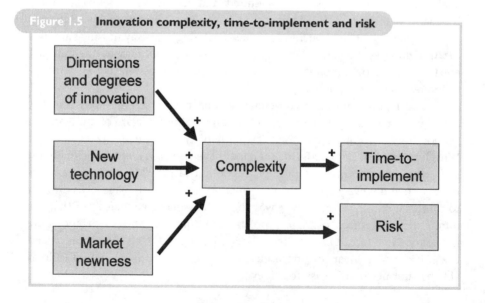

Figure 1.5 Innovation complexity, time-to-implement and risk

Innovation throughout the Organization

An essential point to note is that if an organization is to be fully effective, every part of that organization needs to actively contribute to innovation. Innovation is certainly not just the responsibility of an R&D department in a manufacturing company, or the strategic planning group in a service operation. The main functional areas that should be involved are:

☐ *Research and development*: for many managers, R&D is *the* source of innovation and it is true that this function should drive many of the ideas for new products and services in a company. However, companies that concentrate solely on R&D can fall into the trap of producing sophisticated products that the market does not require. This has been recognized by a leading economist who said 'the proper management of innovation is much more than establishing and maintaining a research and development laboratory that produces a great deal of technical output'.[29]

☐ *Marketing*: has a key role to play in generating ideas for innovation, through creative forms of market research. Marketing can make the difference between a good idea and a successful product. Without marketing and sales, a product innovation, or a new service will not attract customers' interest and developing an effective sales channel is fundamental.

☐ *Operations*: this function, which is often called *production* or simply *manufacturing* in the manufacturing sector, also should contribute to innovation. Unfortunately, many operations managers do not perceive that they have a key role in driving innovation. This limits the ability of a company to obtain longer-term competitive advantage, through process innovations that are often harder to copy than product innovations. Service sector companies often underestimate the potential value of operations' contribution to innovation.

☐ *Finance and accounting*: is normally not perceived as being able to make a contribution to innovation. However, it can provide essential support in calculating return on investment for innovation projects.[30] At leading companies such as Agilent Technologies, the controlling function plays a leading key role in determining which projects offer the best combination of low risk, high return and a good match to the available resources. The finance function can make a considerable contribution to developing effective pricing packages. An example of this is the 'power by the hour' leasing offered by major aero-engine manufacturers.

☐ *Human resource management*: hiring, developing and motivating good people are essential and challenging aspects of innovation management. The creative atmosphere of small teams can easily be lost as organizations grow and so the human resource function can and should proactively support the maintenance of an innovative culture in their organization.

☐ *Outside resources*: are very necessary. For example, suppliers in the automotive industry conduct significant parts of the product development for car manufacturers. Similarly, universities and research institutes can enable small organizations to economically partake in the development of new technologies, and develop new core competencies.

The task of general management is to stimulate the cross-functional teamwork that is needed for effective innovation. Researchers have identified the friction and lack of understanding that commonly arise between different functions, particularly marketing and R&D.[31] Ensuring the active involvement of the different functions is a task for management, and Akio Morita, the late Chairman of SONY, recognized this saying, 'this is the job of top management – to arrange good communications [between functions]'.[32]

Our discussion on the characteristics of innovation shows its broad nature. Earlier we discussed the different ways companies are attempting to stimulate innovation. This shows that managing innovation involves many aspects. Next we will discuss the research findings in order to understand how innovation can be managed.

Key Research on Innovation

Innovation is an area in which both economists and management researchers have been active. Throughout the chapters of this book, the pertinent research will be presented but here we will give an overview of the field, in order to understand how the different topics interrelate. This will help us develop a framework through which to view and plan the management of innovation. The three levels at which innovation has been researched are:

◻   The *macro level*: research on the sources and impact of innovation within economies and industries.
◻   The *micro* or *company level*: investigations of how companies manage innovation and the advantages that it brings them in terms of revenues and profits.
◻   The *project level*: which looks at the management of innovation projects, particularly NPD.

Before the theory is discussed it is important to introduce some concepts about management research.

Research Methodology

Many popular articles on innovation management are based on anecdotal evidence – often pure opinions, or a single company example where improved performance was achieved. Although such evidence can be interesting, it leaves open the questions whether the improvements were the result of the actions taken (or of extraneous factors), and are the results applicable to another organization? Management research tries to address these points by taking scientific approach to gathering and analysing empirical data. Conclusions based on hard data should allow us to have confidence in our understanding how innovation can be better managed, provided they are based on research that has high *validity*.

There are two related concepts here: the *internal* and *external validity* of research. Internal validity refers to how systematically, or rigorously, a study was conducted and, consequently, whether the finding can be believed. Consider, for example, a study of the influence of teamwork on product time-to-market. Did this research accurately determine how good the teamwork was and show whether there was, indeed, a clear link to the faster NPD? Many management articles assume links are clear – especially links between management actions and profitability – whereas systematic research is necessary to prove such links exist. Often it is nearly impossible to establish that direct – causal – links exist. Some studies have low internal validity and, if repeated by a different researcher, very different results would emerge. Therefore, in assessing the value of research it is important to consider internal validity; or in other words how reliable were the findings for the sample studied.

External validity refers to how broadly the findings of research conducted with specific organizations can be applied, for example, to organizations outside those which were included in the study. Has the study been conducted with organizations that are *representative* of the population to which we want to apply the results? This is a crucial point and the relevance of research based on a single company to other organizations is questionable. Only if findings are *generalizable* – they can be reasonably assumed to apply to other companies – are they interesting to managers looking for approaches to use themselves. It is surprising how many of the articles in the popular management press are based on cursory investigations that have questionable external validity because, for example, they looked at a very limited number of companies or companies in very specific business environments. As a result, innovation management is plagued with 'quick fixes' – approaches that have worked at one company and which their proponents claim are universal solutions. There are no panaceas for the management of innovation and the context in which an organization finds itself plays a key role. In assessing research, it is important to consider both the internal and external validity of the studies that are being described and we will consider the validity of research throughout this book.

Macro-Level Investigations

For many years economists have researched innovation, and in the 1800s it was recognized that new products have an impact on the economy. Schumpeter, realized that process innovations in manufacturing also have a strong influence plus, when innovations emerge, they can threaten established industries. In their studies, economists have normally used measures of innovation such as R&D expenditures, the number of major innovations generated in an industry over time, and patent counts.[33] The studies made at the macro-economic level fall into two categories: research on the factors that influence innovative performance, and the spread and influence of innovation.

Typical of the studies on the factors that influence performance are those looking at the affect of the size of companies. Part of Schumpeter's work was the recognition that larger companies are at an advantage when it comes to innovation, because of the economies of scale they have in R&D.[34] Much of the subsequent research has focused on the size of companies and innovation. It has been shown, for example, that entrants are more likely to develop pioneering products and small firms are important innovators.[35] The effects of educational levels and national culture on product innovation have also been investigated (by looking at the correlations between qualification levels and patent counts), and the success rate of government policies that aim to support innovation.[36] The field of *development economics* is also relevant to the study of innovation. This has looked at the reasons why developing countries remain behind advanced countries. Factors such as infrastructure, human capital (in turn, determined by health and education), and the availability of credit to fund innovation all influence growth.

Studies on the impact of innovation are numerous and Everett Rogers has led much of this work. Innovations are adopted slowly at first but, at they become known and information is more widely communicated, the market quickly embraces them.[37] As an innovation is widely adopted, this stimulates growth through sales of new products and services. It may also change the basis of competition; change the structure of an industry. Innovations have been shown to be a driver of long-term business cycles, and to directly influence employment levels.[38] The work of economists on innovation is useful in demonstrating the interaction between the market environment and the firm. It indicates to firms the gravity of conducting a thorough analysis of their business environment and so Chapter 4 will focus on this topic.

Although the relationship between industry structure, company size and innovation has received considerable attention, economists have seldom investigated the actions of individual companies.[39] Management researchers from a number of disciplines including marketing, strategy, organizational behaviour and operations management have been active in this area and their findings provide many insights.

Micro-Level Investigations

Managing innovation is a challenge because of the wide range of factors influencing its success or failure, including the allocation of resources, the skills of key staff, the generation of ideas and the organization of development teams.[40] Also, innovation is not necessarily a logical process and it is far from clear how companies can best improve their performance,[41] or what the key aspects of innovation management are.

One of the most common forms of research at a company level has been the quest to unearth the characteristics of innovative organizations. The companies chosen for these studies are normally large, have a reputation for being innovative and exhibit high market share and growth. For example, leading companies develop over twice as many new products, develop them faster, use more technologies, and compete in more geographical markets.[42] The limitation of such studies has been demonstrated by a meta-study, which showed that over half the key factors identified were unique to specific studies.[43] This strongly demonstrates the need to carefully consider context when taking ideas or innovation best practices from one situation to another. In this book we will point to the contextual issues related to applying ideas and best practices.

It is important to ensure that innovation plays a central role within the business strategy.[44] It should be fully evaluated during strategic planning and clear processes are defined to manage the path from ideas to new products and services. Technology can be a prime component of innovation and therefore it should be given full management attention.[45] The work of Kim Clark of Harvard shows that general managers must investigate the value of technology to their companies.[46] In manufacturing firms, R&D needs not only to develop new products but it must also give a lead to other departments in becoming a continuously innovating company.[47]

Michael Tushman of Harvard has been a major contributor to the study of organizations and innovation. He and others determined that the formal organization and the underlying culture of a company have widely been identified as playing a key role in innovation.[48] This requires firms to be good at not only the internal coordination of the work of different functions but also at managing the linkages to other organizations. It has been shown that leading companies often change their formal organizations and so executives need to create organizational architectures that are both efficient and adaptive.[49] Company culture is recognized as being fundamental in supporting innovation, however, culture is a concept that can be difficult to manage.[50] Studies have concluded that the innovative companies display certain key cultural attributes. These include the propensity to experiment with ideas and the capability to motivate individual employees to be creative and to develop radical ideas. Successful projects are often discussed within such organizations and these 'stories' help focus the organization on the values of innovation.

Most of the literature on innovation concentrates on product innovation – new products – and either neglects or totally ignores other aspects. There are limitations to this because for manufacturers, 'the traditional emphasis on [product] innovation is no longer enough to succeed in an environment of increasingly intense competition'.[51] New services are also essential, and process innovation – developing efficient manufacturing – is often a key source of competitive advantage because it is difficult to copy.[52]

Project-Level Investigations

The third level at which researchers have investigated innovation is the project level. Most of the projects studied have been new product development ones but we should bear in mind that the challenges faced are similar for new service products and also in the management of process innovation projects.

New products are a key source of competitive advantage and so studies at the project – new product development – level are common. Unfortunately, the success rate for new products is considered by many observers to be very low.[53] This is due to the many problems with product innovation, which can occur at every stage of development: from the creation of ideas, to NPD, to the introduction of products onto the market.[54] The literature has looked at these problems and the main findings can be grouped into articles on the benefits of faster NPD, the need for robust NPD processes, teams, techniques for accelerated development, and evaluation of product development.

Faster New Product Development

The need for companies to develop new products faster is widely recognized.[55] The time required to develop and introduce a new product to the market is referred to as *time-to-market* or *cycle time*. It is becoming increasingly important for companies to reduce cycle time, and faster NPD has been a key focus in manufacturing for nearly twenty years.[56]

Fast cycle time is considered to have two main advantages. If a product is a totally new concept, then being first-to-market enables a company to define key market requirements before competitors enter the market. In established markets, being faster leads to increased profit and market share. Although the advantages of short cycle times appear clear in the popular business literature, they are not backed by unequivocal evidence and the link between fast cycle time and profitability is weak. To make NPD not only fast but also efficient, there are a number of requirements. These include the process, teamwork organization and leadership, specific techniques, and project evaluation.

The NPD Process

Much has been written about the need for a clear new product development process, which defines the responsibilities of different functions, such as R&D and marketing, at different phases of NPD. Robert Cooper and Eltjo Kleinschmidt of McMasters University in Canada have published many definitive studies on the NPD processes. One investigation looked at companies' practices and led to a recommended *Stage-Gate*™ approach.[57] In this approach, management meets at the end of each stage of product development and has to approve the progression to the next stage. At each stage the various functions of a firm have clearly defined responsibilities, to ensure that an effective new product or new service product is developed. Many companies in both the service and manufacturing sectors have developed formal processes based on Cooper and Kleinschmidt's recommendations. Companies with formal processes were more satisfied with their performance.[58] However, having a process alone will not necessarily lead to faster NPD. Firms need to collect data on NPD projects, so that companies can learn from the past and improve by, for example, avoiding bottlenecks in the process.[59]

Team Organization and Leadership

The skills and the motivation of people working on product development are crucial and such teams need to be well-organized and led.[60] Steven Wheelwright and Kim Clark have investigated many aspects of product development teams. One approach that has been widely applied to projects is to form NPD teams, drawing members from a number of functions. Including manufacturing and marketing and not just R&D ensures that all aspects of the business are considered in parallel at the design stage. For example, R&D and manufacturing will consider how to make the product easy to manufacture. Although they can be difficult to implement, it has generally been recognized that cross-functional teams have made NPD more efficient.[61] The people chosen to lead NPD teams need particular skills in motivating the team and managing communications both within the team and externally. Relatively recent research has shown that problems in managing new product teams are also prevalent in the service sector.[62]

Techniques for NPD

After the importance of faster NPD was recognized at the end of the 1980s, there followed a wave of prescriptive articles on which techniques could be used to achieve it. Many of these were based on anecdotal rather than hard evidence.[63] One technique hailed as a major advance in reducing cycle time was *Quality Function Deployment* (QFD) – a Japanese method for ensuring that customer requirements are accurately captured – but this method is not a panacea.[64] (We will discuss the advantages and limitations of QFD in Chapter 7.) There are many techniques for improving NPD but the use of any of these will not, in itself, guarantee reduced cycle times. Bringing products to market faster is just not that simple – the situation and the way techniques are implemented play a key role.[65]

Overall, tools and techniques for new product development is a contentious area. Whilst many of the articles in the popular management literature have extolled the benefits of certain tools, the evidence on the utility of such tools is sparse. Managers need to deal with this by recognizing that there are no 'quick fixes' and the application of any tool or technique to speed NPD will take time and effort to make it effective within the particular situation faced by the organization in question.

Evaluating NPD Projects

If NPD is to be improved, then the efficiency of the process and not simply the success of the product needs to be evaluated. Several studies have found that many companies do not evaluate their projects effectively and to evaluate NPD, suitable measures are necessary. Few companies capture accurately the time-to-market and this type of measurement is essential because, without it, valid comparisons are impossible. Abbie Griffin of the University of Illinois has studied the topic of NPD measures extensively and recommends that metrics should cover the outcomes and characteristics of the project (inputs), and the process of NPD itself.[66] However, it has been recognized that 'the performance of individual projects can be influenced by idiosyncratic factors . . . that may be difficult to duplicate from project to project'.[67]

Service Innovation Research

Throughout this book we will be lamenting the fact that most of the research on innovation has focused on products and not services.[68] Although from a historical perspective this is understandable – most economies were manufacturing-driven when innovation research first started – today, the developed economies are mainly service-driven. Fortunately, researchers are now catching up and our knowledge of the impacts and management of service innovation is improving.

A major issue in the macro-level studies of the service sector is that the categories of innovation used in manufacturing studies (product, process and service innovation) are difficult to apply in services. Often innovations in the service sector do not neatly fit into these categories as, for example, a service product is often difficult to differentiate from the way it is delivered.[69] Measures of 'innovation' in services are also more difficult than in the manufacturing sector; for example the spending on innovation related activities is difficult to ascertain.[70]

Studies in the service sector have looked at the nature of innovation (and how it is different from the manufacturing sector). Such research has concluded that in addition to new service products, ways to improve the quality of the service, the process of its delivery, achieve lower costs, and make innovations harder to copy are all important aspects of service innovation (see box case on Singapore Airlines). Because of the intangible nature of service products, service innovation can be very challenging to manage and it is recommended that managers adopt formal process management to increase service innovation levels.[71] In Chapter 3 we will focus on the contrast between the service and manufacturing sectors.

Box case 1.5   Singapore Airlines – sustainable competitive advantage[72]

Singapore International Airlines (SIA) has often been voted the world's best airline in surveys by travel magazines such as *Condé Nast Traveler* and the quality of its services is legendary. Its business strategy is based on a solid service product and attention to every detail of way it is delivered. A first-to-market innovation strategy has been an important part of SIA's approach for years.

The SIA product itself – air travel – is reliable and the range of routes offered has been extended through alliances with other airlines. The way the service is delivered by SIA is designed to achieve maximum customer satisfaction and includes both people and technology-related ideas. Cabin staff are renowned for being friendly and helpful and this has been strongly promoted through the *Singapore Girl* advertising. Staff receive longer and more detailed training than that offered by other airlines. For example, all cabin trainees spend time in homes for the aged in order to understand the problems faced by older travellers (a growing segment worldwide). Technology is also constantly updated and the aircraft fleet is one of the most modern in the industry. Having more modern aircraft has helped SIA differentiate their service product; passenger areas have larger than average seating, and a French fashion house designed the décor and all of the service ware (including the tableware). In-flight services have been constantly enhanced and the list of firsts here is long: first in-flight telephones; first in-flight fax machines; first Dolby surround sound and personal video screens in coach class. SIA has also led in the introduction of electronic tickets, but it is also flexible in allowing flight confirmations by telephone, fax or email.

It is interesting to note that competitors have quickly copied the technology-based innovations, whereas the quality of the service provided by staff has been harder for competitors to follow. In managing service innovation, a key question to ask is which dimensions of innovation can bring a sustainable competitive advantage?

Managing Innovation – The Challenge

The theory illustrated the number of levels at which research has been conducted and it also demonstrated the complexity of managing innovation in firms. Many aspects of the nature of innovation need to be considered, as do different functional areas of a company. This leads us to the question of how can an integrated approach be achieved? How can the recommendations from the different fields of research be related to the situation facing an organization?

Need for a Framework

The skills required to manage innovation effectively are different from general management principles in various respects. Innovation management often requires managers to match 'technical' expertise, in areas such as technology and project management, with 'soft' skills in people management, to promote creativity. The skills needed for technology management relate closely to engineering and the physical sciences, whereas the soft skills are closer to the social sciences. Few managers have been educated in both of these areas. Developing new products, services and processes is inherently uncertain and dealing with risk and uncertainty is central to innovation management. This also requires managers to be aware of techniques for dealing with risk. Another point is that innovation often requires significant investment and the interplay of financial and technical considerations are complex but essential, if good decisions are to be made. The management of innovation requires a distinct mix of skills and this is what makes it such a fascinating challenge.

In many ways innovation management is in its infancy. Although there are tools, theories and approaches, there is not yet a clear methodology to help managers improve innovation performance. A similar situation existed in the 1980s in the area of quality management, where even the meaning of 'quality' was being debated (for example should an 'internal' or 'customer' viewpoint be adopted?).[73] Quality management tools, such as Statistical Process Control (SPC) and cause and effect figures, were emerging, as were approaches to people management such as quality circles (groups of manufacturing employees meeting on a regular basis to discuss how their manufacturing could be made more efficient). Today, this collection of tools and techniques has been combined into the widely recommended methodology of 'Six Sigma' quality management.[74] The Motorola Company was largely responsible for creating this integrated approach. Currently, innovation management has not reached this level of maturity. Therefore, no integrated methodology is available and managers are faced with the challenge of having to merge ideas from different areas of research.

In research interviews with managers, it has emerged that they identify many facets to managing innovation: they cite strategy (for example, whether to be first-to-market, or to follow); people management (for example, motivating teams); and good project management (for example, in striving to meet challenging time-to-market goals).[75] Integrating the many facets of innovation management is a major challenge. For example, the director of one company in the manufacturing sector said he really needed a 'systematic way to encourage and manage innovation'. Taking the main areas of the research literature at the company and project level, we have developed a framework to illustrate the main elements of innovation management and their relationships.

The Innovation Pentathlon Framework

Figure 1.4 gave a simple representation of the way a business generates and implements innovation; the process of innovation within an organization or, as Wheelwright and Clark termed it the *development funnel*. The development funnel is a simplified representation of what may not be a strictly chronological flow, as iterations are common. The development funnel illustrates the process of ideas, through selection, to implementation but it does not show the link to a firm's strategic intent (the importance of which emerges from the literature), or the link to a company's culture. However, the development funnel does offer a very useful simple visual representation of a key business process – innovation.

To build on this work, two extra elements – *innovation strategy* and *people and organization* – need to be added because top managers perceived the importance of both linking the portfolio of projects to their overall strategy, and supporting the innovation levels of their organizations through effective people management. As its name suggests, the *Innovation Pentathlon* framework identifies five what we will term main *areas* or *elements* of innovation management, as shown in Figure 1.6. In each of the five areas, there are a number of key topics to be managed:

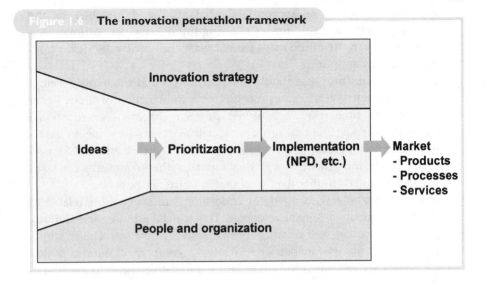

Figure 1.6   The innovation pentathlon framework

- *Innovation strategy.* Developing and achieving the goals of the innovation strategy is the responsibility of top management and this requires a focus on a number of issues. Assessing market trends and determining how these drive the need for innovation in the company's chosen sector(s) is the first step. The role of technology, the opportunities it can open, and how to acquire expertise in the relevant technologies needs to be considered. Management needs to communicate the role of innovation within a company – product, service, process and business process innovation – and match the resources to the strategy. For example, first-to-market approaches require particular capabilities in R&D and market development. Lastly, gauging innovation performance, through the use of appropriate measures is essential.

- *Ideas.* Ideas are the raw material for innovation and managers need to focus on creating an organizational environment that supports creativity at both the individual and team level, and the use of suitable creativity techniques. Creativity should harness the knowledge both within and outside the organization. A large enough volume of creative ideas needs to be generated, which addresses either existing or latent customer requirements for products and related services, or streamlining processes that serve customers. Good ideas blend technical, customer and market requirements. As innovation includes new products, services and new or improved processes, the scope for idea generation needs to be kept wide.

- *Prioritization.* An efficient process is required to ensure that the best ideas are chosen for development into new products, services and process innovations. This requires the use of suitable tools to analyse the risk and return of individual projects. Limited resources for the implementation of innovation projects need to be carefully assigned. Managers need to collate the information from across the range of projects, to check that the portfolio of innovation projects is appropriately balanced and matched to the company's innovation strategy. Collecting information on portfolio decisions, so that in the future management teams can review and learn from their previous decisions.

❏ *Implementation*. This phase should focus on quickly and efficiently developing new products, services or processes, or a combination of these. Faster development times can be achieved through effective cross-functional teams, prototyping and testing. Commercialization is the last step in implementation and, for example, a successful market launch is essential for new products. The implementation process is an area where companies can learn from each project, so that the future performance can be greater.

❏ *People and organization*. Underlying innovation are many issues related to the management of human resources. These include hiring and training policies, job design, and creating effective organizational structures, which will increase innovation outputs. Creating a company culture in which employees are motivated to be constantly innovative is also fundamental. Effective reward and recognition programmes will need to be maintained.

The Pentathlon Analogy

Innovation management has been previously compared to a marathon race.[76] Innovation management needs constant and long-term attention from managers and, in this sense the analogy to a marathon is valid. However, the implication that innovation management consists of high performance in a single discipline is misleading. Innovation management is far more complex and requires good performance in all of the different disciplines. Consequently, a better analogy is a pentathlon, where good performance in five disciplines – the five areas – is essential.

There are two key points to note from Figure 1.6 and the above discussion of the five elements. Firstly, each of the elements is, in itself, a complex area and so it is not surprising that innovation management – which is made up of these inter-related factors – is hugely challenging. Secondly, top performance in one area alone will not lead to long-term competitiveness. Therefore, the focus of many companies over the last decade on NPD alone, to the detriment of the other areas, is misguided. Similarly, many companies make the mistake of confusing innovation with creativity and so start initiatives to increase the volume of creative business ideas, without considering how the best ideas can be selected and quickly implemented. Overall, the framework allows us to split a large topic into more understandable and manageable parts.

The Pentathlon essentially represents the innovation processes within one organization. The context – the business situation – strongly influences innovation management and this is shown in Figure 1.7, where the market and other forces directly impact how an organization should manage its innovation. The figure also indicates that an organization must look outside its boundaries to increase innovation levels. Innovation networks, such as links to suppliers and

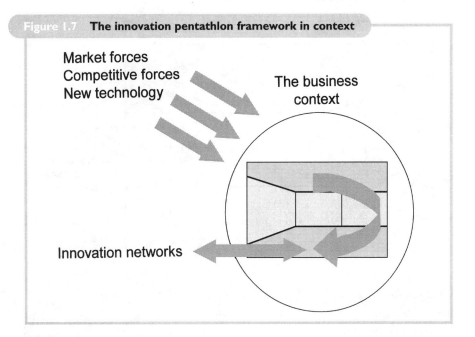

Figure 1.7 **The innovation pentathlon framework in context**

Market forces
Competitive forces
New technology

The business
context

Innovation networks

technical institutes are increasingly important (the main case study at the end of this chapter on NTT-DoCoMo looks at partnerships and alliances).

Applying the Framework

The Pentathlon Framework can be applied to identify the areas of innovation management in which an organization is both strong and weak. To demonstrate this two examples will be given, one from the service sector and one from manufacturing. Each of these has been disguised, to ensure confidentiality and Figures 1.8 and 1.9 indicate the areas of innovation management where the companies were relatively weak.

Example 1   International Bank – innovation processes

A business division of a major international bank spent time considering the lessons it could learn from innovation management in the manufacturing sector. Two conclusions were quickly reached: the bank's innovation strategy needed to be re-thought and new service product development needed a more formalized process.

Having observed that most manufacturing companies have Stage-Gate™ processes, the bank identified a weakness in NPD management. This was the result of no formal processes being applied at the bank, although an NPD process had been defined several years previously. The old processes were too bureaucratic, with many approvals required (for example, over ten managers

Figure 1.8 Innovation management at an international bank

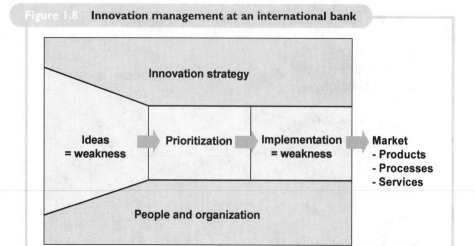

needed to agree to new advetising copy). A new process was defined with the aim of implementing new service products faster, with appropriate but streamlined levels of approval.

Idea generation was also identified as a weak element in the bank's innovation management. Regular cross-functional workshops were introduced to generate initial ideas. The bank's management was impressed by the way that leading manufacturers used prototype products to get qualified feedback from customers. Consequently, the bank focused on turning ideas as quickly as possible into ' service prototypes' (with, for example, material on explaining the new service to customers and proposed advertising).

The improvements at the bank were also closely linked to the overall innovation strategy, which was then clearly communicated to all staff.

Example 2   VehicleCo – cross-functional creativity

Setting the right atmosphere for creativity is essential and the physical environment, the people and the business culture can all play a role. At a UK specialist vehicle manufacturer, which we will refer to as VehicleCo, the charismatic founder still takes an active role in generating technical ideas and ensuring that they are commercially feasible. By asking critical questions about new products – acting in some ways as a devil's advocate – he has created a culture that blends three distinct elements. A focus on developing first-to-market technical solutions is blended with a strong commercial awareness in R&D and an emphasis on constant 'prototyping', right from the concept stage. Prototypes are used as the basis for both internal discussions on new concepts and for discussions with customer groups.

The factory has an ideal physical environment for creativity; it is open plan with marketing and R&D sitting together, separated from production by a

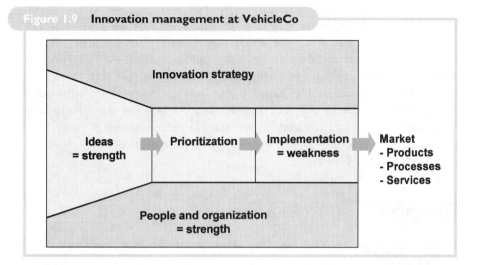

Figure 1.9   Innovation management at VehicleCo

glass wall. Similarly, only a glass wall separates the workshop used for producing prototypes and so its work is clearly visible to all.

At VehicleCo it is normal for different departments to contribute to ideas. For example, although most companies use continuous improvement teams, these are normally only staffed by manufacturing employees. At VehicleCo, marketing and other functions are represented in kaizen projects, to bring a commercial focus and 'outside ideas' to brainstorming sessions. Similarly, production people are present in new product development discussions. Brainstorming has become synonymous within the company with mixing different functional perspectives. With such a strong cross-functional orientation, it is not surprising that the functional R&D organization has gone – replaced by business teams where R&D and marketing are combined in small groups with clear target markets. Over the last decade, the organization has been changed several times and is expected to change again. Employees see this as inevitable and not negative; it means the organization is flexible enough to react to market changes.

It would be wrong to leave the impression that VehicleCo have no issues with innovation management. For example, they only recently introduced a formal NPD process and so still have challenges to face.

Limitations of the Framework

The Pentathlon Framework has limitations that we need to consider. Firstly, it is a categorization of the main elements of innovation management and not a predictive model of innovation performance. The framework provides a visual means of assessing the different aspects of innovation within an organization and can be used as a diagnostic tool for determining priorities for improvement.

However, the five different elements of the pentathlon are difficult to assess quantitatively and so care much be taken in concluding whether performance in one area is sufficient. Also, the interaction between the elements of the pentathlon, for example how changes in a company culture will influence the generation of ideas, are hard to predict and context specific. Within these limitations, the framework enables clearer discussions on the nature of innovation (just as the development funnel enabled managers to better understand how ideas are developed into products). It also can be used as a communication tool, to explain to employees where, why and how improvements in innovation management are to be made.

The Structure of this Book

The structure of this book is based around the Pentathlon Framework with chapters as follows:

- *Chapter 2: Innovation and Economics* presents the macro-economic theory of the influence of innovation on markets.
- *Chapter 3: Contrasting Services with Manufacturing* discusses the innovation management issues in service industries, compared to those in manufacturing. It also introduces much of the terminology of innovation.
- *Chapter 4: Developing an Innovation Strategy* explains the first element of the Pentathlon framework. It covers the importance of companies setting an appropriate innovation strategy based on their market situation, and determining the resources required to achieve it.
- *Chapter 5: Ideas: Managing Creativity and Knowledge* discusses how to generate ideas for new products, new service products, and new processes. It covers approaches to improve both individual and organizational creativity.
- *Chapter 6: Prioritization: Selecting and Managing the Portfolio* discusses how the decisions can be reached on the best ideas which should be selected for commercialization.
- *Chapter 7: Implementation* explains how innovation projects can be managed to ensure that they are quickly and efficiently completed and commercialized.
- *Chapter 8: People, Organization and Innovation* discusses the role of people management in supporting increased innovation performance, including the influence of company culture.
- *Chapter 9: Boosting Innovation Performance*. This chapter on innovation change management first discusses how to audit innovation performance. It then indicates how improvements can be made to increase overall performance – as in a pentathlon, good performance in one area alone is not enough. Performance measures are also discussed at length.
- *Chapter 10: The Future of Innovation Management* concludes with directions for the future. As companies are becoming more effective at managing innovation, where will the leaders be looking for competitive advantage? This and other key trends are covered.

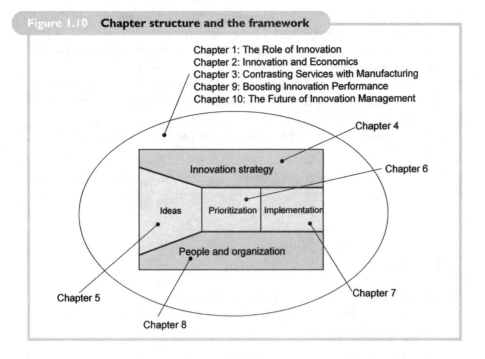

Figure 1.10   Chapter structure and the framework

Chapter 1: The Role of Innovation
Chapter 2: Innovation and Economics
Chapter 3: Contrasting Services with Manufacturing
Chapter 9: Boosting Innovation Performance
Chapter 10: The Future of Innovation Management

Chapter 4

Innovation strategy

Chapter 6

Ideas   Prioritization   Implementation

People and organization

Chapter 5

Chapter 7

Chapter 8

Figure 1.10 illustrates the structure of this book, showing the five Chapters 4, 5, 6, 7 and 8 as being directly related to specific elements of the Pentathlon. The outer circle indicates that Chapters 1, 2, 3, 9 and 10 discuss topics that are related to the whole topic of innovation management.

Format of the Chapters

Each chapter follows a similar style:

☐   The most relevant management tools and concepts, are presented covering both service and manufacturing. These have been selected from an extensive review of the literature, through our own experience in both managing innovation directly, and in teaching and consultancy.

☐   The relevant theory is discussed, in order to provide a solid theoretical understanding of the issues involved and insights into the latest research.

☐   The theory and tools are backed by examples, including four or five short 'box cases' (mini case studies) per chapter, selected to illustrate key aspects of how companies manage innovation in both the service and manufacturing sectors.

☐   At the end of each chapter a several-page case study is given with a set of questions for readers to consider. These main chapter case studies have been carefully selected to illustrate the challenges facing companies, how solutions have been developed, and the main learning points from each chapter. Half the chapters have main cases based on manufacturing companies and the other half focus on the service sector.

❑ A summary recaps the main points and gives practical recommendations for the management of innovation.

❑ Two or three annotated recommendations for readings – either books or papers – are given for readers who want to go deeper into the topics covered in chapter.

❑ The references for the chapter are listed in the order in which they were cited at the end of the book.

For this introductory chapter, we start with a main case from the service sector, looking at the innovation management challenges facing a Japanese mobile telephony service provider, NTT-DoCoMo.

Summary

The aim of this book is to present ways to improve innovation performance through the development and successful implementation of an innovation strategy. This chapter has showed that:

❑ The need for innovation is increasing and being driven by technology, customers, new forms of competition, and the business environment.

❑ There are four main dimensions of innovation – product, service, process and business process innovation. Companies need to identify which types of innovation are important for them and how successful they have been in the past.

❑ Innovation has different degrees. It consists of not only of breakthroughs (radical innovations) but also incremental improvements, which are equally important to companies in both the manufacturing and service sectors.

❑ Extensive research has shown that innovation management is complex and multi-facetted. Its scope is wide, ranging from business strategy, managing technology and new product development, to organization and people management. The Innovation Pentathlon Framework is a diagnostic framework for managing innovation.

Management Recommendations

❑ Determine the intended role of innovation in your organization and clearly communicate this to employees.

❑ Consider how innovation can be enhanced from contributions throughout the organization.

❑ Use dimension & degree analysis to identify whether your products or service products can be made more competitive.

❑ Use the Pentathlon Framework to pinpoint the areas of innovation management that your organization needs to improve.

Recommended Reading

(1) Tidd, J., Bessant, J. and Pavitt, K., *Managing Innovation: Integrating Technological, Market and Organizational Change* (Chichester, UK: Wiley, 2nd edn 2001), ISBN 0-471-49615-4. An Excellent introduction to the issues in managing innovation. Chapter 2 shows how a clear understanding of innovation is needed within an organization.

(2) Kim, W. C. and Mauborgne, R., 'Value Innovation: The Strategic Logic of High Growth', *Harvard Business Review*, vol. 75, no. 1 (January–February 1997), pp. 103–12. Presents how product innovation needs to be complemented by service and other forms of innovation.

Main Case Study NTT-DoCoMo, Japan – partnerships for innovation[77]

Before reading this case, consider the following generic innovation management issues:

☐ How can partnerships and alliances help a company in the service sector achieve its innovation strategy?

☐ How can service and product strategies of different companies be aligned to target specific customers segments?

☐ How can a service provider make it harder for competitors to copy innovations?

Today, NTT DoCoMo is the top Japanese mobile telephone service provider with an enviable 60 per cent market share. The company was formed in 1992 when the Japanese government broke up the monopoly of Nippon Telephone and Telegraph (NTT). The name comes from both an abbreviation of '*Do Co*mmunications over the *Mo*bile Network', and is a play on 'dokomo', the Japanese word for 'anywhere'. Although now the market leader, ten years ago the company was facing a serious situation. The Japanese economic situation was poor, handsets were heavy, subscriptions and call charges exorbitantly high, transmission quality was infamously bad and, to cap it all, DoCoMo was losing money.

Technical Quality Up, Price Down

Some managers might have decided to try and manage the crisis through cost-cutting alone, but CEO Kouji Ohboshi made heavy investments to develop both the transmission quality and DoCoMo's total coverage in Japan. Parallel to this, a pricing strategy was adopted with the aim of making mobile telephone services affordable for everyone. DoCoMo slashed prices and, although competitors followed, DoCoMo raised the number of its subscribers significantly – to the point where it has 44 million today. This growth was at the expense of what the industry refers to as ARPUs (average revenues per user) and so, from an early stage, it was clear to management that a strategy based solely on increasing call quality, market penetration, and cutting prices was not sustainable.

One of the unusual characteristics of the Japanese mobile telephone market is that there is no direct channel by which mobile telephone ('handset') manufacturers can market their products. Every handset in Japan is provided as part of a service contract. Additionally, Japanese law prevents DoCoMo from manufacturing equipment for retail sale.[78] Maybe this is what caused DoCoMo to take a broader view of innovation than many of the other service providers around the world and, in particular, to develop not only new services but also to take steps to strongly influence the design of manufacturers' handsets. Fortunately, through its history as part of NTT, external links to handset manufacturers such as NEC and Fujitsu were strong and this enabled DoCoMo to push for handsets with special features for specific market segments.

Matching Services, Segments and Products

With aging populations worldwide, many companies are trying to target what is often called the 'silver [haired] market' or 'silver segment' but DoCoMo has been particularly successful. Millions of new senior subscribers in recent years have adopted the Raku Raku ('easy-easy') range of mobile telephones, which have a set of features aimed at the particular needs of this segment. Today, 22 per cent of Japanese owners of mobile phones are over 50 years of age. The handsets were developed for DoCoMo by Fujitsu and have:

☐ Larger keyboards.
☐ Larger text on the display and simpler user interfaces than most cell phones. In addition, a synthesized voice explanation can be enabled, for each key pressed.
☐ Colours available include 'traditional silver' and 'eternal pink'. The handset comes with a set of standard ring-tone options to match users' tastes including the Japanese song 'Kawa no Nagare no Yoni', 'Raindrops keep falling on my head', and 'When the Saints go marching in'.
☐ The latest version of the Raku Raku includes a pedometer function that measures how far the person carrying the phone walks, and sends daily e-mails to subscribers telling them how far they walked and how many calories they burned. According to the press release, this 'is particularly relevant to users wishing to regularly update their doctors with this data'.

In marketing the Raku Raku, DoCoMo has trodden a careful path. The company 'highlights its technical features but in its advertising always cleverly links these to emotional benefits', says industry watcher Daniel Scuka of Wireless Watch Japan. 'For example, their adverts show grandparents operating the handsets easily and keeping in easy contact with their families . . . and, of course, "age" is never directly mentioned in their marketing'.

It is not only for the silver segment that specific products have been deemed necessary. Japan has extensive mountains and many of its population enjoy outdoor activities, such as hill-walking and mountaineering. This is a segment that DoCoMo is also addressing with a corresponding handset, the 'Geofree II'. This has a set of features designed to appeal to those with an interest in outdoor activities:

- It is lightweight.
- It floats, is water resistant and shock-proof.
- It has a large (1.8 inch) liquid crystal display.
- It supports 'i-Area', a function that gives local information based on the unique base-station in which the handset is located.
- Matching its usage, the handset is marketed in colours such as 'active red' and 'dynamic blue'.

To understand its target segments, DoCoMo undertakes regular market research. Recent studies have looked at urban usage of mobile phones by 1,000 adults,[79] how adolescents use wireless services and the particular functions they most want in their handsets – 600 young people were interviewed.[80] John Lagerling, a manager in the DoCoMo strategy team, says that the company is careful to make sure that its approach to market research is broad. 'We regularly conduct research outside the mobile telephone market, as we are interested to see how "lifestyle" changes affect customers' needs. Take for example the Geofree. Users' ideas provided the inspiration for the handset, supplemented with by research looking at the developments in the digital watch industry, where rugged designs combined with "outdoor" features had been very successful. Combining a range of features in a handset offers outdoor sportspeople added safety – easy access to weather, local information and emergency services. You do not get these sort of insights for new products if you only research your own industry'.

Although the robust Geofree II, the handy Raku Raku, and handsets aimed at young people increase market penetration, this is not enough. 'Voice-based revenues' from these segments will not generate growth, as the Japanese market has matured and call rates remain an area of strong price competition. So non-voice services are also being developed.

Non-Voice and the Portfolio of Services

'Non-voice services have become a fundamental part of DoCoMo's strategy', says Scuka. Initially, these services were simple ones – such as downloadable, changeable ring-tones (these have become a success story worldwide for service providers, generating surprisingly high revenues). Once the downloadable ring-tone feature had been strongly marketed and the market educated, further downloadable services were added such as '30K Applications', relatively small Java games, paid for on a one-off download fee. DoCoMo introduced their most prominent non-voice service in February 1999. This is 'i-mode' (Internet mode), a service that is generating significant revenues.

The idea behind i-mode involved making Internet access mobile and easy and now it is the world's largest mobile Internet service with 38 million subscribers. Handsets with an 'i' button and special menus were developed to meet DoCoMo's requirements for fast and efficient Internet usage. Not only the handsets have been optimized but also the websites that are available have been coordinated – including those 'authorized by DoCoMo' – and a new business model created. Internet access is priced on the amount of information downloaded rather than the access time and this, combined with the low basic rate of 300 yen ($2.4) a month for i-mode service, and one yen for a typical email, mean that it is good value for money.

Four categories of i-mode service are provided:

☐ 'Transaction' (e-commerce, banking and ticket booking through the websites of Amazon.com, Northwest Airlines and Citibank).
☐ 'Information' (for example CNN news, Bloomberg market updates).
☐ 'Entertainment' (for example Pokemon games, Hallmark e-greeting cards, and hit songs).
☐ 'Databases' (for example telephone directories, restaurant guides, etc.).

Each of these categories has a number of websites providing what the industry refers to as 'content'. DoCoMo has carefully selected content partners for the quality of their services, a willingness to optimise their websites for i-mode access, a willingness to accept site development risk, and an interest in forming a partnership (in which DoCoMo brings more traffic to the content provider in return for a commission on the information charges levied).

Fast and easy access has been achieved by reprogramming websites using a subset of the programming language HTML, which increases access speed. The version of HTML used also allows new websites to be quickly created and this focus on keeping it simple has allowed independent programmers to create a wealth of unofficial i-mode content. Although 'unofficial' sites do not generate content commission for DoCoMo, the availability of extra content has been well received by customers and does generate a great deal of data traffic revenue for the carrier.

Stimulating and Coordinating Innovation

Over 1,100 engineers are employed in DoCoMo's R&D and spending on development has increased by four times since 1998. This investment pays for a very wide range of projects, from improvements to handsets to better networks to support the uninterrupted availability of services. DoCoMo R&D has adopted a central coordinating role – including stimulating innovation – between the equipment manufacturers, content providers (websites) and platform vendors (network providers) as shown in Figure 1.11. In his role in the i-mode strategy department, Lagerling is responsible for managing some of these international collaborations. 'Our strategy is to view the value chain as an 'ecosystem', in which all of the partners need to have a fair margin. If we as a company are too greedy, the system will not function well and relationships will suffer. Therefore, we share both risk and gain'.

Handset vendors receive information from DoCoMo on specific product requirements and the potential sales volumes. This encourages close collaboration on handset NPD and often DoCoMo makes direct investments in such work, to ensure that new handsets are developed on time and these are 'integrated to the content' available. Close links with the content providers include joint work on website operability and co-marketing. The platform vendors are the third set of partners with which DoCoMo R&D has constant contact, as networks determine the availability and reliability of services. Availability is a key concern for Japanese users, as the country suffers from earth tremors and following these there is extreme usage of mobile telephones, as people check whether their relatives are OK. Therefore, network capacity needs to be planned to match these 'spikes' in usage. Overall, Lagerling says that 'subscribers judge the value of mobile Internet services on the basis of the quality of content'.

Figure 1.11   DoCoMo's i-mode collaboration concept – the 'ecosystem'[81]

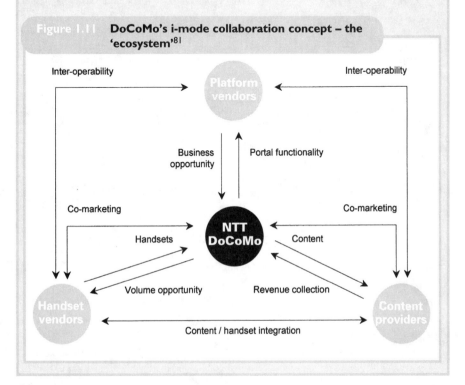

Mobile telephone service providers worldwide are looking for what they term 'killer applications' – services that mobile telephone users will use extensively and that will generate significant revenue growth for providers. DoCoMo is somewhat different in that it is not searching for one solution. Instead it is looking to be the coordinator that can constantly create the best mix of innovative services, handsets, content and reliable network platforms that provides customers with services that they will find essential to everyday life. 'We aim to provide our customers with the best possible range of services. That's only possible by developing our position within a sustainable network of innovative organizations', says Lagerling.

2 Innovation and Economics

'Today, no one needs to be convinced of the importance of innovation . . . How to innovate is the key question.'

(Peter Drucker)

Introduction

In Chapter 1 we gave an overview of research on the subject of innovation and identified the main areas of the literature. One of these areas covers how innovations diffuse through markets, their impact on economic growth, and how innovation helps companies become more competitive. Product or service product innovations can generate growth through increased sales but also they radically change existing market conditions, or can create completely new markets. Process innovations can alter cost structures significantly. It is important to understand the sort of impact innovation can have and so this chapter will present this part of the research literature in detail and discuss its implications for management. This presentation will take the reader on a journey from the early ideas of the economist A.F. Riedel in the 1830s, to some of the leading edge ideas of today. Most of the research discussed in this chapter is at the macro level, as the presentation at the micro level (how companies can manage innovation) and the project level (how to manage innovation projects such as new product development) will be reserved for inclusion in later chapters.

This chapter:

▸ Explains the methodology by which most economic studies were conducted.

▸ Discusses the factors which appear to influence innovation levels in organizations.

▸ Describes the links between innovation and economic performance, including a discussion on long-term business cycles.

▸ Presents the findings of research on how individual innovations are adopted and the typical changes that they bring to a market.

▸ Discusses the challenges facing an organization that needs to improve its performance: the Richardson's kitchen knives company – developers of the well-known *Laser* brand.

Research Methodology

Economic Measures of Innovation

There is a long history of innovation research by economists. A major influence has been what became known as the Austrian school of economic thought. The earliest work was by A.F. Riedel in 1839; who first recognized that new products have a significant impact on the economy. Surprisingly, he did not identify the importance of process innovation even though the industrial revolution had included process innovations which made a big impact, such as the loom.[1] The most significant work on innovation from the Austrian school was that of Joseph A. Schumpeter, who later moved from Vienna to become a professor at Harvard University. His work, which was already mentioned in Chapter 1, laid the foundations for our understanding of both the nature and impact of innovation, and his book *The Theory of Economic Development*[2] is one of the classic texts of economics. It discusses the importance of not only product but also process innovation, such as new manufacturing techniques that can drastically alter the cost structures of an industry. Many of Schumpeter's ideas are still relevant today and these, together with other key insights from economics will be presented. Firstly, however, it is important to understand how macroeconomics studies have been conducted.

Innovation studies by economists have normally focused at the macro level and have examined various industries, in order to develop theories that are applicable to whole communities or nations. This approach has acknowledged limitations because, 'when we look at technological change in the aggregate – as a socioeconomic process – we are obviously forced to simplify an enormously complicated set of activities'.[3] In addition, Paul Geroski of London Business School has pointed out by that research into the causes and consequences of innovation has been complicated by the problems with measuring 'innovation' itself. Economists have used various measures of innovation such as R&D expenditure, the number of major innovations generated in an industry over time, and patent counts. All three can give insight into innovation performance but they also have significant limitations.[4] Patent counts may indicate the level of inventiveness in an organization but until commercialized, an invention is not an innovation. Table 2.1 summarizes the main measures of innovation performance used by economists, with their advantages and limitations. From the table it can be seen that information on patent counts is readily available but it is not a very good measure of commercial success (that is not a good measure of innovation performance).

The issue of measuring innovation performance is not just of concern to economists; it is also a major issue for managers. How can managers select effective measures of innovation? Which measures can not only gauge but also stimulate innovation in an organization? Table 2.1 provides notes on whether the different measures of innovation chosen by economists are relevant for managers. For example, R&D expenditure is not an ideal measure of innovation

Table 2.1 Typical measures of innovation level used in macro-economic studies

Measure	Advantages of the measure	Limitations of the measure	Implications for managers
Number of patents, per employee, or over time	□ Data on the number of patents are readily available and can easily be analysed by industrial sector, country, etc.	□ Patents are more a measure of invention than of innovation. □ Some companies may chose not to apply for patents, as it is a time-consuming process and it does not always offer good protection to small organizations.	□ Useful measure of R&D perform-ance in research laboratories but it needs to be supplemented with other measures. □ It is very useful to monitor both the number and contents of patents filed by competitors. □ Patent counts are also used as an indication of a knowledge base in mergers and acquisitions.
R&D expenditure and intensity (percentage of company revenues invested in R&D)	□ Data on investment levels are normally published in company annual reports.	□ This is an 'input' measure, rather than a measure of R&D output.	□ R&D intensity in a sector is a useful benchmark for companies.
Number of new products	□ Is a measure of the output of R&D (but not strictly of innova-tion, unless product success is considered).	□ The meaning of 'new product' is equivocal (for example six different degrees of product innovation were discussed in Chapter 1) and this can lead to measurement problems. □ Figures on the numbers of new products developed by companies are not easily accessible.	□ Companies need to carefully define what they will count as a 'new product'. □ Often utilized as the measure 'revenues from new products', by companies such as Hewlett-Packard and 3M. □ Few companies use this measure to check the performance of their competitors.

because, as Marco Iansiti of Harvard Business School has pointed out, 'after all, what a company gets for the money it spends on R&D is what ultimately matters'.[5] Where percentage R&D expenditure is useful to managers is in providing a benchmark of the research and development investment typically required to be competitive in a particular industrial sector, as we will see very soon.

Despite the difficulties in trying to study innovation at the macro level, the findings of this type of research have strongly influenced our understanding of the subject and give important pointers to managers. The research at the macro level can be classified into studies looking at the factors that mediate innovation levels and further studies on the impact of innovation on both companies and markets.

Factors Mediating Innovation

Economists have looked at the precursors of innovation. *Development economics* is the study of why developing countries economies have lagged and this looks at all of the factors that are necessary for economic growth, such as infrastructure, the health of the workforce, education levels and economic aid. Whilst the development economics viewpoint is important in that it indicates some of the factors that must be present to develop economies, we shall concentrate on the macroeconomics of innovation itself. Most of the macroeconomic studies of innovation have taken product innovation as their focus rather than process or service innovation. Product innovation levels have been found to be related to:

- The size of companies.
- Education levels and traits of national culture.
- Government policies to support innovation.

Company Size and Innovation

There is a significant body of research that has investigated the influence of company size on innovation performance. Normally, the number of patents awarded, the levels of R&D investment, or the numbers of new products developed have been used to determine the innovation performance of companies (although these measures have the limitations discussed earlier).

Once again, the work of Schumpeter is important in this area of research. In one of the earliest studies, he identified that larger companies are at an advantage when it comes to innovation, because of the economies of scale that they have in R&D.[6] Much of the subsequent macroeconomic research has focused on the relationship between the size of companies and innovation. For example, several studies have found that R&D expenditures increased almost in proportion to firm size.[7] Similarly, an investigation of nearly 600 companies in the USA showed that both the size and age of companies are determinants of the number of new products produced per dollars of sales.[8] Yet another study determined that in larger companies both R&D expenditures and the number of patents awarded is higher than in small ones.[9]

The conclusion that larger organizations are more innovative than smaller ones is not universally accepted. Empirical evidence has also been gathered showing that whilst the scale of research activities increases with the growth of a company, it decreases as a company reaches medium size.[10] Other studies have found no differences between the innovation performance of large and small companies because, although larger companies can have higher R&D expenditures, small companies may have more innovative employees. For example, young graduate scientists bring with them the latest scientific knowledge and ideas.[11] Research by London Business School has concluded that small firms are the most important innovators.[12] Similarly, the number of new products developed in smaller companies tends to be proportionally higher.[13]

What is clear is the key role of start-ups in new industries. High-technology start-up companies are well-known for the innovations they develop and there are many examples where such firms have been responsible for the breakthroughs, rather than the market leaders. One case is the bag-less vacuum cleaner, which was developed by an entrepreneur-innovator – James Dyson – rather than the market leaders such as Hoover (which developed a bag-less product much later). So, the hypothesis that large firms with market leadership are more effective innovators has increasingly been questioned and studies have shown that innovation is by no means the sole territory of market leaders. One study showed that small companies backed by venture capital are disproportionately successful. Of the nearly one million companies formed in the USA each year, only a few hundred are successful at obtaining backing from venture capitalists.[14] Although they make only a fraction of the total number of companies that are founded, over a third of companies that go public were originally backed by venture capital. Similarly, of the biotechnology patents filed over the last two decades, 85 per cent originated from companies that had used venture capital. A partial explanation of the high success rate of such start-ups is that they have to go through a very demanding approval process to obtain venture capital. Companies have also recognized the importance of demanding approval processes for innovation and Texas Instruments has mimicked the tough approaches used by venture capitalists, in the company's internal new venture approval process.

The investigations by economists of company size and innovation illustrate well the need to consider the external validity of research. Although the internal validity is high for the samples of companies studied, the results cannot be generalized to all companies, in all markets, at all times. This helps to explain the contradictory results of the various studies. For managers trying to make their organizations more effective innovators, the messages might appear mixed. What is clear is that at a certain time, in a certain sector, the size of a company may be correlated with the (average) level of product innovation. However, leading companies want to stimulate higher than average levels of innovation because 'the introduction of innovations is the single most important determinant of a firm's competitiveness'.[15] Continuing to innovate at a fast rate may not be easy in large organizations, and research by organizational theorists shows that as organizations grow, this can stifle innovativeness. Overall, economists themselves have construed that the research investigating the influence of company size on innovation is inconclusive.[16]

Although the research on the influence of company size is inconclusive, data on worldwide R&D investment levels are interesting. These normally give an indication of the levels of the investment required to remain competitive within an industrial sector. Table 2.2 gives details of the 50 companies that invest most in R&D. These are grouped into 10 sectors and data is given on the actual R&D spending in 2000 and the percentage of sales (the R&D intensity). For example, the companies that are investing most in Aerospace R&D are BAE Systems in the UK and Boeing in the USA. In the whole sector, the average R&D intensity is 4.4 per cent, but large differences can be seen. BAE Systems is obviously attempting to become more innovative as the investment level is much higher at 10.2 per cent. A more homogeneous picture is seen in the automotive sector, where it appears that 4 per cent of sales is the normal level. Obviously, an organization might consider investing more than the industry average in order to take a lead. Also in Table 2.2 are the *capital investment* (capex) figures; this is the percentage of sales invested for example in new production equipment. Food-processing companies such as Nestlé often invest more in replacing production equipment (4.1 per cent) than they do in R&D (1.3 per cent).

Comparing the different sectors summarized in Table 2.2 shows that the software sector is the most R&D-intense, with 14.3 per cent of revenues being invested in development. Pharmaceuticals also require high levels of investment.

The service sector is of vital importance to developed economies. Most European economies generate well over 60 per cent of their gross domestic product from services; in the USA the figure is 80 per cent, whereas in China it is still only 33 per cent. Moving from an agricultural-led economy to a manufacturing-led one, and then to a service one is a natural progression. As services become dominant, the investments of this sector in R&D also increase. It is now estimated that 24 per cent of the total spent on R&D in the USA is in the service sector, compared to only 5 per cent in 1983.[18] (It should be noted that the 24 per cent figure is probably an underestimate of the true investment, as it is difficult to obtain accurate figures on R&D[19] and innovation spending in services.)

Despite the equivocal findings in the literature on innovation and company size, there are some learning points for management. Large companies appear to have lots of advantages: resources, slack time to develop ideas, readily available funding, knowledge of markets and technologies, management experience and so on. So, why is it not overwhelmingly clear that large companies are the main source of innovation? Specific barriers to innovation can arise within a large established organization and management has the challenge of recognizing and dealing with such barriers. The amount that is invested in research per industry sector appears to be reasonably similar and so the challenge for management is to increase investment, or to ensure that investment which matches the industry 'norm' leads to more innovative products than those of the competition.

Table 2.2   How R&D investment and capital expenditure depended on industrial sectors in 2000[17]

	Sector – top five companies (by R&D investment)	R&D spend (€ 000s)	R&D intensity	Capex intensity	Employees
1	Aerospace and defence sector	11,843,945	4.4%	3.0%	883,479
	(1) BAE Systems, UK	1,550,327	10.2%	3.9%	84,900
	(2) Boeing, USA	1,515,227	2.8%	1.8%	198,000
	(3) United Technologies, USA	1,369,067	5.0%	3.6%	153,800
	(4) Aerospatiale (now EADS), NL	1,063,223	5.5%	4.2%	88,879
	(5) TRW, USA	932,690	5.1%	4.3%	102,900
2	Automobiles & parts sector	53,371,804	4.0%	8.0%	4,229,477
	(1) Ford Motor, USA	7,158,593	4.0%	4.9%	345,991
	(2) General Motors, USA	6,948,045	3.6%	5.3%	386,000
	(3) DaimlerChrysler, Germany	6,263,216	3.9%	18.2%	449,594
	(4) Toyota Motor, Japan	4,159,313	3.6%	9.1%	215,648
	(5) Volkswagen, Germany	4,087,581	4.8%	18.5%	306,417
3	Chemicals	15,252,020	4.1%	7.9%	817,683
	(1) Bayer, Germany	2,354,265	7.7%	7.4%	118,932
	(2) El du Pont de Nemours, USA	1,869,656	6.3%	6.8%	93,000
	(3) BASF, Germany	1,508,034	4.2%	10.1%	104,091
	(4) Dow Chemical, USA	939,039	3.9%	5.9%	41,900
	(5) AKZO Nobel, NL	780,802	5.6%	5.2%	68,200
4	Electronic and electrical	29,554,604	5.8%	6.2%	2,000,102
	(1) Siemens, Germany	5,527,879	7.1%	7.6%	430,200
	(2) Matsushita Electric, Japan	4,844,760	7.2%	6.2%	292,790
	(3) Sony, Japan	3,636,440	6.3%	6.9%	181,800
	(4) Philips Electronics, NL	2,733,795	7.3%	8.4%	231,161
	(5) Canon, Japan	1,793,446	7.0%	6.1%	86,673
5	Engineering and machinery	8,553,390	2.8%	6.3%	485,747
	(1) Mitsubishi Heavy, Japan	1,196,245	4.5%	3.3%	n/a
	(2) Caterpillar, USA	683,224	3.2%	6.9%	67,200
	(3) Deere, USA	570,687	4.9%	n/a	n/a
	(4) Volvo, Sweden	544,021	3.7%	8.2%	54,264
	(5) Komatsu, Japan	391,411	4.0%	5.5%	32,002
6	Food processors	2,463,565	1.8%	3.6%	941,901
	(1) Unilever, UK	1,173,180	2.5%	2.9%	261,000
	(2) Nestle, Switzerland	674,323	1.3%	4.1%	224,541
	(3) Ajinomoto, Japan	222,043	2.9%	n/a	n/a
	(4) Kellogg, USA	124,644	1.7%	n/a	n/a
	(5) Danone, France	123,545	0.9%	5.6%	86,657
7	IT hardware	83,174,629	8.1%	8.3%	2,979,383
	(1) IBM, USA	5,159,450	5.5%	6.4%	338,189
	(2) Ericsson, Sweden	4,677,177	15.3%	4.5%	101,553
	(3) Motorola, USA	4,670,981	11.8%	11.0%	147,000

Table 2.2 *continued*

	(4) Cisco Systems, USA	4,291,997	21.5%	10.2%	38,000
	(5) Lucent Technologies, USA	4,229,885	11.9%	8.0%	126,000
8	IT software	13,048,668	14.3%	11.8%	245,390
	(1) Microsoft, USA	3,974,071	16.4%	4.4%	47,600
	(2) Oracle, USA	1,063,137	10.0%	n/a	n/a
	(3) SAP, Germany	958,091	15.5%	n/a	n/a
	(4) Computer Associates, USA	731,650	16.6%	n/a	n/a
	(5) ADP, USA	484,548	8.0%	n/a	n/a
9	Oil and gas	4,133,784	0.4%	7.4%	1,090,566
	(1) TotalFinaElf, France	678,012	0.6%	5.8%	123,303
	(2) Exxon Mobil, USA	593,743	0.3%	4.1%	100,000
	(3) Schlumberger, USA	569,211	5.6%	13.8%	60,000
	(4) BP Amoco (now BP), UK	456,886	0.3%	5.9%	98,000
	(5) Shell, UK	409,514	0.3%	4.0%	95,000
10	Pharmaceuticals	47,143,896	12.8%	6.6%	915,440
	(1) Pfizer, USA	4,668,876	15.0%	7.4%	90,000
	(2) GlaxoSmithKline, UK	3,972,323	14.0%	5.6%	108,201
	(3) Johnson & Johnson, USA	3,080,300	10.0%	5.6%	98,500
	(4) AstraZeneca, UK	3,045,561	16.0%	7.5%	57,000
	(5) Novartis, Switzerland	3,025,356	13.0%	3.8%	83,031

Education Levels, National Culture and Innovation

Economists stress the importance of technological capability for economic growth. This, in turn, is strongly dependent on national culture and educational levels. For example, the number of new products developed and the number of high-tech and start-ups within a country appear to be dependent on these factors.[20]

As education is recognized as an important factor for increasing the innovativeness of nations, investments in human capital are essential. Several studies found that high investments in education make it possible for countries to create more innovative products.[21] Education levels play a role not only in the level of innovativeness but also in the spread of innovations. Without the ready availability of skilled employees, the diffusion of innovations can be slowed. For example, currently the shortage of IT skills is a major problem in most countries and this is disrupting the ability of countries to take full advantage of such technologies.

With rapidly changing technologies, it is also becoming increasingly recognized that employees' qualifications at the time they enter the workforce is not the only factor. Investments in maintaining and increasing employees' skill levels and motivating employees to personally take responsibility for honing their skills – *lifelong learning* – are crucial. Transfer of know-how from science into industry can be an important source of ideas for new products, services and processes.

It is not only educational factors that influence innovation. Certain characteristics of a national culture also play a key role. Many studies have found that entrepreneurial thinking and personal autonomy are strongly related to the national cultures and influence innovation levels.[22] Examples of the entrepreneurial spirit of particular groups abound in history. For example, several studies have identified the positive impact of the work of Asian entrepreneurs on the US economy. More recently, it has been argued that the secret of US economic success continues to be its innovative and entrepreneurial culture, which was founded on the industries started in Massachusetts. It is widely recognized that innovation needs a supportive social and political climate.

Some countries focus more on R&D and innovation than others. For example, Figure 2.1 shows the percentage of gross national product that is invested in R&D by business in European Union countries, the USA and Japan. This averages 1.3 per cent worldwide, but some countries such as Sweden and Finland invest significantly more (2.8 and 2.1 per cent respectively). The effect of these high levels of investment by companies in these countries is very visible around the world – the ubiquitous IKEA furniture and Nokia mobile telephones are the best-known but by no means the only examples of successful Scandinavian-designed products. In contrast, countries such as Italy and Greece do not have a strong R&D tradition and both local companies and multinationals conduct very little R&D in these countries. The generation of knowledge is generally seen as fundamental precursor to national innovation levels, with the strength of the links between universities, industrial R&D laboratories, marketing specialists and consumers being the key factor.[23]

Although the influence of education systems and national cultures on innovation activities appears clear, it is difficult to make specific recommendations

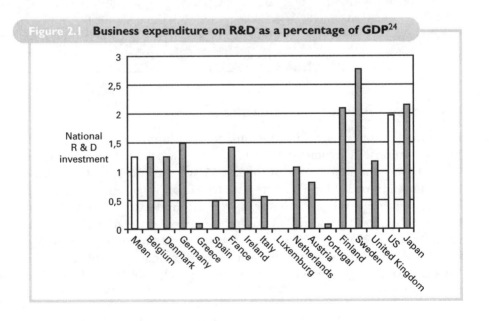

Figure 2.1 **Business expenditure on R&D as a percentage of GDP[24]**

for managers. It can be argued, however, that companies need to find ways to take advantage of the national cultures and different laws that apply in the countries in which they operate. National cultures can have very direct influence on innovation and, for instance, Japanese engineers are far more open to taking and adopting existing ideas than engineers from other countries.[25]

Box case 2.1   Australian Medical Care – changing the culture[26]

Several categories of culture have an influence on innovation: national culture, business culture and sometimes the culture of a profession. Medical care is a major part of the service sector, with both public and private hospitals in most countries. Hospitals have been relatively slow to adopt management techniques, such as process flow analysis (which can be used to optimize the speed at which a patient receives treatment) and quality management. The use of quality management techniques boomed in manufacturing in the 1980s and approaches such as *zero defects* (analysing product manufacturing problems with the aim of eliminating them) were widely and successfully used. Only now is formal quality management becoming widespread in the healthcare industry.

The Australian Resource Centre for Healthcare Innovation supports the implementation of effective and quality improvements in healthcare. It does this through seminars, publishing reports, producing case studies, and communicating new ideas to healthcare professionals. The Centre's website offers some interesting insights into the reasons that quality management has been slow to be adopted in healthcare. Reports speak of a culture in the medical profession that was reluctant to recognize mistakes, 'adverse events' were kept quiet, and learning from mistakes was impossible without 'greater openness'. Fortunately, the culture of the medical profession is now changing and, worldwide, the quality of treatment is being improved not only by improved drugs and medical technology but also through suitable use of quality management techniques. Innovation is not possible without a culture of openness.

Government Policies and Innovation

Ever since economists identified the link between innovation and economic growth, national governments have taken steps to stimulate technological developments and innovation. In the last 15 years, particularly, technology and innovation policy have become an integral part of government support for business and developed countries invest a considerable portion of their budgets in supporting research and technology in science and industry.[27] For example, since 1996 there has been an action plan with measures to speed the transfer of ideas from research establishments into industry in the European Union.[28] Typically government programmes fit into the following three main categories:

▫ Programmes to optimize the interface between science and industry. These include measures to strengthen the links between industry and universities and, for example, allow scientists to move between academia and industry more easily.

▫ Political measures to support the foundation and growth of more innovative companies. These include the creation of a favourable financial climate for companies needing start-up capital. Such measures are often focused on *new technology-based firms* (NTBF) and sometimes these are also focused on a particular range of technologies or innovations. Key technologies supported by governments in Europe, North America and Japan include biotechnology and aerospace. China is also investing significantly in biotechnology. Studies have shown that government support for specific areas can be particularly effective.

▫ The creation of new public bodies with a focus on innovation. For example, Spain formed a new ministry for science and technology in 2000 and a national R&D strategy was developed for the first time in 2000 in Italy, as investment in research had been comparatively low for many years (as shown by Figure 2.1).

Governmental policies can have a positive influence on product innovation. An investigation of the support for research and technology development in the USA, Japan, Sweden and the Netherlands concluded that this has helped increase the number of new products developed by industry.[29] The role of non-university research establishments, focusing on knowledge transfer is also seen as important and, for example, the Fraunhofer Gesellschaft has helped to close Germany's technological gap with North America and Asia.

Biotechnology and multimedia technologies have created significant employment in the 1990s and will continue to do so. Politicians and policy-makers regularly try to support innovation through, for example, grants for relocation, lower taxes for start-up companies and changes in education. A key factor in the success of such schemes is how easy it is for small companies to apply for financial support (see box case on Dutch Government policy). However, despite the actions of governments to support innovation, it is still individual organizations that are at the sharp end of managing innovation. This book is focused on the frameworks, actions and measures that companies can directly take to improve their own performance. If political changes support companies in their drive towards innovation, then this is positive. However, it is better for managers to focus on the areas of innovation management that they themselves can influence.

Empirical studies have identified that the availability of credit can inhibit innovation and because of this, many governments are moving to encourage the improvement of credit mechanisms.[30] The European Union has produced a number of studies which show the importance of finance for innovation.[31] Generally, governments are attempting to encourage entrepreneurial innovative companies by making capital available for technology-based ventures to be launched (often called 'pre-seed capital'), and supporting a climate in which venture capitalists are active. The influence of venture capitalists has been found to be positive in that they not only provide capital but also impose a demanding set of selection criteria.

> **Box case 2.2   Dutch government policy and R&D**
>
> Many governments have used taxation, or rather its relaxation, as a means to stimulate innovation. There are various mechanisms but for these to be effective, especially for SMEs, a key factor is that they are easy for companies to operate. In Holland, where companies must deduct income tax and social security payments directly, this has been achieved by allowing organizations to pay lower tax amounts on behalf of their R&D staff. It has proved popular with SMEs – who receive 60 per cent of the budget allocated to the scheme – and a total of nearly 15,000 organizations benefited in 1999. Research conducted on behalf of the Dutch government has shown that both R&D expenditures and the number of R&D employees have increased.[32]

Impacts of Innovation

Four main topics have been studied related to the impacts of innovation. These are:

- Innovation and business cycles.
- Product innovation and growth.
- Innovation and employment.
- The diffusion of innovations through markets.

Innovation and Business Cycles

Much of the work of Schumpeter and other economists has looked at the complex relationship between business cycles and innovation. Business cycles are the macroeconomic oscillations between prosperity and depression, popularly referred to as 'boom and bust'. Schumpeter viewed the underlying slow and continuous increase in economic performance as important and in his opinion the primary driver of cyclical patterns of economic performance is innovation. Essentially, economic development only takes place as a result of innovation and innovation implies irreversible changes in the way things are done. Schumpeter introduced the term *creative destruction*, which accentuates both the novel ideas behind innovations and their power to disrupt markets and industries. Statistically speaking, innovations are able to provoke upturns in an economy and 'create waves'.[33]

To understand the impact of innovation on economic performance, it is useful to take a historical perspective. Table 2.3 summarizes the characteristics of the 'long waves' of economic cycles, which are also called Kondratieff cycles, after the Russian economist. We will describe these at length. The table shows the approximate dates of the groups of innovations that stimulated industrial revolutions (see second column). The Industrial Revolution started in Britain and lasted from about 1780 to 1845 and was the result of the innovations based on steam technology developed around 1760 (these influenced a number of industries) and the loom (which affected the textile industry).[35] The disruption in the textile industry was stark – the loss of jobs caused by the loom led to riots in Lancashire, England, which was at the time a centre of textile production. The workers, who were known as *luddites*, tried to stop the adoption of the technology. (The word luddite is now used in English to refer to anyone who resists change, including new technology.) Strong protests against the arrival of the new technology were also seen in Europe, with textile workers desperate to retain their jobs and willing to destroy the looms. (In fact the word *sabotage* is derived from *sabot* – the name of the wooden clogs commonly worn by workers in Benelux countries.) Overall, the creation of the loom led to the destruction of the workings of the old clothing industry. The prosperity resulting from the innovations of the Industrial Revolution was seen between 1782–1802 and, as

Table 2.3   Economic cycles – long waves[34]

Long waves	Important innovations	Schumpeter's first phase of innovation		Schumpeter's second phase of innovation	
		Prosperity	Recession	Depression	Recovery
1	The Industrial Revolution (division of labour, steam engine, loom)	1782–1802	1803–25	1826–36	1837–45
2	Railroads, steel, mechanization	1845–66	1867–72	1873–83	1884–92
3	Electricity, automobiles, chemical industry, water supply	1892–1913	1914–29	1930–37	1938–48
4	Atomic energy, computers, robots, electronics, civil aviation	1948–66	1967–73	1974–82	1983–95
5	Information and communication technologies biotechnologies	1995–2000	2000–?	?	?

Schumpeter identified, innovations spread and in doing so led to recession (1802–25), depression (1825–36), followed by a recovery phase.

The second industrial revolution was the result of what is referred to as the 'Group of Five' innovations: electricity (both electric light and motors), internal combustion engines, chemical processing, communications (including the influence of the telegraph in 1844, the telephone in 1876, and the phonograph in 1877), and the widespread availability of clean water. As shown in Table 2.3, these innovations were responsible for two long waves with years of prosperity in 1845–66 and 1892–1913. Since the Second World War, the main innovations have been atomic energy, the computer, robots, microelectronics and commercial aviation.

The innovations since the 1990s have been seen as creating the 'Information Age' and recently the Internet has been portrayed as creating the 'New Economy'. The New Economy has been hyped and is controversial; economists view the Internet as having significantly less impact on people's lives than, for example, the availability of running water.[36] Similarly, economists believe medical treatment and technology have made far less of an impact on longevity than the diffusion of the refrigerator, which has drastically reduced serious illness caused through eating food stored in unhygienic conditions. The boom created by the telecommunications and Internet technologies has currently been replaced by a recession, with low levels of growth in all of the economies of the major countries of the world. How long the recession will last and whether the long waves of the past, all of which were about 60 years in length, will continue into the future is unclear. Long waves, 'constitute an interesting interpretation, but one that cannot be taken as a well-established fact; there haven't been enough of them to serve as convincing evidence'.[37]

The historical perspective allows us to understand several concepts. Economists refer to *basic innovations* and *general-purpose technologies*. The loom had an enormous impact on the textile industry but it was a basic innovation that did not impact other industries. In contrast, steam was a general-purpose technology that was applied in a vast range of industries. The implication for managers is that they need not only to monitor the development of the technologies that are commonly used in their sectors but also be aware of the potential of general-purpose technologies.

Schumpeter's explanation of the impacts of innovation fits closely with the cycles of growth and recession discussed above. He believed that there is a significant difference between invention and innovation and there is often a time lag between an invention and its widespread adoption (for example the lag between the invention of steam technology and its diffusion during the Industrial Revolution, mentioned earlier). Additionally, he believed that the number of discoveries and inventions is high and information about them is relatively easily available. In contrast, innovations are limited in number and normally very few individuals identify the relevant issues necessary to create market successes. These individuals are the *entrepreneur-innovators*, who apply the ideas from inventions and drive them to commercial success. This requires a particular type of leadership, which Schumpeter believed is seldom found in management or amongst the owners of existing firms. Consequently, he believed that incumbent organizations are more likely to be followers rather than leaders of innovation.

There are two main phases following an innovation founded on entrepreneurship. First, the diffusion phase in which the innovation leads to new products with higher utility and often reduced production costs. The enhanced value or lower production costs quickly disrupts the pricing structure of the existing market and radically changes customers' expectations. Similarly new largely automated manufacturing processes can rapidly reduce employment levels – creative destruction. Innovation can also spread across industries as successful innovation in one field enables faster innovation in other fields, as the ideas can be directly copied. Through the enhanced value that innovations offer, entrepreneurs are able to generate higher profit levels. This stimulates economic growth, particularly as competitors copy the innovation (or modify it to work around patents). As others follow, the diffusion path becomes easier as barriers are broken and experience is accumulated. The *market equilibrium*, as economists refer to it, is disturbed and this triggers a process of market adaptation with many new products being developed and competition intensifying.

Innovations do not last forever and the second phase is recession (column 4 in Table 2.3). Once innovations have diffused throughout an economic system, for example a market, they lose their power as a source of growth. This leads to depression and, in a depressed market, a form of equilibrium is reached in which the value of products and their pricing is largely stable. Until new technologies emerge and are applied as innovations, this market stagnation continues. Entrepreneurs who invest in innovation at times when the economy is slow can help to break this stagnation. The rate of technological change is broadly recognized by economists as being the single most important determinant of the economic growth rate of countries.[38]

Figure 2.2 illustrates the impact of innovation at the macroeconomic level. Here there are a number of points that are noteworthy for managers:

◻ In times of low growth and increased competition, investments in R&D are likely to be lower as companies strive to maintain their profitability. There is the argument for 'anti-cyclical' R&D investment (that is investments at times of low growth may be essential to provide the opportunities for growth).

◻ Being first-to-market with an innovation may bring increased profits. This is called the *Innovation Theory of Profit*.[39] The improved product utility or significantly reduced process costs disrupt the pricing structure of markets and allow the innovating companies to earn higher profits.

◻ The increased profits achieved by the entrepreneurial organizations will quickly attract interest and innovations will be copied. Therefore, there is an argument for making it as difficult as possible for a competitor to copy an innovation. As discussed in Chapter 1, there is a need to create multi-dimensional innovations where the essence of a product innovation is embedded in the manufacturing or service delivery process (see box case on Tetley's Teabags in Chapter 1).

Figure 2.2 The macroeconomic impacts of innovation

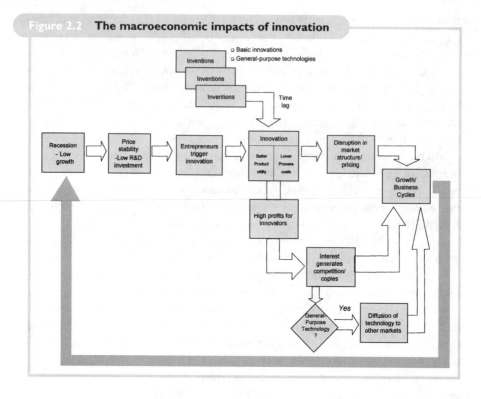

☐ As innovations diffuse to more companies, competition increases and prices are forced down.

Box case 2.3 Repsol YPF – offering full service in Argentina[40]

Economic downturns create an environment where innovations that save money are particularly attractive to consumers. Argentina had already been in recession since 1998, when in December 2001 it suffered an economic crisis and the peso plummeted by 45 per cent. The affect for the 'man in the street' was drastic – real salaries for workers fell by 25 per cent and the cost of living soared by 75 per cent. Petrol and the cost of owning a car became prohibitive and car sales fell by half within one year. Although a natural-gas do-it-your-self car conversion kit had been on the market for some time, this had not been widely adopted. This was mainly because the modification of the engine was too complicated for someone who was not a mechanic and, in addition, the conversion required a time consuming reregistration of the car with the relevant authorities (the Argentine Chamber of Natural Compressed Gas).

Enter Repsol YPF, the Spanish-Argentinian oil company which also distributes natural gas to more than 9 million clients in Spain and Latin America. Working in partnership with Volkswagen (VW), Repsol YPF introduced the Polo CNG (compressed natural gas) in November 2002. This model uses modern CNG equipment designed and installed by Repsol YPF, official registration papers are included, and the car is ready to drive with a one-year guarantee regardless of the kilometers driven. With the Polo CNG, the popularity of gas-powered cars has rocketed and there are now nearly a million on the roads. So, too, has the number of petrol stations offering gas. There are now over a 1,000 such stations supplied by Repsol YPF in 205 towns and cities in Argentina.

The *relative advantage* of an innovation compared to what the consumer is currently using is one of the factors that influences the rate of adoption. For the Polo CNG the advantage is clear. For a family driving an average of 1,000 kilometres a month, the annual saving is the equivalent an average earner's monthly salary. No wonder that the Polo CNG has become a top seller in Argentina. Repsol YPF and VW have met customers' needs in terms of not only the product but in also offering a full service (including installation and registration).

Innovation and Employment

Both product and process innovations can influence employment levels, and new products and services have been shown to have a positive influence on employment. However, improvements in processes in either the manufacturing or the service sector can also significantly reduce labour requirements.[41] In Schumpeterian terms, this creative destruction is irreversible and so actions to try and save industries based on old technologies may meet with limited success. For example, cheaper and effective automation has removed nearly all of the manual painting tasks in automotive production, as hand-spray painted cars are not perceived by customers as superior to ones that have been painted by robots. Similarly, currently information technology is still making many of the processes in banking more efficient and the number of employees in this sector has dropped significantly in many countries in the last few years.

It is not only large incumbent companies that influence national employment levels. It has been established that *small and medium-sized enterprises* (SMEs) contribute significantly to employment.[42] Such small firms that are founded to promote new technologies are important generators of new employment[43] and consequently the policies of many governments are aimed to be particularly supportive towards SMEs.

Product Innovation and Growth

Just as the macroeconomic studies have shown the benefits of innovation, studies have identified several potential advantages at the company-level. These are the role of innovation in providing market share, revenues, growth and profits.

Product innovation appears to be closely linked to market share.[44] A comprehensive mail survey of over 3,000 companies showed that the main objectives of manufacturers' product innovations were to increase market share and improve product quality. Innovating companies were also found to have faster growth, and on average companies earned approximately 23 per cent of their revenues from products less than four years old.[45] Several other studies have confirmed these points. For example, one found that, on average, new products generated nearly 30 per cent of manufacturing companies' revenues.[46] In the service sector, new products were found to generate nearly 50 per cent of revenues.[47] Companies that introduce more product innovations have been found to exhibit higher growth levels.[48] The reliance of companies on innovation, particularly product innovation, is clear from research: they 'are increasingly relying on new products for profitability'.[49] However, the profits that can be generated from new products do appear to be highly dependent on the particular market sector.[50]

Box case 2.4   Extricom GmbH – small but innovative[51]

Extricom, based in Lauffen am Neckar near Stuttgart in Germany, is a small company competing in the 'twin-screw extruder' market. Twin-screw extruders are large machines used to mix and form a wide variety of materials, such as plastics, chemicals, pharmaceuticals and foods. The manufacturing process for such products is normally continuous, and the twin-screws are often exposed to high temperatures and abrasive or corrosive materials, which means that replacement parts are required regularly.

The original twin-screw extruder was developed in the 1950s. Patents protected the technology and the monopoly this provided allowed high margins on both the machines and the replacement parts. Attracted by the margins, further players entered the market and several of these copied the original technology (with small variations), or produced replacement parts that fitted the market leaders' machines. Because of this, customers became aware of the over-pricing of replacement parts and competition forced prices down by 70 per cent. Today, there are over 100 companies worldwide offering twin-screw extruder technology, including Extricom. The technology has largely become a commodity, margins are relatively narrow and this has led the market leaders to also produce replacement parts for their competitors' machines.

With intense competition, innovation can be a differentiator. Extricom has developed the latest technology – 12-screw extruders – which allow materials to be processed more efficiently through improved flow dynamics. Micha Dannenhauer, Sales and Operations Manager at Extricom says, 'we are only a small company with about 50 employees and do not have the R&D resources of the big players. However, we do have a great deal of process know-how, which has enabled us to quickly develop the 12-screw technology. Our challenge is to continue to be faster than our competitors at making innovations that make our customers' processes more efficient'.

Diffusion Theory

The last area of research on innovation at the macro level that we will consider concerns diffusion, the way in which innovations spread through markets. Everett Rogers at the University of New Mexico has been particularly active in this area and his book *Diffusion of Innovations* is a classic text.[52] It is highly relevant for managers, as it gives indications on how product and process innovations can be planned so that they are adopted more quickly.

The first and fundamental lesson from diffusion research is a simple one that managers should always keep in mind: just because an innovation offers a better method for doing something this is no guarantee that customers and users will adopt it. Companies and organizations need to identify the many potential reasons why their innovations may not succeed. Diffusion theory provides a practical framework for understanding barriers to diffusion and taking steps to minimize these. An example of an innovation that from the engineering perspective is a significant improvement but which was not widely adopted by the market is the Dvorak keyboard (see box case).

Box case 2.5   Dvorak versus QWERTY[53]

The most common type of computer keyboard is the QWERTY design. However, it is not the most efficient design. A faster alternative was developed using an engineering approach years ago. However, the alternative Dvorak keyboard is virtually unknown and demonstrates the uncertainty involved in the diffusion of innovations.

Consider the difference in how the two keyboards were designed. The QWERTY version was actually designed to slow the rate at which you can type! This was because it was developed for mechanical typewriters, where there was a problem of the levers catching together and jamming. People who have used typewriters will remember the annoying problem of two levers jamming, and the need to flip the levers back (which nearly always resulted in you getting ink on your fingers). To minimize the chances of two levers jamming, designers looked at the most common sequences of letters in words and deliberately moved letters that commonly come together (for example 'e' and 'r') close together. Consequently, the sequence of keys on the keyboard led to its name, QWERTY. Since letters that come together are very close, this means that they cannot be pressed simultaneously. Thus the QWERTY layout was engineered to slow typing, in order to prevent levers jamming. Professor Dvorak, an American, analysed the process of typing with the aim of maximizing the speed of typing. To do this he considered how the letters could be distributed on the keyboard to take advantage of the fact that most people are right-handed. Therefore, approximately 55 per cent of the work is allocated to the normally stronger right hand, by the locating more of the common letters on right hand side of the keyboard. The central row of keys was reserved for the most common letters, with the less common letters allocated to keys further away from the strongest fingers. Despite the clever ideas behind the Dvorak keyboard, it has not been widely adopted although a number of computer manufacturers offer it as an option.

Diffusion theory can be used to understand the failure of the Dvorak innovation. Although once trained, a touch typist is faster on the Dvorak keyboard, the *relative advantage* of the device is too low – it will not make them twice as fast. In addition, potential users are aware of the effort that they must make to learn the keyboard. Similarly, the *observability* of the innovation is low, that is potential users cannot perceive the advantage that the keyboard can bring to them until they have taken the time to learn to use the keyboard. *Trialability* is good and it is easy for users to try the keyboard but the compatibility does not allow the keyboard to be tried by users with their own computers. Superficially, the *complexity* of the keyboard is the same as a QWERTY one but to a user the *compatibility* with their current modus operandi is low. It is perceived as too high for the return in terms of increased typing speed. Clearly, diffusion theory is a useful way of assessing the viability of any new product or innovation.

Diffusion is defined as the process by which an innovation is communicated through certain channels over time among the members of the social group that adopt it. Mass communication, such as advertising, can be an effective form of marketing innovations particularly in the early phases. Of notable importance is the influence on potential adopters of near-peers, opinion leaders and role models. The decision process on whether to adopt an innovation involves customers being provided with knowledge about the innovation, being and being persuaded.

Research shows that the adoption of innovations by users and consumers takes time. From marketing theory we also know that the users and consumers that are quickest to adopt have particular characteristics. Figure 2.3 shows how adopters are categorized. The first 2.5 per cent are termed *innovators*, the next 13.5 per cent *early adopters*, while the next 34 per cent are the *early majority*, who have all adopted the innovation by the average adoption time (t). These categories are followed by the *late majority* (34 per cent) and finally the *laggards* (16 per cent). Diffusion research has also investigated the characteristics of each of the adopters and this can be used to improve marketing plans. How this can be applied to new product or new service product launches will be presented in later chapters.

Just as the theory on adopter characteristics is relevant to management, so is the research on the main six factors that influence the rate of adoption. These are the *relative advantage* of the innovation to the user; the *observability* of the innovation (that is how easy it is to perceive the advantages of the innovation); then *trialability* refers to how easy it is for users to test the innovation for themselves; *compatibility* is not just the technical compatibility to the users' existing equipment but also how well-matched the innovation is to the way users work; finally, the perceived *complexity* and *risk* of the innovation influences how quickly it will diffuse, as consumers or users are less likely to adopt technologies

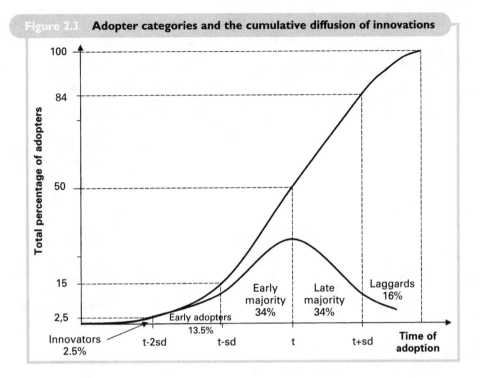

Figure 2.3 Adopter categories and the cumulative diffusion of innovations

or innovations that they think will be difficult to learn or use (see box cases on Repsol YPF and Dvorak versus QWERTY).

Diffusion theory has largely looked at the macro level and investigated how innovations have changed markets. However, it is interesting how applicable the ideas are to innovation at the project level. The six factors that influence the adoption of an innovation, for example, offer an excellent framework through which to analyse the strengths and weaknesses of new products. Table 2.4 lists the factors in a form that can be used in this way.

Summary

The literature on the impacts of innovation has been reviewed, including the precursors of innovation, and its influence on markets and industries. This chapter has showed that:

☐ Large companies or small start-ups can generate innovations. For managers in existing organizations, the challenge is to maintain or increase innovation levels. For entrepreneurial managers in start-ups, the challenge is to generate an innovative idea that can dislodge the incumbents.

☐ Innovation has a major impact on the economy, it drives business cycles and employment levels.

Table 2.4   **Factors that influence the diffusion of innovations (based on the ideas of Rogers)**

No.	Factor	Relationship	Questions to ask
1	Relative advantage	The greater the perceived advantage, the faster the diffusion	▫ What new benefits does the innovation offer? ▫ Does the innovation cover all of the benefits of the existing product, process or service? ▫ How much better is the innovation, in terms of financial, time saved and other measures?
2	Observability	The easier it is to observe the advantages, the faster the diffusion	▫ How can the benefits of the innovation be made as tangible and demonstrable as possible?
3	Trialability	The easier it is for users to test the innovation, the faster the diffusion	▫ Is the customer easily able to trial the innovation to perceive the benefits first hand? ▫ Can a trial on a small scale be used?
4	Compatability	The closer the match to the existing product, process or service, the faster the diffusion	▫ In what ways can the innovation be made similar to the customer's current way of working?
5	Complexity	The simpler the innovation appears, the faster the diffusion	▫ How can an innovation be designed to be simple? ▫ How can extra features and customization be developed in the product, process or service without adding unnecessary complexity?
6	Perceived risk	The lower the risk the faster the diffusion	▫ What are the customer's perceived risks of adoption? ▫ How can they be minimized?

▫   Economic cycles can make business conditions harder, but lead to opportunities for particular innovations.

▫   Diffusion theory showed that customers perceive an innovation positively or negatively in terms of five factors, such as the relative advantage of the innovation compared to the existing solution. Positive perceptions across all five factors raises the potential of an innovation.

▫   Most studies have focused on the manufacturing sector, and only in recent years has innovation research started to look at the service sector in detail.

❑ Even companies that have a very successful innovation need to avoid becoming complacent and to keep innovation alive, as shown by the issues faced by the Richardson's kitchen knives company. Expertise in a particular technology can lead to inflexibility.

Now that the meaning of innovation and the diverse issues facing managers have been introduced, Chapter 3 will look at the specific issues of managing service innovation.

Management Recommendations

❑ Analyse market conditions and identify where innovations can have strong impacts.

❑ Review your markets using the Economic Theory of Profit. This should determine when and where profit margins are likely to be squeezed, and where suitable counter-actions will be necessary.

❑ Determine how economic cycles are influencing companies' investment levels. This should identify opportunities to innovate when others are focusing on are cost-saving.

❑ Apply the insights provided by diffusion theory to individual innovation projects; managing the six factors that can lead to faster rates of adoption.

Recommended Reading

(1) Rogers, E.M., *Diffusion of Innovations* (New York: The Free Press, 1995), ISBN 0–02–926671–8. This is one of the classic texts on innovation, with a wealth of fascinating examples of innovations in both the manufacturing and service sectors.

Main Case Study   Richardson – strategy and NPD[54]

Before reading this case, consider the following generic innovation management issues:

❑ How can successful companies avoid becoming trapped with one technology or product concept?

❑ How can links between the innovation strategy and new product development be made effective?

❑ How can the product concepts be selected that are most likely to be successful?

❑ Should new technology be developed in parallel to new products?

Richardson Sheffield is part of the American-owned McPherson's Houseware products group and manufactures kitchen knives and scissors. Until fairly recently the company's success was primarily based on one main product range. In 1980 the company's then owner invented the 'Laser' knife. With its fine serrated edge profile, this product had a 25-year 'stay sharp' guarantee, and created the market segment that is now known as 'never needs sharpening' (NNS). The Laser with its patents provided the company with a technological advantage that enabled it to grow dramatically throughout the 1980s. While the Richardson's name may not be that well-known, the company – through the Laser brand and the production of own-label products for major retailers – commands a significant share of the European NNS market.

In recent years new entrants to the market, weakening intellectual property rights, and the growing importance of 'fashion' in all kitchen products have started to weaken the company's position. Technologically advanced products were developed to counteract this trend but many were not as successful as anticipated. In fact the company was suffering from a number of key problems – many of which were confirmed by consultants brought in by the parent company.

Major problems

One of the key issues facing Richardson was, in common with many companies that have one highly successful product, a reluctance to move on. Designers were happy with the technology and the sales people wanted to stay with what they knew they could sell. In order to generate sales with the existing products, the company had adopted a strategy of giving every major retailer exactly what they wanted, no matter how difficult these product variations were and, as a result Richardson had ended up producing more and more niche variations of the same product.

As David Williams, group technical director for McPherson's, explains: 'We had ended up with an increasing number of customer-specific variations – and enormous business complexity, and all within a block of business that actually had not grown at all. Therefore, one of the factors we realized we had to change was the clinging to old technology and an old definition of what constituted "customer service" '.

Another key factor was that the new product development process, which supported the whole division's development effort, was poorly managed. For many years development had been reactive, not proactive. The main R&D department had increasingly become overloaded by the demand for product variations; one-off special designs were pushing out core product development. Even when an early filtering system was set up, it was far too bureaucratic. The result was that although the R&D function based at Richardson Sheffield was the main development unit for the whole of the Houseware Group, work often ended up being undertaken by other engineering departments within Richardson, leading to duplicity of effort.

The NPD process itself suffered from many typical problems; in particular there was no 'front-end' coordination and control, and no real R&D focus. 'Instead of focusing on major projects, we used to start and develop many projects, and then cherry pick the best ideas for final design', explains Williams. 'Many ideas almost got to market before being dropped, because only right at the end did we get any marketing input'. Also, when NPD projects did pass through the proper system, decision-making was very slow and poor. 'All major project decisions had to be taken by the Group's senior executives at regular business review meetings', notes Williams. 'Not only did this mean that considerable time was wasted preparing for the meetings, but R&D was only one item on the agenda at these reviews – and usually the last one. Consequently decisions were often rushed; there was poor decision making, with executives acting as judge and jury, dismissing ideas and re-directing projects without full and proper consideration'. Also the reasons why some projects were chosen in preference to others were not transparent to most of the organization, as only those present at the business review meeting were informed.

An example of the inefficiency of the process is that one project went round in a loop through the concept, design, and modelling stages for two years. It started life as a replacement for a previous project – which had been running for some time – completely changing the specification for what the required knife should be. By the end of the two years the specification for the replacement project had changed so much that the final product was almost exactly what the original project would have delivered. In effect, a lack of front-end focus meant that two years were wasted on this project and several million pounds in potential sales were lost.

Another key problem was a poor understanding of the market and consumers. As with many companies that grow through technological domi-nance, and with products that effectively sell themselves, Richardson Sheffield had lost contact with its customers. As its technological lead dimin-ished, the company found it increasingly difficult to develop new products that met consumers' expectations. As Williams explains: 'for example, on the back of another innovation – a tungsten carbide edge coating that stays sharp 11,000 times longer than a normal knife – the company launched its 'Fusion Edge' professional knives in the 1990s. However, while initially successful, the product did not meet sales expectations. What the market wanted – and initially thought it was getting – was a proper plain edge/professional chefs' knife that never needed sharpening'.

The Innovation Process

Having taken the biggest step towards change – recognizing and under-standing the problems – Richardson Sheffield has over the last few years brought about significant changes in the way it develops new products. As well as adopting many new practices to speed up NPD – a structured process, teams, empowerment, CAD/CAM and rapid prototyping – it has reorganized its predevelopment process to overcome the key issues of slow and poor decision-making and portfolio control. Moreover, marketing is now a major player in this process, ensuring that product ideas are market-led and meet with both customers' (retailers') and consumers' requirements.

The changes to managing innovation at Richardson Sheffield are summarized in the company's Three-Stage Model: this consists of a front-end process, the NPD process, and tooling to production process. The predevelopment 'front-end' is based around a process framework developed by Williams (see Figure 2.4). 'Essentially the first key ingredient was to establish that there was only one process . . . and all projects should follow this route, and be subjected to the same filter screens – no more product extensions, or projects being completed by the back door route', he says. To enforce this, marketing has become the originator of all new product projects, and as an initial project filtering process – the marketing audit – works jointly with R&D to develop product ideas that can be presented to retailers as a combination of technology, consumer and customer-driven concepts, rather than simply asking what retailers want and trying to produce this accordingly. A

Figure 2.4   Linking strategy and new product development at Richardson Sheffield

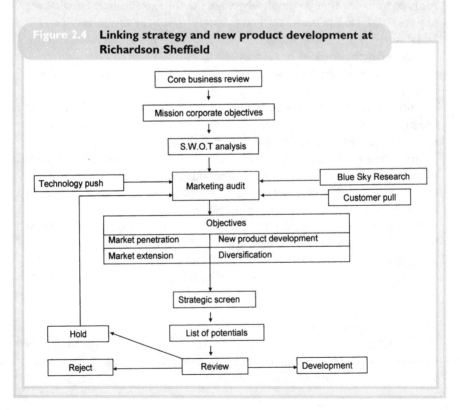

focus is also placed on *Blue Sky* research, long-term projects with the potential to exceed customers' expectations.

A key part of this approach is the off-line development of new technology. Rather than put together concepts that require technology still in development, the approach is based on technology push. 'We have found in the past that it is very difficult to get new technologies to work, and impossible to say when the technology will be ready. So we have formalized the approach whereby I keep the technical developments on one side, only pushing them forward when they are ready', explains Williams. 'Once I have proved the material technology and the benefits of it, and if I can sell those benefits to the marketing people – and through concepts to the customer – then the technology is taken up and developed into a full project brief. This way customers are not left waiting for promised new technology, and from the market's point of view the development cycle from them seeing a technology to the finished product is very short'.

After retailers' reactions to concepts have been collected, these concepts are put through further screening and review – which takes into account the desired market positioning; how the product fits within the portfolio; the requirements of other companies within the division for this product; and strategic fit. Depending on the outcome of this process, concepts will be reworked, dropped or drawn up into a full development brief. This brief will include the product's price point, features, general shape and style required, and packaging. For all projects that are to be progressed the company now appoints a new product manager – from within marketing – who is made responsible for that project, and who works directly with the R&D team once they are given the brief.

By doing much more coordinated work up-front, only those projects which are likely to actually have a high market impact come into R&D for development, and those that have no real business merit no longer waste development resources. 'As a result of the changes, R&D no longer get bombarded with hundreds of half-baked and badly thought through ideas', notes Williams. To enforce this, authority for specific projects has been delegated to the marketing product managers and the development teams by the group's executives. Teams now have the responsibility for determining the project's objectives and, if a product is to be sold by other companies within the group, they must liaise with them to determine if their market requirements can be accommodated or not. Moreover, projects no longer have to be continually assessed by senior executives.

'Development projects are now very much in the hands of the marketing product managers. This means that projects are no longer being driven by senior executives – and in particular not by those that shout the loudest. Therefore projects are much less likely to be 'political solutions' – a design which tries to harmonize all the division's requirements and customer demands into one product, which often led to products that did not really meet anyone's requirements', says Williams. He adds: 'The senior executive review now only looks at future product strategy rather than specific projects, and this was again something that we dramatically needed to achieve'.

Stronger Market Analysis

However, it is pointless introducing a market-driven process, if marketing does not have a good understanding of the consumer and its marketplace. Therefore, alongside the changes in the development process, Richardson Sheffield has undertaken a substantial marketing review and invested heavily in consumer research. These two initiatives have helped the company to identify a much clearer programme of product and market development, which are now bringing about significant sales growth. 'We commissioned a major piece of independent research costing £35,000, looking at consumer usage and attitudes; this produced a number of key findings on what people felt were important', says Williams.

One of the key findings was that, of the different sizes and types of knives in a particular product range, the majority of consumers only use three or four, and even confident cooks rarely use more than six. Yet, up until then, most of the kitchen knife sets produced by Richardson Sheffield had 13 or 14 different knives. Another important issue was design and packaging. The research highlighted that when people go into a shop they first of all judge a knife on whether it has rivets in the handle. They instantly regard it a better quality knife than one with a plastic handle if it has these rivets. Then they like to be able to hold the knife to find out whether it is comfortable and well-balanced. These factors had clear implications not only on design but also on how the product is packaged and sold.

'Another point that was made clear was that consumers do not want a lot of fancy marketing jargon on the packs. They want a very clear brand, they want to know where it came from and they want a guarantee – those were the three things that they are really looking for on the pack', notes Williams. This was all vital information, and feedback that was hard to come by when we simply concentrated on talking to the retailers. We have obviously taken all this on board, and gone down the route of using this and other information in our product planning process'.

The research also had more immediate results in highlighting the problems with the company's 'Fusion Edge' professional product. While there was a definite interest in the edge technology, the research showed that people wanted a plain-edged knife rather than the serrated fusion-edge product. Crucially, rather than just finding out the reason for past problems, the company immediately used the information to redesign the product. 'Based on the research and with marketing working closely with the technical team, we re-launched the product – Fusion Edge – but this time with a fine plain edge which was what the market wanted. This was the first new product to be driven by the research', says Williams.

The same combination has been used since to drive another new product, with new technology into the market. As Williams notes: 'we could see that there was also a real need for a product with a *switchable* edge technology to provide a longer lifetime, but which would be at a lower price point. This was a market area dominated by our biggest UK rival – Kitchen Devils – and where up until now we hadn't really had a presence'. Knowing exactly what the market required, marketing went to R&D only to be informed that the necessary technology – a long-lasting titanium nitride edge coating – had already been developed as part of the off-line research projects. The result was the rapid development and successful launch of a market-driven, technologically advanced product – Excell – aimed specifically at satisfying a range of known consumer requirements.

Seizing Future Opportunities

Richardson Sheffield now concentrates on consumer requirements and driving a targeted programme of product development. This combines technology with a new focus on attractive designs, and aims to generate much more market pull – rather than the company's previous pushing of products through retailers. The result has seen a total repositioning of the product range to match the various levels of market and customer expectations better in terms of quality, cost and design. New products are being introduced – such as a new stainless steel knife aimed at the top end of the market – to fill recognized gaps. 'We've achieved a significant change in the culture of the business', concludes Williams. 'Instead of being reactive and clinging to old technologies, we have now changed our approach to the market. The approach is now very much based on style and design excellence combined with technological excellence. We are also now in a position to broaden our scope outside kitchen knives, and into the development of associated kitchen products'.

3 Contrasting Services with Manufacturing

'In services, although the service product is important it is not the key success factor.'[1]

Introduction

The contrast between services and manufacturing warrants a chapter in its own right for several reasons. Firstly, the service sector is of increasing importance in many countries and often accounts for 60–70 per cent of gross national product. Secondly, services can also be used to differentiate manufactured products – for example research has shown that manufacturers' services play a key role in the achievement of high customer satisfaction levels.[2] So manufacturers need to concentrate on developing high quality services, such as product maintenance and repair. Thirdly, services have some distinct characteristics that mean that there are significant differences to managing innovation in the service arena, such as the intangible nature of services and the challenges of ensuring consistent quality. These characteristics need to be understood; otherwise the challenge in managing innovation in a service environment could be underestimated. Unfortunately, the study of service innovation has lagged behind that of pure product innovation[3] and so the most effective ways to manage it are still emerging.

Chapters 4–8 present the key elements of managing innovation, looking at each of the elements of the Pentathlon Framework in detail. Before moving to these topics, this chapter will:

▸ Look at the important role of services in the economy.
▸ Introduce the terminology of services and manufacturing and describe the characteristics of services.
▸ Discuss the challenges of managing quality for services.[4]
▸ Identify the key issues to be addressed in developing new service products.
▸ Present a case study of the management of innovation at a service company – AXA Insurance in Ireland.

The Importance of Services

The importance of the service sector to many countries can be demonstrated by looking at its contribution to GDP, its role in providing employment, and the increasing levels of investment in R&D in the sector. Services are also essential for companies in the manufacturing sector because of the competitive advantage they can bring and the differentiation they allow in commodity markets.

Service and the Economy

Table 3.1 indicates the contribution of services to the economy in 21 selected countries in the Americas, Asia Pacific, Europe and Africa. It can be seen that in the USA the service sector contributes 80 per cent of GDP, whereas in Finland it is 62 per cent. In contrast, the service sector is currently of less importance in countries such as Nigeria (28 per cent) and Indonesia (39 per cent). Studies by economists have shown that as economies grow, the proportions of the GDP that are generated by the three main sectors – agriculture, *industry* and services – change significantly[5]. (The term industry refers to manufacturing, mining, construction, electricity, water and gas.) Typically, developing countries are dependent on agriculture and it typically generates in the order of 25 per cent of GDP (in India, for example). As countries develop, they first *industrialize*, as the demand for food is satisfied and demand for industrialized goods rises. In parallel, agricultural labour productivity rises and consequently agricultural products become less expensive and account for a lower proportion of GDP. Later, *post-industrialization* sees a shift, as the demand for tangible products saturates and people start to focus on services, such as health care, education and entertainment. Since services are labour intensive, their cost can be relatively high. They also provide employment for a high proportion of the workforce. The shift to the service sector is accelerated by technological advances, which reduce labour requirements in manufacturing and agriculture. Most developed countries in the world have service sectors that contribute over 60 per cent of GDP.

The term *services* covers a wide range of offerings, as is illustrated by Table 3.2 that summarizes the main types of services and the levels of employment in the total service sector in Europe. Note that the research that generated these figures looked only at what were termed 'market services' (52 per cent of the EU economy), and this excluded healthcare and education, two fields that provide significant employment. It can be seen that the retail sector provides over 25 per cent of the employment in market services, followed by 11 per cent provided by hotels and restaurants and 10 per cent by wholesalers.

R&D in Services

Research and development used to be a term associated only with the manufacturing sector. But the amount spent on R&D by service companies has increased significantly in the last 20 years. In the USA it is now estimated that 24 per cent of the total spent on R&D is in the service sector, compared to only 5 per cent in 1983.[8]

Table 3.3 lists the 10 international companies from the service sector that spend the most on R&D, and the dominance of the telecommunications

Table 3.1   The service sector: selected international economic comparisons (2002)[6]

	Country	Total GDP (billions)	Population (millions)	Agriculture (%GDP)	Industry (%GDP)	Service sector (%GDP)
Africa	Egypt	$258	70.7	14%	30%	56%
	South Africa	$412	43.6	30%	25%	45%
	Nigeria	$105	129.9	39%	33%	28%
	Kenya	$31	31.1	24%	13%	63%
Americas	USA	$10,082	280.6	2%	18%	80%
	Brazil	$1,340	176.0	9%	32%	59%
	Canada	$923	31.9	2%	27%	71%
	Mexico	$920	103.4	5%	26%	69%
	Argentina	$391	37.8	5%	28%	66%
Asia Pacific	China	$6,000	1,284.3	18%	49%	33%
	Japan	$3,550	126.9	1%	31%	68%
	India	$2,660	1,045.8	25%	25%	50%
	Indonesia	$687	231.3	45%	16%	39%
	Australia	$538	19.5	3%	26%	71%
	Hong Kong	$180	7.3	0%	14%	86%
Europe	Germany	$2,184	83.2	1%	31%	68%
	France	$1,540	59.7	3%	26%	71%
	UK	$1,520	59.7	1%	25%	74%
	Italy	$1,438	57.7	2%	30%	68%
	Holland	$434	16.0	4%	23%	73%
	Finland	$136	5.2	4%	34%	62%

Table 3.2   Employment in the service sector in Europe[7]

Sectors	% total employment
Retail trades	25.7
Hotels and restaurants	11.3
Wholesale trades	9.9
Land transport	7.1
Motor vehicle sales, service	6.0
Post and telecommunications	4.8
Ancillary transport services	3.4
Real estate services	2.3
Other financial services	2.3
Financial intermediation	2.2
Computer services	2.2
Research and development	1.1
Insurance and pension funding	1.4
Air transport	0.7
Machine rental, etc.	0.6
Water transport	0.5
Other business services	14.8

industry can be clearly seen. This shows the heavy reliance on technology in this industry. Banks are also starting to invest heavily in R&D and it can be seen that Deutsche Bank invested 0.6 per cent of its revenues in 2000, largely in the development of information technology. In the e-commerce sector, Amazon.com is well-known for its interactive website and the company spent over 10 per cent of revenues on R&D in 2000. It should be noted that the revenues invested in R&D (termed R&D intensity) are not always easy to identify, as formal R&D departments with separate budgets seldom exist in the service sector. With increasing competition in the sector, it is likely that forward-looking companies will use R&D and innovation as a means of developing services that can be more effectively differentiated from their competitors. For example, the construction industry is now looking at how it can be more innovative in the management of the key stages of typical construction projects.[9] R&D in the service sector is more difficult to manage effectively than in manufacturing. This is because few companies know how to apply technology to create new services and due to a lack of personnel who understand both technology and business opportunities in the service environment.[10]

Table 3.3 The top ten investors in R&D in the service sector in 2000[1]

	Company	Field	R&D spend (€1000s)	R&D intensity	Employees
1.	NTT, Japan	Telecommunications	3,291,319	3.4%	224,000
2.	Deutsche Telekom, Germany	Telecommunications	690,716	1.7%	205,000
3.	BT, UK	Telecommunications	571,480	1.8%	133,000
4.	France Telecom, France	Telecommunications	443,046	1.3%	188,000
5.	AT&T, USA	Telecommunications	422,505	0.6%	165,000
6.	Amazon.com, USA	General retailers	299,880	10.3%	9,000
7.	America Online (now AOL Time Warner)	Internet services	238,578	3.3%	15,000
8.	Deutsche Bank, Germany	Financial services	177,612	0.6%	104,029
9.	CMGI, USA	Financial services	161,827	17.1%	98,311
10.	Great Universal Stores, UK	General retailers	135,491	1.4%	69,708

Manufacturers Need Services

Today few manufacturers market purely a product; most have some form of services that they offer to support the purchase and use of their products.[12] For example, car manufacturers offer leasing and other financial services, and repair and maintenance. Increasingly, food manufacturers offer nutritional advice services to support their products. Services that help the customer derive maximum value from their purchase are normally referred to as *after-sales service*. It is important for manufacturers to note that service has a major impact on customer satisfaction and, for example, 50 per cent of car owners who switch brands do so because of poor after-sales service.[13] Services are not only important for achieving customer satisfaction, they can also make a significant contribution to revenue, and profit margins on after-sales service are normally higher than those on the products themselves. For example, after-sales accounts for 13 per cent of revenues in electronic systems but 39 per cent of profit.[14] Manufacturers need to become more efficient at matching services to their products to remain competitive. Such services are best designed in parallel to new product development.[15] Many manufacturers fail to adequately consider services during the development of their (tangible) products.

Characteristics of Services

The United Nations has recognized the diversity of what is commonly referred to as the *service sector*. It describes services as being 'a heterogeneous range of intangible products and activities that are difficult to encapsulate within a simple definition'.[16] In 1991 the General Agreement on Tariffs and Trade (GATT) produced a classification of the 12 major categories of service, as shown in Table 3.4. Considering the variety in this list, it might be concluded that there is little

Table 3.4 GATT classification of services[17]

	Categories
1.	Business services
2.	Communication services
3.	Construction and related engineering services
4.	Distribution services
5.	Educational services
6.	Environmental services
7.	Financial services
8.	Health-related and social services
9.	Tourism and travel-related services
10.	Recreational, cultural and sporting services
11.	Transport services
12.	Other services

that can be said about services that applies across the board. Nevertheless, some generic characteristics can be identified and these allow services to be better understood. Before we discuss these generic characteristics, it is important to establish the vocabulary that we will be using to discuss services and manufacturing in this chapter and throughout the rest of this book.

Terminology of Services and Manufacturing

Most service companies refer to their *products*, which are produced and delivered to the customer. These are best referred to as *service products*. As service products cannot be stored, the customer's perception of the quality and utility of a service product is also dependent on what is termed the *service augmentation* – the production and delivery mechanisms for the service product. Much research shows that the competitive advantage is often gained from the service augmentation and not the service product itself.[18] The total package, consisting of the service product and the service augmentation, is called the *augmented service offering*, which is what customers perceive when making their judgements on the quality of the service (as a whole), as illustrated by Figure 3.1. Since the service product cannot be thought of in isolation, designing and implementing an effective service augmentation is crucial. As a result, the scope of service product development is broader and more complex than that for a tangible product.

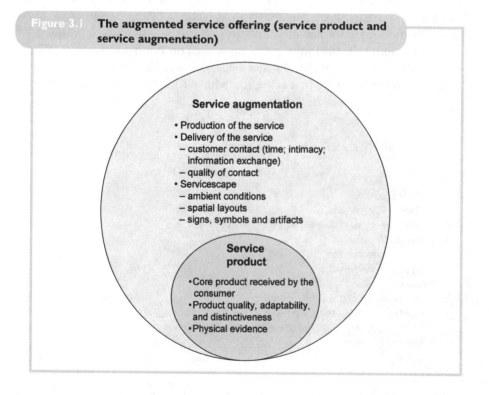

Figure 3.1 The augmented service offering (service product and service augmentation)

Service augmentation

• Production of the service
• Delivery of the service
  – customer contact (time; intimacy; information exchange)
  – quality of contact
• Servicescape
  – ambient conditions
  – spatial layouts
  – signs, symbols and artifacts

Service product

• Core product received by the consumer
• Product quality, adaptability, and distinctiveness
• Physical evidence

Service Delivery

In the service sector, we refer normally to *consumers* as the end-persons receiving the service (the equivalent of end-users for manufactured goods). Not all of the employees in a service operation have contact with consumers and therefore the terms *front office* (contact with consumers) and *back office* (supporting functions that do not have direct customer or consumer contact) are often used. Some service companies base their organizational structures on this distinction. The front office is normally responsible for most aspects of the production and delivery of service products (this is often called the *operations* function). The attitude and behaviour of front-office staff is crucial as it directly influences how positively consumers perceive the service. Innovation is normally one of the responsibilities of the back-office function. In the service sector, innovations consist of *new service products*, new ways of producing or delivering these service products (*new service augmentations*), as well as significant changes in service products, or their production and delivery.[19] The term *new service development* (NSD) will be used in this book to differentiate from new product development for tangible products. (It should be noted that some companies use the term *new product development* when referring to the development of new service products and service augmentations.) Table 3.5 summarizes the key terms, contrasted between the manufacturing and service sectors.

The Servicescape

A key concept in the management of services is the *servicescape*.[20] This is the environment in which the consumer receives the service. It is important in many ways, as psychologists have identified that all of our social interactions are dependent on the environment in which they occur.[21] The physical environment gives the consumer clues as to the quality of the service and influences customer satisfaction. A functional and pleasant environment can increase the satisfaction of service employees, boost their performance, which in turn can mediate further increases in consumer satisfaction.

The servicescape has three dimensions: (1) ambient conditions such as odours, air quality and temperature; (2) spatial layout of the facilities and their suitability for delivering the service; (3) signs/symbols and artefacts, such as the quality of the signage provided to travellers at an airport and the uniforms and appearance of staff. These three dimensions generate physiological responses in the consumer; cognitive responses (consumers' perceptions of a service); and emotional responses (leading to satisfaction or dissatisfaction). For example, supermarket design will take account of the ambient conditions (as appropriate background music and the smell of freshly baked bread can influence our willingness to purchase); the spatial layout to make finding goods easy (the French chain Carrefour has researched the order in which customers prefer to buy food and arranged their stores accordingly); and the signs and symbols (the appearance of staff at the meat counter strongly influences our perception of how fresh

Table 3.5 Terminology overview for innovation in manufacturing and services

Term	Usage in manufacturing	Usage in service
Product innovation or products	Refers to tangible products developed by R&D departments	When used in the service sector, this term is synonymous with service innovation
Process innovation	New or improved ways of manufacturing products	New or improved ways of producing and delivering service products
Service innovation or service products	New or improved services associated with the manufacturer's products	New or improved service products (including enhanced service augmentations)
New product development (NPD)	The process of developing new or improved (tangible) products	Sometimes used to refer to as the development of new or improved service products
New service development (NSD)	The process of developing services to support customers gaining maximum value from products (for example after-sales). Often overlooked by manufacturers	The process of developing new or improved service products. The augmented service offering consists of both the service product itself and the service augmentation
R&D	The organization that conducts basic research (for example to develop technology) and product development	Relatively seldom used in the service sector. Groups conducting research and new service development may be termed innovation departments
Manufacturing	Production facilities and organizations for the preparation of products	Not applicable to services
Operations	Normally only used as the term manufacturing operations, which is synonymous with manufacturing	The facilities and organizations used to produce and deliver a service. Includes the human resources required in the front-office. The terms service delivery and service operations are also used
Supply chain	The network of organizations that supply materials and components to the manufacturer, plus the distribution channels that delivers the products to customers	The network of organizations that supply materials and components to the service provider, plus the distribution channels that delivers the service products to customers

the produce is). The servicescape is an aspect of service management that should be considered during new service development – it is a key and often overlooked component of the augmentation.

Manufacturers may also need to manage servicescapes. For example, a large number of European DaimlerChrysler customers personally collect their new cars from the factory at Sindelfingen in Germany. The Sindelfingen customer centre has been carefully designed to make not only the collection process easy but also to be a pleasant environment. The building supports the overall impression of DaimlerChrysler quality and customers are encouraged to make a trip round the factory. In this sense, both the customer centre and the factory itself are servicescapes that have a strong influence on customers' perceptions.

Box case 3.1   Boeing and Airbus – creating the feeling of space[22]

Sometimes attributes of manufactured products can have a major impact on the servicescape of service providers. An example is passenger aircraft design. Airlines need to influence the design of airliners, as the passenger cabin is a major element of their servicescape. Aircraft manufacturers Boeing and Airbus are being challenged to provide more innovative cabin designs, within the limitations of costs and the space available. The ambient conditions, such as air quality and temperature are already well controlled in aircraft and so the focus is on the spatial layout, more comfortable seating and cabins that give the impression of being spacious. Innovations such as luggage bins that lift out of the way provide extra space. However, as in all services, perception plays a key role and so the subtle use of décor, mirrors, dividing walls and lighting can give the impression of more space (through reducing shadows and other effects that make passengers feel more cramped). The size of windows also has been found by psychologists to have a strong influence on passenger well-being and so aircraft interior design is developing into an area of strong competition between Airbus and Boeing.[23]

Service Characteristics and Innovation

Many textbooks discuss the generic characteristics of services and it is useful for management to recognize these and their implications for the management of innovation. There is some controversy as to whether services are really different from manufacturing. Five characteristics of services have the greatest influence over how they can be managed:[24]

☐   *Intangibility*. Service products are normally intangible; they do not have components that can be perceived by touch (in contrast to manufactured products). Banks provide the service to their customers of being able to collect cash from anywhere in a network of automatic teller machines (ATMs). The ability to collect cash is intangible although some aspects of the service delivery, for example the ATM itself and the printed receipt, are tangible. The perception of the quality of a service is more subjective that that of a tangible product. It also means that the customer may find it difficult to judge the quality of a service in advance. Customers may be forced to take their cues about the quality of a service product from the tangible aspects (the *physical evidence* of the service product as shown in Figure 3.1) and the servicescape. For example, the appearance of the ATM itself, can act as a surrogate for the quality of the banking service itself. More directly, we look at the style and appearance of a restaurant, its staff, and menu when we choose whether we want to eat there for the first time.

☐ *Customer contact.* The level of customer contact in the consumption of a service is an important characteristic and it is normally divided into three categories: *interpersonal service, remote service* and *self-service*. On the one hand, many service products require a high degree of contact between the customer and the employees responsible for the delivery. For example, a business consultancy project will require regular contact between the employees and managers of the client company and the consultants. On the other hand, some services are designed for low contact; such as the telephone help lines for answering customers' questions on computer problems. The extreme is self-service, where customers are willing and able to cooperate in delivering most of the service themselves. In this case the contact with the service provider's staff is minimized to perhaps the checkout operator. Managing the level and nature of customer contact is important as it impacts the perceived quality of the service. Recent research has shown that the customer contact can be better understood as consisting of three dimensions: the contact *time*, the *intimacy* of the contact, and the information exchanged.[25] This is also indicted on Figure 3.1. Internet retailers may have no direct contact with the customer but they still need to manage the contact. For example, Amazon.com tries to develop a level of intimacy with its customers by monitoring previous purchases and making helpful suggestions on books and music that the individual customer will probably enjoy. Managing remote contact can be dependent on good staff training (see box case on Dial-a-Flight).

☐ *Inhomogeneity.* The output from service providers is often variable because the augmented service offering is dependent on both the employees responsible for delivery and the consumer. There can be differences in the service delivered from one employee to another, or from the combination of the employees and the consumer. This can have positive aspects, as leading service companies give their front office staff some discretion to be flexible in the service provided to the consumer. Inhomogenity can influence service quality positively or negatively and so it must be managed appropriately.

☐ *Services are perishable.* Since services cannot be stored, the location and timing of the delivery are crucial. This means that the delivery mechanism must provide geographical availability to match the distribution of consumers and a clear example of this is the franchised chains of fast food restaurants around the globe. The rapid advances in the past 20 years in transport, particularly air travel, computing and telecommunications have also enabled services to be globally more available. The production, delivery and consumption of a service are essentially simultaneous; this is one reason why the consumer does not differentiate between the service product and the augmented service. In the eye of the consumer, they are inseparable and if the quality of either one does not meet expectations, then disappointment or dissatisfaction will result.

☐ *Service quality is multifaceted.* Quality for manufactured products is a simpler concept, largely because the customer is able to base their opinions on a tangible product. The customer's perception of services will be strongly influenced by their tangible aspects. In addition, the delivery mechanism and in particular the employee working with the customer influences the overall quality. Managing service quality has a number of facets that need to be considered simultaneously and will be discussed in the next section.

Box case 3.2   Dial-a-Flight – managing customer contact

Dial-a-flight is a successful European Internet retailer of travel and tourism services. They have succeeded in a competitive, low-margin sector through a strategy that includes a conscious attempt to improve customer contact and provide a degree of customization. Similar to other internet travel retailers, the company has a fast search engine to identify locations, flights and other information. For confirmation, however, the customer telephones the company and is connected to a call centre employee, who clearly identifies him or herself by name. In the process of the discussions with the customer, Dial-a-Flight employees are skilled, personable, and enthusiastic about offering advice on travel destinations, flights, and budget packages. In the event of further questions, it is the original employee who phones back and, similarly, repeat customers are encouraged to return to 'their representative'. Although based on a simple idea, the Dial-a-Flight approach is very well implemented and leaves the customer with a very different impression to that left by many (anonymous) call centres.

Managing Quality in Services

Research shows that one of the main goals of innovation in the service sector is to improve service quality.[26] The key aspects of managing service quality include recognizing that customers' and consumers' *expectations* and *perceptions* of a service depend on both the quality of the service product and the augmentation. One of the leading researchers in this area, Christian Gronroos from the Swedish School of Economics in Finland, uses the term *perceived service quality* (PSQ) to stress that it is the customer's or consumer's perception that counts and not an organization's internal view of how good their services are. PSQ is dependent on both the quality of the service product and the augmentation.

The Gap Model of Service Quality

In order to design and deliver high-quality services, it is necessary to understand how a consumer's expectations are derived. The team of 'Parsu' Parasuraman, Valarie Zeithaml and Leonard Berry (often referred to as PZB), from the universities of Miami, North Carolina and Texas A&M respectively, have been very active in researching service quality and developed a widely used approach, which builds on the ideas of Gronroos. This is called the *Gap Model*, which can be applied to analyse the quality of service products. The model covers the differences – termed *Gaps* – that may exist between an organization's view of their service products, and customers' perceptions. The intuitive idea behind this model is that managers must accurately understand their customers' requirements, if customer satisfaction is to be achieved.

The Gap Model shown in Figure 3.2 is a useful diagnosis tool, and there are several key things to note. In the customer domain, the customer's expectations of a service product are based on previous experiences, communications and the image of the service product. The customer's expectations lead to the customer's own specification of the quality of service they expect (an informal 'specification'). A central point of the Model is that if the customer's perceptions of what

Figure 3.2   The gap model[27]

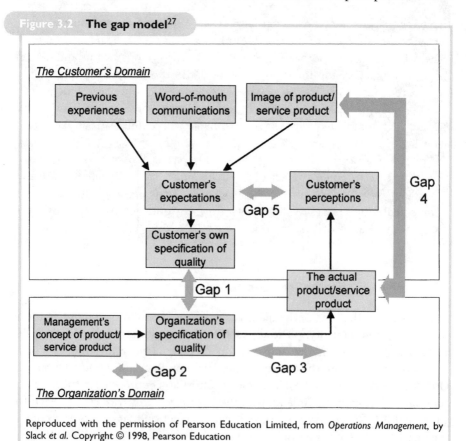

they receive do not match or exceed their expectations, this will lead to customer dissatisfaction – Gap 5. To identify the root causes of Gap 5, the Model defines four contributing gaps. These are:

- *Gap 1*: the differences between the customer's informal specification of the quality they expect and the actual specification of quality in the organization.
- *Gap 2*: the difference between management's concept of what customers expect and the organization's internal quality specifications. Management's internal views can often be very different to what is actually specified in a service.
- *Gap 3*: the difference between service-quality specifications and the service product actually delivered (this is determined by how the service product is implemented, including the service augmentation). Too often the product delivered differs considerably from what was intended.
- *Gap 4*: the difference between service delivered and what is communicated.

The Gap Model provides a logical process by which service organizations can check whether customers' expectations are being met and it has been extensively used to diagnose service quality problems in a wide range of industries, including both pure services and services provided to support manufacturing products. The size of the gaps can be estimated using the *SERVQUAL* questionnaire, also developed by PZB. Once problems have been identified, management can take actions to close the gaps or even better, prevent them occurring by suitable design of the service product and the augmentation.

Researchers have extensively tested the validity of the Gap Model. The main limitations have been found to lie in the ambiguity of terms such as 'expectations', from a customer's perspective. This can result in inaccurate estimations of the gaps when these are measured via the questionnaire.[28] However, the basic idea of the Model – the need to look at the relationship between what the customer expected and the service they received – has been successfully applied in a wide range of service industries (see box case on Malaysia Airlines).

Box case 3.3   Malaysia Airlines – airfreight service quality[29]

Airfreight is a significant business. Currently one third of the dollar value of all goods shipped globally is air freight and the growth rate of this market is estimated to remain at over 6 per cent for the next 20 years The competitive Asian market is currently estimated at 42 per cent of the world market and is identified by the business press as *the* region for growth. Typical shipments from Asia include high value electronics and perishables such as seafood for top restaurants. The region is particularly dependent on airfreight because of the distances to markets and the, as yet, underdeveloped infrastructure in many countries.

What are the most important factors when shipping airfreight and how can these be addressed in new service offerings? Management at Malaysian Airlines had their own opinions on what these factors were but rather than rely on an internal view and prompted by the Gap Model, they decided to conduct interviews. An innovative market research technique was used to unearth customers' true needs, and in-depth discussions with 19 airfreight managers revealed a total of 44 attributes of airfreight. Many of these were previously unknown and were related to the service augmentation. Next a sub-set of attributes was used to identify how shipping managers make trade-offs between price and other service attributes when choosing between different airlines. This information allowed Malaysia Airlines to decide on how to enhance service augmentation and also how it should be priced. Finally, as prompted by the Gap Model, the enhancements to the service augmentation were clearly communicated to customers, in order to set expectations realistically and gain a competitive lead.

Innovation in Services

The Need for Innovation

There is widespread recognition of the necessity for innovation in the service sector and the challenges facing companies striving to achieve this.[30] Just as many manufactured products fail in the market, so it is with service products. Often competitors can easily copy new service products, and the speed with which new service products can be introduced to the market can create an over-supply (which in turn causes more failures).[31] Service augmentation should be explicitly included in the new service development process, in order to minimize the risk of the innovation being quickly copied.[32] It also helps counter the problem that services are hard to protect through patents.

A study of innovation at over 150 companies in the financial services sector identified the factors to be considered during the development of new services.[33] The research found that new service products can open new opportunities but such products are perceived by managers to have only a modest impact on sales and profit. It is only the new service products that have distinct attributes and are difficult to copy that bring a competitive advantage. Conversely, innovations in the service augmentation are perceived by managers to have a big impact on both sales and profit (and also to positively impact the success of other products from the same service provider). The aspects of service augmentation that managers perceived to have the most potential for innovation included distribution channels, effective communications about the new service product, improving the interaction between customers and service employees, and enhancing the overall customer experience.

Research in Germany has shown that the majority of service companies make innovative changes not only to their service products but also to their operations (the processes and organizations that deliver services). It can be seen from Figure 3.3 that nine per cent of innovating companies focus only on the service product,

Figure 3.3 **Innovation in the German service sector**

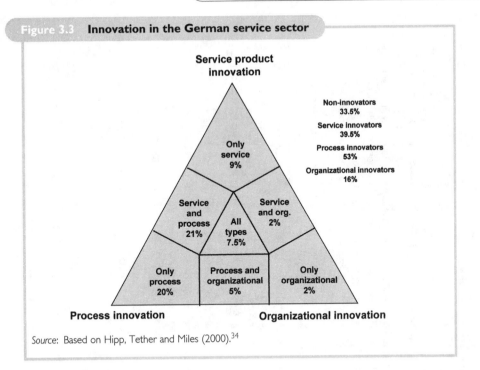

Source: Based on Hipp, Tether and Miles (2000).[34]

whereas others combine service product innovations with either process or organizational changes.

Managing Service Innovation

The generic characteristics of services, including the intangibility and the difficulties in managing quality, can all have a direct impact on innovation. To clarify these links, Table 3.6 gives the implications for the management of innovation for each of the characteristics and we will discuss each of these.

In managing service innovation, intangibility has four major implications. Firstly, it means that the design of a service product should be considered inseparable from the design of the production and delivery system. Second, particular care must be taken in designing the tangible aspects of the augmented service product including the servicescape when a new service product is designed, because these provide vital clues to the customer about service quality. Thirdly, many organizations do not have a well-defined new service development processes. A disciplined NSD process is just as important for services as for physical products and for the same reasons, such as defining the responsibilities of all departments. Intangibility also makes market research harder.

Services are dependent on both the consumer and the main persons in the delivery chain and so management action is necessary to ensure consistency. Alternatively, service providers may use the interaction between their employees

Table 3.6 Characteristics of services and their implications for innovation management

Characteristics	Implications for innovation management
Intangibility	□ The design of the production and delivery mechanisms (augmentation including the servicescape) must be carefully planned at the same time as the service product.
	□ Tangible and intangible aspects of the service concept must be both identified and managed appropriately. The tangible components of services (physical evidence) need to be carefully managed to give customers a positive perception of the service product. Tangible elements should be used to give a positive impression of the intangible.
	□ Intangible products can easily lead to informal processes. Managers in the service sector need good processes for the development of new services.
	□ The intangible nature of services can make it more difficult to conduct effective market research than for physical products, as customers may find it harder to articulate their ideas for improved services.[35]
Customer contact	□ Deciding on the appropriate degree of customer contact is essential. What is the current level of contact and does this match the expectations? Consider timing, intimacy, and information exchanged.
	□ New service products may change the nature of customer contacts and so staff retraining may be necessary.
	□ Innovations in the way the customer contact is managed can give opportunities to improve the perceived quality of the service product.
	□ New service prototypes can only be tested with customers; 'laboratory testing' is not possible.
Inhomogeneity	□ Service innovation must take account of the dependency of the service offering on both the consumer and (often) the main persons in the delivery chain. Either consistency or customization can be a valid aim.
	□ Different customer segments can require changes to both the service product and the service augmentation. It is important to identify the main market segments.
Services are perishable (simultaneous production and delivery)	□ The production and delivery mechanisms must ensure easy access for consumers. The experience of both front and (simultaneous) back-office staff needs to be considered in new product development.
	□ Capacity issues need to be considered at the design stage.
	□ To achieve high customer satisfaction, the quality of the augmented service must be high.
Service quality is multi-facetted	□ Expectations and perceptions need to be managed. Internal perceptions need to be matched to those of the customer and/or consumer.
	□ Managing service quality requires good cross-functional interaction between the front and back office.

and customers to deliberately provide heterogeneous (customized) service offerings. These may also be required if certain different customer segments are to be served. Potentially, each segment will require not only a variation on the service product but also a modified service augmentation.

The form and quality of customer contact can be the deciding factor in whether customer satisfaction can be achieved. Therefore, managers need to make decisions on the appropriate level of customer contact at the design stage of new service products. This can be a trade-off as, although customers generally perceive high levels of contact positively, the provision of this may be labour-intensive and too expensive. It is important that customer expectations are set realistically. As innovations are introduced to the market, staff will require product specific training. Customer contact itself is also an area where there are opportunities for innovation: either in the timing, intimacy, or information exchanged.

Services cannot be stored and so the degree of access provided by the delivery channel and its capacity to deliver services is important. For many services, the capacity is directly related to the number and accessibility of service outlets. Therefore, a mantra for many managers in the service sector is 'location, location, location' (attributed to the founder of the UK retail chain, Selfridges). The staff members who are regularly involved in service delivery (the front office) have information that can be vital in developing effective new service products. The Internet has now altered our understanding of location, as some successful companies have achieved a considerable 'presence' via the web ('clicks and mortar', to use the jargon), without resorting to physical outlets ('bricks and mortar'). Products where the physical experience of the product is not essential in the buying decision (unlike clothes, furnishings, etc.) can be effectively marketed via the Internet.[36]

Many innovations in services aim to improve quality levels. Therefore, the development of new service products and augmentations requires an analysis of how service quality is influenced by expectations and perceptions. The Gap Model is a useful tool for the concept stage of new service development. In particular, the Model forces organizations to compare their internal views of service products with their customers' expectations and perceptions, to ensure that discrepancies do not occur. The back and front offices need to be closely coordinated as, 'the interface between these functions becomes critical for a successful service offering'.[37] Teamwork leads not only to an enhanced augmented service offering (consisting of both the service product and service augmentation) but also speeds development and improves quality.

Box case 3.4   Innovating in Healthcare – not just treatment[38]

The importance of customer perception in the service sector is paramount and nowhere more so than in healthcare. In healthcare the service product is diagnosis and treatment and these have traditionally been the focus to the exclusion of almost all other aspects of the service (that is, the service augmentation has been largely neglected). For example, the waiting times in many healthcare systems are long, staff members are overworked and may have little time to concentrate on how the service is delivered, and drab décor is not unusual in many hospitals and clinics. However, now the role of the augmented service and, in particular the servicescape, has been linked directly to the 'bottom-line' in recent research in the USA. Hospital departments that have been redecorated in pastel shades and where attractive artwork was hung on the walls were found to have higher levels of well being in their patients and certain patients were found to require less medication. Perhaps it is not surprising that patients stated that they preferred the atmosphere in the different surrounding (and perceived the service as better) but what is enlightening is that these same departments found that dosages of self-administered painkillers were up to 45 per cent lower and this leads to significant savings.

New Service Development Processes

NSD has often been found to be less well-organized than product development in the manufacturing sector. Research, including the work of Dick Chase, a leading authority on services from the University of Southern California, has identified three enablers of effective NSD: information technology, cross-functional teamwork, and formal processes.[39] The information technology capability of an organization, for example its usage of database information to generate ideas for new service products and improved delivery, can be very important in the early stages of NSD. Typically information technology is also one of the limiting factors in the capacity of services that can be delivered by an organization. Cross-functional teamwork is necessary to create an effective service product and augmentation and this requires managers to coordinate the front-back-office boundary between marketing and operations. A well-defined formal development process is less common in service companies but just as important as in manufacturing. There are normally four stages in the development of a new service product: generation of a concept; business analysis and planning; development; and market launch.[40]

In generating a concept for a new augmented service offering, ideas can come from a number of sources. An EU survey of the service sector found that over 80 per cent of organizations gained most of their ideas from customers.[41] This indicates that companies are talking to their customers but raises the question of whether they are doing it in an effective way (Chapter 5 considers how to take a more innovative approach to market research). High-quality market research is needed to gain insights not only for new service products but also for possible service augmentations. Often internal ideas based on anecdotal evidence are used rather than decisions about service innovations being appropriately based on facts gathered from the marketplace.[42] It should be noted that service consumers, just as product users, might not be able to clearly articulate their future product needs, particularly due to the intangible nature of service products. (Ways of identifying hidden needs of both manufacturing and service customers are discussed in Chapter 5.) A new service can often be easily designed and discussed (often purely on paper).[43] In generating a new service concept it may be difficult to imagine how the customer will perceive it. To counter this, HSBC Bank make discussions about concepts for new service products more tangible by using role-plays to show how the new product will be presented to the customer. This way of making 'service prototypes' has been found to be particularly effective at the concept stage.

Box case 3.5   Halifax Building Society – new service development

The Halifax Building Society in the UK focuses on the fast development of new service products. These include new lending packages for house purchasers, which for instance allow borrowers to customize repayment levels to their needs over a number of years. Halifax have reduced the time to develop and introduce new mortgage packages from six months to a matter of a few weeks, in response to a more competitive market. There are four main steps to their development process and in each of these the responsibilities of each department are clearly defined:

(1) *Concept development.* This takes account of previous products, competitive products and perceived customer requirements. The concept will be refined, taking particular account of the views of marketing and operations. An initial check is made on whether the concept can be delivered with existing systems or whether it will require changes at the operational level.

(2) *Trial.* Customers (in focus groups) are asked their opinions of the new service. This market research largely replaces the market piloting of new mortgage packages, which was common in the industry a few years ago.

(3) *Delivery system definition.* The delivery of a new service requires that a suitable system is set-up. The *system* means all resources involved in the delivery, which typically will include computer resources (for tracking payment level, etc.) and human resources (for marketing and administering the service).

(4) *Introduction.* Once the delivery system has been defined, the introduction of the new service largely involves the implementation of training programmes to explain it to staff, preparation of necessary software to run systems, etc.

Services and Innovation Management

The discussion in this chapter has shown how the management of innovation for service products is different to that for manufactured products. In reading the next chapters on the elements of the Innovation Pentathlon, the main points that

Figure 3.4 **Summary of service issues to consider in the next five chapters**

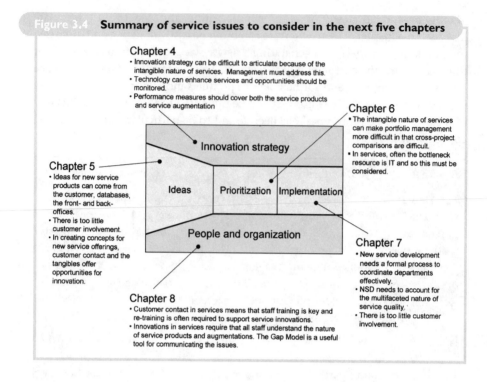

Chapter 4
• Innovation strategy can be difficult to articulate because of the intangible nature of services. Management must address this.
• Technology can enhance services and opportunities should be monitored.
• Performance measures should cover both the service products and service augmentation

Chapter 6
• The intangible nature of services can make portfolio management more difficult in that cross-project comparisons are difficult.
• In services, often the bottleneck resource is IT and so this must be considered.

Chapter 5
• Ideas for new service products can come from the customer, databases, the front- and back-offices.
• There is too little customer involvement.
• In creating concepts for new service offerings, customer contact and the tangibles offer opportunities for innovation.

Innovation strategy

Ideas   Prioritization   Implementation

People and organization

Chapter 7
• New service development needs a formal process to coordinate departments effectively.
• NSD needs to account for the multifaceted nature of service quality.
• There is too little customer involvement.

Chapter 8
• Customer contact in services means that staff training is key and re-training is often required to support service innovations.
• Innovations in services require that all staff understand the nature of service products and augmentations. The Gap Model is a useful tool for communicating the issues.

should be kept in mind are summarized on Figure 3.4. This shows for example that an innovation strategy can be more difficult to articulate in a service organization because of the intangible nature of service innovation and normally the lack of a single department such as R&D, which is seen as having the main responsibility for innovation. Similarly, technology increasingly impacts the service sector and so monitoring technological advances and identified potential impacts need to be done.

Summary

Managing service innovation raises some particular challenges but, as manufacturers are facing the need to provide more services, these challenges are very relevant to both the service and manufacturing sectors. This chapter has shown:

☐ The role of the service sector in developed economics and the increasing importance of services for manufacturers.

☐ That service products are intimately linked to their production and delivery – the service augmentation. Service augmentation, including the environment in which the service is delivered, has a strong influence on customer satisfaction.

□ The management of innovation for services is complicated by their inherent nature, especially by their intangibility and non-storability.

□ Managing service quality requires an awareness of the customer's perception and careful management of both the core service product and the service augmentation.

□ That new service development is challenging because of the nature of services. A suitable management process is required and this must consider not only the product itself but also the augmented service offering. The process also needs to ensure good teamwork, spanning the front and back office boundary.

In the next five chapters, each of the elements of the Pentathlon Framework will be considered.

Management Recommendations

□ Irrespective of whether your organization is in the manufacturing or service sector, identify the role of services in your business. Consider which customer segments require particular services.

□ Identify where innovations in both the service product and the augmentations can lead to competitive advantage. Make these improvements as tangible as possible to customers.

□ Use the Gap Model to gauge the current quality of your services and identify potential improvements.

□ Recognize the need for an efficient process for new service development (parallel to NPD if in the manufacturing sector).

Recommended Reading

(1) Johnston, R. and Clark, G., *Service Operations Management* (London: *Financial Times* – Prentice Hall, 2001), ISBN 0-2736-39226. Leading textbook on the management of services, including useful discussions on quality and new service development.

(2) Johne, A. and Storey, C., 'New Service Development: A Review of the Literature and Annotated Bibliography ', *European Journal of Marketing*, vol. 32, no. 3/4 (1998), pp. 84–251. Key review of the research into new service development.

(3) Tidd, J. and Hull, F.M. (eds), *Service Innovation: Organizational Responses to Technological Opportunities and Market Imperatives* (London: Imperial College Press, 2003), ISBN 1-86094-367-5. Very useful collection of readings on the latest research on innovation in the service sector.

Before reading this case, consider the following generic innovation management issues:

▢   What sort of ideas lead to the most important innovations? Are they the 'brainwaves' that lead to radical products or are they more pedestrian?
▢   How can the best ideas be selected?
▢   How can the nature of innovation be effectively communicated within an service organization?

Introduction

The French company AXA is the largest insurance company in the world with approximately 150,000 employees. Their Irish subsidiary was formerly part of the Guardian Insurance Group and today it has high market shares in the motor and household insurance sectors and distributes its service products through a network of branch offices, insurance brokers and tele-sales operations. Although the insurance sector is not normally known for its innovativeness, the parent company has established innovation as one of its company core 'values' and the Irish operation has created a reputation for creativity over the last few years. In Ireland the focus on innovation started in January 2000, when AXA created a new position of 'Innovation Manager'.

The responsibility of this role was broadly defined as 'to raise the innovation capability of the organisation through staff involvement and shared knowledge' and a service manager Catherine Whelan was quickly asked to accept the challenging position. Her task was not simple, especially as there had been no previous incumbent, on whose ideas she could build. Furthermore, the Irish AXA organization did not have a tradition of innovation and colleagues greeted her appointment as the Innovation Manager with some scepticism. In contrast, Catherine had the full support of the Chief Executive Officer, John O'Neill, who had joined the Irish operation in late 1999. He had immediately announced that one of his main business targets was for AXA Ireland to become more innovative, to match the worldwide emphasis that AXA placed on innovation. However, his aim was also strongly influenced by the need to find ways of addressing factors such as the significant inflationary pressures in the Irish economy, cut throat competition, market consolidation in the insurance industry, and the urgent need to reduce costs.

The MadHouse

O'Neill had acted quickly to stimulate innovative thinking within AXA Ireland, both through the appointment of an Innovation Manager and, shortly before, through the launch of an initiative which he christened the 'MadHouse Programme'. It was a team-based way of stimulating innovative ideas, with members meeting regularly over a period of two–three months. Typically, it brought together half a dozen employees from different areas of the business and different levels in the organization, on a part-time basis with the stated objective of coming up with innovative business ideas. This activity was carried out in a way that involved both learning and fun and there was a dedicated room for the use of the MadHouse teams. This contained a PC, internet access, information on creativity techniques, books and magazines, coloured hats hanging from the ceiling as a reminder of Edward de Bono's 'Thinking Hats' and other symbols and decorations from around the AXA organization.

In its first six months the MadHouse Programme generated over 200 business ideas. These ideas were passed to Catherine, who as Innovation Manager was responsible for choosing the best ideas for further development. She realized that the MadHouse programme had achieved a lot in a short time and had helped to raise the profile of innovation within the organization. It had generated enthusiasm among staff. It had created an environment of shared learning and was helping to build cross-functional business relationships. It had also generated a significant number of business ideas. Nevertheless, Catherine was worried whether the Programme would continue to be successful for a number of reasons:

☐   Firstly, given the time and resources allocated to the programme it was the view of several managers that too few really 'new' ideas had emerged and little contribution had been made to the business.

☐   The 200 ideas generated were only at the concept stage. They required selection and development but the business units were reluctant to take on this additional work. Catherine knew that achieving some successful implementations was key to the continuing credibility of the programme.

☐   It was obvious that both the MadHouse and innovation were still viewed as something separate from normal business activity. Catherine perceived her role was to embed innovation activity as part of the way AXA Ireland staff act and think during their day-to-day work. As AXA Ireland was a traditional insurance company, this change looked like being difficult.

Linking Innovation to the Business

In looking for a way to push innovation further, Catherine focused on a number of areas. Firstly, she decided to quickly push the implementation of one of the ideas from the MadHouse. This was the 'TaskMasters' initiative in which every employee at every level in the business would be empowered and encouraged to engage in innovation and continuous improvement on a daily basis, rather than as only part of the MadHouse initiative. TaskMasters encouraged employees to continuously question the value of what they were doing on a daily basis and check if it was supporting the relationship with customers. The focus would be on addressing small problems and issues that could be implemented quickly and at low cost. A reward structure was estab-lished to support the initiative and measures were set to gauge the success of this programme.

Secondly, Catherine actively promoted the awareness of innovation in general and specifically the TaskMasters initiative. Regular communications were sent to all staff and, additionally, an 'Innovation Corridor' was created on the way to the staff restaurant. This created a wider familiarity about the need for innovation, which had previously been restricted to the relatively small number of people involved with the MadHouse. Still, Catherine felt that perhaps too much emphasis was being placed on the generation of new ideas and this kept her thinking about the meaning of innovation in the AXA Ireland business in general.

Thirdly, she realized that the generation of many business ideas was posi-tive but the selection of the best ideas from the 200 concepts already exist-ing would not be easy. To address this problem she worked with management to understand their views on the factors that needed to be considered when choosing projects; such as the potential market impact, the resources available, and the urgency. When viewed from this perspective, many of the ideas appeared less viable and so a set of 'filters' was created for MadHouse participants and a selection process that involved management. The filters consisted of a set of questions that participants were encouraged to use to evaluate their own ideas. A selection process was also created where, at the end of a three-month period, MadHouse participants were required to present their ideas to a management panel that, if convinced, would quickly assign resources for implementation.

Although the MadHouse and TaskMasters initiatives had raised the inno-vation capability of the organization and by doing so had supported the strategy of the business, a number of key issues had to be addressed. Structuring the programmes effectively was going to be important. Convincing staff that they had a key role to play in the development of the company was also still a challenge.

Learning from the Results

With hindsight, Whelan sees that a clear understanding of the meaning of innovation is essential within an organization. This led her to develop the 'Innovation Quadrant' (Figure 3.5), as a categorization of the types of ideas that lead to successful innovations. Initially the Quadrant provided a commu-nication tool, which was used to explain to all employees that innovation has a broad scope and is not simply ideas for new service products. It also allowed more emphasis to be placed on encouraging all employees to contribute to innovation and not just those selected to attend the MadHouse or work on new service products. Now, with the experience of focusing on innovation, it is interesting to see what types of ideas were applied successfully. The figures

Main Case Study *continued*

Figure 3.5   AXA innovation quadrant

Create new customer-focused opportunities (10%)	Improve existing products, services and processes (40%)
Eliminate non-value-adding activities (40%)	Re-use AXA global success stories (10%)

in brackets in Figure 3.5 indicate the percentage of ideas successfully implemented over the last two years, and it can clearly be seen that new customer-focused opportunities (new service products) represents only 10 per cent of the implemented ideas. In contrast, improving processes through the elimination of non-value-adding steps has had a major impact on many areas of the AXA business. Similarly, many improvements to existing service products have been made.

Overall, AXA Ireland has come a long way since the role of Innovation Manager was created and the company has discovered the importance of communicating the role of innovation, creating well understood and effective filtering mechanisms, and knowing the types of ideas that are most likely to generate business returns.

4 Developing an Innovation Strategy

'I have always found that plans are useless, but planning is indispensable.'
(Dwight D. Eisenhower)

Introduction

Innovation strategy is part of overall strategy. It determines where and when innovation is required to meet the aims of the organization and lays out in broad terms what is to be done about it. It is a key element of the Pentathlon, shaping and influencing all the other elements, as is shown by Figure 4.1

The first step in developing an innovation strategy is to identify where innovation is most needed. This is perhaps the most difficult task because the need for innovation often arises from long-term trends that may develop slowly or outside the immediate scope of the business. As a result they may be difficult to

Figure 4.1 The influence of innovation strategy on other elements of the Pentathlon

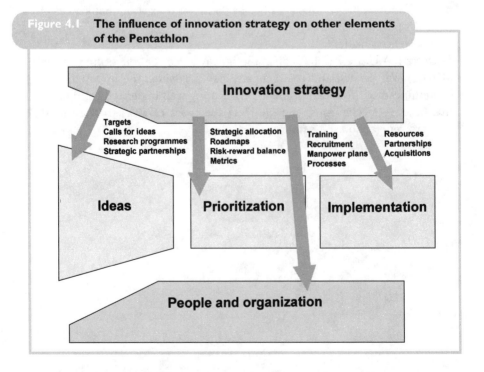

recognize and painful to confront. The second step of an innovation strategy is to determine what type of innovation is needed to address the issue: for example new products, new business processes, or a new route to market? And is a major change required or will an acceleration of existing trends suffice? Finally there are issues of implementation, particularly timing, resources and partnerships.

In this chapter we cover the following topics:

▸ The key elements of strategy.
▸ Linking strategy to customer needs.
▸ Technology maturity and dominant design.
▸ Disruptive technologies and strategies.
▸ Timing of innovation.
▸ Tools for assembling and communicating the strategy: road-mapping and scenarios.
▸ A main case study of Domino Printing Sciences.

The Elements of Strategic Management

Johnson and Scoles[1] define strategy in the following way:

> Strategy is the direction and scope of an organization over the long term: which achieves advantage for the organization through its configuration of resources within a changing environment, to meet the needs of markets and to fulfil stakeholder expectations.

The term *stakeholder* covers all those to whom the organization is important. For a company it is usually taken to include customers, investors, employees, suppliers and the local community. These authors propose that strategic management has three main elements, all of which must be addressed in any strategic plan. These are:

1 *Strategic analysis.* Understanding the competences, assets and capabilities of the organization, the environment it operates in (including competition), and the goals and expectations of the people with power to guide it. The latter point is crucial for the subject of this book because the need for innovation arises when there is a mismatch between these goals and the expected future.
2 *Strategic choice.* This covers the broad choices the organization makes about its activities: What business are we in? What markets do we intend to serve? What is our competitive stance compared with other players? What emphasis or priority shall be given to the various parts of the enterprise?
3 *Strategic implementation.* The resources, organization and management processes that must be put together to implement the strategy.

Johnson and Scholes draw these elements in the form of a triangle (Figure 4.2), emphasizing the fact that strategic management is not a linear process from

Figure 4.2 **The strategy triangle**

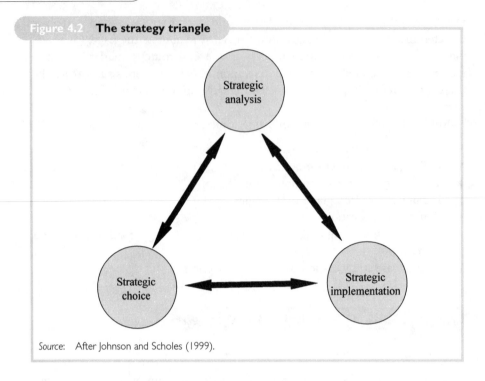

Source: After Johnson and Scholes (1999).

analysis to choice to implementation, but rather a cyclical one, where all the elements interact and affect one another. This means that in practice strategy must evolve continuously as the world and the organization change. Field Marshall Von Moltke rightly said of military strategy 'No battle-plan survives first contact with the enemy'. Nevertheless, every successful general has given the closest attention to strategic planning, not in order to predict every move of the battle but to ensure they had the understanding and the capabilities to exploit the turn of events. The lesson for management is that strategy is not a group of decisions taken once and never altered. Rather it is an adaptive process of learning and analysis aimed at giving the organization the best possible scope for success now and in the future. This means it must be reviewed regularly and altered when required. No strategy lasts forever.

We will now consider the elements in more detail, giving particular emphasis to strategic analysis. Strategic choice and strategic implementation are discussed further in Chapters 6 and 7 respectively.

Strategic Analysis

In the most general sense the need for innovation comes from a mismatch between the aims of the organization and what it actually expects to achieve by continuing with its present policies. The gap, if any, points clearly to where innovation is required (Figure 4.3). The aims of the organization, namely to

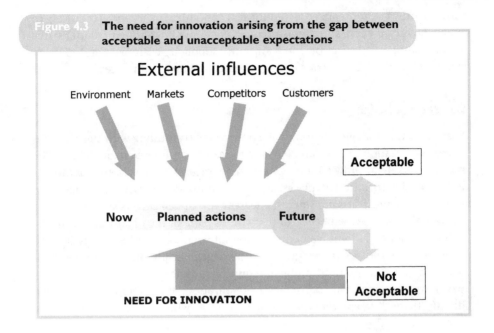

Figure 4.3 **The need for innovation arising from the gap between acceptable and unacceptable expectations**

satisfy the needs of stakeholders, are crucial in this analysis because innovation is required only, and to the extent that, the expected performance falls short of what the stakeholders want. For many organizations strategic impetus is provided by the needs of customers combined with the demands of investors for growth and profitability. However the ambitions of the key leaders in the company often play a vital role, as the fortunes of Microsoft,[2] the Virgin group and (less happily) Enron attest.

The analysis of long-term trends is a particularly important part of innovation strategy because slow trends may not be easy to spot, and, if spotted, are too often ignored. Organizations (and individuals) will often react imaginatively to a crisis but may fail to recognize and confront a slowly developing threat. One is reminded of the schoolboy question: 'how can you boil a live frog?'. The answer is 'slowly': drop the frog into hot water and it will jump out, but heat the water slowly and it will not become uncomfortable enough to jump until it is too late. Most of the great companies that dominated the electronics industry in the 1950s failed to make the transition to the new world of integrated circuits. This was not because they lacked the resources to develop new technologies but because they failed to react until it was too late. Similar things have happened in countless other industries. For this reason we give considerable attention in this chapter to how long-term trends, particularly in technology and customer behaviour, can demand innovative responses. Viewed from the perspective of meeting the needs of stakeholders (of whom customers are usually overwhelmingly the most important) the key strategic challenges are how to judge customers' future needs, and how to satisfy them better as time goes on, compared to the competitors. The influences affecting these challenges may conveniently be summarized as Political, Economic, Social and Technical, to which Environmental and Infrastructural are sometimes added.[3] Porter's five forces analysis[4] (substitution, new entrants, suppliers, customers and existing competitors) is helpful in considering broad competitive influences.

Strategic Choice

Analysis of the strategic situation will show where continuing with the activities of the organization as they are, is likely to lead to an unacceptable future. The analysis is likely to show a number of such opportunities, of various magnitudes and urgencies in different places. Managers must decide which to tackle. In doing so they must first consider the degrees and dimensions (see Chapter 1) of innovation that may be needed in the various parts of the organization. In one activity incremental improvements may be sufficient; in another it may need to be accelerated with extra resources and management attention. Another business unit may face a serious problem requiring radical new solutions; and these may have to come from outside the organization. Innovation strategy must identify these different themes and make it clear where the emphasis is to be placed.

It is in the nature of innovation that the answers to the problems raised by the strategic analysis may not necessarily be at hand. One role of the innovation strategy should therefore be to indicate what new ideas are needed. In practice this is not often done. Indeed many would say that creativity cannot or should not be directed; that the aim of innovation management is just to develop the culture and processes for innovation, leaving it to the creative energies of the staff to throw up ideas that the organization can use. We disagree. We believe it is absolutely the job of management to point out as clearly as possible where the organization faces problems (or opportunities) that require innovative solutions; and thereby to guide or direct inventive energy to where it is most needed. Few people produce new ideas spontaneously but most can be inventive when faced with a problem they really want to solve. And there is no reason to think that directed creativity is in any sense inferior, as the long and honourable tradition of commissioned paintings, sculptures and symphonies makes clear. Of course, in pointing out particular needs for innovation, managers must avoid giving the impression that these are the only ideas that are welcome.

As Figure 4.1 indicates, innovation strategy influences all the other elements of the Pentathlon. It guides idea generation through setting goals for internal work, approval of research programmes and sponsorship of partnerships with others to explore new opportunities (Chapter 5). It guides project selection and prioritization (Chapter 6) through the criteria used in selecting projects, particularly the balance of risk and reward and perhaps directly by earmarking funds for strategically important work. Innovation strategy also guides training and recruitment (Chapter 8) and provides the framework for major investments in implementation (Chapter 7).

Strategic Implementation

The first issue to be addressed in implementing an innovation strategy is that of the resources needed to generate and carry through the innovations looked for in the plan. If these are all available internally it is only a question of allocating budgets and responsibilities. However, an increasingly important dimension nowadays (see Chapter 10) is whether the organization has the capabilities to generate the innovation and carry it through itself. The more radical the change, the more likely it is that outside help will be needed. This may range from advice or facilitation from consultants, through sponsored research or technology licensing to partnerships and acquisitions. An innovation plan should identify where the organization expects to need help, or at least where it is prepared to consider it. In doing so, managers not only indicate a willingness to face the cost and possible upheaval but also signal that radical thinking is acceptable, even expected.

The second issue in implementing an innovation strategy is the question of whether the organization has the internal processes to handle the type of innovations called for. For example, a company may have a well-developed NPD process, and competent staff able to generate a string of new products; but this is unlikely to be a good mechanism for handling, say, a series of acquisitions. New staff, new processes and new organizations may well be needed to support innovative change and these must be catered for in the innovation plan.

Box case 4.1   Allianz-Versicherungs-AG – innovation networking[5]

Increasingly companies need to bring in a fresh, outside perspective into the way they define their innovation strategy. Too often organizations view their field too narrowly and this prevents them generating breakthrough ideas. Creativity is often the result of a market being viewed from different standpoints and this approach has been very successful at Allianz-Versicherungs-AG.

Allianz is the largest insurance provider in Germany. Dr Karl-Walter Gutberlet, an Allianz board member with responsibility for private customers, also serves on the board of Mondial Assistance Deutschland GmbH. This company is a business-to-business service provider focused on consumers' service needs related to travel, car transportation and living. Gutberlet's idea was to add this service philosophy to the insurance viewpoint. The result is an innovative new product that has taken the German market by storm and won an innovation prize from *Capital* magazine.

The new product is officially called 'Allianz Haus- und Wohnungsschutzbrief' (House and home emergency cover) but is better understood as the equivalent of a car breakdown service – a 'household emergency service'. Normal house insurance may cover the costs of solving a problem (for example, a blocked water pipe) but the consumer is still left with the hassle of finding someone to do the repair. Taking the analogy of the breakdown services available for cars, the new product covers the costs and also provides a hotline at Mondial, which organizes a quick repair by a qualified tradesman and the payment; and this is for about 5 euro per month.

Klaus Stemig, a member of the board of Mondial Germany, was appointed to be the project manager for the 24-hour household emergency service. A cross-functional team was assembled for the project comprising personnel from Allianz, Mondial and Agemis, a facility management company which provides part of the service provider network for the product. The kick-off was in July 2003 and the product was introduced (with the full supporting networks of service providers) in April 2004. Despite a time-to-market of only eight months, extensive market research was used to test and improve the initial ideas generated in brainstorming sessions involving the two companies. Over 400 inputs from interviews and focus groups for example defined the key product features. The completed product includes cover for being locked out, heating failures, plumbing problems, removal of wasps' nests, storage of copies of crucial documents such as passports, emergency babysitting, and emergency looking after of animals.

The cross-functional team had to solve many unexpected problems during the development, but having all functions represented and both companies' networks meant that these could be quickly addressed. 'For example, information technology is typically the bottleneck in the development of insurance and service products but our representatives from IT were on board from the beginning'. Overall, Stemig says, 'we are proud that we not only developed a new concept but that we developed it on-time, matching a very challenging schedule. For example, it wasn't easy to create a new network of tradesmen set up to respond 24 hours a day across all of Germany but we did it'.

The product has sold more than double the first year's goal of 25,000 policies and has established a reputation for Allianz as an innovative player in a conservative market. Spotting strategic opportunities is often about bringing in a different perspective and it is management's role to ensure that an organization's paradigms are challenged. Allianz are continuing to try and do this and are now rolling out further new products, such as 'Accident 60 Active' for senior citizens who need not only health insurance but also help in finding and organizing the services they require.

Innovation Strategy and Stakeholder Satisfaction

It is revealing to consider how innovation strategy will deliver increasing satisfaction to the stakeholders, and particularly the most important of these: the customer. This involves analysing the important features of the products and services that an organization offers to its stakeholders and asking how their value is to be maintained and enhanced into the future. The approach is essentially the same regardless of the stakeholder or the type of product, and starts with an analysis of customer satisfaction.

Kano's Feature Analysis

A helpful and influential framework for thinking about the strategy for customer satisfaction comes from the work of Noritaki Kano. The focus of Kano's work was how the features of consumer products contributed to customer satisfaction but his framework is equally instructive in thinking about services of all types, to customers and to other stakeholders. It is also a useful strategic tool. His original paper was published in Japanese in 1984 but was made available in English in 1996.[6] Kano classified the features of a product into three categories according to the effect they have on customer satisfaction.[7]

1 *'Basic' features*. These are attributes without which a product or service would simply be unacceptable. The customer takes them as prerequisites and may not even mention them, though they are essential for any successful product. Cars must start readily, window-glass must not distort the view, factory effluent should not poison local wildlife. All of these features are expected nowadays (though it was not always so). Failure to provide them would cause great dissatisfaction. However, providing extra performance beyond the basic requirement gives no extra satisfaction to the customer. A car that fails to start only once in 10 years has no competitive advantage over one that fails once in nine years.

2 *'Performance'* or *'one-dimensional' requirements*. These are features that provide a real benefit to the customer, and the more of them you get the better. Typical examples would be fuel economy in a car, battery life in a portable phone, reliable and increasing dividends for shareholders. For many products reliability or ease of use will also be performance features.

3 *'Excitement' features* or *'Delighters'*. A customer is unlikely to demand these features because they are not part of the way the product is normally viewed, but when offered them he may be surprised and pleased. Such features often respond to hidden needs (see Chapter 5). They give an extra, unexpected value and may be attractive out of all proportion to the objective benefits they give. When it was first introduced, the remote control on a television was a classic example of a Delighter. We doubt it was invented in response to complaints about the chore of getting out of the seat to change channels, but once it was available it made a big impact. A major new initiative such as an acquisition or expansion into a new market may have the same effect on investors.

Figure 4.4 illustrates Kano's classification of features in schematic form. The horizontal axis is the degree of implementation of a feature and the vertical is the customer satisfaction conveyed by it. The three categories of feature follow different curves reflecting their different effects on customer perception. A successful product needs to have an appropriate combination of basic, performance and delighter attributes. Thus a sufficient level of basic features is essential but must be accompanied by an attractive level of performance and, if possible, excitement. It is probably true to say that customer

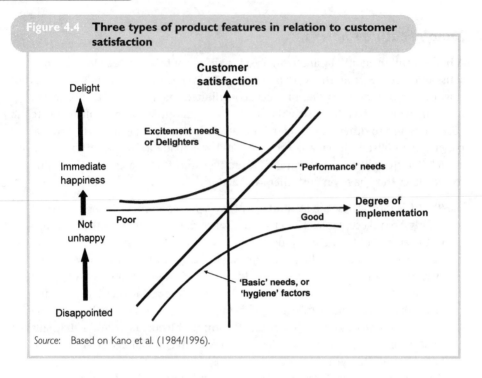

Figure 4.4   Three types of product features in relation to customer satisfaction

Source: Based on Kano et al. (1984/1996).

or stakeholder satisfaction comes from the Basic and Performance features, while their loyalty depends on delivering superior Performance together with some Excitement.[8] Excitement features are often needed to capture market share.

The features of a company's product may be allocated to the Kano categories by a simple questionnaire in which customers are asked how they would feel about a significant increase or decrease in its level of implementation (or possibly its presence or absence.) The answers are interpreted using the matrix shown in Figure 4.5. Thus if a respondent is unconcerned if the feature is absent but pleased if it is present, then the feature is clearly a Delighter. If she expects the feature to be present, but is unhappy if it is absent, then it is Basic. Features that fall into the central four boxes (shaded gray) cause no particular response either way and so the company can choose whether or not to implement them on other grounds, such as cost or convenience.

A key strategic question for any organization is how it can enhance the value it delivers to stakeholders as time goes on. The Kano diagram raises two vital questions. The first is whether the organization can continue to enhance the Performance features of the products and services it offers to stakeholders at the rate they require (or, at least, as fast as competitors do). The second, and more subtle, issue is whether stakeholders, particularly customers, will continue to demand the same balance of features in future. We consider these two challenges in some detail in the following two sections.

Figure 4.5 Matrix for allocating product features to their Kano categories

		Answers to negative question			
		Good	Expected	Not important	Bad
Answers to positive question	Good		Delighter when present	Delighter when present	Enhancement is performance feature
	Expected	Delighter when absent			Basic when present
	Not important	Delighter when absent			Basic when present
	Bad	Reduction is performance feature	Basic when absent	Basic when absent	

Source: Based on Kano *et al.* (1984/1996).

Box case 4.2   Formule 1 Hotels – a new strategy for customer satisfaction[9]

In the early 1980s the board of Accor, a French hotel chain, challenged its managers to come up with a new concept for low-cost hotels. They asked them to reconsider what customers really valued from a night's stay and to see whether it was possible to find a better overall value proposition than the one generally on offer. The analysis showed that a number of features that were traditionally provided by even the lowest cost hotels were of comparatively little value to customers making an overnight stop. These included lounges, eating facilities, availability of a receptionist, and spacious rooms. Such features were important for people staying in two or three-star accommodation, for whom a hotel stay was in part a cultural experience. However, most users of low-cost hotels simply wanted a good night's sleep. The other features were being oversupplied.

By moving to small rooms with only basic facilities, cutting out lounges and restaurants, and having receptionists available only at peak times, the company was able to reduce construction and operating costs for the new hotel chain significantly. But rather than reduce the price they used the money to raise the standards of the features most important for overnight customers – comfort, cleanliness and quietness in the rooms – well-above that usually available in the sector. The result was a new value proposition giving a much higher level of customer satisfaction. The 'Formule 1' hotel chain, launched in 1985, quickly became the market leader in the sector. Within 10 years its market share exceeded that of its five nearest rivals combined.

The Challenge of Meeting Expectations

One of the most serious strategic threats an organization can face is for it to be unable to continue to improve the value it delivers to its stakeholders: in other words not to be able to move its products and services up the performance curve on the Kano diagram at the rate demanded. An organization that has reached such a limit risks being quickly left behind by any competitors who are not constrained in the same way. Such limits on performance are in fact very common and they pose a particular threat because they are usually approached gradually and so may not become apparent until it is too late. A vital part of innovation strategy is to see if key parts of the company's capabilities are approaching the limits of what they can do. Such limits frequently demand an innovative response.

Capability Maturity: the 'S'-curve

An important idea in the management of technology is that all technologies have a natural upper bound on their performance beyond which it simply cannot be pushed. The same applies to any kind of competence or capability, not just those that are overtly science-based and we will use the terms technology and capability more or less interchangeably in what follows.

Foster[10] points out that, viewed over a sufficient length of time, the progress of any technology is likely to follow a recognizable path as illustrated in Figure 4.6. On the vertical axis we plot the progress of the key characteristic of the competence. It might be a physical attribute of a product, such as speed, price or comfort; the scope of a service (for example the number of customers a sales-person can serve in a day); or any other parameter that is of value to the customer. On the horizontal axis is the cumulative investment made in developing that aspect of the technology. The curve tends to be 'S'-shaped. In the early stages, when the technology is in its infancy (the *emerging* stage), the performance is modest and the rate of progress is relatively slow. But each advance provides the basis for further improvement and so progress accelerates and the slope of improvement becomes steeper. This improving trend may go on for a very long time, but eventually it comes to an end when some natural limit is approached, beyond which the capability simply cannot go. As a technology approaches this ceiling – and all technologies have one – progress becomes slower and investment in it becomes less and less productive until eventually it is clear that the way ahead is blocked. The technology has now reached its limit and the organization that depends on it is vulnerable to attack from a better

Figure 4.6 **The S-curve of technological progress showing the typical performance of a technology against investment in it**

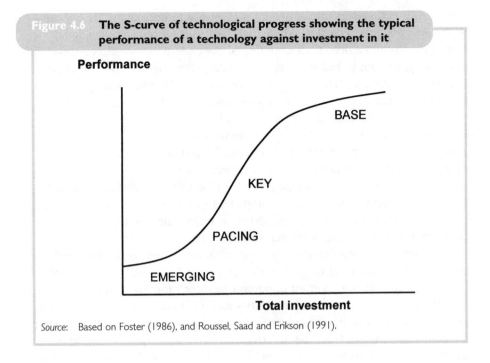

Performance

BASE

KEY

PACING

EMERGING

Total investment

Source: Based on Foster (1986), and Roussel, Saad and Erikson (1991).

idea. Innovation is the only way out. The various stages of development have been labelled *emerging, pacing, key* and *base*[11] to indicate their competitive significance.

History is full of examples where this drama has been played out. Foster quotes the example of commercial sailing ships.[12] They showed steady improvement from Roman times through the middle ages and into the nineteenth century, but the flowering of the great clipper ships like the Cutty Sark in the second half of the century signalled the top of their S-curve. Further attempts at improving their speed were unsuccessful, and indeed counter-productive: the only possibility was to add more sail, which led to instability in windy weather and a number of well-publicized disasters when the overdeveloped monsters capsized. Sail could improve no more, and gave place to steam.

A similar thing has happened in many modern instances: propeller-aircraft reached an absolute speed limit and jets took over for faster travel; waxed cylinders gave way to vinyl discs, and so to CDs as each reached its limit of audio fidelity; detergents replaced soap for washing clothes; steam trains replaced canal transport and were themselves superseded by diesel and then electric power. In manufacturing, the traditional method of glass manufacture that involved grinding and polishing each pane reached its limit and was replaced by plate glass; and production lines superseded individual construction for many products.

An organization that relies on a capability that is approaching the top of its S-curve may be catastrophically vulnerable to a competitor with a better approach. It is therefore imperative for a company to understand its key capabilities well enough to be clear where their limits lie. Of course this may not be easy, for it requires a deep understanding of the underlying principles of a vital technology. Certainly, just looking at the competitors is not enough, because sometimes progress in a technology will slow down not because a limit is appearing but for transient reasons, such as a temporary reduction in investment.

A maturing technology is always potentially at risk but the threat is *real* only if the limit to the capability is truly unavoidable and there is a genuine market demand for further improvement. It is *real* and *urgent* only if an alternative technology exists that does not have disadvantages that outweigh its benefits. If no such alternative is in sight managers may breathe a sigh of relief – but not a big one, because competition does not stop; its focus just moves elsewhere. The company must now concentrate its efforts on improving other features such as price (always remembering, however, that the core vulnerability still remains).

The question of possible disadvantages of a competing technology is illustrated by two contrasting cases. The first (Figure 4.7)[13] concerns the chemical phthalic anhydride, which is an important feedstock for the manufacture of a number of other chemicals used in plastics and paint manufacture. The original process for making it, using naphthalene, was challenged by a new one, using orthoxylene. This new process offered only a small improvement in yield compared to the old one – from 95 per cent to 105 per cent. However, the naphthalene process could not match it; over $100 million was spent on efforts to raise the yield but with no results because the technology had simply reached its limit. The orthoxylene process offered a cost improvement of only 10 per cent but the end product was absolutely unchanged so there were no barriers to adopting the new method.

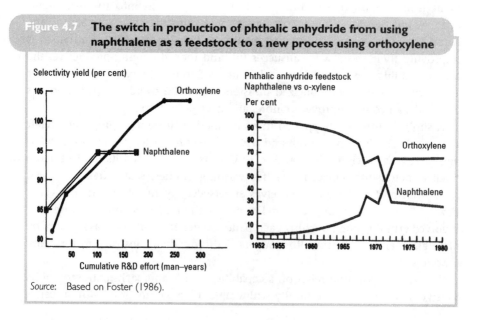

Figure 4.7   The switch in production of phthalic anhydride from using naphthalene as a feedstock to a new process using orthoxylene

Source: Based on Foster (1986).

The second case is the introduction of fluorescent lights around 1940. The ordinary incandescent lamp had by then reached the limit of its efficiency as a source of light. Fluorescent lamps were significantly more efficient when they were introduced and quickly became almost 10 times better. However, as we all know, they have by no means replaced the old technology. There are many reasons for this, among them the higher initial cost, the different quality of the light and perhaps most important the fact that (for a long time) fluorescent lamps would not fit into the available light sockets and so required extensive rewiring.

Fluorescent lamps are not simply a direct replacement for incandescent lights. They have great and desirable benefits, but disadvantages too. The result is that the two still coexist, and will probably continue to do so, at least until they are both threatened by a further innovation.

Of course, technologies are not vulnerable to replacement *only* if they are reaching the top of their S-curve. Sometimes a better alternative appears while there is still plenty of scope for improvement in the incumbent technology. The two technologies may then jostle for leadership for some time until one becomes dominant. For example the first video discs were launched by Philips in the 1970s as an alternative to video tape[14] but failed to make much progress and were eclipsed; but the technology formed the basis of the CD and then reemerged as a video format with the DVD. Petrol engines never entirely displaced diesel power for automobiles, and, indeed, diesel seems to be making a comeback after 100 years or so. The arrival of a new technology may itself trigger a burst of improvement in the old one.[15] Often the old will respond by adopting features of the new, as when conventional cameras quickly acquired a host of electronic features as established companies tried to stem the advance of digital imaging.

There are cases where companies have introduced a new competence with improved performance only to find that their competitors accelerated investment in the established technology and pulled ahead again. An example of this is gallium arsenide, a semi-conducting material that was tipped in the 1960s and 1970s to replace silicon as the material for integrated circuits because of its fundamental advantages in speed. However, every time it seemed poised to take a significant share of the market, further improvements in processing methods allowed silicon to catch up and pushed gallium arsenide back into the tiny niche it still occupies today.

The Predictability of Technical Advance

Many authors have observed that technologies often advance at an apparently regular rate for many years.[16,17] This implies that the S-curves may have predictive value. The most famous example is Moore's Law.[18] Gordon Moore, one of the founders of Intel, first suggested in 1965 that the number of transistors that could be put on an integrated circuit chip would double every 18 months (later revised to 24 months). This 'law' has continued to work for nearly 40 years, as Figure 4.8 shows, and is now expected to continue at least until around 2010–15.

Many other technologies show similar steady improvements over time, although the speed of advance of integrated electronics is unparalleled. Figure 4.9, for example, shows the advance in the size of astronomical telescopes.[19] There may be changes of slope from time to time when significant new approaches to the technology are found, but in between regularity appears to be surprisingly common.

The data in Figures 4.8 and 4.9 are plotted on logarithmic scales and the fact that they tend to follow straight lines shows that the improvement in the

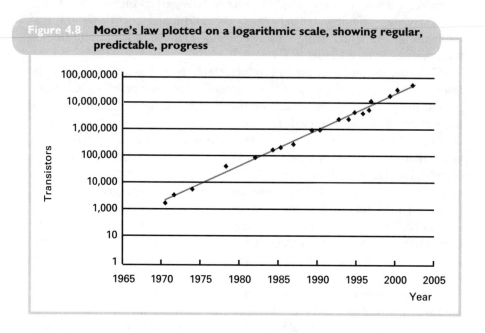

Figure 4.8 Moore's law plotted on a logarithmic scale, showing regular, predictable, progress

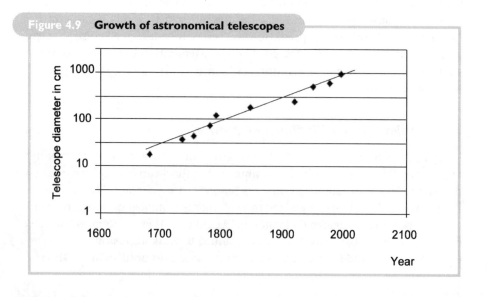

Figure 4.9 Growth of astronomical telescopes

technologies is not linear, but *geometric*; that is to say there is a certain proportional, or percentage, improvement each year rather than a simple addition. This is understandable: adding an extra 100 transistors is a much bigger step if the present chip holds only 100 than if it already holds 1,000,000. The important thing is not the actual number added, but the relative increase.

How do we reconcile these straight-line progress plots with the S-curve in Figure 4.6? It is just a question of the scale that is used. Figure 4.6 is plotted on a linear scale and on this a geometric increase gives a concave curve, getting steeper as it rises. This is just what the first part of the S-curve is: a Moore's law-type increase but plotted in absolute rather than relative terms. So rather than thinking of technology improvement as starting slowly and then accelerating, it is more helpful to think of it as a steady *relative* improvement slowing, perhaps rather abruptly, as the limit is approached. Plotting the S-curve on a logarithmic scale, like Figures 4.8 and 4.9, shows what is really happening (Figure 4.10).[20]

It is, of course, not the passage of time that drives a capability forward but the amount of effort put into it. To predict future progress one needs to foresee both the level of investment and the productivity of the effort. Neither is easy. Even with hindsight it is difficult enough to find out what levels of effort have gone into developing a particular capability, and it is even more difficult to know what the future holds. Clearly companies will put the investment into a technology only if they believe that the market will justify it. It has been suggested that Moore's law is now to some extent a 'self-fulfilling prophesy' because all the players expect it to continue and put in the investment to make it happen. Indeed there is evidence[21] that recently the continuing progress of Moore's law is now requiring higher levels of investment than before, implying that the

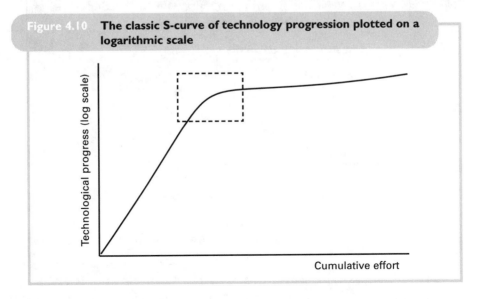

Figure 4.10 **The classic S-curve of technology progression plotted on a logarithmic scale**

productivity of the investment is declining as the technical limit for integrated circuits approaches. There is clearly scope for more research here, but the evidence is that the recent rate of technical progress is likely to be a good pointer to the future until a limit is approached, provided only that commercial need and investment continue.

The S-curve has traditionally been applied to technology-based manufactured products but we stress that it is equally valid for services. New bar-coding technologies allowed Federal Express to improve their service in ways that had previously been impossible – for example by offering on-line shipment tracking. Service companies need to be aware of the how the maturity of the technologies on which their products are based affects their competitiveness.

Box case 4.3   Fiat – customize . . . but not at any cost

Mass-customization has become one of the manufacturing buzz-words of the 1990s. For example, Nippon Bicycle (owned by National Panasonic) revolutionized the mountain-bike industry in Japan by offering customers the capability to 'design' their own bike from an almost endless selection of frames, wheels, gears and colour schemes; and to receive delivery in less than two weeks. This *mass-customization* has influenced many companies and they have attempted to use it to more exactly meet the needs of customers. However, mass-customization has a price, and engineers must be aware of the investment required to offer more variety to customers.

Fiat has developed a simple matrix for engineers to analyse the trade-offs between cost and customization of components in car design. The matrix below shows the *cost of variety* against the *importance to the customer of variety* of car components, and is used to focus engineering choices on those components where variety has a high perceived value to the customer. Variety that has low value is eliminated where possible. Components whose variety can add high perceived value are given high priority, and engineering resources are assigned to identify how their cost can be reduced.

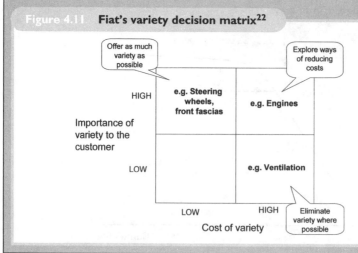

Figure 4.11   Fiat's variety decision matrix[22]

Evolution of Strategy as Technology Matures

As a company's core technology evolves through the stages shown in Figure 4.6 from Emerging, Pacing and Key to its ultimate maturity as a Base technology, so the strategic focus of the company (or its business unit handling the technology) changes with it (Table 4.1).

To start with, the R&D department concentrates mainly on mastering the technology, while the market stance of the company as a whole emphasizes its technical competence and ability to supply the new product. Later on, as the technology moves up the S-curve, technical attention turns towards pushing forward the performance of the product and exploring the new applications that the extra capabilities open up. At this stage the company typically seeks to gain a strong market share and the marketing message concentrates on the competitive advantages of the product. Then, as the technology reaches its later stages, attention inevitably moves away from the core performance (which has gone about as far as it can) to emphasize other aspects such as price, quality and reliability. The company now positions itself as a competent and reliable supplier, not only of the product itself but also perhaps of a range of supporting products and services. In a sense the competition is no longer between products so much as between whole companies, or brands.

Table 4.1 How commercial and technical focus evolves with technology maturity

Technology phase	Typical R&D focus	Typical company focus
Emerging	Technical understanding Patents and IPR	Find early adopters. Gain practical experience. Publicise capability
Pacing	Demonstrate capability Establish standards Explore variations Understand limits	Respond to early market feedback Speed of response Flexibility Readiness to learn
Key	Performance improvement Customer focused features Technical mastery Design for manufacturing	Product performance improvement Market share Exploit new niches and applications
Base	Reliability Cost Ergonomics Scan for new technologies	Reliable and respected supplier Brand image Quality Value Complementary products/services Business process improvement

Dominant Design

Abernathy and Utterback[23] describe the evolution summarized above in a slightly different but illuminating way. They say that the focus of innovation moves away from product design towards process improvement (which should be understood to mean all business processes, although their emphasis is on the manufacturing element). They point out that when a new type of product is launched there usually follows a period of ferment and experimentation during which many different designs are tried out, often by many different companies. Eventually a preferred, or *dominant*, design arises that becomes an actual or *de facto* standard and is eventually adopted by all serious players. Thereafter the emphasis of innovation moves from the design to the processes by which it is made, marketed and supplied. This change of focus is illustrated schematically in Figure 4.12. Such an evolution has been observed in many products from typewriters to automobiles and from aircraft to portable phones.

Once a dominant design has emerged, it benefits from the accumulated efficiencies of scale and experience among the suppliers, and among the companies that provide components to them. As Utterback says 'A dominant design has the effect of enforcing or encouraging standardization so that production or other complementary economies can be sought'. As the automotive and PC industries demonstrate, design standardization allows manufacturers to use many common components, often specially designed for the purpose, with all the advantages of volume supply and specialization that go with it. The whole supply chain rides down a learning curve, incrementally improving efficiencies and trimming costs. All this helps to maintain the advantages of the dominant design though the specialization that drives the improvement may also store up trouble for later (see later sections 'Disruptive technology' and 'The Success trap').

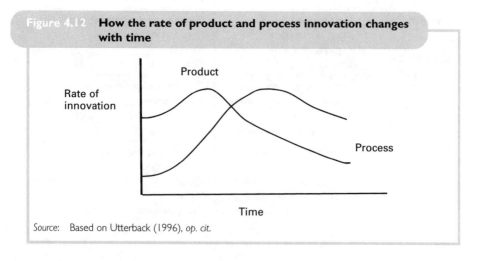

Figure 4.12 How the rate of product and process innovation changes with time

Rate of innovation

Product

Process

Time

Source: Based on Utterback (1996), *op. cit.*

A dominant design may emerge simply because it is the best way available at the time to perform the function. Axes, needles, woodscrews, roller bearings, light-bulbs and fork-lift trucks are all examples of designs that are dominant simply because nobody can (as yet) improve on them. In the natural world there are many examples of animals and plants that occupy similar environmental niches in different parts of the world and have strikingly similar forms and yet have evolved from very different starting points. The 'Tasmanian wolf' that inhabited Tasmania until recently looked very like an American wolf and yet was a marsupial, having evolved quite separately to the optimum form for its way of life. This convergent evolution is surprisingly common. Perhaps the best-known example is the camera-like form of our own eyes, which has evolved quite separately at least seven times.[24] It is one of nature's dominant designs for vision (the other is the compound eye of insects).

Another way for a dominant design to arise is by way of a formal standardization agreement at the national or international level. We all drive on the same side of the road, at least within each country; all postal systems use stamps; rails are now the same distance apart on virtually all public railways. Such agreements are particularly useful when interfacing between interested parties is an issue. Thus 405, and later 625, lines became the standard format for European television broadcast signals by government decree so that transmitters and receivers would work together. Similarly, the way mobile telephone systems work has been laid down by international agreement, rather than emerging in the marketplace, because it is more important that the way of operating should be agreed than that it should be optimum in any other sense. Once the choice has been made, innovation in the standard necessarily stops and competitive attention moves elsewhere.

In between the two extremes – a design that becomes dominant simply because it is the best and one that is imposed by formal standardization – come a variety of situations where a leading design is held in place by other effects that make it difficult for people to change even if a very much better one were to come along. It becomes, in effect, a 'frozen accident'. The forces that cause this may be summarized as *threshold* effects and *network* effects.

Threshold Effects

A dominant design is often held in place simply by the high cost of making a change. An excellent example is the attempt to replace the Qwerty keyboard (Box case 2.5) with the more efficient Dvorak configuration.[25,26] It failed, because anyone who wanted to change over had to unlearn a painfully acquired skill and relearn a related one, passing through a time when they were not much good at either. The cost of making the change outweighed the benefits of the more efficient design. Fluorescent lighting is another example of an innovation whose considerable advantages are counterbalanced by the cost of the changeover – in this case to a different set of fittings.

Network Effects

Another, more powerful, way in which a dominant design becomes locked in place is through so-called network effects. These occur when the value of a design becomes greater the more people adopt it. Telephones, email and the internet are modern examples of products which are valuable because many people use them. The more popular they are the more valuable they become. The network effect may be direct, when the value is directly related to the number of customers, as in the case of fax machines. Or it may be indirect, when the network value is generated by related products and services associated with the standard. Thus the VHS video standard and the CD format have become unassailable not because of the hardware but because of the huge amount of software products that are available to use on it (see Box case 4.4).

Products with network effects show a characteristic adoption curve: slow at first but reaching a rapid 'take-off' point when enough people have adopted it so that the network effects kick in. The explosive growth of the internet is a familiar example. This is what is known in chemistry as *autocatalysis*, a reaction whose products themselves accelerate the reaction. If two or more standards are competing in a market where network effects are prevalent the network effect may be enhanced by the competition so that a 'tipping point' is reached[27] when one first emerges as the acknowledged leader and then grows rapidly at the expense of the others.

Box case 4.4   The case of Betamax and VHS

The tussle between Sony and JVC for supremacy in the home video recording market illustrates the power of network effects in a mass-market product.[28] The video recorder was pioneered for professional purposes by RCA and Ampex in the USA, with the latter eventually emerging as the dominant player. Many companies, including Philips, Sony, JVC and Matsushita took an interest in the technology from the 1950s but competition quickened in 1971 when Sony brought out the U-Matic, a cassette model that was suitable for semi-professional users such as schools, though not yet for home use. Sony, Matsushita and JVC agreed to cross-licence their patents in 1970 and the race was on to open up the domestic market.

Sony launched the Betamax, the first video recorder designed for the home market, in 1975. JVC followed with the VHS a year later. Both designs used ideas from the U-Matic and so neither had a fundamental advantage of cost or technology. Nevertheless they used incompatible cassettes and recording formats. Sony had the advantage of being first to market but their one-hour recording length was felt by many to be too short. VHS offered two hours from the start and a number of major companies, including Matsushita, decided to wait for it. In fact Sony launched a two-hour machine only five months after the launch of VHS and thereafter the two formats matched each other with innovations, neither drawing ahead for more than a few months at a time.

The market for VCRs grew dramatically, from around 20,000 units a year in 1975 to nearly 20 million in 1983 and 40 million in 1987. Sony's sales also grew until 1984 but their initial 100 per cent market share dropped to 61 per cent when VHS arrived in 1976 and was down to 50 per cent in 1978, 30 per cent in 1981/2 and below 10 per cent by 1985.[29]

Sony did not lose their initial advantage because of significant price or product disadvantages; their problem was that JVC, a much smaller and perhaps less arrogant company, gave much greater emphasis to signing up partners and distributors. They consequently gained a small but significant market lead early on, which was amplified into a greater dominance by network effects. These became particularly strong in the early 1980s when the market for prerecorded videotapes took off. The higher market share of the VHS system made it the more attractive format for suppliers of the software. The better range of pre-recorded films in turn made VHS more popular with buyers of machines and so an upward spiral developed that turned JVC's 60/40 lead in terms of installed base (total machines sold) into a monopoly within a few years.

Where they occur, network and threshold effects both serve to make an established dominant design very difficult to shift. Together they can make an almost insuperable barrier, as people who have tried to persuade the world to adopt a new language, such as Esperanto, have found. A new language is useful if many people know it, but there is little point in learning it unless many others have already done so. Moreover, the effort required is considerable. As a result artificial new languages, however efficient they may be, have never made progress against the network advantages of established tongues.

Perceptive companies are well-aware of the advantages of standardization and often promote it deliberately either with monopoly intent, as in the case of Microsoft, or to help the growth of the market as Philips and Sony did with the CD following their disastrous experience with lack of standardization in video recorders.

The Challenge of Changing Expectations

The second strategic issue that is illustrated by the Kano diagram (Figure 4.4) is that customer requirements change with time in a regular and at least partly predictable way. The features on the diagram tend to rotate clockwise so that Delighters become Performance features and Performance features become Basic (Table 4.2). This trend leads to important strategic challenges.

Consider the typical lifecycle of a new Performance feature such as a TV remote control or an in-car radio. When it is first offered it causes admiring comment, and generates well-deserved sales advantage for the originator. But in the course of time it will be copied by competitors, become widespread and lose its special impact. Its mere existence is then no longer a surprise and the scramble starts to make improved and refined versions. It is now a Performance feature, the focus of competitive improvement.

Often the improvement continues until the performance of the best products completely meets the needs of even the most demanding of users. The products in the market will now be spread out along the Performance line and customers can choose what level they are willing to pay for. Eventually the market becomes so used to the feature that it is no longer a competitive element and drops below the axis as a Basic need. Few people now would consider booking a hotel without first viewing pictures and even movies, of the rooms on the internet, a facility unheard of until recently. Here are some other everyday examples of these movements:

Table 4.2 Examples of movement of products on Kano's diagram

Delighters that became performance features	Delighters that became basic:
▢ Climate control in cars	▢ Self-starters and heaters in cars
▢ Package holidays	▢ TV remote controls
▢ Internet banking	▢ Seat-back TV on long-haul flights
▢ Size of portable computers	▢ Lounges for business class travellers
▢ Index-tracking investment funds	▢ 'Cash-back' at supermarket tills

Performance features that became basic	
▢ Price of ball-point pens	▢ Resolution of desktop printers
▢ Accuracy of clocks and watches	▢ Service interval of (most) cars
▢ Size of portable phones	▢ Fidelity of audio systems

When a Performance feature starts to run out of steam as a competitive advantage it heralds a structural change in the basis of competition. Companies often find it very difficult to adapt to this change because the old focus of competition may be, quite literally, built into the fabric of the organization. It may be its core competence; and may very well be where management has habitually looked to protect and enhance margins. These pressures make it surprisingly easy for a company not to notice that the game is changing and to continue to develop the familiar features of its products well beyond the point of interest to its customers. Customers themselves may not be helpful, either. When asked about the relative importance of various features they will continue to rate basic features highly. Is it important that the car should start reliably in the morning? Of course it is. But that is not the same as saying that ease of starting is something that makes a customer choose one new car rather than another.

Continuing to develop Basic features as if they were still Performance features can be disastrous on three counts. First the extra but useless performance can add unnecessary cost to the product; second the chance to pursue features that will be of real interest to the customer is foregone; and third the company may become vulnerable to an alternative, so-called *disruptive*, technology.

Disruptive Technology

The concept of disruptive technology was first identified by Clayton Christensen[30,31] at Harvard. He pointed out that companies often fall prey to a new technology whose performance is inferior to that of the incumbent technology. This can happen if the performance attribute that has previously been the focus of competition is starting to surpass the needs of a significant part of the market. (In other words the feature drops from the Performance category towards Basic.) Then, a new approach, which perhaps offers less of this feature but has other advantages, can alter the basis of competition in a dramatic way. A disruptive technology can be a particular threat to well-established companies because its inferior performance can mean that it is initially entirely unsuitable in their market. It only becomes suitable as its performance improves. So it attacks from below in a way that is difficult to combat.

Christensen's initial research was conducted on computer disc drives, a fast moving market sector in which product life-cycles are shorter than most. But further investigations have shown that the principles apply in other sectors from retail to earth-moving equipment.

Christensen's ideas on disruptive technology are based on the following observations:

- Companies succeed by serving their customers in markets that they understand well. They seek to improve the performance of their products to stay ahead of competition and protect their margins.
- The pace of technology development often exceeds the demands from the bulk of the market. This may be because the technology is developing particularly fast, or because the requirements of the most demanding users are much higher than those of the majority, or because, as already described, customer demand for the feature is becoming saturated.
- Disruptive technologies initially offer products that have poorer performance on the accepted features in the established markets. For this reason they are usually first used elsewhere, in markets too small or offering too low margins to attract established companies.
- In the course of time a disruptive technology may improve enough to offer performance that is acceptable to most of the customers in the established market (although often never fully matching that of the existing technology). It can then compete with the established technology and its other features can catastrophically change the basis of competition.

For these reasons, past success with a particular technology reduces a company's ability to objectively assess the attractiveness of new technologies.

The performance of a product is normally dependent on the main technology used. For example, the speed of a personal computer is related to the characteristics of the processor chip. Similarly, the size and the operating time of a mobile telephone depends on the characteristics of the batteries used. Key product performance characteristics often become the basis of competition in a market

Figure 4.13 The development of sustaining and disruptive technologies

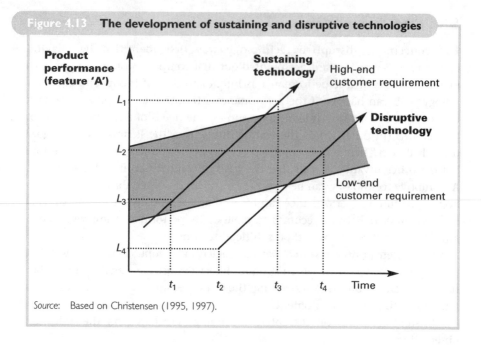

Source: Based on Christensen (1995, 1997).

and companies strive to achieve higher performance in their products. Once the basis of competition is focused on particular product features, the underlying technologies on which these are based are referred to as *sustaining* technologies, because the further development of these technologies allows competition to be sustained in its current form.

Figure 4.13 illustrates the concept of disruptive technology. The speed at which the sustaining technology is developed is driven by the competition between the established companies competing in the market. High growth enables increased R&D investment and faster development of the technologies and products. Frequently, competition drives the pace at which sustaining technology is developed faster than the rate at which customers' needs develop. Figure 4.13 shows the performance curve of a sustaining technology related to user needs on a particular 'Feature A'. Over time (from t_1 to t_3) the technology enables product performance to increase from level L_3 to L_1. The rate of increase of product performance is greater than the speed at which both 'high-end' and 'low-end' users' demands increase, which is indicated by the shaded band on the diagram. Nevertheless companies that develop products with improved performance will often be successful and their market shares increase.

Disruptive technology is very different. The performance of a product developed at time t_2 using the new technology measured on Feature A is worse (only L_2, as shown on the diagram). This means that the product using the new technology is not normally attractive to customers in the established market, simply because they will not accept what is for them inferior performance. However, the new (disruptive) technology may offer other advantages that are particularly attractive to new customers in some other market and, to them, outweigh the reduced performance on Feature A. For example, when physically smaller disc drives became available they were unattractive to PC manufacturers who were looking for high storage capabilities. However, they were very attractive in the emerging market for laptop computers, where size was more important than storage capability. Their initial application was in this new, and at first rather small, market.

Often disruptive technology develops rapidly and, although it may never match the performance of the existing one, it may adequately meet the needs of low-end, and eventually of most users in the original market. Now the performance on Feature A is no longer a disadvantage, and the other advantages (which often include lower price) give it the edge. At this point, the technology will start to disrupt the established market and customers may start to switch in significant numbers. Established companies may not have time to react and develop or acquire an expertise in the disruptive technology.

The danger posed by disruptive technology for successful companies in established markets is that they may easily miss all the warning signs. Established companies are strongly linked to their customer base, to their competence in the sustaining technology and therefore the inertia to change may be great. For example, early mechanical diggers were based on motors linked to the digger buckets by drums and cabling and the key product features in the market were the reach of the arm and the capacity of the bucket. Over the years the established manufacturers improved the motors, drums and cabling to the extent that the reach of the arms and the bucket capacity more than met the needs of, for example, the open-cast mining industry. In the 1940s an entrant, the British company JCB introduced hydraulic technology into the design of mechanical diggers. Both the reach and the bucket capacity achieved with this new technology were inferior to that of the established products. But the mechanical arm using hydraulics was lighter and could be mounted on the back of farm tractors used for pipe-laying – a new market. The success achieved by JCB and other entrants established the new market and over time hydraulic technology was developed to the level that the reach and capacity required in the traditional market was met and then exceeded. Of the thirty-four established companies using the sustaining technology in 1945, only four were able to successfully adopt hydraulic technology and survive to 1965. Over the same time period, over twenty new companies entered the mechanical excavator market.[30]

Why were thirty manufacturers of mechanical excavators unable to make a successful transition from one technology to another? Christensen explains this with reference to the key principles from his research. First, companies depend on both their investors and their customers for their resources. Therefore, the thirty manufacturers tended to invest in technologies and products that would satisfy their existing customers, in markets they understood. Second, small markets by definition do not solve the growth needs of large, established companies and so the growth market of diggers attached to the back of tractors was not attractive. The third principle is that the speed of technology development may well exceed the rate of increase in market demands. So although the established companies observed the emergence of hydraulic technology, they largely discounted it as unviable and forgot that its performance could increase rapidly. Consequently, the thirty companies that concentrated their research on their existing customer base were unable to follow the needs of the emerging market. Finally, the disruptive technology, being initially inferior, developed in other sectors of the market. But its capability eventually improved to the point when it was attractive to many existing users even though it never fully matched the capacity of cable-based systems. There is a certain sense in which the better managed a company is the more vulnerable it is to a disruptive technology. Successful companies focus on their customers and are well informed of their needs; they look for the highest growth opportunities and seek to protect margins. All these excellent things help them to miss the potential of disruptive technology.

Responding to a Disruptive Technology

The future of a company that faces a threat from a disruptive technology sounds bleak. It seems as if they must either pour investment into something that cannot be used in the current business or stand back while it develops elsewhere into an overwhelming threat. This is too alarmist. Of course the disruptive technology *may* precisely replace the functions of the old, bringing advantages but no disadvantages (as in the case of phthalic anhydride synthesis in Figure 4.7). This is indeed a difficult situation but it is an extreme case. More usually the disruptive technology will have desirable features that the incumbent did not, but vice versa too. There is no reason to assume that the newcomer will necessarily sweep all before it; the two are more likely to coexist,[32] sharing the market according to the different baskets of capability. And even if one does 'win', the victory may take a long time: for example, it took minicomputers 10 years even to match the sales of mainframes.

A study of a group of companies facing disruptive innovations found a variety of responses:[33]

1 Adopt the disruptive technology and find a way to use it at once

This is the 'classic' response to a disruptive technology and is the most appropriate if the disruptive technology really has the capability to exactly replace the functions of the incumbent technology at a level that satisfies the market (Christensen's example of disc drives of various sizes falls neatly into this category).

The difficulty facing a company that takes this route is that by definition the disruptive technology is not suitable for the existing markets. So the company must set up a new division operating in a new market where the technology's attributes are immediately useful. The new unit will need a high level of autonomy from the rest of the company because its customer base, business model and overhead structure are likely to be very different. Hewlett Packard took just this approach with its ink-jet printer activity (see Box case 4.5).

Banks and building societies faced a similar situation with internet services but with the important difference that the new competence was not at all a simple replacement for the old. One desktop printer may seem much like another, whatever the technology inside, but nobody could mistake an internet bank for a high street bank. In these cases the new approach results in a very different experience for the customer so most of the companies not only separate the new business operationally but also give it a different brand identity as well. Disruptive *technologies* have led these businesses into disruptive *strategies*.

Many companies find it very difficult to manage radically different approaches to customers at the same time. British Airways and KLM both started low-cost companies to compete with Ryanair and Easyjet but ended up selling out to them when the internal contradictions in running such contrary business models proved too great to handle.

Box case 4.5   Hewlett Packard and inkjet printing

When it first emerged inkjet could not rival the quality of laser printing, but it had other attributes such as low cost, low noise and low power consumption. Rather than trying to get existing customers to buy the inferior technology HP set up a separate division tasked with exploiting inkjet in whatever applications it could find, operating whatever business model allowed it to make money. The strategy paid off handsomely when the quality of inkjet printing eventually rose to be good enough to displace laser from much of the desktop market. But if the improvement had not happened HP would still have had a profitable, if modest, business.

---

2   Focus on and invest in the existing business

Since disruptive technologies seldom precisely replace the incumbent one, an aggressive response may be successful, emphasizing and enhancing the features of the existing technology that are not shared by the new one. This will minimize the impact of the new competition and perhaps roll it back. Examples of this are all around us: cinema responded to television with ever more impressive visual and sound experiences and is now more successful than ever; established airlines such as BA and Virgin are introducing full-length beds to emphasize their difference from their low-cost competitors. And our clothes are *not* all made of artificial fibres. Disruptive technologies do not always win all the business. Often, they co-exist with existing approaches or even reach a peak and decline.

A disruptive innovation starts in, and maybe creates, a new market sector. Sometimes it's best to let it stay there. Edward Jones a leading U.S. retail-brokerage firm decided not to respond to the rise of internet brokerage. The CEO said[34] 'You will not buy securities over the internet at Edward Jones . . . if you aren't interested in a relationship and you just want a transaction then you could go to E*Trade . . . we just aren't in that business'. Edward Jones recognized that the new technology offered some things that theirs could not, but only some. They could not adopt it without weakening their brand position, and they did not need to because it was not a substitute for all they could offer.

3 Wait and see

Innovations do not always live up to their promise so a 'wait and see' strategy may be best, combined perhaps with partnerships or investments designed to keep options open. The new technology may fail completely, or at least it may not develop far enough to be a threat. And in any case a late entrant may be able to buy in the new capability when it is sufficiently matured and use it to good effect.[35,36] We discuss this approach further in the next section.

4 Attack back – disrupt the disruption

A final strategy is for incumbents not only to emphasize and enhance their intrinsic advantages against the new entrant, but to add further ones, changing the basis of competition yet again. This is equivalent to reinvigorating a performance feature on the Kano diagram and adding some complementary delighters as well. The Swiss watch industry is a classic example of the aggressively transforming approach. Its previous success had been based on a long tradition of craftsmanship in making clockwork timepieces that were more accurate and reliable than any others. This advantage was wiped away by the arrival of extremely accurate electronic watches based on quartz crystals that were also very much cheaper and could provide a variety of new features. Faced with this dramatic change they neither continued their previous competitive focus on accuracy and craftsmanship nor attempted to follow the new one introduced by the competition (price and features). Instead they redisrupted the market by turning to a new way to compete – on style. The Swatch became a byword for novel visual design, a fashion accessory rather than a timepiece. To retain their valuable brand name Swiss Watch reengineered the design of the watch, reducing the number of assembled components by 40 per cent so that it could still be made cost-effectively in Switzerland.

Timing of Innovation

Timing of innovation is an important strategic choice. Companies, like people, have their own preferred approaches to innovation: some will be 'early adopters', who always like to take on new things, others will be innately more conservative.[37] For individuals it's a matter of personal psychology, though much influenced by education, wealth and social standing.[38] For a company, culture certainly plays a part but more important are the strength of its position in the market and the extent to which the innovation may be protected from competition.

In the long run a company's ability to profit from an innovation depends on how easily the innovation can be imitated and also, crucially, on the company possessing other business capabilities such as manufacturing, distribution, brand image or financial assets. These factors are called *complementary assets*.[39] The innovator is in a strong position if the innovation is not easily copied – for example because it is protected by strong *intellectual property rights* (IPR) or requires a great deal of specialized tacit knowledge. If he lacks the required complementary assets then, protected by his IPR, he can take time to develop them or can acquire them from elsewhere. However, if the innovation is readily copied, success is likely eventually to go to those with the strongest position in the key complementary assets. This was the case for IBM's venture into the PC market. IBM did not invent the PC but their strong position in all the related parts of the business allowed them to take a dominant position because the idea was not difficult to copy. By contrast EMI, who invented the body-scanner, found that their intellectual property was not strong enough to protect them for long against GE, Siemens and others who had far stronger complementary assets in knowledge of the medical equipment market and access to it.[40] Although initially successful, EMI lost market leadership in six years and withdrew from the market after eight.

When embarking on an innovation, companies need to consider what the dominant source of competitive advantage in the market will be in the long run and to use their advantage as innovators to build up strong protection for their IPR or the complementary assets that will underpin later success.

There are three generic postures that an organization may adopt towards timing its approach to innovation:[41] Shape the Future; Adapt to the Future; and Reserve the Right to Play.

Shaping the Future involves trying to push the uncertainty in a particular direction or attempting to take a controlling position in an emerging technology. This strategy holds out the hope of large rewards but also the possibility of expensive failure. It usually requires significant resources, either alone or with others, or a privileged position, perhaps in the form of strong intellectual property. It is a particularly appropriate strategy when the market is subject to threshold or network effects. These, as mentioned above, can give an enduring advantage to the first players to establish a significant lead. Sony and Philips took this approach to the CD market by collaborating to get their data format adopted as a world standard. This resulted in a rapid take-off of the market and a continuing dominant position for the two companies.

Adapting to the Future means entering the market at once but not attempting to manipulate it. This stance requires good intelligence to understand how things are moving, coupled with the agility and resources, especially complementary assets, to respond as quickly as the scene develops. It is often the only sensible approach when the market is still uncertain and the only way to learn about it is to participate.

Reserving the Right to Play is an option strategy. A company makes relatively

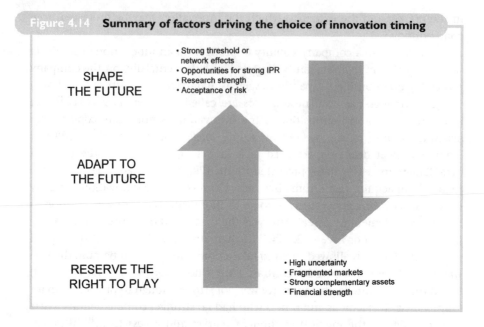

Figure 4.14 **Summary of factors driving the choice of innovation timing**

SHAPE
THE FUTURE

- Strong threshold or network effects
- Opportunities for strong IPR
- Research strength
- Acceptance of risk

ADAPT TO
THE FUTURE

RESERVE THE
RIGHT TO PLAY

- High uncertainty
- Fragmented markets
- Strong complementary assets
- Financial strength

small initial investments that put it in a position to scale up quickly if things turn out well or to withdraw if they do not. This reduces the investment risk but may put the company at a disadvantage compared to others who are building up experience and brand awareness in the new market. It is an appropriate strategy for companies with strong complementary assets; and also when the market is uncertain or liable to fragment into sectors that can be tackled separately. Pharmaceutical companies habitually follow this strategy by making strategic investments in small companies with interesting technologies. These investments give them up-to-date knowledge of the new field and a strong position from which to build up their investment if the prospects are good. They have strong complementary assets in the market and need only to secure their technical position and of course the IPR that protects it.

Figure 4.14 summarizes the drivers for each of these strategies.

Linking the Components of Strategy: Roadmapping

In an effective strategic plan the components must be linked together in a coherent way that commands the understanding and engagement of all those involved. And it must clearly drive the actions that will make it happen. An effective way of achieving these aims is to construct a *roadmap*. This is a graphical representation of strategy that aims to lay out the key aims of the organization, the means it will use to deliver them, and the new resources needed to make it all possible, in a single document. The roadmap format can be used as a way of presenting a strategy arrived at by other means, or as a vehicle for developing it.

Figure 4.15   Generic design of a product-technology roadmap[42]

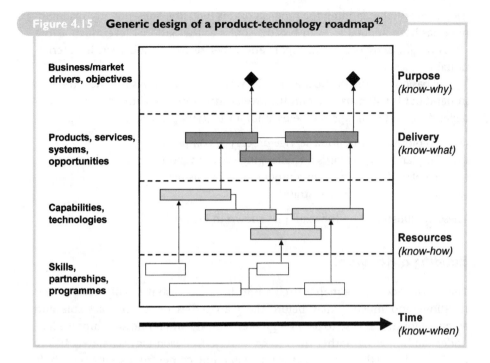

The map is typically structured in a series of layers representing the elements of the business issue being addressed, with links showing the dependencies between them. The upper level might show specific business aims such as a planned entry into a new market sector. Below this might be the physical or service products the company would need to achieve these aims; and below that the capabilities, resources or technologies it would have to develop to deliver these. The axis is timing (too often missed out in so-called strategies!). Thus know-how (capabilities) is linked to know-what (products and services), know-why (aims) and know-when (timing). A simple and generic example is shown in Figure 4.15.

Describing their use in Rockwell Communications, McMillan[43] comments, 'Roadmaps are formal mechanisms for collecting data and sharing information in an open, partnering environment. Thus, roadmaps become knowledge-capture and communication tools for the company.' A roadmap is in many ways like a Gantt chart but at a rather high level of abstraction, the emphasis being on the logical structure and interdependencies rather than on completeness of detail.

The first consistent use of roadmapping in business was by Motorola and Corning in the 1980s.[44] The technique was adopted by a number of electronics companies in the 1990s, notably Philips,[45] BP,[46] Lucent and Hewlett Packard, and this led to its use by communities of companies collaborating to plan the evolution of technologies for complete industry sectors. The roadmap for the semiconductor industry is perhaps the best-known of these.[47] It has certainly been influential in guiding the progress of this industry. Subsequently roadmapping has been applied to even broader topics at the national level, such as the UK Foresight activities for transport and other sectors,[48] and even in international politics.

The basic structure of the map can be varied in many ways to reflect the task in hand but it will usually retain the layered structure with links showing interdependencies. Roadmaps can be used for a variety of purposes, for example:

(a) To plot the future for a service process or competence.
(b) To plan a way towards a challenging goal or vision.
(c) To plan the evolution of a product line or business.
(d) To explore a particular strategic issue.

These are illustrated by the examples shown in Figure 4.16.[49]

Building a Roadmap

The act of building the map is itself a learning process so it usually takes several iterations and much review before the plan settles down into a stable and accepted form. It is wise to do a rough draft quickly and refine and improve it as understanding grows rather than to try and perfect each part separately before putting it all together. Much of the understanding comes from seeing the whole picture. Moreover, building the map takes a lot of effort and it is motivational to have an output early on so that participants can see the sense of what they are doing. Roadmaps gain much of their value from the process of review and critique.

In our experience representatives of all relevant technical and commercial departments must be involved because the purpose is to stimulate understanding and debate about how the parts of the strategy work together, and ultimately to generate commitment to the plan. And it must have the active participation of the management team responsible for the aspect of the business under review. After all, the subject is nothing less than the future of their business.

The Cambridge 'Fast-Start' process

Although it is easy to imagine how useful a roadmap can be, getting started on it may not be so simple. Researchers at Cambridge University[50,51] have devised a quick way to generate a coherent 'first-cut' roadmap, which is particularly suitable for product planning. The process consists of four stages, the first three of which are concerned with identifying the key market drivers, product features and technologies. A pair of *cross-impact matrices* are used as an analytical tool (Figure 4.17).

The first stage is concerned with understanding the market, to determine a prioritized set of market and business drivers. These are listed and given a weighting out of 10 according to the team's view of their importance.

In the second stage participants consider the features of the product that drive

Figure 4.16 A variety of roadmap formats

(a) Roadmap for the development of a service process or core competence; exploring the knowledge flows required as the process develops

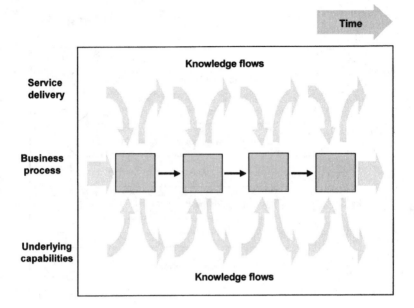

(b) Roadmap for planning the way towards a vision: exploring the vision, defining the requirements for moving from the current state towards the vision and identifying gaps

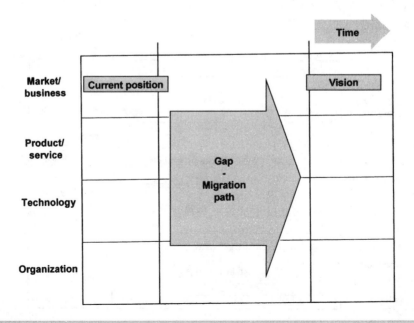

Figure 4.16   *continued*

(c) Product-planning roadmap; identifying the products required to meet particular strategic needs and the competencies needed to achieve them

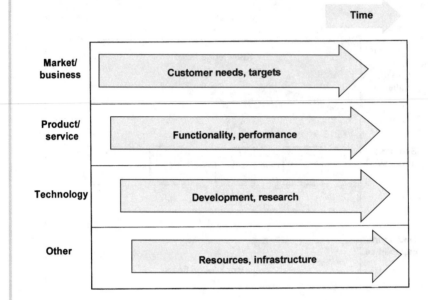

(d) Roadmap for a research activity; linking general market requirements with the applications and capabilities to be demonstrated and the technologies required

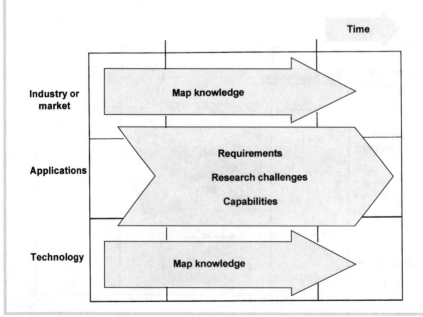

competitive advantage. These will be the things that will be emphasized in the company's brochures, advertising and sales promotions. The first cross-impact matrix is used to check how well they support the key market and business drivers, using a process analogous to Quality Function Deployment (see Chapter 7 for a more complete description). Each feature is given a score according to the strength of its influence on each driver and these scores are multiplied by the weighting factor of the driver to give an overall score. This score shows how well that feature contributes to satisfying the set of drivers. This is a useful check that the right features have been chosen, but it is highly approximate so the precise rankings should not be taken too seriously. Any surprises should be carefully reviewed, though. This process is illustrated in Figure 4.18.

In the third stage a similar analysis is done linking the product features (which now have weights derived from the first process) to the competences that the company has available. This shows what the critical competences are and how they contribute to the performance of the products, and so to the needs of the company and the market.

In the fourth stage the information derived in the first three is used to generate a first roadmap. This is not an automatic process, however. The basic structure of the map – the key market events and their timing, the number of product lines and the frequency of new products and so on – are matters for top management judgement bearing in mind all the circumstances of the company and the market.

A useful starting point for the mapping session is for the participants to estimate what level of performance is achievable for each of the agreed product features at various times in the future. Extrapolation of past improvement trends, as we described earlier, is a useful tool to use at this stage. The team must also be aware of any possible limits to progress (are we reaching the top of an S-curve?) and, of course, must make some assumptions about what level of resources they can employ. In practice the performances proposed are unlikely to be entirely acceptable, so the debate begins, tradeoffs are made, and the team eventually homes in on a set of performances features that are both adequate and achievable. During the debate managers should ask explicitly whether each feature is a Satisfier, a Performance feature or a Delighter in Kano terms; and more important whether they will continue to have the same status during the life of the map. Very probably some features whose performance has driven success in the past may, with time, become mere Satisfiers. So it is worth establishing a vision for each feature: 'how far should we go with this?'; 'can we envisage a time when it will no longer give us competitive advantage?'; 'what new Delighters can we introduce to replace it?'.

Keeping a Roadmap Alive

Roadmaps are sometimes used as a way of analysing individual issues, but more often they are intended have a continuing life as part of the organization's strategy debate. If this is so then one cannot overemphasize the need to review

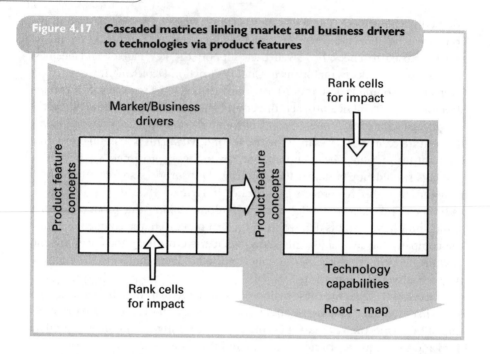

Figure 4.17 **Cascaded matrices linking market and business drivers to technologies via product features**

Figure 4.18 **Cross-impact matrix for first stage in roadmap development**

Driver weight	4	10	2	6	6	10	8	4	
	Market driver 1	Market driver 2	Market driver 3	Market driver 4	Market driver 5	Business driver 1	Business driver 2	Business driver 3	Score
Feature 1	✓✓✓	✓		✓✓		✓✓✓	✓		72
Feature 2	✓	✓✓✓						✓✓	42
Feature 3			✓		✓✓✓	✓	✓		38
Feature 4	✓	✓		✓	✓	✓		✓✓	44
Feature 5	✓	✓✓✓		✓✓		✓✓✓	✓✓✓	✓	104
Feature 6	✓✓			✓✓✓		✓	✓✓	✓	56

and update regularly. There are four principal reasons for this. First, the world changes, often rapidly. A roadmap is not a page from an atlas but a sketch-map of a changing battlefield so the assumptions behind it are constantly being made obsolete by the march of events. The roadmap must adapt to new facts. Second, our own understanding of the world changes as we learn, think and debate with colleagues. The roadmap must adapt to new insights. Third, the process of thinking about strategy is more important than the strategy itself. At the head of the chapter we quoted Dwight Eisenhower's wise words 'I have always found that plans are useless, but *planning* is indispensable' (our italics). Reviewing the roadmap deepens understanding and reinforces commitment to what has been agreed and so prepares us to meet the next challenge. Finally, old colleagues move on and are replaced with new. The act of reviewing the strategic roadmap with newcomers is an excellent way to acquaint them with the strategic thinking.[52]

Looking Further Ahead: Scenario Planning

The strategic planning techniques discussed so far in this chapter assume a certain level of predictability about the future. Scenario planning is a group of techniques designed to help organizations approach a future that contains large and genuine uncertainties. It first arose after the Second World War, given impetus by the success of Operations Research. Their adoption in business was pioneered by Shell who used scenarios to examine what would happen if there were to be a political change in the Middle East leading to a sudden rise in the price of oil. This work did not allow them to predict the Yom Kippur war of 1973 but it left the company to some extent prepared for the price shock and able to react to it faster and more effectively than their competitors.[53]

Many scenarios have been developed to address the impact of major geopolitical and social changes but they can be used on a smaller scale to examine the consequences of, say, the collapse of a competitor, a major regulatory change or a significant shift of customer behaviour. The aim of scenario planning is not to predict the future, but to:

□ Understand the range of futures that might plausibly occur.
□ Find indicators that will give early warning of how things may turn out.
□ Avoid strategies that could be disastrous.
□ Prepare the way, if only mentally, for possible disruptive changes.
□ If possible find some strategies that are valid for all likely scenarios.

The approach is to build up a group of scenarios, each of which is a description of how the world would be if the uncertainties under consideration turned out in a particular way.[54,55] The scenarios are made as complete as possible and are presented in a colourful and compelling way so as to stimulate interest. Each one is, in Porter's words, 'An internally consistent view of what the future might turn out to be – not a forecast, but one possible future outcome'.

The quality of a scenario depends very much on the skill and knowledge of those participating in its definition. The key steps are:

1 Identify the issues of concern and the timescale of interest.
2 Analyse the internal and external forces at work.
3 Identify trends in key factors and extrapolate to the chosen time.
4 Agree any baseline assumptions.
5 Identify a small number of key events or developments whose outcomes are uncertain but that will have important consequences.

6 Consider all possible combinations of the key events. Reject any combinations that are incompatible or that contradict other assumptions.

7 Analyse the remaining scenarios in depth.

When Stanford Research Institute carried out a scenario exercise for Norway's Statoil they identified three axes of uncertainty. These were: the structure of the energy market (a seller's or a buyer's market); the Norwegian economy (heavily energy-dependent or more diversified); Technology (slow and fragmented development or integrated and rapid). The combination of these gives eight scenarios that were reduced to four by removing contradictory or uninteresting combinations.

Managers using the technique at ICL emphasized that to be useful, scenarios must be carefully publicised and widely discussed in the company. Effective presentation graphics and attention-grabbing names for the scenarios all help to engage the debate and fix the issues in peoples' minds.[56]

The Success Trap

A company that makes an innovative strategic change is likely to be changed by the experience. As the new capability moves up its S-curve the competitive focus of the company typically moves away from dramatic service or product innovation towards improvements to business processes.[57] Financial, quality and manufacturing disciplines tighten. Organization, capital investment and margins now dominate management discussions, which previously had concentrated on technologies, customers and markets. The disciplines of running a complex and efficient organization are very challenging and they become deeply embedded in the culture and thought patterns of the company. The trouble is that the ways of working that are essential to survival in a mature industry can be quite wrong for handling the challenges of something really novel.

A related source of inflexibility in established companies is that the structure of the firm itself often comes to reflect the structure of the product it makes or the service it delivers. Whole divisions of the organization may be formed to specialise in one module of the product. For example, Airbus makes the fuselage of its aircraft in France and the wing in Great Britain, a division of labour that has political as much as technical origins. Recently a radical new aircraft design was proposed, which is simply a single wing with the passengers and cargo inside. Needless to say the proposal came from Boeing, not Airbus. It is almost impossible to imagine Airbus proposing, let alone developing, a concept that would destroy the very structure of the company. Any well-established company faced with a major change to the architecture of its product or service may face similar, though less extreme, issues.[58]

To a lesser degree, any new technology or approach to business is liable to present a somewhat different collection of characteristics to the customer, overlapping those of the old but not simply substituting for them. The extreme case is a disruptive technology that, initially at least, forces a totally new approach to the business. We have already seen how difficult that can be to handle. But in between a sustaining and a fully disruptive technology lies a whole spectrum of cases where the different capabilities of the new technology cause a greater or lesser reorientation of the business. The main case for this chapter, Domino Printing Sciences, is an example of this. This company sought to escape from the limits of its core inkjet technology by adopting laser markers, among others. The move was successful but the new products were sufficiently different to demand new business models and strategies, radically changing the shape of the company. The more effective a company is in its existing business the more difficult such a reorientation will be.

A study[59] of 27 firms that faced a radical innovation and adopted it, found that only seven were successful. Their own established approaches, divided loyalties and the priority given to existing businesses all stood in the way of the success they sought. Experience of spin-outs at Xerox[60] found that radical new activities kept within existing divisions seldom prospered because professional managers tried to force the new businesses to work within the patterns of the old. Hewlett Packard had the same experiences with small disc drives.[61]

In summary: 'An unhappy by-product of success in one generation of technology is a narrowing of focus and a vulnerability to competitors championing the next technological generation . . . firms seem to fail by learning the lessons of survival in the short term too well.'[62]

Summary

This chapter has covered the first element of the Pentathlon – innovation strategy. We have discussed the various factors, some subtle and some not so subtle, that demand innovative change. These have the common feature that they stem from the blocking of pre-existing routes to competitive advantage either through loss of scope for improvement or through satisfaction of market demand. This chapter has shown that:

- An innovation strategy should identify and prioritise the needs for innovation, in the various parts of the organization, showing what dimension and degree of change is required.
- Innovation strategy must be an ongoing process not a single point event.
- The need for innovative change often comes from slowly developing trends, which may be difficult to recognize and respond to. Among these are technology maturity and threats from disruptive technologies. Kano's analysis provides a useful structure for understanding these.
- As companies and competencies mature the focus of innovation moves from products and services to business processes.
- Organizations should choose the timing of innovations with care. Network and threshold effects can give advantages to earlier entrants.

❑ Roadmapping is a flexible way to formulate and communicate innovation strategy. Different formats are available for different strategic issues.

❑ Successful organizations acquire disciplines and ways of working that are vital to continued success in their current operations but make change more difficult.

Management Recommendations

❑ Understand the limits of your existing technologies or competences.

❑ Be clear whether these limits may put the organization at a competitive disadvantage.

❑ Be alert to the possibility that the market's demand for further improvements may be not as strong as it was. Avoid going further than required and find new sources of competitive advantage as the old run out.

❑ Choose a competitive stance to each innovation: whether to shape the future, adapt to it, or reserve the right to play.

❑ Recognize how the management style and focus for success in established businesses is inimical to new ones. Set up separate activities for new businesses as far as possible.

❑ Plan ahead, using tools such as roadmapping and scenarios that encourage participation from all concerned.

Recommended Reading

(1) Bower, J. L. and Christensen, C. M. 1995, 'Disruptive Technologies: Catching the wave', *Harvard Business Review*, Jan–Feb (1995). Summary of the theory of disruptive technology. Christensen has also written two books on the subject: *The Innovator's Dilemma* (1997) and *The Innovator's Solution* (2004).

(2) Courtney, H., Kirkland, J. and Viguerie, P., 'Strategy under Uncertainty', *Harvard Business Review*, Nov–Dec (1997) pp. 67–79. Analysis of timing and company stance in a new market.

(3) Johnson, G. and Scoles, K., *Exploring Corporate Strategy* (London: Prentice-Hall Europe, 1999). Classic text on corporate strategy.

(4) Teece, D. J., 'Profiting from Technological Innovation: Implications for Integration, Collaboration, Licencing and Public Policy', *Research Policy*, vol. 15 (1986) pp. 285–305. Seminal paper on the role of IPR and complementary assets in determining the distribution of advantage from innovations.

(5) Utterback, J. M., *Mastering the Dynamics of Innovation* (Boston, Mass.: Harvard Business School Press, 1996). Covers the evolution of markets and technologies, and the concept of dominant design. Good case studies.

Main Case Study **Domino Printing Sciences – facing the limits of technology**

Before reading this case, consider the following generic innovation management issues:

- How can companies recognize that their technological basis is facing a technical limit?
- Do such technological limits necessarily matter?
- What issues face a company adopting a new technology that fully replaces their current one?
- What issues face a company adopting a new technology that overcomes deficiencies of their current one but does not fully replace it?
- What problems may a single-technology company expect to face when it adopts new, overlapping products?

Domino was founded in 1978 as a spin-out from the technology consultancy Cambridge Consultants. Graeme Minto had led a project developing Continuous Inkjet (CIJ) technology for a client. Minto's client eventually lost interest but he believed the technology had promise so he licensed the know-how and set up on his own, working literally out of the garage of his home. The technology was not totally new: there had been academic work in the USA and Sweden in the 1960s, but only one company, Videojet in the USA, had yet applied it industrially.

Fortune favours the brave and by the early 1980s the company was prospering, helped by EU legislation requiring the date marking of perishable goods, an application for which CIJ was ideally suited. In 1985 Minto floated Domino very successfully on the UK stockmarket and set about handing over the reins to a new management team with experience in running large companies. He himself became chairman and after four years moved on to other things leaving a thriving company with a technology much in demand, albeit in specialist applications.

Approaching the Limits of Technology

It was in the early 1990s that Domino management started to be concerned about the restrictions that the technology itself would place on the growth of the company. As Howard Whitesmith, Domino's MD at the time, commented: 'CIJ is a great printing technology. It's fully flexible, character by character; it can print at high speeds – up to 5 metres a second – and the drops fly up to a centimetre through the air. It's ideal for printing simple information onto products bouncing along a high-speed production line, like putting codes onto Coca Cola tins, for example. But it has serious limits: it's low resolution – well below what is acceptable on a printed page – and you can't make images more than about half an inch high. In fact as the characters get larger the printing speed goes down sharply (Figure 4.19). By the end of the 1980s we'd made a lot of progress with better resolution and bigger images but it

Main Case Study   *continued*

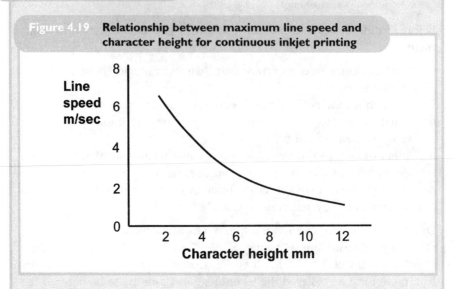

Figure 4.19   Relationship between maximum line speed and character height for continuous inkjet printing

was becoming more and more difficult. The technical guys were quite clear that we were starting to push up against the laws of physics.'

'Many of our customers already wanted to print larger characters, as well as images such as bar codes and logos, while keeping the flexibility of non-contact printing. But we couldn't do it. And there were other things about CIJ that were less than ideal, such as the fact that we used solvent-based fluids. It's not as fundamental as the print size issue but here, too, we couldn't meet what our customers wanted.'

The Domino board recognized that the fundamental limits on CIJ performance posed both a threat and an opportunity for the company. Without a new technology Domino's rapid growth could soon come to an end. But there was obviously a demand for better performance if only it could be done. The big danger was that if a competitor moved in with something better Domino would not only miss out on a new business opportunity but could lose many of its existing customers.

Meanwhile competition became more intense. As David Cope, Domino's Operations director says 'In the 1980s we could still make regular improvements in product performance but in the 1990s there was less and less chance to keep a competitive edge in terms of the actual printing. These days the focus is on the quality and reliability of the product, and the back-up we give in service, distribution, and sales competence. And price, of course.'

The Search for New Technologies

During the 1990s Domino staff looked for ways to print larger, higher-definition images onto moving products. 'It wasn't a big, concerted, project', says Steve Marriott, Domino's R&D manager at the time, 'Everyone knew about the limitations of CIJ so we kept our eyes open for anything that might be better. We followed up magnetography, ion deposition and various kinds of contact printing such as mimeography. We even played with spraying a light-sensitive layer onto the surface and projecting an image onto it. But we didn't find anything that would replace and surpass CIJ.'

The nearest thing was 'binary' inkjet, a technology related to CIJ but using over 100 jets for each inch of printing width instead of the single nozzle used in CIJ. This gave great printing speed and could be expanded to large printing widths. The equipment would be much more complex than Domino's existing products but there would be good applications in the commercial printing industry for addressing and personalizing magazines and envelopes, markets in which Domino already had some presence.

Another possibility was 'drop on demand', the technology used in desktop printers. This was a high-resolution technology and the print-heads could be stacked together to print large images. But it was slow, very sensitive to the distance from the print-head to the surface, and could print only onto paper or cardboard. Not a suitable technology for coding Coke tins.

A final possibility was laser marking. This works by rapidly scanning a small spot of laser energy over the product. It makes a mark by removing a layer (for example of printed ink) and exposing the surface beneath; or by changing the colour of the surface itself. This technology would be fast, reliable and environmentally friendly but it wouldn't be suitable for all surfaces. One further drawback was that laser marking requires no ink, so Domino would forgo a very important source of revenue. Another was that nobody in the company knew much about lasers, either from a technical or marketing perspective.

The Domino board realized that there was no simple solution to their problem. No single technology would replace CIJ. 'I don't think we ever asked ourselves how many different technologies we might have to take on', says Whitesmith, 'we just took each one on its merits and made separate business cases'. Binary inkjet was easiest to decide because it was within the technical capabilities of the Domino R&D team, and there was a clear commercial demand for higher speed and higher resolution printing in the commercial printing market where the higher price would be acceptable. Developing binary technology proved more of a challenge than expected, but Domino launched a product in 1997 which became successful and substantially replaced CIJ in the commercial printing sector.

Laser was clearly a case for acquisition. In 1994 Domino bought Directed Energy, a small laser company in California that had a unique small high-power laser tube already used in marking equipment. Domino's international distribution and knowledge of the marking market with Directed

Energy's technical expertise allowed Domino to take the leading position in the expanding laser marking market.

Drop on demand proved more complex. Domino's technical team surveyed all the available examples in the early 1990s and found none that met their requirements. They adopted a 'watching brief' waiting for something suitable to be developed elsewhere. Eventually Xaar in UK and Spectra in USA, and others brought suitable print-heads to the market and Domino began to build them into products. They chose to act as integrators, selecting whatever type best suited each application.

The Difficulties of Becoming a Multi-Technology Company

Within a few years Domino changed from being a single-technology company to one with a variety of technologies and products. The problem was that since none of the newcomers exactly replaced CIJ the company now had to handle four product lines with overlapping capabilities (Figure 4.20). 'To start with', says Whitesmith, 'we were very aware that the new technologies, especially laser, meant a big change and a big challenge to the company, especially to our distributors. So we set up separate divisions to drive the new products along, complete with their own sales forces. That didn't last long: it was too expensive and our customers were confused when they got calls from several Domino salespeople apparently in competition with each other. But most salesmen couldn't master the finer points of all the new products so they couldn't really sell them all properly. We ended up

Figure 4.20 Characteristics of Domino's new product range

	Cost(£)	Consumables	Reliability	Installation	Familiarity
CIJ	5,000–10,000	Yes	High	Easy	High
Laser	12,000–20,000	Some	Very high	Easy	Low
Binary	20,000–30,000	Yes	Medium	Difficult	Medium
D.O.D.	5,000–12,000	Yes	Medium	Easy	Medium

with a hybrid arrangement where every salesman offered the complete range but they had local specialists in each technology to call on for support'.

Domino retained a divisional structure to give independence and focus to each product business. The CIJ-based coding and marking business continues to grow but the competitive focus is less on the product and more on price, quality, service and business processes. The newer technologies are still developing rapidly and their concentration is on new products and new applications. Their management has to be correspondingly more exploratory and entrepreneurial. All the divisions still sell through the established sales channels but the newer technologies are also moving into new markets with new distribution. For example lasers now sell into the semiconductor and clothing markets, entirely new ground for the company. Cope says this all makes for a more complex operation 'but that just reflects the real complexity of the markets and products'. By taking on new technologies to overcome the limits of their original one Domino have protected their existing customer base as they hoped. The new capabilities have driven them into new organizations and new markets that will change the very nature of the company.

5 Ideas: Managing Creativity and Knowledge

'. . . chance favours only the prepared mind.'

(Louis Pasteur)

Introduction

Companies that want to improve their innovation performance levels intuitively concentrate on generating more ideas through suggestions schemes and brainstorming. However, there is more to the second element of the Pentathlon than simply introducing creativity techniques to an organization. Innovation requires creativity that is closely linked to the knowledge in an organization; it requires effective ways of recognizing customers' requirements, and protection of the resulting ideas. Unfortunately, many of the commonly held views on creativity are incorrect. Too often it is only perceived as producing 'completely new' ideas. This neglects the creativity involved with recognizing and clarifying issues. It is necessary to understand the nature of creativity and the implications for organizations and, here, the substantial research on individuals and groups gives useful pointers.

The potential of customers and users in generating innovative ideas should not be overlooked. Many researchers have recognized that customers are not adept at articulating their needs. Therefore, it is necessary to move from traditional market research – which relies on direct questioning – to enhanced techniques, such as observation and indirect questioning. These can identify breakthrough ideas that either revitalize existing markets or create new ones.

In concentrating on creativity, knowledge and ideas, this chapter aims to:

▶ Explain the nature of creativity and how managers can take steps to enhance the levels of creativity in their organizations.
▶ Discuss how knowledge is generated in organizations and how it can be harnessed to increase innovation performance.
▶ Give a detailed understanding of the leading edge tools and techniques for identifying customers' needs.
▶ Summarize the most effective ways to protect innovative ideas.
▶ Explain how the leading US company Texas Instruments manages creativity, knowledge and ideas.

Creativity

Managers in both the service and manufacturing sectors 'need training if they are to be effective sponsors [of creativity and innovation]'[1] and an understanding of the following areas:

▸ The different types of business creativity.
▸ The factors which influence individual creativity.
▸ How group creativity can be managed.
▸ Key creativity techniques.

Types of Business Creativity

It is important to differentiate business creativity from invention and innovation. They are not identical. 'Business creativity is not only original thinking but also thinking that is appropriate and actionable'.[2] In other words, creativity can lead to inventions but until these are commercialized, they are not innovations.

There are three types of business creativity: *normative*, *exploratory*, and *serendipitous creativity*. In normative creativity, original thinking is used to solve known problems. Research has shown innovation projects to be a series of problem-solving exercises, including solving customer needs and solving the many technical problems that arise in, for example, the design of a car.[3] Normative creativity is often required for process innovation, where customers are dissatisfied with service delivery, or a manufacturing facility that is not producing high enough quality. In the service sector the opportunities for normative creativity are enormous, as solving customer issues is a major catalyst for service innovation.

Exploratory creativity is closer to most people's normal understanding of creativity, where the goal is to identify new opportunities. It is 'unconventional thinking, which modifies or rejects previous ideas, clarifies vague or ill-defined problems in developing new views, or solutions'.[4] A financial services provider might conduct discussions with customers to generate ideas for new service products. Identifying problems which create real business opportunities is not easy. Problems are often articulated in a vague or indirect way. Therefore, an important task for managers is to identify the problems that their employees should focus on.

Serendipitous creativity is accident and good fortune in, for example, identifying an existing idea that will solve a new problem. A famous example is the 3M 'Post-It', where a glue that was being developed for permanent fixing failed but for which a very successful alternative use was found is. Serendipitous creativity, by definition, cannot easily be managed although looking for ideas from different sectors or bringing in experts from other fields can help because 'the best innovators aren't lone geniuses. They're people who can take an idea that is obvious in one context and apply it in not-so-obvious ways to a different context'.[5]

Recognizing that there are three types of business creativity gives managers a greater ability to positively influence it. For example, generating ideas for new products and services is an exercise in exploratory creativity, whereas determining the technology or other means to develop that new product or service is a normative task. Depending on the task involved, the most appropriate combination of individuals and creativity techniques can be selected.

Individual Creativity

Creativity can be the result of individual ideas and often certain individuals play an indispensable role. In the academic literature individual creativity is a contentious subject. This is because some researchers take an *elitist* perspective and argue that most of the creativity in an organization originates from a few individuals. Others contend that creativity is a social process, and everyone has the potential to be creative under the right circumstances. We will look at some of the factors that influence individual creativity and then how all individuals' potential for creativity can best be unleashed in teams.

From his extensive research, Mihaly Csikszentmihalyi a psychologist at the University of Chicago, stresses the importance of knowledge to make creativity possible. Both individuals and teams need experience, and access to relevant experts and information (*knowledge domains*) to be creative.[6] For example, in the complex field of pharmaceutical research, where hundreds of chemicals may be considered in the search for an effective medication, the volume of ideas being considered makes it necessary to have good data management – even highly talented individuals with good memories simply cannot remember all of the data that might be relevant. Similarly, with the growth of material being published, it is becoming increasingly difficult for scientists to have a grasp of more than their own specialized field. So, knowledge management is an important springboard to creativity.

A myth has developed that individual creativity is normally the result of a flash of inspiration and the metaphor of the light bulb has become inseparable from creativity. The American inventor Thomas Edison developed the light bulb and his creativity was legendary. However, the second element of the metaphor is the instantaneous way a bulb lights and, for many, this stands for how creativity happens without precedent, or planning. The view that creative ideas emerge spontaneously originates from the romantic era, where poems and other great works of art were credited by their authors to moments of inspiration (for example, Samuel Coleridge claimed that he wrote his famous poem Kublai Khan in one attempt), rather than through hard work over a period of time. Closer scrutiny of the many similar stories about spontaneous creativity shows them to be untrue (and earlier drafts of the poem were found in Coleridge's papers after his death). The quote at the beginning of this chapter from Louis Pasteur also indicates the role of knowledge and hard work in creativity, in contrast to pure chance.

Just as creative individuals are normally extremely knowledgeable and hard working, they may also exhibit definite personality traits. Much of the research looking for the typical traits of creative individuals is inconclusive and the search for *the profile* of a creative person is probably similar to alchemy. Csikszentmihalyi's work does show, however, that extremely creative individuals have 'complex personalities', by which he means that such people display contradictory traits. For example, they may switch quickly from being humble to being proud, introvert to extrovert, and traditional to rebellious. This may make the job of managers harder but if this is the price to pay for more highly creative individuals, then it almost certainly worthwhile. Csikszentmihalyi and others' work shows managers need to nurture the creativity of their key individuals by:

1   Giving them full access to the knowledge domain in which they are working. This could mean ensuring that company research scientists visit the leading conferences in their field and even allowing them to spend time at universities each year. In the service sector, it could mean allowing key individuals to visit top service providers in other sectors, to gain a different perspective.

2   Motivating them to develop and passion for the subject on which they are concentrating.

3   Providing the time for key them to immerse, even indulge themselves in the issues. Initially the process of creativity is *divergent*, when ideas, information, and alternatives are being collected. Then the process becomes *convergent*, as alternatives are rejected. Providing sufficient time is often a very difficult point because of the pressure for results in business. Managers need to be aware of the importance of avoiding extreme time pressure, as a recent business study has showed just how detrimental it can be.[7]

4   Avoiding the impact of uncertainty. For example, the threat of redundancy has a massive negative impact on personal creativity.[8]

Team Creativity and Culture

The level of creativity in an organization is not only dependent on individual creativity. Companies need to take all possible steps to create a culture of creativity and innovation in which innovation project teams can excel. As this is intimately connected with the management of people (the fifth element of the Pentathlon) we will save our main discussion of this for Chapter 8 – People, Organization and Innovation. It will be stressed that the right culture for innovation is necessary; otherwise creativity levels will be low. The vast majority of innovation projects involve teams of people. The lone inventor, striving to develop a successful product, is an exception as in the case of James Dyson's bagless vacuum cleaner. He worked in isolation on countless prototypes, before finding the right design. However, such cases are rare as few can finance their sole endeavours. Therefore, managers need to be able to stimulate creativity in teams.

From research it appears that nurturing team creativity is largely a question of avoiding barriers to creativity. Teresa Amabile of Harvard has conducted a number of studies and found that managers need to focus on six issues:

1   Providing the right group of individuals with the right challenge. Too often, the match of people to projects is poor.

2   Giving teams the autonomy to choose the means by which they meet the challenge but not the freedom to choose the challenge themselves. A vague or ill-defined problem is where discussions should start; as such problems often mark the starting point of successful innovations. Project strategy should be developed in discussions with the employees themselves, as this achieves 'buy-in'.

3   Making suitable resources available (including time and money). A certain amount of time pressure can be positive but, as recognized for individuals, team creativity plummets when unrealistic schedules set by management lead to mistrust and employee burn-out.

4   Building effective teams, through diversity, shared excitement in achieving the goals, supporting and recognizing the contributions of all colleagues.

5   Ensuring timely and appropriate supervisory encouragement. For example, if management takes too long to respond to team proposals, this has a negative impact on team motivation.

6   Guaranteeing support from the whole organization, particularly for innovation teams working under time pressure. Similarly, protecting teams from organizational politics is important.

Box case 5.1   PA Consulting Group – the 'garden'[9]

'Creativity is a free spirit . . . it is an elusive subject to harness effectively into the delivery of business benefits'. With this philosophy, John Fisher, Technical Director of PA Consultancy Group's Technical Division manages nearly two hundred engineers, scientists and technicians in Cambridge, UK. The Division develops both product and process innovations for clients, often organizations that have got into difficulties developing the innovations themselves. Fisher perceives his role as tending the 'garden' in which creativity can flourish. This requires leadership (including the communication of challenging goals); managing the politics to free the time for individuals to focus on the technical issues; providing excellent resources in terms of equipment, services and support; and providing access to information. The Division has been extremely successful in developing products and processes fast, even though this has often involved the solution of problems that others have failed to solve. As a result, the Division has been behind a number of hugely successful product innovations for well-known companies.

Researchers have warned that very strong company cultures – *cults* – can decrease creativity.[10] Pressure for uniformity or elitism can block creativity, especially the openness to using and modifying others' ideas. At the team level, management must avoid *groupthink*, in which a team develops an unrealistic view of the issues and disdains opposing views. Strong leadership can make groupthink more extreme.[11]

The diversity of teams helps creativity, as identified by Amabile. Process innovation in manufacturing companies has largely been the responsibility of quality teams. Groups of manufacturing employees meet regularly to identify opportunities for improving the efficiency of processes. However, if the group is consists only of manufacturing people, the ideas generated may be too narrow. For this reason, the JCB company which designs and manufactures earth-moving equipment (with manufacturing operations in the UK and Savannah Georgia) always includes representatives from other functional areas in their manufacturing quality meetings. For example, a sales representative is responsible for stimulating discussion on which of the process improvements being considered is likely to have a direct positive impact on customers.

Creativity Techniques for Innovation

A wide range of creativity techniques is relevant to innovation projects. The choice of which technique is most appropriate depends on the type of creativity needed (for example, exploratory or normative), and the number of individuals involved. J. Daniel Couger from the University of Colorado describes 22 creativity techniques, with recommendations as to whether they are best used with individuals or teams, and whether they can be used for exploratory or normative creativity.[12] Companies that are aware of the many possible techniques can turn this to their advantage in two ways. Firstly, in choosing the most suitable techniques to match the issues at hand and, secondly, to provide variety. For example, constant use of only *brainstorming* can cause interest levels to drop.

Arthur Koestler wrote one of the classic books on creativity in the 1960s and his central premise provides a useful tool for innovators.[13] When we think we do so using frames of reference – using particular ways of thinking (rules, habits, associative contexts) that have been useful in the past. These are the mental equivalent of the physical reflexes and movements, which our bodies apply, unconsciously, to particular situations. Frames of reference and physical reflexes are highly efficient tools but can be difficult to shake off. According to Koestler, the creative act is bringing a new, previously unassociated, frame (F_2 in Figure 5.1) of reference to bear on a topic with an existing frame (F_1). Frames of reference are similar to the philosopher Thomas Kuhn's concept of paradigms: patterns and rules that define boundaries, and shared sets of assumptions. All creativity techniques help bring a new frame of thinking and we will discuss four techniques that are effective for innovation projects.

Brainstorming

The original and most widely known creativity technique is brainstorming, which was developed in the 1950s for use with groups. A group of people are asked to describe any ideas that come to mind as solutions to a problem (normative creativity), or as opportunities for new products, services of businesses (exploratory creativity). The ideas are written on a flip chart where everyone can

Figure 5.1 **Creativity as the intersection of two different frames of reference**

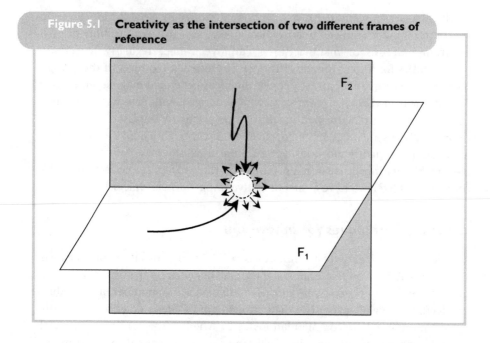

read them and one idea leads to another. An experienced moderator typically records the ideas and reflects these back to the group to stimulate further discussion. The evaluation of the feasibility of each idea is suspended during the idea collection phase, so that potentially good ideas are not prematurely rejected because superficially they appear unsuitable. An appropriate use of brainstorming would be, for example, to identify the reasons why certain customers are unhappy with a product whereas others are very satisfied.

Brainstorming is based on the assumption that people are naturally creative and that by deferring judgement on the quality of ideas until a sufficient quantity has been thought up, means that from the volume of ideas some really good ones can be selected. One limitation of brainstorming is that certain people may dominate the discussion and so in the variation *brainwriting*, ideas are written down by individuals before they are shared with the group.

Left–Right Brain Alternations

This technique helps a whole-brain approach to identifying an opportunity or solving a problem. Typical left-brain functions include speaking, writing, calculating, logic and deliberating, and so on. In contrast, our right brains control our abilities for intuition, spatial perception, art and visualization. The creativity task at hand can be formulated to require thinking driven from both our left and right brains and two columns on a flip chart are used to summarize the contrasting ideas.

For example, the technique can be used to improve a service product by analysing the service from a left (analytical) perspective, asking such questions as: What is the core product? How quickly is it delivered? What are the key performance indicators? In contrast, the right brain approach would lead us to ask questions such as: How does the customer perceive our service? How do they feel about the service? The contrast between the insights gained from the left and right brain focused questions help to generate new ideas.

Attribute Association

Attribute association can be used to solve a known problem with a product, process or service (normative creativity), or identify new opportunities. The starting point is to create a list of the attributes themselves. This can be based on looking at the attributes of existing products, or managerial judgement, or it can be based on the results of market research, which exposes the customer's perception. For a vacuum cleaner the list of attributes would include the ability to clean carpets, smooth surfaces, stairs, corners, and so on, plus other factors such as the manoeuvrability, design, and so on. Each of the product, service or process attributes is then reviewed using one or more of the approaches summarized in Table 5.1.[14]

The process of reviewing and modifying the attributes requires practice and there are no hard and fast rules for which of the approaches given in Table 5.1 (for example subtraction or multiplication) is the most appropriate for a particular service or manufactured product. Complex products will most benefit from subtraction or task unification. Of course the review of product attributes does not simply have to be conducted internally; it can be conducted with customers or users.

Five 'W's, One 'H' Technique

This is versatile technique that can be used at all stages of innovation. It helps enhance our understanding of a problem or an opportunity by asking 5 'W' questions ('who', 'what', 'where', 'when', and 'why'?) and one 'H' ('how'?). Specific W and H questions are developed for the topic and the answers to the Ws tell us more about the issues. The answer to the H question provides ways to implement the ideas generated by the Ws. The technique is very useful for in investigating reports of product problems.

A medical electronics company received a limited number of complaints that a widely sold blood pressure measuring device was not working properly. Investigation using the Five Ws, One H technique helped understand the problem better. The 'where' and 'why' questions prompted an analysis of what was different about the hospitals that were filling complaints, compared to the majority of hospitals that had no problems. It emerged that the device worked well, except if the patient was shivering. The hospitals making complaints were found not to heat their recovery rooms (where patients are placed following operations), as a warm ambient temperature slightly slows the recovery from an anaesthetic. Most hospitals heat their recovery rooms to near normal room

Table 5.1 Approaches to attribute association

	Approach	Explanation	Service and manufacturing examples
1	Modifying the nature of attributes	Also called product morphology analysis, this approach takes the main product attributes and sees how these can be modified.	▶ Home insurance normally covers the costs of repairs. The German Allianz Group has gone further and offers a home 'breakdown' service, with fast call-out of qualified tradesmen guaranteed for any household problem. ▶ Originally domestic coffee machines had a simple glass pot to hold the freshly brewed coffee. However, companies such as Braun have changed this attribute to a vacuum flask, which keeps the coffee warm until needed.
2	Subtraction or simplification of attributes	Removing certain attributes may simplify a product and make it more attractive to certain segments. This is an attempt to prevent what some writers have called *feature creep* – the tendency for development teams to always add more features to products.	▶ Some mobile telephone companies have success-fully marketed a 'receive calls only' contract, which is popular with parents that want to be able to contact their children but prevent outgoing calls. ▶ Not every subtraction attempt will be successful or positively perceived by customers. For example, the colourless Crystal Pepsi failed when it was introduced to the market in 1993.
3	Multiplication of attributes	An existing product attribute is copied and offered, with a modification of the function of the repeated attribute, multiple times in the product. The multiplication leads to a specific benefit.	▶ A classic example is the Mach 3 razor from Gillette. The three blades all cut but the first two, which are set at different angles, drag across the skin to raise the beard for cutting by the third blade. ▶ A service example is Europcar's multiple rental agreement. Busy executives can purchase rental agreements of, for example, five days a month but these can be multiple rentals, such as one-day at five different airports.

4	Division of attributes	This essentially looks at the product architecture and how physical or functional components are grouped together.	▶ In the automotive sector 'mechatronics' – the combination of software-driven electronics and mechanical components) is making a big impact. Companies such as DaimlerChrysler are moving previously mechanically controlled functions into software, to optimize vehicle performance. ▶ Dial-a-Flight, an internet retailer of travel and tourism services, has carefully divided its service augmentation between its website and its call centre to give a personalized service (see box case in Chapter 3).
5	Unification of attributes	Assigning new functions to existing attributes. This can, for example, also lead to simplification.	▶ The US lawnmower manufacturer Toro has designed a cutting blade that circulates and cuts grass into much smaller pieces. Therefore, the pieces can be left on the lawn and the need for a grass-box has been removed. Effectively, a mixture of task unification and simplification.
6	Introducing cross-attribute dependency	Investigating how pairs of attributes are dependent and, through the development of new dependencies, adding useful functionality.	▶ Two attributes of drinking vessels are their height and diameter. Normally, these attributes are not related, however, if the diameter increases with height then a cone-shape cup results. These have the characteristic that they do not stand up and for this reason they are often used as the free drinking cups in shops (where it would be a disadvantage if people left half- empty cups around the store). The attribute dependency creates a new product for a particular application.

Source: Based on[15, 16] supplemented by examples collected by the authors.

temperature. The H question was: how can the device be made to work when the patient is shivering? The answers to this led to improvements in the device and accurate blood pressure measurements in all conditions.

Managing Knowledge

Csikszentmihalyi's work shows that creativity is dependent on knowledge and over the past 15 years much has been written about the *learning organization*; how an organization can stimulate and effectively utilize knowledge. In this section we will look at links to managing innovation. The first of these is an understanding of the nature of knowledge.

Nature of Knowledge

The sharing and interaction of individuals' knowledge is an important source of innovative ideas within organizations. Knowledge has two main forms: *explicit* and *tacit*.[17] Explicit knowledge (which is also known as *articulated*, or *declarative knowledge*) is formal and systematic, easily communicated and shared. For example it can be *codified* and brought into a written or symbolic form that can easily be communicated. Examples of explicit knowledge are instructions manuals, textbooks and service operations or manufacturing *standard operating practices* (SOPs). In contrast, tacit knowledge is hard to express, formalise or write down. It is highly personal, often based on individuals' mental models (which they may not even be aware of themselves), and is usually taken for granted. A commonly quoted explanation of tacit knowledge is the master craftsman who can create a perfect artefact but cannot readily explain all of the steps taken, or the particular ways the materials are chosen, formed and worked. Master craftsmen have a high level of knowledge, most of which they do not and cannot write down. Tacit knowledge is practical, context specific, and not easily shared as it is 'in the heads' of certain individuals. Another example of tacit knowledge is the experienced cook who has a favourite dish that they can cook without weighing the ingredients or timing the stages of cooking. In order for the dish to be cooked by someone else, the recipe needs to be prepared, and the timings, weights and other details codified.

The two types of knowledge reside in various locations within an organization. Artefacts such as databases, computer systems, and publications are the repositories of explicit knowledge. Sometimes, however, what tends to be stored is information as opposed to knowledge. Information alone, without interpretation, recognition of its validity, or experience is of limited use. Tacit knowledge resides with individuals, their expertise and heuristics ('rules of thumb'). The interaction between individuals, their shared understanding and 'routines for doing things' is also a zone for tacit knowledge.

Managers must deal with the implications of the nature and locations of knowledge. On the one hand, tacit knowledge can give a company competitive advantage, as it is difficult to articulate and to copy. On the other hand because it is concentrated in individuals, this knowledge can be lost if they leave the organization. Therefore, managers must take steps to decide where the conversion of tacit to explicit knowledge is important, such as in documenting SOPs. Explicit knowledge can easily be stolen. The problem for managers is how best to stimulate the knowledge transfer that is needed for innovation.

Knowledge Transfer

There are four possible modes of knowledge transfer: *socialization, externalization, combination* and *internalization.*[18] Tacit to tacit knowledge transfer is called socialization. The most commonly quoted example of tacit to tacit knowledge is the apprentice who over several years learns from the master through observation, discussion, and trial and error under the master's supervision. Once the apprentice has learned, their knowledge is also largely tacit. In an organization, managers can promote socialization by taking the time to interact extensively with their employees and by creating a work environment where peers can easily observe and learn from their most experienced colleagues. An example of this are the programmes used by some R&D departments, where new project managers are allowed to 'shadow' more experienced peers. Finally, after-work meetings in a social setting are also a key means by which tacit knowledge is transmitted.

The next mode of transfer is to convert tacit to explicit knowledge and an example is music. Troubadours, the travelling medieval musicians, learnt both their music and texts through apprenticeships, travelling for years with older musicians. However, the sponsorship of Pope Gregory led to the development of the first efficient written notation for music. This allowed music to be accurately defined and enabled the wider transfer of songs and music including the Gregorian chants named after Gregory. Further developments such as the metronome allowed more accurate knowledge capture to occur (on how fast the composer intended a piece of music to be played). Externalization is the name given to the process of converting tacit to explicit knowledge and this, as was the case with music, can be a complex process involving the development of new symbols and methods of codification. Individuals with tacit knowledge may be reluctant to support the process of externalisation because of the time required for this task. Evotec OAI, a German-owned provider of chemical services to the pharmaceutical sector, found that arranging informal weekly tutorials where their top scientists explained how they had solved specific problems, allowed experience to be externalised and passed on to newer colleagues. (This is also much easier than asking the most experienced scientists to document their knowledge in writing.) Metaphors, analogies and models are often effective means by which tacit knowledge can be made understandable.

The third mode is combination and this transfers explicit knowledge without changing its form. There are many examples, such as the preparation of manuals, documents and databases about customers, products, suppliers and the like.

Presentations, a regular part of organizational life, present explicit knowledge. Combination involves the gathering of explicit knowledge both internal and external to the organization, the collation and preparation of the knowledge in a suitable form for dissemination and application within the organization. Consultants McKinsey found that their first attempt at knowledge management, which was a database of reports, slide presentations and checklists, did not enable their employees to solve problems. Therefore, the system was changed to become a sort of 'annotated yellow pages', where a précis of business problems were given, with the contact details of the relevant consultant. This combination enabled McKinsey employees to make contacts and transfer knowledge via socialization.[19]

The final transfer mode is from explicit to tacit and is called *internalization* and is closely related to learning-by-doing. Practice gives experience, resulting in sub-conscious mental models of what is effective and what is not effective. Thus, for example, explicit production tasks enable a manufacturing employee to gather not only knowledge of the current process and its output but also to develop ideas on what could be improved.

Promoting Knowledge Transfer

Although it is intuitively easy to understand the different forms of knowledge and their sources, managers need to find viable simple mechanisms to promote knowledge transfer and creativity. Hard and fast rules cannot be given due to the complexity of the topic and the strong influence of context. However, by looking at both theory and practice three key ideas can be recognized:

1 *Knowledge brokering.*
2 *The Learning Organization.*
3 *Communities of Practice.*

From practice, an anecdotal study of product design consultants IDEO in California showed that it brokered knowledge through four steps.[20] Firstly, by bringing together people with knowledge of different markets, countries, products and technologies, the chances of good ideas emerging are higher. Ideas need to be kept alive and IDEO have found that providing easy access to information is important but simple Internet databases are not sufficient. Collections of tangibles, prototypes, toys and a multitude of other items are kept prominently in the company's offices, to remind people of ideas and stimulate further ones. IDEO also focus on creating new uses for old ideas. Finally, constant testing provides data on what works and what does not, which is essential information if the intent is to commercialize an idea.

Probably the best-known theoretical contribution to the knowledge management debate is organizational learning. This is 'the capability, which enables an organization to acquire and process new information on a continuous basis to elevate knowledge and improve decision making'.[21] Peter Senge,[22] an expert on organizational learning, identifies five key elements of learning organizations:

1 Promote and value the *personal mastery* (expertise) of their individual employees. Recognition of individuals helps generate a high level of individual commitment to the organization and its learning.

2 Develop *mental models*, which illustrate the way in which an organization and its processes work. Drawing and discussing key processes helps discover new ways of thinking.

3 Promote *team learning*, that is teams continuously adopt and adapt successful practices from other teams, both internal and external to the organization.

4 Have a *shared vision*, which is the collective form of personal mastery. This focuses on providing the goals for learning, which is only possible if people try to achieve something that deeply matters to them.

5 Utilize *systems thinking*, the ability to understand the cause and effect relationships inherent in the variety of systems in which individuals and groups operate. It is the cornerstone of organizational learning and inter-links the other four elements.

Another key concept of knowledge management is *Communities of Practice* (CoPs). These are groups of independent participants who share a common context to their work, use common practices, share identities and can provide the social context for transfer of knowledge across organizational boundaries. For example, engineers form a community with a common background, similar experiences and ideas that can make the communication between engineers in different organizations more effective than between engineers and marketing people within one organization. CoPs are important as they can be viewed as the means by which companies can profit from their employees' networking with broader communities. The ideas for a 'Graphical User Interface' passed through the community of engineers from Rank Xerox to Microsoft, where they finally were implemented in the ubiquitous Microsoft 'Windows'. A novel approach is that of the US company greeting card manufacturer, Hallmark Cards, which has created what it calls 'customer communities of practice'.[23] These consist of customers who are particularly interested in cards and similar products. Ideally, about 100–150 are linked via a website and encouraged to exchange ideas, comments and experiences. Typically, only 20 per cent will be active but monitoring their exchanges has been a valuable way for Hallmark to understand consumers. Hallmark's approach is a useful example of how internet technology is being used to stimulate customer ideas. Similarly, Beiersdorf the German company which developed Nivea skin care products, uses its website to collect ideas directly from consumers and the idea of using virtual communities to improve NPD is gaining popularity.[24]

Ideas and Innovation

Innovations often fail. One study found that 34 per cent of new product developments do not fully reach their business objectives,[25] while another study found the figure to be 90 per cent.[26] These studies show that a decisive factor is how clearly new products can be differentiated from existing ones. It is not only product innovations where problems can occur; process innovation is also difficult to manage effectively.[27] Companies that are successful at selling and implementing process innovations (for example production line equipment) have been found to interact more intensively with their buyers during development.[28] Service products without original features (either in the service product or augmentation) also have high instances of market failure. In product, service and often process innovation, it is essential to obtain effective customer input through new approaches to market research.

Identifying Customer Needs – Traditional Approaches

Traditional market research uses direct questions to obtain customers' inputs. However, customers and users may not be able to recognize or articulate their needs, as their ability to comment on the products and services is limited by their prior experience. As customers and users have difficulty in articulating their future requirements, these are termed *hidden needs* (or *emerging needs* or *latent needs*). To determine hidden needs, quality input from customers and users is indispensable. It should be noted that in some markets the customers and users may be different persons and, in addition, the purchase decision may not be made by a single person but rather by what is called the *decision-making unit* (DMU) – this can consist of several people. In business-to-business markets particularly, the DMU can be complex as the individuals involved can have different expectations and requirements.

Traditional market research uses mainly *surveys* and *focus groups*. Current knowledge of products, markets and customers is used to frame the questions to be asked. In parallel, a suitable sample is determined. In selecting a sample, companies strive to identify a representative group of customers or users, whose answers will be indicative of the whole market. Survey methodology is well known and will not be discussed here. Suffice to say that the design of a good questionnaire is not easy and, to be effective, questionnaires need to be pre-tested (normally referred to as *piloting*). For an overview of the crucial aspects of designing and using questionnaires, refer the classic texts on the subject by Oppenheim[29] and Dillman.[30]

Focus groups are small groups of customers or users who have sufficient experiences in common to discuss a specific topic, related to products or services.[31] Normally, they are invited to meet at a neutral location, the discussion topic is introduced and, visual examples of the subject matter are often on display. The discussion is stimulated with a broad question posed by the moderator, who also ensures that all participants contribute equally, and that all topics are discussed. Focus groups mix survey and interview techniques with, often, observers being hidden behind a two-way mirror. Video-recordings may also be used. Once the data have been collected, the analysis of surveys or focus groups leads to a list of product attributes required by customers.

Increasingly companies have found that traditional approaches lead to disappointment, as the output of such market research leads to incremental improvements rather than the breakthroughs that management hopes for.[32] The importance of new approaches to understanding customers has also been found in the service sector.[33]

Hidden Needs Analysis

The recognition of the limitations of surveys and focus groups has led to a range of enhanced techniques, which we will collectively term *hidden needs analysis*. It is important to understand how these techniques relate to each other.

Figure 5.2 shows how the techniques can be used in combination. The first point to note is that an organization consciously decides that it wants to identify radical product attributes and not just incremental ones. This decision immediately influences how the market research is linked to product development and also the techniques used for attribute identification. In addition to the traditional survey and focus group research, techniques such as *repertory grid analysis, empathic design* and *lead users* can be used, individually or more likely in combination (see Figure).

Another key difference to traditional market research is that ideas are tested early in a practical way. Once potential attributes have been identified, it is increasingly common to quickly produce simple prototypes that can be tested by customers and users. Such approaches often rely on new technology and allow intense interactions with customers; *experimentation, rapid prototyping* and attribute association all allow ideas to be further enhanced by obtaining customer reactions. This, in turn, leads to better product definition and then these product attributes can be prioritised using *conjoint analysis*. As shown by Figure 5.2, hidden needs analysis should lead to more radical products but there are no guarantees. There is anecdotal evidence that empathic design is generating ideas that

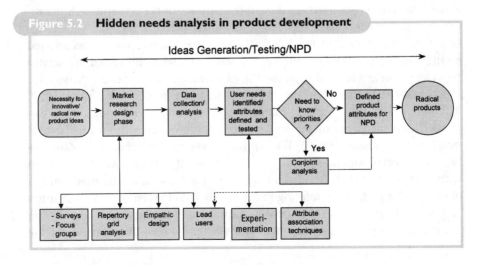

Figure 5.2   Hidden needs analysis in product development

lead to breakthrough innovations but hard evidence is yet to come. (This is an area where there is an urgent need for reliable research.)

Surprisingly, considering the high percentage of product failures, the adoption of enhanced market research techniques is slow. A survey of 70 Finnish companies producing business-to-business products showed the usage to be very low: 58 per cent of respondents do not use any technique and 27 per cent use only one technique.[34] The reasons these companies do not use innovative approaches to market research were that management did not have the resources and perceived the data difficult to collect and analyse. Specialized consulting companies, such as IDEO in California, and PDD and WhatIf! in London, are leading the way in promoting empathic design and similar methods. We will look at each of the enhanced techniques in detail, so as to understand their potential for discovering hidden needs.

Repertory Grid Technique

Repertory Grid Technique is a powerful market research tool for identifying customer needs. It was developed for use in psychology and is very effective at helping interviewees to articulate their perceptions on products and services and in accessing their tacit knowledge. The technique is a highly structured form of interviewing which leads to a matrix of quantitative data – the *repertory grid*.

To understand how the technique can be used, consider how an information technology (IT) service provider would use it. Such providers install and maintain computer networks for companies, including such tasks as upgrading personal computers and training employees in the operation of software. An IT service provider could use repertory grid analysis to gain creative ideas for improving its service offerings (consisting of both the service product and the service augmentation). Interviewees would be members of client companies who have experience of the services that they had outsourced (for example, purchasing managers). The interviewee would be asked to name six outsourced services with which they are familiar – these we will call service products A, B, C, D, E and F. The services are what are termed the *elements* of the test and each is written on a separate (postcard-sized) card, as shown in Figure 5.3(A). A wide range of services can be selected and Table 5.2 shows that the interviewee has selected a range, including facility management and financial auditing. The IT service provider's own service is also on the list, as is one direct competitor (Service E).

Note that the cards have been pre-numbered in a random sequence (5, 1, 4, 3, 2, 6) to enable the selection of random sets of cards. From the diagram it can be seen that the name of the first service ('A') has been written on the card numbered '5', whereas Service B is written on the card numbered '1'. After the cards have been annotated with named services, the interviewee is presented with a set of three cards (termed a *triad*). Figure 5.3 (B) shows the triad consists of cards 1, 2 and 3, corresponding to Services B, E and D respectively. The interviewee is asked: 'Why is using two of these services similar and different from the third?' A typical response – a service attribute – could be that two of the

Figure 5.3 Example of a repertory grid interview

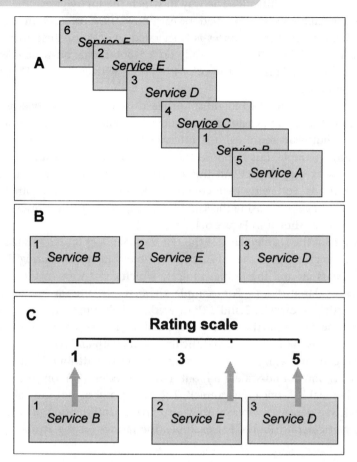

Notes: (A) The elements of the test – services – written on cards; (B) the first triad presented to the interviewee; (c) the rating of the services in the first triad.

Table 5.2 The augmented service offerings chosen by the interviewee

Service products
Service A – Facility management (security and cleaning)
Service B – IT Services (IT service provider)
Service C – Data warehousing
Service D – Financial auditing
Service E – Competitor's IT services
Service F – Employee training seminars

service providers are 'easy to work with, good communications', whereas working with the third 'is difficult'. The way in which the interviewee differentiates between the elements in the triad reveals how they perceive the different services. Each of the three services is then rated against this first attribute. As shown in Figure 5.3(C), this is normally on a 5-point scale on which Service B has been highly rated on 'easy to work with' (a '1'), whereas Service D was given a minimum rating ('5').

Further triads are used to identify further attributes. The interviewee is not allowed to repeat attributes and so each new triad elicits at least one new one. As each attribute is determined, the interviewee is asked to explain what they mean by, for example, fast response and they will give details such as timings and the actions they expect. All this is recorded, as it gives insight into the customer's needs. Following each construct, the interviewee is required to rate all the services against it using the same 1–5 rating scale. These ratings form the repertory grid, as shown in Figure 5.4.

In Figure 5.4 the six elements of the test are – Services B to F – shown across the top of the grid. Down the side are the attributes identified during the interview. The stars around the ratings indicate which cards were in the triad that elicited particular attributes. For example, the first attribute was elicited using a triad consisting of cards 1, 2 and 3 (indicated by the ratings with stars: *1*, *4*, *5*). It can be seen that the Service B is rated as '1' ('easy to work with, good communications') but Service D is difficult to work with and received a rating of '5'. Looking at the ratings, it can be seen that on the attribute 'fast response' Service C is rated mid-scale ('3') but rated as poor ('5') on the attribute 'absolutely reliable service (guarantee)'. The ratings tell us not only about how an interviewee perceives services; they also give us information on the importance of particular attributes. For example, the ratings on the attribute 'clearly

Figure 5.4 A repertory grid on outsourced services

Attributes	Card 1 Service B	Card 2 Service E	Card 3 Service D	Card 4 Service C	Card 5 Service A	Card 6 Service F	Poles
Easy to work with, good communications	*1*	*4*	*5*	5	1	1	Difficult
Fast response to problems	1	4	5	*3*	*4*	*4*	Slow
Professional employees	*2*	5	*3*	4	*1*	1	Little knowledge
Clearly defined service product	3	*2*	1	*3*	1	*1*	Poorly defined ...
Service is good value for money	*3*	*3*	5	1	*5*	5	Expensive
Absolutely reliable service (guarantee)	5	4	*4*	*5*	5	*5*	Difficult

defined service product' are not as widely spread (they only range from 1 to 3) as those for 'good value for money' (where the ratings range from 1 to 5). This shows that this latter attribute differentiates more strongly between the elements. Hidden needs tend to be indicated by low ratings for all elements

---

Box case 5.2   Equant – repertory grids in practice

One company that has used repertory grid technique to its advantage is Equant, the world's largest data network provider – offering network design, integration, maintenance and support services in over 180 countries. The company always placed a high emphasis on being 'customer-focused' and regularly reviewed the results of customer satisfaction surveys, comparing their performance to competitors'. Although such surveys provided useful 'benchmarks', Equant recognized that they did not measure performance against the criteria, which were most important to customers.

In 1996, the company offered excellent network performance and global service availability. Consequently, it received better ratings than its competitors in surveys and this could have led to complacency. However, a project was launched to investigate whether there were aspects of service quality that were important to customers but were not covered by the surveys. Liam Mifsud, Business Support Manager at Equant, designed and conducted repertory grid interviews, in which the elements of the grid were a range of the customer's current service providers. Interviewees (IT Directors and Managers) were asked to name nine suppliers that their companies did business with, and these elements were presented in triads. The constructs elicited typically included a wide range of service quality criteria (far wider than those covered by the customer satisfaction surveys).

The results showed that customers' perceptions of service quality were not based solely on technical measures (such as coverage or network performance). Equant were able to identify ten new criteria on which their performance was being judged. For example, customers emphasized intangible elements of service quality, such as the responsiveness and flexibility of account management teams, and the quality and competence of the support staff they came into contact with. 'This provided us with a valuable means of understanding the changing needs of customers', says Mifsud.

The grid also can be used to derive a *cognitive map* of an interviewee's perceptions of products and services. Deriving and interpreting this map is beyond the scope of this discussion but suffice to say that it can give further insights for product and service designers. Further details can be found in the book *Essential Skills for Management Research*.[35]

Repertory grid technique can also be used to generate ideas for manufactured products. The Hewlett-Packard Medical Products Group first used repertory grid interviewing over ten years ago and it helped the company identify the emerging importance of product attributes such as 'easy to set up' and 'easy-to-clean' in the medical equipment market.[36] A focus was placed on these factors in all subsequent developments. The box-case on Equant gives a detailed example from the service sector.

Empathic Design

Dorothy Leonard-Barton from Harvard has promoted empathic design and defines it as 'the creation of product or service concepts based on a deep (empathic) understanding of unarticulated user needs'.[37] The terms *ethnographic* or *anthropological* market research are also sometimes used, indicating that the data collection and analysis methods are largely drawn from these disciplines. The foundation of the technique is *observation*, but it also includes *discrete observation, contextual interviews* and what we will term *empathy-building*.

Observation

This technique directly assesses the use and potential of products rather than customers' reported perceptions (as, for example, are derived in surveys).[38] Although observation looks at real situations, it has limitations. Actions can be influenced by the presence of the observer, observation is time-consuming, analysis can be complex and observation is a difficult skill to learn. Therefore, the preparation that is needed for effective observation should not be underestimated.[39] It is for this reason that market research companies are increasingly hiring ethnographers. Their training enables them to observe and interpret situations more effectively (that is accurately, unambiguously and in an unbiased way), as they are used to dealing with a variety of visual and verbal clues.

The key to effective observation is the preparation of a good *coding scheme*. Such a scheme is based on the research question: what is the observer looking to understand? Usually, in product innovation studies, observation aims to understand how users utilize existing products in their day-to-day environment and to identify the problems they currently face with these products. For example, a manufacturer might watch housewives operating washing machines in their own homes and this would yield a large amount of data on where (in the house), how (the process), and when (time of the day) washing machines are used. In the service sector observations can be used to determine the typical stages of consumption of a service. The coding scheme gives the observer points to watch for and therefore prevents oversights. This is particularly important, as the clues to unarticulated needs may be non-verbal.

Table 5.3 gives a generic coding scheme for observation and has seven categories of data; from the observed triggers for product usage up to the unarticulated needs. The table gives the main types of events to look for and the additional columns can be annotated with the timings of when these are observed and additional notes. It can be seen that the seven categories of data force the observer to look at not only how the product fits into the user's overall environment but also to look for signals that indicate unarticulated needs. For example, identifying the triggers for use can give insights. For a vacuum

Table 5.3   Generic coding scheme for observational studies

	Data categories	Events to look for	Observed?	Timings	Notes
1	Triggers for acquiring the product or service	▸ Why, when and how?			
2	Triggers for product usage	▸ Who, what, where, when, why, how?			
3	The environment	▸ Physical layout / objects ▸ Actors ▸ Activities / events ▸ Time sequence			
4	Interactions with user's environment	▸ Physical interactions ▸ Social interactions			
5	Product usage	▸ Wasted time ▸ Doing things right ▸ Doing things wrong ▸ Misuse ▸ Confusion ▸ Dangerous situations (for example physical or data)			
6	Intangible aspects and unarticulated needs.	▸ Emotions ▸ Frustration and wasted time ▸ Fears and anxiety ▸ Linguistic signals ▸ Extra-linguistic signals ▸ Non-verbal signals (for example body language) ▸ Spatial signals			
7	User customization	▸ User modifications of the product ▸ User modifications of the (normal) process			

Source: Compiled by the authors from Leonard-Barton (1995, 1997) and a variety of other sources.

cleaner the trigger for use could be the weekly clean of rooms, or something spilled. The latter trigger for use brings different requirements such as speed, which may influence product design. (The Black and Decker Company created the well-known hand-held 'Dustbuster' vacuum cleaners to address this need.)

Frustration with services or products can indicate that a current design does not meet the user's main needs, or fear of operating a product can indiate a poor user interface. However, the signs may not be obvious. A good observer will look for subtle signs such as *extra-linguistic* signals (for example, the speed and emphasis in speech), *non-verbal* signs such as body language, and *spatial signals* (for example, the proximity of a user to others or objects). Another clue to unarticulated needs can be that users have modified the equipment to better meet their needs. Observers also need to be aware that users may also modify their way of working to get around some of the limitations of the current product or service (modifications of the working process can be hard to spot). Due to the multi-dimensional nature of good observation, often the best solution is to make video recordings, which can be viewed off-line by a number of people all looking for the different clues. The disadvantage of video recording is it may influence the user's actions.

The massive amount of data collected by observation must be analysed and summarized in a form that is useful to management. New technology is helping here and the market research consultants PDD in London produce databases of video clips, categorized by customer segment, for their clients. This database can be made available on a company's intranet to any department involved in product development. This helps to spread the understanding of the customer's world throughout the innovation project team.

Another approach to observation data analysis is to identify typical scenarios of how products are used, with associated problems and issues. Descriptive statistics on the number of times particular events occur, for example, can also be a useful way of summarizing data. Simple drawings and storyboards can also be used to summarize triggers for use and problems encountered. Storyboards are useful communication tools with both users and internally, to help the whole of the NPD team understand users' needs.

Discrete Observation

This approach, in which users are observed without their knowledge or permission, is only viable for consumer products and services that are used in public. For example, Nokia in Japan have had employees observe how users operate their products in public. Similarly, car manufacturers have built miniature cameras into cars at shows to observe how potential customers react to their new products. The disadvantages of discrete observation are that it can raise, depending on the product, significant ethical issues and the type of usage that can be discretely observed might not be typical. As discrete observation often deliberately eavesdrops on users' conversations, it has been colloquially dubbed capturing 'the murmur of the customer'.[40] It should be kept in mind that people normally quickly become aware that they are being observed and often react negatively. Obtaining permission in advance is safer.

Contextual Interviews

Observation is conducted with a coding scheme but without asking questions. Contextual interviews are also conducted in the user's environment but observation and a number of semi-structured questions are used, to understand the situation in which products are used. Questions collect background information on the user, and then to stimulate them to describe their actions. Typical questions are: 'Can you please describe what you are doing?' and 'When is that necessary?' Essentially, this produces verbal data on product usage that might not be generated in pure observation of a single user working alone. Once again, video recording is commonly used. Contextual interviews are particularly useful for gaining insights into how the customer feels during the service delivery process and gaining ideas for improvement.

The London consultancy WhatIf! have made contextual interviewing easy for the manufacturers of consumer products, by negotiating access to all of the residents in one (long) street in Birmingham. All of the houses in 'The Street' can be visited with minimal notice and product managers have been able to both observe their products in use and ask questions. Intel, the microchip giant has a number of projects which make use of contextual interviewing and employ a team of ethnographers, sociologists and behavioural scientists based in Oregon.[41] This team was involved at looking at the need for a device for helping parents keep track of their children's extracurricular activities. Although such a product was known to be applicable in many western countries, social research showed that in China, where families are restricted to one child, there was not a need. Intel now regularly uses such insights on the social background to product usage.

Box case 5.3   Clarks – these boots are (really) made for walking[42]

Clarks Shoes has been renowned for the quality and comfort of its products for over 175 years. Three years ago the company was aware that the market for leisure footwear was significant and growing fast, and decided to enter for them a new market – walking boots. As this was a market about which they had no detailed knowledge of customer needs, they worked closely with PDD, a London-based market research consultancy. Product Manager Chris Towns said, 'I needed to understand the buying habits, end use and expectations of our new consumer. Understanding the motivations of walkers can only be guessed at from within the confines of your own office'.

PDD specialize in ethnographic studies and they conducted contextual interviews with walkers in UK national parks, home interviews with people who were members of walking and rambling clubs, and observed customers buying walking boots. The insights obtained from this market research allowed Clarks to clearly identify their target segments and, for these, to understand customer priorities. For example, 'comfort', 'fit' and 'safety' were quickly identified from interviews as important product attributes. However, the contextual interviews in the national parks allowed the design team to understand the real meaning of each of these terms and develop product characteristics to meet them. Much of the development involved experimentation with prototypes and this was conducted directly with walkers. Similarly, customers in shops were observed to always feel the tongue of walking boots before they tried them on. Therefore, it appeared that the tongue was a feature of a boot that customers closely associated with comfort. This insight led the Clarks team to produce a particularly well-padded tongue in their final product. The Clarks range of 'Active' walking boots has been well received by both hobby and professional walkers and ramblers and is selling well.

Empathy Building

Most authors concentrate on the data collection and analysis aspects of empathic design. However, the other side is the need to ensure that product designers not only develop an understanding of customers and users but also fully empathize with them. As yet, there is no formal methodology for this but a number of examples from industry demonstrate the approach. When the Ford Motor Company developed their Focus model, one target segment was elderly people. In order to get the engineers to understand the difficulties that older people have in getting into and out of cars, designers wore padded suits that reduced their ease of movement and simulated the restricted movement of later life. Similarly, a mobile telephone design team also working on a product for elderly people had its engineers wear thick gloves and glasses smeared with Vaseline for a week, to help them understand how difficult it can be for pensioners to operate today's products. No doubt in coming years the way in which companies attempt to generate true empathy will develop further. It is a case of finding ways in which the designers can 'step into the customer's shoes'.

Lead Users

Another approach to uncovering hidden needs was developed by Eric von Hippel at MIT. *Lead users* are groups of customers or users that face more challenging requirements than most of the current marketplace. Lead users' needs can anticipate the general needs of the market – by months or by years. As the market vanguard, lead users face urgent, challenging needs and can benefit significantly from solutions to these. One word of caution is necessary – the theory on disruptive technology discussed in Chapter 4 shows the drawbacks of concentrating solely on existing customers needs. However, if applied correctly, the lead user technique looks not only at the needs of existing users but also collects ideas from users of similar products and services in other markets.[43] So the central issues are selecting the lead users and determining whether their needs are relevant to a wider range of customers.

In contrast to traditional market research, where the sample is chosen to be representative, lead users face particular issues and are not representative of normal users. The selection of a lead user group normally follows four steps. Firstly, a screening process is used with existing users to identify which of them have more demanding needs. Figure 5.5 illustrates the process in which the starting point is screening normal users. From these, the *extreme users* are at the top

Figure 5.5   Selecting a lead user group

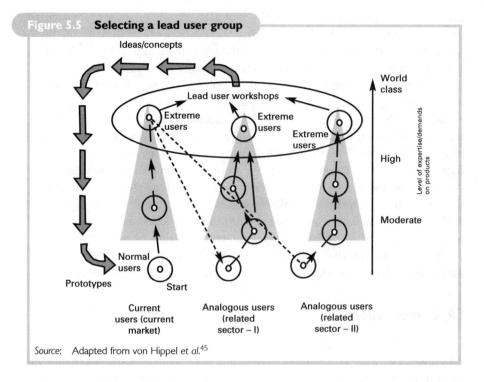

Source: Adapted from von Hippel et al.[45]

of what can be perceived as a pyramid of users. They are extreme in terms of the demands that they place on products or services and also, normally, in their expertise in dealing with the particular challenges they face. For example, extreme users may have the ability to modify standard products or processes in order to cope with the particular challenges of their working environment.[44] Once the extreme users have been identified, the important next step is to identify analogous fields where similar but even more extreme challenges are faced than the ones in the current market.

To understand the process, it is useful to consider an example from the 3M Company, which used lead users to develop improved medical drapes. These are adhesive films applied to the skin to minimize infections during surgery. Firstly, the key attributes of the product were discussed with normal users – these were adhesion to skin and infection prevention. The discussions also identified that an increased risk of infection was a worrying trend in many hospitals. Next, extreme users were identified; surgeons who had to deal with higher risk of infection than in normal hospitals. Here both military field surgeons and surgeons working in developing countries with lower hygiene levels were consulted. Discussions with these extreme users identified two related sectors. The problem of infection is also an issue for veterinary surgeons, who have to operate on animals in non-hygienic environments and have problem fixing drapes on fur and hair. Secondly, an unusual second set of *analogous users* was identified; Hollywood make-up artists, who have to attach masks to skin.

Extreme users from the current market and those from related sectors form the full lead user group. For each of the lead users identified, techniques such as observation and contextual interviewing should be used to understand their working environment and issues. One of the advantages of working with analogous users from related sectors is that they normally do not mind sharing their experience, as competitive issues are not involved, and so it is normal to organize a workshop with the lead user group. This is used to not only tap their individual expertise but also to learn from the discussions that result from bringing together users from what can be very different sectors and backgrounds (referring back to Figure 5.1, this can be seen as the bringing together of different frames of reference). The discussions are moderated and produce ideas for products that address the challenging needs lead users face. The development of these ideas into prototypes can also be conducted in close cooperation – called *co-development* – with the lead users, before the products themselves are tested with normal users. Hilti, a European manufacturer of industrial mounting equipment has found that the combination of a workshop and co-development was particularly effective and less expensive than their normal market research.

Experimentation

Users often cannot articulate product solutions, as they do not have the technical knowledge of what is possible. What this requires is a creative exchange of ideas from the customer or user (their needs) with designers' ideas on possible solutions.[46] By its nature, this is an iterative process, as proposed solutions need to be tested and modified to be effective. Therefore, it is useful to produce both *physical* and *virtual prototypes* that can be tried out and discussed by users and customers. It takes advantage of the much-improved technologies for the production of prototypes. Whether it is stereolithography development of physical models, computer simulations of car crash scenarios, or virtual reality mock-ups of products, which allow users to interact with them, there are many more possibilities today to make prototypes than there were in the past. Allowing customers and users to try and test products at an early stage means that it is still possible to make changes to the final product or service design.

Identifying Priorities – Conjoint Analysis

Essentially all of the techniques discussed up until now identify product attributes. Once these are clear, the priorities from the perspective of the customer can be determined using conjoint analysis, as indicated in Figure 5.2. Conjoint analysis (or *stated preference technique* or *trade-off analysis*) is one of the more widely applied scientific approaches to market research. Provided the product attributes have appropriately elicited from customers, conjoint analysis is a very useful method for understanding the *utility* of each of the attributes. Conjoint analysis can be used in the service sector to understand the trade-offs that a customer is willing to make between elements of the service product and service augmentation.

There are three main stages in conjoint analysis:

1. Identifying characteristics of each of the product attributes and hypothetical product descriptions.
2. Interviewing a suitable sample of customers.
3. Calculating the customer's perceived value of each attribute (the utility).

To understand this, we will consider the example of the development of a new laptop computer. Various methods will have been used to identify product attributes and hidden needs. Let us assume that six attributes were identified in market research with business users: (1) display size; (2) hard-disk capacity; (3) processing speed; (4) physical size and weight; (5) connectivity (ease of integration with other devices); and (6) price. An important question during product development is: on which of these attributes does the customer place most value? Only with this information can development priorities be effectively set. For example, how much effort should be invested in developing a large screen compared to attempting to reduce the overall weight?

The first stage involves the identification of levels for each of the attributes and the typical range of values of existing products. For example, the weight of a laptop is typically around 3 kg. Once the attribute measures and their ranges have been determined, the next stage is to prepare descriptions of a hypothetical set of products, as shown in Table 5.4. Naturally, the values or levels of the attributes change over time and in a fast-moving market such as laptops, the price and performance will need to be checked regularly (and the examples given in Table 5.5 will rapidly become outdated, although at the time of writing 50 Gbyte was not yet available). There are many possible combinations of attributes and so many hypothetical products can be developed, although only three (Product A, Product B ... Product n) are shown in the table. The number of hypothetical products that need to be considered depends on the number of attributes and their possible levels. For example, with six attributes, each with at least three levels (as shown in Table 5.4), results in $3^6 = 729$ theoretical combinations but far fewer need to be used in data collection).

The next stage is to interview customers and to present them with alternative products. In the so-called *pairwise* version of conjoint analysis, the customer

Table 5.4   Attribute levels

	Product attribute	Product A	Product B	... Product n
1	Display size	14 inch	15 inch	14.1 inch
2	Hard disk capacity	50 Gbyte	30 Gbyte	20 Gbyte
3	Processing speed	1.7 GHz	1.5 GHz	1.6 GHz
4	Physical size and weight	3.5 kg	2.5 kg	2.1 kg
5	Connectivity	Network and internal modem cards	Network card, infra red connections	Slot for modem
6	Price	€ 2299	€ 2199	€ 1299

would be presented with simplified descriptions of Products A and B and would be asked: 'Which do you prefer?' Each product has advantages and disadvantages; although Product A is faster it is more expensive and has a smaller display. Therefore, the customer makes trade-offs between the values of the attributes in choosing their preference. Next the customer is presented with another two products and asked the same question. The process of presenting the products and collecting answers is made easier by conjoint analysis software packages (such as the widely used ACA developed by Sawtooth Software), where this is automated and many researchers now administer conjoint analysis via the internet. The sample of customers to be interviewed needs to be representative of the target market.

The interviews collect a significant amount of data on how customers view attributes and make trade-offs. Conjoint analysis software takes this data and uses mathematical principles to determine the value or utility a customer places on each attribute. Figure 5.6 shows the typical output of conjoint analysis, for the attributes speed and hard-disk capacity. A graph of the utility versus the attribute level is shown and the slope of this graph indicates the importance of the attribute. For example, the speed appears to be very important to customers, as the 1.5 and 1.6 GHz speeds have much lower utilities than the 1.7 GHz speed. Similarly, the hard-disk capacity of 30 Gbyte is much better than the lower alternative, but the value of 50 Gbyte memory is not much higher. Although not shown, utility graphs can be derived for all attributes.

The utility graphs give an understanding of how customers make their trade-off decisions, which in turn allows product development trade-off decisions to be made more effectively. In addition, analysis of the results pertaining to price can allow pricing decisions for new products to be made. For readers who want to know more about conjoint analysis, it is recommended to consult the textbooks of Caroll et al.[47] and Gustafsson et al.[48] Referring back to Figure 5.2, conjoint analysis is shown as the last step in using market research for improved product development. It should be stressed that although conjoint analysis is a

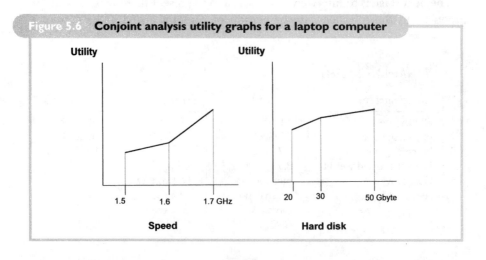

Figure 5.6 **Conjoint analysis utility graphs for a laptop computer**

very effective method, it is critically dependent on the identification of product attributes that are pertinent to customers (including hidden needs).

Choosing the Correct Approach to Market Research

To help choose the most appropriate approaches for a specific piece of market research, Table 5.5 gives the advantages and limitations of the seven techniques discussed in this chapter. To achieve effective results and uncover hidden needs, a combination of techniques is almost always needed. For example, one of Robert Bosch's business units which designs and manufactures production-line equipment used observation of operators working in their customers' factories and repertory grid interviews, thus gaining insights into product requirements. A survey was then used to collect data from a representative sample of users and the results are now being incorporated into a new product design. A fundamentally important part of managing the ideas element of the Pentathlon is designing how to capture the *elusive* voice of the customer, through a blend of the most appropriate techniques.

Protecting Ideas

In order to gain the maximum advantage from their innovations, companies need to protect and exploit their knowledge. The most obvious mechanism for protecting innovations is patents: 'a patent is a legal right granted to exclusive commercial use of an invention, normally for a limited period of time'.[49] Most countries in the world have laws that protect intellectual property – ideas, designs, works of art, literature or music – and allow their originators to establish and defend their ownership of them. The field of *intellectual property rights* (IPR) is complex, constantly changing and varies to some extent from country to country. IPR is a matter of civil, not criminal law and companies must police their own IPR and take action at their own expense to protect it. In this section we will concentrate on the aspects of importance to managers, but we stress that the importance of taking legal advice before making serious commitments.

There are many kinds of IPR, but only the four main kinds need concern us: *copyright, design right, trademarks* and *patents*.

Copyright

Copyright protects writing, music, computer programs, electronic circuit layouts, web pages, photographs, reports, works of art and so on from unauthorized copying for commercial use. It protects the overt content or appearance of the work, not its meaning (if any). So a particular drawing of an invention would be covered by copyright but not the invention itself: another drawing, not obviously copied from it would not be protected. Limited copying for personal use or study is allowed: typically one chapter of a book, one article from a journal, a

Table 5.5 Different approaches to identifying customer problems and requirements

Approach	Overview	Applications/advantages	Limitations
1 Survey research	□ Use of mainly direct questions to determine customers' views on what they think are their requirements. □ Open-ended questions allow respondents some freedom to give creative ideas.	□ Widely used as the method of collecting customer inputs. □ Can be applied as a postal survey, telephone or direct interviews.	□ Questionnaires are often thought to be easy to design. In fact, it is the opposite and many surveys are poorly designed and consequently produce equivocal results. □ Response rates often low, which raises the question of whether the results are representative of the market. □ Respondents may find it difficult to articulate their answers to open questions.
2 Focus groups	□ Small groups of selected users or non-users, paid to discuss product needs. □ Discussions are stimulated by an initial question. □ A moderator guides discussions. □ Market researchers often observe the discussions through a two-way mirror.	□ Help to define customer problems and give background information, rather than identifying solutions. □ 'In vitro' discussions of products (that is users are taken outside their normal environment).	□ The somewhat artificial nature of the situation can limit the effectiveness. □ Particular individuals can dominate the discussions. Therefore good moderation is required. □ Some companies try to save costs by using inexperienced moderators; this wastes the potential of focus groups discussion.
3 Repertory grid technique	□ Users or customers undergo a structured interview. □ Interviewees are stimulated to identify product attributes by being asked to compare triads of different products and/or services.	□ Is powerful at enabling users and customers to articulate their issues. □ Taps tacit knowledge of hidden needs.	□ The technique is not well-known. □ Interviewees need to have experience with 5–6 different products and services to make the technique work. □ Interviewer needs specific training in the technique, although it is easy to apply.

4 Empathic design	□ A range of approaches of which the main ones are observation, contextual interviews and putting product designers 'in the shoes of users'.	□ Effective observation is not easy and using specialists may be the best approach (otherwise base studies on a suitable coding scheme developed from Table 5.3). □ Vast amounts of qualitative data may be generated, which requires effective analysis strategies.
	□ Increasingly used to focus on users' problems. □ Gives an in-depth understanding of customers' and users' product use models. □ Contextual interviews are 'in vivo' and the environment gives valuable information.	
5 Lead users	□ Identification of users that have extreme needs in your current market. Further identification of analogous users in related sectors. It is usual to run a workshop with extreme and analogous users, to develop product concepts.	□ Difficulties in identifying lead users. □ Workshop is time-consuming and lead users may need to be motivated to give their time. □ Workshop is outside the normal working environment (although it can be combined with a visit to a lead user environment).
	□ Workshop brings together very different users and stimulates creative discussions. □ Can be combined with experimentation, to test the concepts identified in the workshop.	
6 Experimentation	□ Customers are presented with early prototypes of products (or services) and base their suggestions on these. □ Seeing and using a tangible product often enables customers and users to articulate their views better.	□ May require expensive virtual prototyping equipment. □ Superficially, services cannot easily be prototyped. However, leaders such as HSBC Bank prototype their services and collect reactions.
	□ Observing in a realistic scenario how customers react to tangible product ideas. □ Can be an extension of the lead user approach.	
7 Conjoint analysis	□ Identifies the trade-offs customers make in deciding between different products. □ Customers are presented with descriptions of products or service products and must choose their preferences.	□ If the wrong attributes are fed into the analysis, then the prioritisation will not be useful (it will encourage a continuous focus on incremental products) □ The somewhat artificial nature of the decisions can limit the accuracy of the findings. □ Relatively complex method that usually needs expert support.
	□ Identification of the product attributes that customers perceive as their key priorities □ Development of pricing models.	

Source: Complied by the authors.

short excerpt from a piece of music. In the UK, copyright for musical and artistic works lasts for 70 years. For published editions the term is 25 years.

Copyright is created automatically when the work is complete and requires no registration or payment. Generally the copyright for anything done by an employee in the course of his or her job would belong to the company, but there may be ambiguity about work done by contractors or freelance workers. Always clarify who owns the IPR in innovation projects; it can be embarrassing to find that a subcontractor owns the copyright to the manual produced for you, the artwork for your sales campaign, or the computer program that runs your new product.

One defence against an allegation of copyright infringement is that the work was separately created and appears the same merely because there was little choice in how the function could be performed. This may be plausible in software and so some programmers deliberately include sections of code that have no function as a way of proving if their program has been copied.

Design Right

Design means the appearance of all or part of a product, especially its shape, colour, texture or ornamentation (or a combination of them). Design protection can prevent another company copying the product directly, or marketing an apparently identical one, even if they can show that they designed it themselves. It is a useful way to protect an original piece of design, and the brand recognition that may go with it, such as the Coca Cola bottle shape. In services, aspects of the servicescape can be used to strengthen the brand, such as McDonalds double arches.

In many countries an *unregistered design right* exists that protects against copying but not against separate creation. More powerful is the *registered design right*, which gives a monopoly right to the design for up to 25 years, and can apply internationally. The design has to be registered through a Patent Office and it is granted only to designs that are novel and would be viewed as 'fresh' by an 'informed user'. Expert advice is essential. There is a one-year period of grace after public disclosure so it is possible to test market a design before registering it.

Trademarks

A trademark is defined as 'any sign capable of being represented graphically, which is capable of distinguishing goods or services of one undertaking from those of other undertakings'.[50] It can be a name, a symbol, a special font or script, a colour, or – more often – a combination of them. There are many familiar examples. A registered trademark can be obtained through the Patent office and typically cost up to €100. Protection is granted separately for different categories of product so the same mark may be used by quite different companies provided their activities do not overlap. Separate protection is needed in each country but there are arrangements to extend cover to many territories for quite modest fees. Failure to trademark in different countries can cause problems. For example, the international clothing company La Chemise Lacosta has a right facing crocodile logo. Crocodile International, a Singapore-based clothing manufacturer, registered its own left-facing crocodile motive across Asia in the 1960s. Now with Lacosta trying to dominate the high-end Asian market, the two companies have become locked in a number of legal actions.[51]

A trademark may not be purely descriptive (like 'bread' or 'washing powder'), or too similar to another one already in use for the same category of product. So it is important to check the availability of the proposed name of a new product or service if you may want to trademark it later.

There are two reasons for seeking protection for a trademark in a particular country. One is to be able to prevent other companies using it and so 'passing off' their products as yours. The other is to establish your own right to use it; because, unlike other types of intellectual property, trademarks are, by and large, granted to the first applicant in each country (the USA and Canada are notable exceptions). So if you do not register early you may lose the chance to do so later.

Patents

Patents are the most powerful and influential way to establish ownership of an innovation because they protect the idea itself. A patent grants the legal right to exclusive use of an invention in exchange for a fee and a full disclosure of it, including a description of how it can be embodied. Protection typically lasts for about 20 years but often with maintenance fees to be paid at intervals, which usually get steeper as time goes on.

Patents are granted separately in each country where protection is required, so such protection can be expensive. In Europe it costs approximately €300 in official fees to get a patent granted but the renewal fees for the full lifetime may be €7,500 (per country). The equivalent fees in Japan are €4,500 and €22,000. The cost of a Patent Agent to draft the legal document and shepherd it through the process may also be considerable in each case.

What Can be Patented?

To be patentable, an idea must pass four tests. It must be *novel*; it must involve an *inventive step*; it must have a *practical application*; and it must not be in an *excluded category* (which includes, among other things scientific theories, mathematical methods, and methods of doing business). The most demanding test from the management point of view is the first, which requires that the invention has never been publicly revealed before the filing date of the patent. Patenting services is consequently difficult. The patent office will search existing patents but this does not guarantee that the idea has not been published in some other way. Of course it also means that the inventor must keep the invention secret until a patent is filed.

Infringement of Patents

If a company manufactures or offers for sale a product incorporating a patented idea they are said to infringe the patent. The owner, or licensee, of the patent can force them to stop and may be able to extract substantial damages. This is the primary power that a patent gives. However, infringement is a quite separate matter from patentability. For example, suppose long ago a company invented the first chair with a back and were granted a patent on it. This would give them the exlusive right to make and sell chairs. However, another company already had a patent on a stool (an essential constituent of a chair) then the first company would infringe this if they actually sell any of their chairs. They will need to seek a licence from on the stool patent before they can market their product.

A company that may infringe a patent has a number of options. One is to seek a licence to use it. Another is to challenge the validity of the patent, particularly if it can find a prior disclosure of the idea. The third, which is often possible, is to work round the patent by finding a way to perform the same function but outside the legal scope of the patent. The full disclosure required in the patent document often helps competitors 'design-around' the patent and copies proliferate.[52] A survey of 600 European companies showed that 60 per cent had suffered from copies of their products but only 20 per cent went to trial.[53]

The Business Use of Patents

Patents have four main uses in a company. The first, as noted above, is to enforce a monopoly by taking legal action to prevent others using the idea. The second is to licence the patent to others in return for a fee, or royalties, or both. This is often a better idea than going to court. The third is as a bargaining counter in relations between companies: large companies often agree to swap rights to each other's patent portfolio, each one using its own IPR to gain access to that of the other. Finally, small companies use their patents as objective proof of their technical depth and inventiveness so as to enhance their value on sale or flotation.

The key points for managers are:

1 When launching a product with new features check carefully whether some could be patented. This must be done, and a patent filed, before the product is shown to any third party (unless covered by a confidentiality agreement).
2 Check new product features to make sure they do not infringe other patents. This requires a professional search of patent databases.
3 Leave enough time to act on the results of these investigations before the product launch.
4 Encourage staff to patent ideas that may be valuable, but choose the countries to file in with care because of the considerable cost.
5 When licensing a patent or when starting a joint venture that may lead to patents, establish who is responsible for: filing costs and maintenance fees; for choosing countries to file in; for detecting and taking action following

infringements; and for defence of the patent if attacked. And establish what the rights of all parties are if the patent is successfully challenged or worked round.

Limitations of Patents

One of the drawbacks of the patent system is that it is less useful for small and medium-sized companies. A survey with results from European SMEs found that patents are used less than they might be, although many respondent companies had suffered financially when copies of their products and services were made, often by larger companies.[54] The perceived limitations were that patent protection took a lot of effort to acquire and gave, in practice, only limited protection, as legal action was both expensive and seldom successful. As patent protection has its limitations, both SMEs and larger companies often adopt other strategies to protect their knowledge. As discussed in the sections on the scope of innovation, the matching of product innovation with process innovation is often a good way to protect knowledge because innovative process technology 'can block or stymie would-be imitator's push into the market'.[55] It is also normally hard to apply patent protection to services and often the best approach is to concentrate on developing a unique augmentation. Some companies operate in markets where patents offer little protection and need to take other measures (see Box case on Micro, and also Sidler, the main case study in Chapter 9).

Box case 5.4   Micro Scooters – success, even when patents don't help[56]

In many cities and towns there is ample evidence of a worldwide revival of the scooter: two years ago it was a smash hit and continues to be popular today. What used to be considered as simply a child's toy has become a high-tech product, aimed at a range of age groups. The story behind this phenomenally successful product is an interesting one, which shows the need for innovative marketing, fast product development and the limitations of international patent protection. Surprisingly, the product idea itself almost failed to get to market.

Wim Obouter is the Swiss inventor of the original Micro City-Scooter. He studied international marketing in the USA and had worked in both financial services and the manufacturing sector in Switzerland. However, it was his love of sports – windsurfing and cycling – that helped him to identify a niche in the transport market. Over ten years ago Wim recognized that when he wanted to go out for a drink or a meal in the evening, it was often too far to walk but not far enough to warrant getting his bicycle out of the cellar, or to drive. Later he was to coin the phrase *micro-distances* for these sorts of journeys. As he often travelled micro-distances, he set about designing a solution to the problem. He considered a skateboard but decided on a scooter, as it would be easier to ride. So he hand-made himself a simple scooter that turned out to be 2–3 times faster than walking and which could be folded together, so that it would be easy to take into a bar. This prototype worked well and turned heads in Zürich. 'When I was on it, people always used to stop and stare at me. So much so that I started to think that it wasn't very 'cool' to be seen riding a scooter! So I stopped riding it during daylight hours'. Soon the prototype fell into disuse and the whole idea might have died, had not Wim still believed that there was a need for such a product.

Over the next few years the idea did not die entirely and Wim even wrote a marketing plan. In this he described a market need for not only an updated children's toy but also for a lifestyle product, which addressed the micro-distance issue. However, friends and colleagues were completely sceptical and told him that he had a respectable job in a Swiss bank so why on earth was he playing around with ideas for children's toys? So the prototype was literally shelved – it was left unused in Wim's garage.

That was until the summer of 1996 when, by chance, the prototype was spotted by neighbours' children, who asked if they could try it out. They were hooked immediately. From then on, all through the summer, up to 20 kids per day took turns to use the scooter – 'they just kept coming to borrow it and my wife kept saying there really is something in this idea'. Finally Wim had proof that the city-scooter had great potential for the kids market, although he still thought convinced that the potential was far greater. The success with the local neighbourhood finally convinced him and his wife to take the idea further. At the time, the launch of the Smart car with its advertising slogans of 'Reduce to Max' and 'The Future of Mobility' inspired Wim to make a video of his prototype and approach the car manufacturer. The Smart organization was impressed and considered integrating a scooter within the boot of the car as an ideal combination – a city car with the city-scooter for the last lap of the journey. Later, however, this decision was reversed at the time that the Smart project – a cooperation between Swatch and Daimler – experienced problems. Therefore, Wim was forced to look for an alternative route to market.

When Smart's backing fell through, Wim turned to Far East manufacturers looking for a source of funding. He found a partner company with enough faith in the project to fund the tooling and other set-up costs and who helped find a Japanese retail partner willing to try the product – with an opening order of 20,000 scooters. These sold immediately and the market grew quickly to sales of 75,000 units per week – almost an instant success.

City Bug UK Ltd handled the UK marketing. One of the partners, Seth Bishop, says they quickly realized that 'the product was great but it would attract competitors quickly. And without many international patents it would need a strong brand to maintain a market leadership position'. This was difficult because City Bug did not have the 'marketing spend' of a big company. Therefore, they adopted what some marketing professionals now refer to as 'stealth marketing' – finding novel ways to reach their target segments, without resorting to conventional advertising. The marketing plan concentrated on establishing the profile of Micro as a premium product. 'We wanted it to achieve cult status quickly, to make it stand apart from the copies'. Therefore, the marketing team concentrated on getting fashion journalists interested so that they would write articles in magazines such as *The Face*, and in selecting distribution channels such as design shops as opposed to retail chains. From the start the Micro product was promoted as a top design.

The Micro product is manufactured in China and Wim knew that by the time production of the Micro had ramped up, word would have spread and a host of Asian copies would be inevitable. However, he knew that the high labour content of his product would make it uneconomical to produce in Switzerland. He also saw a need to increase production volumes fast and his experience in the manufacturing sector told him that the length of time required to gain approval and build new facilities in Switzerland would be a disadvantage. The downside of Asian manufacturing was the speed and frequency with which copies emerged and, as he later discovered, the impossibility of using patents as a protection mechanism.

With hindsight, Wim sees two issues with patents: the time required before cover is achieved and the investment needed to enforce them. Typically it takes up to two years to be granted a patent. During this time a host of copies will be on the market, many from countries where patent rights are difficult, or even impossible to enforce. 'The difference between innovation in my markets and, for example, the pharmaceutical sector is time-scales. Product life cycles are typically six months for me and so the market moves much faster that the bureaucracy of patents. And so I need to compete through constant product innovation, not through law suits'.

With over 15 million units of the Micro brand sold since 1999, the product is an outstanding success. For the future Wim intends to innovate in both the product design (for example, sophisticated suspension mechanisms and ABS brakes are planned) and the brand. Finally the product has achieved the 'cool' image and broad market appeal that Wim intended.

Summary

This chapter has covered the second element of the Pentathlon – managing ideas. It has explained how often creativity is misunderstood as being a question of chance and not something where managers can have a major influence. This was shown to be a misunderstanding and managers need to look for effective ways to stimulate constant creativity through the exchange of information and knowledge. One of the key areas of knowledge is capturing the elusive voice of the customer. Here, traditional market research has serious limitations and, therefore, companies need to understand and adopt appropriate enhanced approaches. Overall, this chapter explained:

❑ The nature of individual and team creativity with ideas on how to stimulate creativity levels.

❑ Some of the most useful techniques to invigorate the process of generating ideas for new products and new services.

- The main types of knowledge and how they can be best utilized and, as necessary, protected.
- The most appropriate ways to conduct market research into customers' and users' needs, so that radical innovations can be developed.
- If the strategic goals of the organization focus on achieving product and technology breakthroughs, then creative links need to be made between the strategy and the generation of ideas. This is the subject of the main case study for this chapter, which looks at Texas Instruments.

Management Recommendations

- Foster an understanding of the different types of creativity in your organization and use this to stimulate a constant flow of ideas.
- Take active steps to establish and constantly maintain a 'culture of innovation'.
- Promote the exchange of knowledge within and between innovation project teams. Recognize and protect knowledge that is vital to the organization.
- Employ an appropriate combination of market research and creativity techniques to identify your customers hidden needs.
- Identify suitable ways to protect innovative ideas from competitors.

Recommended Reading

(1) Squires, S. and Byrne, B. (eds), *Creating Breakthrough Ideas: The Collaboration of Anthropologists and Designers in the Product Development Industry*. Bergin and Garvey: Westport Connecticut, USA, 2002, ISBN 0-89789-682-3. Interesting perspectives on how product design studies can be improved through ethnographic methods.

(2) Couger, J.D., *Creative Problem Solving and Opportunity Finding*. Boyd and Fraser, 1995, ISBN 0–87709–752–6. Comprehensive coverage of many creativity techniques and their applications. Unfortunately, gives little information on empirical research into creativity.

Main Case Study   Texas Instruments – defining innovation[57]

Before reading this case, consider the following generic innovation management issues:

- How does the chosen innovation strategy impact the management of ideas?
- If end users do not understand the technology, how can they generate useful inputs for product designers?
- How can managers match market trends to technological advances?
- How can customers be encouraged to give ideas that are not simply based on improving current functionality?

Texas Instruments Incorporated (TI) is based in Dallas. It is a world-leader in semiconductors, producing a wide range digital signal processing (DSP) and analogue devices and has over 34,000 employees worldwide. Revenues of $8.4B revenues were earned in 2002, of which a massive $1.6B (19 per cent) was invested in R&D – a clear demonstration of TI's commitment to technology and new products. Its products provide the processing capability for a multitude of consumer devices such as mobile telephones, digital stereo, car navigation systems, interactive toys, and digital cameras. Developing technology that will satisfy the demands of manufacturers such as Nokia and NEC, technology experts themselves, constantly tests TI's ability to anticipate requirements. However, the company has a tradition of going beyond existing customer needs.

For example, TI is famous for developing the first integrated circuit (chip) in 1958. Back then inventor Jack Kilby knowingly broke 'the customer is always right' rule. He was specifically asked by a customer to develop some discrete circuits but he thought of how, by packing these onto a single piece of silicon, a more efficient overall device could be manufactured. As a result of his foresight, the applications of electronics have multiplied and, today, millions of chips are produced every day. A brilliant idea, for which Kilby won the 2000 Nobel Prize for physics, and the sort of feat that is difficult to repeat. Today, just as in 1958, it is important to exceed customer needs. But how can radical ideas be generated?

With the increased complexity of electronics, TI has recognized that technical intuition alone is seldom sufficient. Trying to extrapolate customer needs in the isolation of the laboratory was found to be too risky. 'For a while, we had a bunch of engineers who used to figure out what the customer wanted and throw it over the wall to the sales guys, who would figure out how to sell it . . . but not now', says Bob McKune with TI's Wireless Marketing team. Over the past ten years, TI has developed a variety of approaches to support the process of anticipating customers' needs and predicting technology trajectories. These are based around a new function and its interface to people in the business units, both in marketing and technology management.

Strategic Marketing

One of TI's most effective means for stimulating innovative ideas has been the Strategic Marketing function, which is staffed by technical, business and market experts. They collect and develop ideas for new markets and evaluate potential projects very much in the way venture capitalists work. The group was founded in 1998 and has been responsible for developing some major new businesses, such as the OMAP – family of applications processors for mobile telephones. Ideas are honed by comparing data from the market, technology and financial scenarios. Every idea has to undergo top-management scrutiny and, if approved, seed funding is available, resources are quickly identified and high-level priorities are set. To accelerate new business development attention is focused on the 'top-three priorities'. And to speed progress even further, the strategic marketing people most closely associated with the development of an idea transfer to the 'start-up' business unit. 'Being in one of the strategic marketing teams is about as close as you can get to external start-up mentality . . . inside of a big company', is how one of the original members of the OMAP team described it.

One of the ways Strategic Marketing and the business units go further than many of TI's competitors is in studying end-users and not just direct customers. It is recognized that end-users determine what will be needed in the future and, although these end-users understand little if any of the technology going into a mobile phone, for example, identifying trends in requirements is vital. Therefore, Strategic Marketing closely follows markets and conducts significant consumer research. Doug Rasor, VP of Strategic Marketing, says that understanding end-user trends helped TI recognize very early how 'the combination of convenience and increased functionality would transform gadgets from "luxury" or "techie" items to "must-haves" for today's busy consumer'. Similarly, tracking the consumer gave an early prediction of the need for every mobile phone to support high-quality photographic capability. Such insights into the world of the consumer have had a major impact on how TI products are designed, often pushing R&D to deliver what could be called 'over the horizon performance'.

Marketing and Lead Customers

Just as Strategic Marketing focus on new markets, marketing in the business units is tasked with developing ideas for radical new products. McKune says, 'TI has shifted to become not only technology-oriented but also customer- and end-user oriented'. In the process, new approaches have been adopted to help customers articulate the future and a strong focus on end-users comes from close cooperation with Strategic Marketing. Lead-user technique has also been used extensively and the view of McKune is that choosing the right people for lead-user groups is the critical part of the process. 'Literally, you have to look years ahead and a lot of our customers can only look out about 12 months. Others can only look out six months to the next introduction'. Therefore, 'industry thoroughbreds', as McKune calls them, are carefully chosen and experts are also brought in from related sectors. This stimulates broader discussions around technology and emerging customer issues, which in turn identifies real opportunities. Leading these discussions is a role shared by McKune and the Chief Technologist.

Chief Technologist

The Chief Technologist for the OMAP platform, Michael Yonker, works in an office directly opposite to McKune's. Their respective doors are always open and they constantly trade jokes, accusing each other of either an inability to properly interpret the market, the technology, or both. Behind the jest, however, both Yonker and McKune are very serious about their goal of matching future technology to hidden needs. Yonker describes his role as 'the technical guy, who also understands the business side and who has a prominent role with our customers. In a sense I have to bridge the gap, acting as an evangelist to both R&D [convincing them about the importance of interpreting and leading the market] and marketing [convincing them of the potential of new technology]'.

'A lot of technology managers are pure R, or pure D but I put a premium on internal and external communication', says Yonker. Product technology roadmaps are used extensively as an internal planning and communication tool. By using roadmaps to show the links between the market and technology, Yonker aims to avoid 'technology being developed that is not effectively applied. That's what we call 'nerd products' – nobody wants to buy them and we don't want to develop them'. This in turn has led to the 'customer is always right' rule being broken regularly. Usually customers have a tendency to demand ever more functionality. However, McKune and Yonker have found that appropriate communication can identify product simplification opportunities. Removing product features can be a tough negotiation with customers but when all five key criteria – cost; size, weight and volume; power consumption; performance; and time-to-market – are discussed in unison, as opposed to features alone, TI have found that interesting alternatives emerge more easily than might be expected. 'Through introducing this broader view and discussing all five criteria with customers, the whole technical thing has taken on a different light', says Yonker.

Innovation: Define not Refine

In common with their competitors, each year TI is introducing new chips that are half the size, one-quarter of the price of previous ones, and have half the power requirement (and therefore require fewer battery changes). In terms of performance, however, the work of Strategic Marketing, lead-user discussions and end-user studies are providing TI with ideas for exceeding expectations. For example, the OMAP – team is now working on a 'super-chip', which will offer manufacturers the capability of designing all of the features they want to include in a mobile telephone from voice-only to multimedia. This is one product but the result of what Yonker and McKune see as the clear innovation philosophy of their business unit; 'our goal is to *define* new customer needs, not just *refine* existing ones'.

6 Prioritization: Selecting and Managing the Portfolio

'As living and moving beings we are forced to act . . . [even when] our existing knowledge does not provide a sufficient basis for a calculated mathematical expectation.'

(John Maynard Keynes)

Introduction

Any organization is likely to have a number of innovation projects running at any one time. Allocating resources between them to achieve optimum returns is always difficult, the more so when some are innovation projects with high levels of uncertainty. Managers face two challenges: the first is deciding which projects are intrinsically worth doing in themselves (the *Valuation problem*); the second is choosing a group, or *portfolio* of them that best meets the overall needs of the organization (the *Balance problem*). Choosing and managing a portfolio is a dynamic activity because innovation projects change and develop as they proceed and as a result some may be pushed forward, some delayed and some stopped altogether. The very ability of the organization to absorb change may itself be a constraint. Service companies often do not have an R&D department dedicated to innovation projects, so may find it particularly difficult to manage fluctuating demands without disrupting the core business. Setting and managing the priorities among innovation projects is the third element of the Innovation Pentathlon.

A key difficulty in selecting the right innovation projects is that many of the facts on which the decision is based may be unknown, or at least uncertain, at the outset. A very great deal of preparatory work may be needed to resolve the uncertainties, and indeed some important risks may remain until very near the end of projects. So project selection is often not a single decision made at the start of the project, but rather a series of exploratory steps followed by a review, a further choice about whether to go on, another review and so on. In innovation, project selection is not usually a 'one-off' event.

Management action plays a vital and creative role in steering innovation projects to success. As a project progresses and the uncertainties unravel, managers will face not only unanticipated obstacles but also unexpected opportunities. There will be upsides to exploit as well as downsides to manage. The first step in successful portfolio management is to accept the inevitable uncertainty, embrace it and turn it to good account. This requires a flexible and open attitude backed up with some strong management disciplines, and a few simple tools. This chapter covers:

▸ The aims and processes of portfolio management.
▸ Financial valuation of innovation projects.
▸ Ways to value projects when the numbers are unreliable.
▸ Accounting for uncertainty in project valuation.
▸ Balancing the portfolio, for example with respect to time and risk.
▸ Aligning the portfolio with overall company strategy.
▸ Management processes.

Management, and especially financial management, is notorious for its use of obscure acronyms. Portfolio management has more than its fair share of these and we give a glossary in Table 6.6 at the end of the chapter.

The Principles of Portfolio Management

The Need for a Process

Portfolio management is not just about making the right decisions about which projects to start. It is also about reviewing those decisions regularly, changing them when necessary and helping staff and colleagues to understand and accept the decisions. Stopping projects is particularly difficult because people may have invested much energy, enthusiasm and even their personal credibility in them. So it is very helpful to have a clear and objective process for making these difficult selection decisions. The process should:

▸ Clarify the logic involved.
▸ Expose the key issues for debate.
▸ Help to make sure that nothing relevant is overlooked.
▸ Encourage clarity and, where appropriate, quantification.
▸ Leave scope for exercise of management judgement.
▸ Create a record of the lines of reasoning so that the arguments can be explained to others and built on in later reviews.

An inadequate portfolio management process leads to slow decisions, a tendency to choose low-impact 'me-too' projects and a failure to stop projects that have lost their way. The typical results of these are summarized in Table 6.1.

Portfolio management is a complex and multifacetted task. Management judgement is required but appropriate tools also help structure the decision process. In selecting the tools to use it is vital to remember that their role is to help managers come to judgements that are not only good but can be justified and communicated.

Box case 6.1   The World Bank – the vision for selecting programmes[1]

Most people expect innovation to be particularly difficult in large, bureaucratic organizations. The World Bank, with its headquarters in Washington D.C., might be seen as such an organization and not a hub of innovation.

Table 6.1   Portfolio management issues and their impact

Management issue	Resulting problems
Slow decision-making	▢ Projects that start late will be late to complete ▢ Late to market means lost profit ▢ Rush to make up for lost time causes excess cost and temptation to cut corners ▢ Frustrated staff
Unadventurous, low-impact projects	▢ Poor profitability ▢ Lost opportunities to gain market share ▢ Poor morale
Too many projects	▢ Resources stretched so that some or all projects run late ▢ Lack of management attention ▢ Bottlenecks
Poor projects never killed	▢ Lack of profitability ▢ Lack of resources for good projects

However, appearances can be deceptive as during the last four years the World Bank has built a reputation for being creative and innovative. How?

Much of the credit must go to the insights provided by the team at the corporate strategy unit that has radically changed the way projects are chosen for World Bank funding. The aim of the Bank is to alleviate poverty and traditionally only large, relatively conservative programmes were funded. Due to the large amounts of money involved, everybody involved wanted to make the best use of the cash available and avoid funding anything with a high risk. The decision process was normally complicated, conducted at the highest levels in the organization, and was slow.

Now the Bank has completely changed the way it selects the best proposals from the myriad it receives. The vision was to base the selection process on the way venture capitalists make funding decisions in stages and spread their risks over a range of projects rather than 'just going for the big one'. Initial funding is now available for the first stages of a programme and subsequent financing is dependent on defined results being achieved in a set timeframe. Now the World Bank is experimenting more, and running pilot programmes to test radical ideas. The range of projects being considered and the selection process have also become highly transparent. Decisions are made by a panel of judges drawn from industry and a variety of non-profit organizations, such as Oxfam and World Vision and centres on a 'Development Marketplace'. This is a day in which proposals are presented and selected in the style of an industrial show, with booths set up for each proposal, presentations and the like. Not only does this make the selection process transparent to all employees and applicants but the resulting exchange of ideas spurs everyone involved towards the production of better proposals, year for year.

Elements of a Good Portfolio

The overall purpose of portfolio management is to ensure that the company's collection of innovation projects makes the best use of its resources and will deliver the best value to the company over time. This is very important because the portfolio represents nothing less than the total innovation efforts of the company and therefore its long-term survival. The key issues that must be considered are:[2]

☐   *Valuation criteria*:

(1)   Each individual project should represent good value to the organization.

(2)   The collection of projects must make efficient use of the resources available. Where projects compete for scarce resources it must be clear how the allocation between them is to be made.

☐   *Portfolio balance criteria*:

(3)   The portfolio may need to be balanced in other respects; for example any high-risk projects will have to be balanced by an adequate number of low-risk ones to ensure that the company's overall exposure to risk is acceptable. The company may also want to maintain a balance of projects over time and possibly across the areas of the business.

(4)   The innovation portfolio must fit and respond to the company's strategic needs. Perfectly good projects may have to be delayed or aborted in favour of others in more strategically important parts of the business.

We will examine each of these requirements in more detail later in this chapter.

Types of project

In discussing valuation methods it is convenient to distinguish three generic types of project. The simplest is a *single-stage* project that is expected to run through from start to finish without interruption, as shown in Figure 6.1a. Small or low-risk projects are generally treated in this way. The second is a *multi-stage* project, which is conducted in phases with a progress review after each one when a decision is made whether or not to continue. This is obviously appropriate for high-risk projects and especially those where preliminary investigations are needed to establish what can (or should) be done. Projects with

Figure 6.1 Single stage, multi-stage and network projects

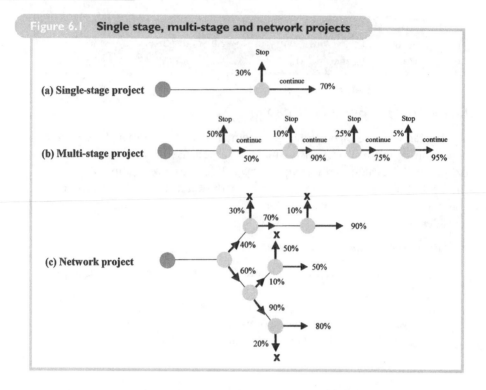

high levels of technical novelty, such as drug development, would be examples. It may be possible to give figures for the probability of cancellation at each phase, as shown schematically in Figure 6.1b, and these figures can be useful in valuing the project. The third type of project is one where the reviews after each phase may lead to alternative courses of action, rather than a simple go or stop decision so that the project plan could branch into a network of possibilities (Figure 6.1c). Such *network* projects require more sophisticated valuation methods.

Valuing Individual Projects: Financial Methods

The most obvious way of valuing a project is by financial analysis. Indeed this is the most common, and often the only, method used.[3] We shall argue later that it may be necessary to supplement it by other techniques, especially in the early stages of projects when the financial information is often unreliable. But appropriate financial assessment is obviously important at any stage and should, of course, dominate the argument as the project nears fruition. The analysis can be done with varying degrees of sophistication and somewhat different methods are appropriate for simple and for complex projects.

Single-Stage Projects

The most straightforward and the most commonly used method of valuing a potential project is simply to estimate the financial benefits accruing from it and subtract the costs to give a net value.

Project value = project benefits − project costs   (6.1)

Many levels of sophistication are possible in estimating the components of this simple equation, but before we discuss them further it is worth remembering that extra sophistication does not necessarily make for better decision-making. If the basic data is flawed or uncertain, elaborate computation is unlikely to make it any better. Indeed, it may obscure the logic or, worse still, it may lend a spurious authority to a fundamentally unsound deduction.

That said, some enhancements are certainly useful. The first is to take account of the time-related value of money. Income today is worth more than income next year because money in hand today could be invested to earn one year's worth of interest. For the same reason early expenditure is more costly than later. The first modification of Equation 6.1 is therefore to take account of this effect by using Discounted Cash Flow (DCF). In this approach every element of income or expenditure is discounted by a factor that takes account of when it occurs.[4] An income or cost in one year's time is multiplied by a discount factor $1/(1 + s)$, where s is the yearly cost of money: so if money costs 10 per cent a year, the discount is $1/(1.1)$, or 0.9. Income made in two years' time is multiplied by a discount factor of $1/(1.1)^2$, or 0.88, and so on.

Net Present Value

When discount factors are included for both income and costs the value of the project is called the Net Present Value, or NPV:

$$NPV = C_1 + C_2/(1 + s) + C_3/(1 + s)^2 + C_4/(1 + s)^3 +$$ (6.2)

Here C_1, C_2, C_3, etc. are the cash flows (costs or incomes) into the project in the first, second, third years and so on.

The discount rate, s, should be the average cost of capital to the organization and so should include the cost of equity and of debt in the proportions found in the balance sheet.[5] Some financial managers choose a higher discount rate on the income stream as a way of taking account of a high level of risk in the project. However, this practice is subject to three criticisms:

❏ The particular figure used tends to be a 'gut feel' that can seldom be justified.[6,7]
❏ The assumption is that uncertainty is always a negative factor, which is not necessarily the case. In practice there may be as much chance (maybe more) that the uncertainty will result in a better result than expected.
❏ The risk in a project is not merely an aspect of income. It is an entirely different thing, requiring specific management. Burying risk in a financial discount hides it from scrutiny and so undermines the whole management process.

Net present value is widely used[8] and is worth the comparatively small amount of effort involved in the calculation, especially if the timescales of the project are long or money costs are high.

Sensitivity Analysis

The next enhancement is to calculate how robust the value of the project is. The simplest and most useful approach is to re-run the financial calculations several times with different assumptions about the major component parts. This basic and valuable step is surprisingly often omitted, even in these days of easy spreadsheet analysis. Yet this information is very important and can be critical in deciding whether to go ahead if the project turns out to be very sensitive to some factor that cannot be relied on. It is also very useful in managing the project because it points out the critical elements that the project manager must control if the project is to be a success. We will discuss this further in Chapter 7 on implementation.

An alternative approach to estimating robustness is to calculate how quickly the project delivers its results. A convenient measure for this is the 'payback time', or Time to Break Even (TBE). The financial returns from most projects will follow a curve broadly like that shown in Figure 6.2, starting with a period of loss when expenditure is made but income has not yet begun, and moving eventually to the 'break even point' when the income balances the expenditure. Other things being equal, a project that aims to deliver financial results quickly is less risky than one that takes longer and so faces more of the inevitable uncertainties of the future. A more complete approach is to calculate the Internal Rate of

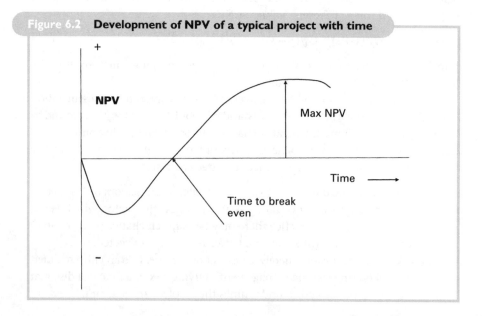

Figure 6.2 Development of NPV of a typical project with time

Return or IRR. This is the value of the discount factor, s, in equation 6.2 that would reduce the NPV of the project to zero.[9] It gives an idea of how secure is the return on the investment in the project. Clearly, the higher the IRR is, the more robust the project. Companies often reject projects that do not meet a threshold value for TBE or IRR.[10]

Including the Possibility of Cancellation

Innovative projects may face the risk that they will prove unsuccessful and be cancelled before coming to fruition. Then there are really two possible outcomes: a loss equal to the costs if the project is stopped; and a profit equal to the difference of income (I) and cost (C) if not. One can work out the expected outcome over a large number of such projects by adding the two possible outcomes multiplied by their probabilities. If the Probability of Success is p, the effect is to reduce the income by a factor p, while leaving the costs unchanged:

$$\text{Outcome} = p(I - C) + (1 - p)C = Ip - C \tag{6.3}$$

Notice that the effect on profit can be quite severe: a healthy 50 per cent profit margin is reduced to zero if p is 0.5.

A Warning about Probabilities

The objective assessment and management of risk is a relatively recent development in the history of human thought, let alone of business management.[11] The classical Greeks, who thought deeply about many aspects of philosophy and mathematics, had no concept of probability. The dice they used in games of chance were not even cubical, as ours are: they had square ends and rectangular sides so that they were inherently biased. Nobody seemed to notice because there was simply no framework within which to think about these things. They were regarded, literally, as 'in the lap of the Gods'.

The modern concept of probability as applied to games of chance and similar situations was eventually formulated in the mid-seventeenth century by Pascal and Fermat, who built on the earlier work of Galileo, Huyghens and others.[12,13] The fact that such illustrious names were involved should remind us that this is not an easy topic to think clearly about. Even today we are easily misled, as the number of people who believe in winning systems and 'runs of luck' at roulette makes clear.

In applying probability to innovation projects it is important to bear carefully in mind how probabilities can be measured and what they really imply. What do we really mean when we say 'I give this project a 30 per cent chance of success'? Thirty per cent of what? And what use can one legitimately make of that number? Let us start with the question of how to estimate the probability of an event.

Estimating Probabilities in Projects

In most games of chance the probability of an event can be worked out just from the logic of the situation: the chance of drawing a king from a well-shuffled pack of cards has to be 4/52 because there are four kings in a total of 52 cards. No measurement is required, only thought, because all the possible outcomes of the choice are known and can be counted. In the business world, of course, such logical simplicity is rare. Thought alone will not tell us the probability that the dimensions of a part made in a factory will fall in a particular range, or the proportion of the populace who need shoes of a particular size. They must be measured. Yet it is impossible to examine every person's foot or every part made in a factory; instead one must look at a finite number of cases and hope to deduce the underlying proportions of sizes from them. *Sampling Theory* is the study of how the characteristics of a population can be calculated from measurements of a restricted sample of cases. Three considerations are important here:

1   The samples must be representative of the population. There is no point in looking at a sample of Japanese people and hoping to deduce the foot sizes of Norwegians.
2   Sampling measures the state of things at a particular moment. One can estimate the facilities needed for people passing through an airport by counting the use made of them at various times spread over several days, but one would hesitate to use this estimate to predict the requirements in five years' time. Nor would a winter estimate help to predict the traffic the next summer.
3   The accuracy of the estimate depends on the number of samples taken. Roughly, because the details depend on the statistics of the underlying process, the relative uncertainty in the estimate from a sample is approximately the reciprocal of the square root of the number of samples.[14] This means that accurate estimation requires a surprisingly large number of samples: 100 are needed to give 10 per cent accuracy; 10,000 for 1 per cent. Opinion pollsters have to interview over 1,000 people to get a measure that is accurate to a few per cent.

We see from this that when we assign a probability to some event in a project, as we did in equation 6.3, we can at best obtain only a *very* rough estimate. How many even approximately equivalent projects are available as examples? And if there were enough, is the current project sufficiently similar to them for their outcomes to give valid pointers to its future? In practice we may have experience from the past but we seldom have many truly representative samples of the future.

The lesson for managers of innovation projects is simple: recognize that in practice you can have only very, very approximate estimates of probabilities in projects – probably much less accurate than you think. Therefore use them with great caution and beware of basing any decisions on detailed differences between them. Fortunately, accurate probabilities are often unnecessary. For example, if there is estimated to be only a 100-to-one chance that my project will fail to meet its target, I would probably go ahead without worrying whether the 'correct' figure should be 50-to-one or 200-to-one. However, faced with a decision between two projects estimated to have 50 per cent and 60 per cent probabilities of success, the best course is usually to regard the difference as too small to be relevant.

Using Probabilities in Valuing Projects

The usual way to value a project where the outcome is uncertain is to multiply the expected result by the probability that it will happen. This is what we did in equation 6.3. If there are several possible outcomes we multiply each by its estimated probability and add them up. The result is the average, or *expected value*.

It is very important to realise that the expected value is the average outcome in the long run. A tossed coin has a 50 per cent chance of showing heads; but toss it twice and there is no guarantee that one will get just one head and one tail, it may easily be all of one or all of the other. Twenty tosses will not necessarily produce 10 of each, but it's rather less likely to generate all heads. In 1,000 trials one can be fairly certain not to find only 1,000 heads. As the number of trials increases, the *proportion* of heads will get closer and closer to 50 per cent. (At least, it will if there are no systematic effects biasing the result. But if I use a machine to toss the coin and always start with the same side uppermost the flipping may be so reproducible that the result comes up heads (or tails) most of the time. If so, the results of the tosses are *correlated*.) To say that a project has a particular probability of success means that if the identical project were repeated in *a very large number of uncorrelated trials*, that proportion of them would be successful.

An individual project may have quite a wide range of possible results, with the expectation value somewhere in the middle, as we will discuss in more detail in the next section. But the total result of a larger number of projects will cluster more and more closely around the sum of their expected values as the number goes up, just as the coin tosses did in the previous example. With a sufficiently large portfolio the sum of the expected values will provide an accurate and reliable measure of what the portfolio is likely to deliver, even though the individual projects are relatively unpredictable. Unfortunately, though, the uncertainty reduces rather slowly as the size of the portfolio increases. Roughly (because the details depend on the statistics) it takes 10 projects to reduce the relative spread to 1/3 of what it was for one project, and 100 to reduce it to 1/10. That is assuming there is no correlation between the factors causing success or failure in the projects, a rather bold assumption if they are happening in the same organization. Any such correlation slows down the reduction of the spread.

Here we see the essential problems in applying probability measures and expectation values to projects.

▸ First, the results are valid only if the company has a great deal of experience of similar projects from which to calculate probabilities, and is running a large number of independent projects simultaneously.

▢   Second, and more important, the whole process concentrates on predicting the mean outcome of a large number of projects and draws attention away from the much wider range of outcomes that are inherent in each individual project. This is where the most important management challenges may lie.

Probabilities apply only in the long run. The outcome of any particular project will not be the mean but somewhere on a spectrum of possibilities. In managing innovation projects the purpose of risk assessment is not to make a more refined prediction but to understand the range of things that are plausibly likely to happen, and to see what actions may be taken to turn the uncertainties to best account.

In spite of all this we still have to make judgements in selecting between projects, and there seems no alternative to using probability figures to reflect the different levels of certainty we feel. Let the foregoing section at least serve as a warning that the figures will be highly inaccurate. If one project is to be selected over another on the basis of small differences in probability figures it pays to reflect on just how tenuous such figures are. Better perhaps to find another basis for the choice. In the words of Kenneth Arrow, Nobel Laureate in Economics[15] 'our knowledge of the way things work, in society or in nature, comes trailing clouds of vagueness. Vast ills have followed a belief in certainty'.

Box case 6.2   Zara – a revolution in fashion

The Spanish fashion retailer Zara is making a conspicuous success from overturning the established practices of the mass fashion business. Low margins at home and cheap labour overseas have driven European retailers increasingly to obtain supplies from the Far East, shipping them, in the main, by sea. Zara, which is the major part of the Inditex group, has reversed this trend. 90 per cent of its goods are made in its own factories in northern Spain and Portugal from where it ships them by truck or air to over 600 stores in 30 countries. The brand is very profitable –its return on sales is 15 per cent, five times the typical level in the sector. It is also growing strongly: from its foundation in 1975 it now has a turnover of €3b. It has been described as 'possibly the most innovative and devastating retailer in the world'.

   The key to Zara's success is the speed with which it can now get new designs to market. 'The vertical integration of our production system allows us to place a garment in any store around the world in two to three weeks, provided the fabric is in stock', says Maria J, Garcia, a spokeswoman for Zara. The norm in the sector is five to ten *months*. No sooner has a new look made the headlines than it is on the hangers in Zara – weeks or months ahead of anyone else, and at a premium price. Moreover the company's speed of response means it can follow the ups and downs of demand very closely. Twice-weekly deliveries mean that Zara shops are seldom short of popular lines and yet need to hold very little stock. So when demand turns down they simply switch immediately to the next thing.

   By contrast, the much longer lead times elsewhere in the sector mean that competitors have to place orders months in advance. Forecasting that far ahead is almost bound to be wrong in such a fast-changing market and the result is a huge cost in obsolete stock that must be discounted or scrapped.

Zara's business model ensures loyalty and premium prices by always offering its customers the most up-to-date designs. The cost of making the clothes in its highly-automated European factories is certainly higher than it would be to buy them from off-shore suppliers, but the savings in inventory costs and discounts more than compensate for this and give the company a unique positioning in its market. The Inditex group now claims to be one of the largest fashion retailers in the world.

Multi-Stage and Network Projects

In a multi-stage project managers can take action to deal with problems as they arise, if necessary abandoning the project if its prospects become unattractive. They can also recognize good fortune and capitalise on it. The scope for management action during the course of a project can radically alter its value and must be taken into account in the calculations. Failing to include this 'undervalues everything'.[16] The following simplified calculation shows how important it can be.

Consider a project, which we will call Project Alpha, which proceeds in five stages with decision points between. Each stage has a different cost and a different probability of being a success, in the sense that the results achieved are good enough for the project to continue. These are shown in Table 6.2. If the project comes to fruition the expected income, appropriately discounted, is €75m.

The total discounted cost of the project is €20m and the overall probability of success is 25 per cent ($0.5 \times 0.7 \times 0.9 \times 0.8$). If the project goes ahead with no intervention the expected revenue is 25 per cent of €75m, or €18.75m. With costs of €20m, the NPV is projected to be a loss of €1.25 Million and so the project looks thoroughly unattractive.

However, the picture changes dramatically if we take into account the option that management has to stop the project after each stage if the prospects for eventual success look poor. The cost of the first stage must be included in full

Table 6.2 Project alpha: a multi-stage project

Stage	Cash Flow (€ million)	Discount factors	DCF	Probability of success of the stage
1 Concept	−1.1	1.1	−1.0	50%
2 Prototype	−2.4	1.2	−2.0	70%
3 Design	−6.5	1.3	−5.0	90%
4 Pilot	−16.8	1.4	−12.0	80%
5 Commercialization	+135	1.8	+75	100%

but there is only a 50 per cent chance that the cost of the second will actually be incurred. The third-stage cost will occur only if both the first and second phases are successful, the probability of which is 0.5×0.7; the final stage costs will be incurred only if all three of the preceding stages are a success and the probability of that is $0.5 \times 0.7 \times 0.9$. The correct calculation for the likely costs is therefore

$$€m(1 + 0.5 \times 2 + (0.5 \times 0.7) \times 5 + (0.5 \times 0.7 \times 0.9) \times 12) = €7.5m \qquad (6.4)$$

Thus the project as a whole has a projected NPV of €11.25m. This straight-forward calculation emphasizes how misleading and oversimplistic financial projections can be. Good management decisions add value (arguably €12.5m in the above example). Neglecting the possibilities for choice and action during a project can lead to serious undervaluation and the likely rejection of potentially excellent opportunities.[17]

The estimated value for a multi-stage project derived in this way is known[18] as the Expected Commercial Value (ECV). The process of analysis itself is called[19] Decision Tree Analysis (DTA). Clearly it is more realistic than a simple DCF calculation for such projects, though one must always remember that the probability figures used are estimates, not facts.

The Expected Commercial Value calculation yields a single figure for the value of the project, taking into account the probabilities of the outcomes at the various stages. It is very convenient to have a single value but it is important to remember that it actually represents what would be the average outcome of a large number of such projects. If one undertook project Alpha it would actually have just one of five outcomes: a profit of €55m if it went to completion; or a loss of €1m, €3m, €8m or €20m if it stopped at an intermediate stage. This is illustrated in Figure 6.3. Adding up all of these with appropriate weightings for their probabilities gives us the ECV, which is the average result of the five possible scenarios. But no single project would itself produce the Expected Commercial Value.

Monte-Carlo Simulation

The range of possibilities for a project can be explored more completely using a Monte-Carlo simulation.[20] This used to be considered a rather esoteric technique but it can now be done very easily using a spreadsheet and a simple application package.[21] The idea is to run a large number of calculations using a random number generator to represent the probabilities. For example: the probability of success of the first phase of project Alpha is 50 per cent, so the simulation would first generate a random number between 0 and 100 and if this is more than the 50 the phase has failed so the simulation records a project loss of €1m and stops. Otherwise it stores the €1m cost and generates another random number to decide whether the next phase is successful. If this number exceeds 70 the second phase has failed so a project loss of €3m is recorded. Otherwise the accumulated cost would increase to €3m and the simulation would move to the next phase, and so on until completion. The simulation is then repeated. Each run

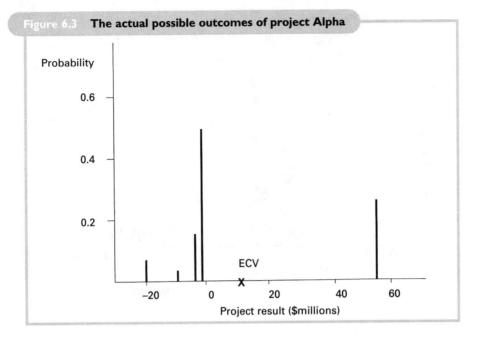

Figure 6.3   The actual possible outcomes of project Alpha

will probably have a different outcome, but repeating the process a very large number of times and accumulating the results generates a full view of all the possible outcomes and how relatively often they occur.

A simple calculation such as we have just done does not strictly require the Monte-Carlo treatment. But it is very useful if we wish to make the model more realistic, for example by replacing the single values for the costs of each phase by a range of possibilities. For example instead of putting €5m for the cost of phase three of project Alpha the model would allow, more realistically, a distribution of cost between perhaps €4m and €6.5m. This is the only practicable approach for a network project, with more complex decisions at each stage or for a multi-stage project with more complicated logic: for example where the outcomes of one stage affect the costs of later stages. Figure 6.4 shows the result of a Monte-Carlo simulation of a project similar to that in Table 6.2, where a range of costs and of income have been allowed in place of the single-point estimates.

The Monte-Carlo simulation is a helpful and surprisingly easy technique and gives much more information for managers than is provided by a single point valuation. It has the healthy effect of showing not just the average outcome, but the full range of possibilities that management may actually face on the partic-ular project. Of these outcomes the 'average' may itself actually be very unlikely. For example any action (such as organizing sales and production capacity) based on assuming that the average will happen in the project shown in Figure 6.4 will undoubtedly be disastrously wrong. Management must be aware of the full range of possibilities and must be prepared to take action both to limit the downsides, and to exploit the upsides.

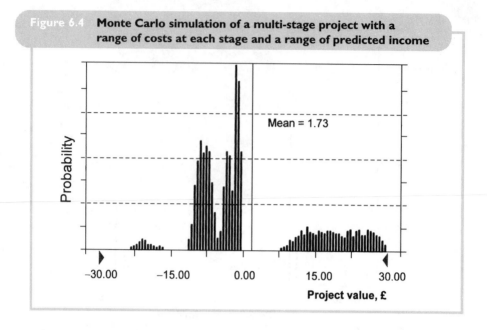

Figure 6.4 **Monte Carlo simulation of a multi-stage project with a range of costs at each stage and a range of predicted income**

The additional information provided by this more complete analysis is very helpful in managing a single project but it does make the task of choosing between several competing projects more difficult. Consultants Ron Dembo and Andrew Freeman[22] have suggested combining the upside and downside relative to a performance benchmark to produce an overall figure of merit. They apply weighting factors to the upside and downside to take account of the attitude of the organization to risk, but it is not clear how the weighting can be calculated. Certainly it will depend on the magnitudes involved: outcomes that may have a transforming impact (for good or ill) on the organization must be treated differently from those that are merely part of normal business. There is a clear need for further research to provide better tools for managing small portfolios of projects in a logically satisfactory way. The 'state of the art' is simply to use the mean expectation of projects as a measure of the potential overall value, while the range of outcomes can be used as a measure of the project's risk (see the section on risk–reward diagrams).

The Real Options Approach

Many authors[23] have noted that projects in the physical world have much in common with financial instruments called *Options*. An option on a stock is a contract that allows, but does not compel, the holder to buy that stock at a fixed price at some point in the future. If the price of the stock goes up, the holder of an option can make money by exercising the option and then selling the stock at the (higher) prevailing price. However if the stock goes down, the option holder does not have to make a purchase and loses only the cost of purchasing the option itself, which is usually much less than the price of the stock. Many innovation projects have the same logic that they give management an option, but not the obligation, to make an innovative change. The stock price corresponds to the value of the project while the option cost corresponds to the cost of the preliminary work (perhaps a concept study). This analogy suggests that the extensive theory developed for valuing these financial options might be applied to valuing the flexibility that managers have in managing projects. This is known as the *Real Options* approach to valuation.[24] Its application to innovation projects, and especially to new product introduction, is an area of active research at the moment.[25]

The fundamental insight for innovation management is that uncertainty provides options for management which, properly managed, can be a source of profit. In fact, provided there is the possibility of movement up as well as down, the option actually becomes more valuable as uncertainty increases. But there must be management intervention at the appropriate point to acquire this value.

The Expected Commercial Value and Decision Tree Analysis calculations described earlier are fundamentally option-based valuation methods. Other researchers have used the option philosophy more explicitly. For example Ian MacMillan and Rita McGrath[26] describe different kinds of projects as representing different kinds of options and give pointers to appropriate actions in each case.

The theory of option valuation for financial stocks was worked out fully in the 1970s by Fischer Black, Myron Scholls and Robert Merton (BSM). The full treatment involves an elegant partial differential equation, the Black–Scholls equation, which allows analysis of a large range of varied cases.[27] The analysis has been extremely influential in the financial community. Black and Scholls received the Nobel Prize for their work, though Merton died too soon to share it. It would be most helpful if the mathematical tools they developed for financial options could be carried over for use on real innovation projects, but attempts to do so have not so far been particularly convincing. Indeed, we consider that the idea is actually fundamentally flawed because the realities of the financial and project domains are seldom closely comparable.[28]

The first discrepancy is that in the BSM treatment the value of the stock follows a 'random walk' path so that the range of values it may assume spreads (upwards and downwards) as time goes on. This means that the value of the financial option also grows with time. However, this is not generally true of innovation projects, which generally have no realisable value until they are complete. And certainly the value of the options that they provide is more likely to decline with time because of competitive pressures, expiry of patents or market lifecycle. If it were not so managers would be observed diligently slowing down their innovation projects! The second discrepancy is that the BSM analysis relies on being able to identify a *hedge position*. In essence a hedge is a mirror image of the stock: an asset whose value tracks it in reverse, going down if the stock goes up, and up if it goes down. A suitable combination of a stock and a hedge will be impervious to movements of the market and so will be free of risk. Holding such a combination of assets is just like putting money in the bank and this allows the option to be valued.[29] In the world of innovation projects, however, much of the risk will be within the project itself (so-called *specific*, or *private*, risk). This cannot usually be hedged. How could one arrange to profit fully from a project that simply proved to be unworkable?[30]

Financial option methods are a powerful tool in their place, and can, indeed, be useful in evaluating 'real' projects where the risks are mostly in market conditions. But they have not yet proved useful for valuing the majority of innovation projects, where most of the risks are internal, and we cannot, yet, recommend their use.

Valuing Individual Projects: Scoring Methods

In an ideal world financial calculations would be all you need in selecting projects in a portfolio. Unfortunately the financial information available in the early stages of a project may well be incomplete or unreliable; or more likely, both. There are two reasons for this: the first is that the completion date may lie far in the future so there may be much genuine uncertainty about what can be achieved and what the customer's reaction will be. The second is that developing a detailed business plan with reliable financial information requires a lot of effort that companies feel is not justified when the project is still in the concept stage. So even if realistic financial projections could be made, the fact is that they seldom are.

This fact is well attested by research. In a wide-ranging study, Robert Cooper and co-workers[31] found that of all the possible ways of selecting projects, practicing managers had the least faith in financial projections. One company tracked the estimates that managers made of the NPVs of 30 projects at various points in their development and found that the estimates fluctuated greatly as time went on, suggesting that they were never very reliable. More damning still, the exclusive use of financial methods was most popular among less successful companies, though admittedly not by a large margin.

This distrust of financial projections has led companies to look for more broadly-based approaches to portfolio management in which financial forecasting is often included but as only one of a variety of indicators. The approach is analogous to the Balanced Scorecard approach to measuring company performance.[32] The argument is that where financial figures are considered unreliable one can improve the project selection process by including other criteria that are known to be well-correlated with the success in new products.[33,34] The simplest set of such generic factors for a new product might be:

- A unique, superior product well-differentiated from the competition in an attractive market.
- Leveraging the company's internal strengths.

In practice more specific sets may be used, that give the factors that have previously been found to be pointers to success in the particular industry or organization.

Table 6.3　Du Pont's project scoring matrix

		Score	
	15	10	5
1 Strategy alignment	Fits strategy	Supports	Neutral
2 Value	Significant differentiation	Moderate	Slight
3 Competitive advantage	Strong	Moderate	Slight
4 Market attractiveness	Highly profitable	Moderately profitable	Low profitability
5 Fit to existing supply chain	Fits current channels	Some change, not significant	Significant change
6 Time to break even	< 4 years	4–6 years	> 6 years
7 NPV	> $20 m	$4–$20 m	< $5 m

Cooper *et al.* found that more successful companies tend to use a variety of methods, in which scoring systems and strategic considerations augment, but do not entirely displace financial projections. An example of such a scoring process, used by Du Pont,[35] is shown in Table 6.3. Managers allocate a score against each of seven factors, using the statements in the boxes as guidance, and the results are added to give an overall figure. The score is a measure of the expected value of the project and can be used to compare and rank projects just as a financial measure might.

Scoring systems have a number of advantages compared with purely financial analyses; they:

▶ Bring a wider range of relevant considerations into the decision.
▶ Avoid dominance by uncertain financial data.
▶ Provide a useful focus for a broader discussion of each project.
▶ Allow use of learning from other projects and industries.

However, it will be clear by comparing Tables 6.3 and 6.4 that different companies, or even divisions of a company, may need somewhat different systems. One cannot expect to be able to use a standard approach in all circumstances.

Designing a Scoring System

Scoring is an aid to decision-making, not a substitute for it. A scoring system assembles the relevant information and helps structure the decision-making process so as to include all the important factors. But in making the final decision managers may also have to take account of human factors such as personalities, morale and even politics, as well as unique factors that are relevant only to the particular projects concerned. A scoring system must therefore be clear, simple and objective so that the results are open to discussion, and to amend-ment if additional factors must be considered. There is much to be said for constructing one's own scoring matrix, drawing on examples in the litera-ture[36] but taking account of the particular needs and goals of the organiza-tion.

An important part of constructing a project scoring system is to give adequate guidance on how to interpret the scales. It is arguable that Du Pont does not go far enough in this respect: people may have quite different opin-ions on what constitutes 'strong', 'moderate' or 'slight' competitive advantage, or whether the project 'supports' rather than 'fits' the strategy. This ambiguity can be reduced by using a more complete set of *anchoring statements* to help ensure that all participants use the scales in a comparable way. An example of such a set, used by Laserco (Box case 6.3) is shown in Table 6.4. There is a fine balance to be drawn in defining anchored scales, however. The anchoring statements must not be made too prescriptive or the process becomes mechan-ical, and fails to make full use of the experience and judgement of the partici-pants.

The following factors must also be considered in designing a project scoring system:

1 Avoid too many scoring factors. The aim is to bring out all the major rele-vant factors and to encourage discussion of them. You need enough separate points to give structure to the debate and to ensure nothing important is overlooked, but not so many that the exercise becomes mechanical. One must avoid creating a 'black box' where the information goes in and a result comes out without the participants understanding what happened in between. Six factors is probably about right, ten the maximum.

2 The scales for each factor must be appropriate for the organization. For example the NPV scale of $5–20m used by Du Pont would be far too demanding for a small software company, while the time-to-break-even scale might be unacceptably long.

3 Ideally the factors chosen should be of roughly equal importance to the orga-nization, if only because the team will probably spend roughly equal times on scoring each of them. Of course it is possible to allocate a weighting to each factor and then multiply the scores by these weightings before adding them up. But beware of spending more time discussing the weightings than the projects.

4 The scales used for the factors should as far as possible represent equivalent value to the organization. For example in Table 6.4 the scales for Increased Sales and Cost Reduction were chosen so that a particular score on either would yield approximately the same profit level, taking into account the typical gross margin on the products and the fixed/variable cost ratio of the particular business.

5 Require facts and numbers rather than 'gut-feel' responses wherever possi-ble.

Table 6.4 Laserco's project scoring matrix with anchored scales (see also Box case 6.3)

	Rating	0	4	7	10	Total
	Key items					
'HARD'	Increased sales (or lost sales saved) in first 3 years after	None	$2 million (e.g. 100 machines at 20k)	$4 million (e.g. 200 machines at 20k)	$6 million (e.g. 300 machines at 20k)	
	Cost reduction savings over 3 years	None	$0.5 million	$1 million	$1.5 million	
	Price premium/ gross margin in target market	Worse margins than in our main business	Margins similar to our main business. Little or no price premium	Improved margin. Price premium equivalent to $1m over 3 years	Significantly better margin. Price premium equivalent to $1.5m over 3 years	
	Channel cost or efficiency benefits	More difficult to sell or service than existing products. Significant training need	Selling and servicing much the same as existing products	Easier to sell or service than existing products. Efficiencies worth $1m over 3 years	Significant benefits to the channels. Efficiencies worth $1.5m over 3 years	
'SOFT'	Customer impact	Offers no unique customer benefits or features	Some unique benefits. Enhances corporate image	Clear unique benefits. Something to talk about. A 'door opener'	Eye-catching benefits. A talking point at shows. Gives an entry to competitor laser accounts	
	Technology offers a platform for growth	Dead end/ one of a kind	Can be used in other products or for business expansion	Potential for use through-out the business or for diversifica-tion	Opens up entirely new markets	
	Comments					Total %

Using a Scoring System

There are different opinions about whether the scoring should be conducted individually or as a group and whether one should aim to reach a consensus on each factor. The advantages of sharing information in an open way are obvious but it has often been noted that the discussions and conclusions can be driven to a false consensus by one dominant or senior member.[37] The 'Delphi' process[38] avoids this by having each participant put forward his or her opinion (score) anonymously. The group discusses them without seeking to identify who said what. A further vote ensues, and so on until consensus is reached. An alternative is for the team to discuss the evidence, vote separately (but not necessarily in secret) but not to seek to come to a shared view. The range of views as well as the average is recorded. After all the outlying views may be right and it is certainly relevant to know the level of unanimity in the team.

The value of using a scoring system may lie almost as much in the process as in the outcome. The scoring tool requires the team to collect information about all relevant aspects of the project and to review and discuss it in a structured and disciplined way. The understanding that this engenders is valuable in itself, and managers finish up with a better appreciation of all the programmes.

It is important not to overestimate the precision that scoring systems achieve. Helpful as they are, these are rough-and-ready methods designed to aid decision-making in highly uncertain situations. If one project should score a few points more than another, recognize that the precision of the tool is not enough to differentiate them. Find another consideration – the quality of the project manager or the morale of the team perhaps – to separate them.

Box case 6.3   Laserco – portfolio scoring

Simon Bradley, the Managing Director of Laserco a manufacturer of laser systems based in the USA and Germany, became concerned that the company was concentrating too much on small, low-impact projects, possibly to the exclusion of larger but riskier enterprises. The company had between ten and 15 projects in hand, some quite mature but others in the early formative stages. Bradley wanted to include the management of the newly-acquired German subsidiary in the review of the project portfolio to ensure there would be support from all parts of the company for any changes that had to be made. But it would not be easy, as it was clear that managers in the two parts of the company had different tolerances of risk. The two teams also tended to emphasize different aspects of the market, the Americans being more used to seeking high volume opportunities while the Germans tended to pursue applications with lower volume but higher margins. Doing a portfolio analysis together could help to align the views of the two management teams but there would have to be a clear structure to guide the discussion.

Bradley spent some time in preparing a structured risk-reward analysis. It had to be useable for early-stage projects, where detailed financial information was not available, as well as for more mature ones. Carefully anchored scales were clearly needed to help align the approaches of the two teams. The scales used are shown in Tables 6.4 and 6.5.

A trial run for the scoring system quickly revealed a problem. While all the participants were familiar with some of the projects, almost nobody really understood them all. The review could not go ahead without more shared information. Accordingly, three of the participants undertook to collect data on all the projects and circulate it for comment and review so that at the next meeting everyone would start from an agreed set of facts.

The teams met by video link to discuss the projects and assign scores for risk and reward to each one. Richard Blackburn, manager of the US factory commented: 'We started out trying to reach a consensus on each factor but we quickly decided that if there really was a range of opinion about something then we ought not to lose sight of that. So we discussed the facts of each project and then scored them individually. Then we discussed the scores. Sometimes people changed their minds when they understood where the others were coming from, but not always. At the end we recorded the range of each score as well as the mean. People felt much more comfortable not trying to force a consensus'.

Bradley comments: 'The most useful thing about the scoring system was that it forced us to think about all the aspects of the projects – not just the cost and technical feasibility, which had tended to dominate our thoughts before. For example we had a couple of research projects where the biggest risks were actually to do with the market acceptance. So we decided to put effort into the market research first and hold off on the technical work for the moment'.

Applying Valuation Methods

Choice of Method

We have discussed a number of different ways of evaluating innovation projects. Each has its strengths and weaknesses, and the choice of which method to use will depend to some extent on the circumstances. The characteristics of projects that most affect the evaluation method are the level of uncertainty and the amount of choice open to managers as the project progresses. For relatively low-risk projects an NPV calculation is appropriate for a single-phase project. However, if there are many decision points with perhaps many outcomes, ECV or a Monte-Carlo simulation are more useful. Greater uncertainty demands an Internal Rate of Return calculation at least, or a switch from financial methods to a scoring system. These choices are illustrated in Figure 6.5.

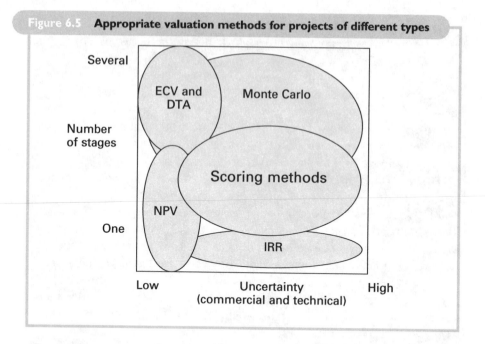

Figure 6.5 Appropriate valuation methods for projects of different types

Ranking Projects for Selection

Assigning a potential value to each project, by financial calculation or scoring, is the first major step in choosing a portfolio. The projects can now be ranked in terms of value or in terms of return on investment (by dividing by the expected cost). In the latter case only the future cost should be included, not money already spent, because the purpose is to make the best use of resources from now on. This has the effect of giving greater priority to projects that are nearing completion, with all the benefits still to come but little cost. This is as it should be.

Money is the crucial measure of course, but other factors may be important. Progress may be limited by the availability of specialist staff such as good project managers; or it may simply be a departmental budget that cannot easily be changed. Portfolio selection then amounts to getting the best return from this bottleneck resource. Return on investment may be replaced by some other ratio such as 'Return on R&D spend' or 'Return on marketing spend'. If a scoring system has been used, rather than financial assessment, the expenditure may already be factored into the score, giving an overall figure of merit directly.

Actually, of course, each project in the portfolio will use a variety of resources, human and material. Mathematical optimization techniques, based on linear programming, are available to calculate how to select the group of projects that will produce the best financial return subject to the constraints on several different resources. However such techniques seem rather seldom used by companies.[39] The main reason for this is probably that the selection process tends to be hidden from view by the mathematics. Managers do not have access to how the selection was actually done so they cannot readily review or justify the results; nor can they adjust or amend them to take account of factors not explicitly put into the calculations. How do you explain to a team that their project has been terminated because an optimization programme said so? For these reasons companies have sought simpler methods that help to clarify the logic without removing the scope for management judgement.

Managers will often start the project selection process by discarding all proposals that do not offer a certain return on investment, or that fail to achieve a required score. Projects with too long a payback period or too low an IRR may also be rejected if the organization requires quick returns or is particularly risk-averse.

The projects may now be ranked in terms of financial returns or score and, if no other considerations were involved, one would simply select from the top as many projects as funds or facilities allow. However, in practice the overall balance and strategic fit of the portfolio must also be considered and we consider these techniques in the next section.

Box case 6.4   Agilent – riding the market waves

Agilent Technologies provides leading technology for communications, life sciences and chemical analysis, automated test equipment and semiconductors. The Systems on the Chip Business Unit (SOC BU) has four sites with manufacturing and R&D: in Boeblingen Germany, Hachioji Japan and Loveland and Santa Rosa in the States. At these sites, over 650 employees develop and manufacture a range of highly sophisticated 'chip-testing solutions'. SOC Systems cost between $600,000 and $4 million. Agilent's customers include 'testhouses' (high volume integrated circuit testers) and many of the major electronics manufacturers worldwide.

Financial management is given much emphasis at Agilent and the SOC BU controller Werner Widmann has deliberately spread his team across the four sites. This ensures the close cooperation necessary with all aspects of the business, from hardware and software R&D, to marketing, to manufacturing and supply-chain management.

Key success factors in the chip-tester business are time-to-market (to have new testing products available to meet the waves of new technology – for example, digital home entertainment), meeting customers' demanding technical specifications, and achieving fast, low-cost chip testing. In addition to these, the business is highly volatile – within a year the quarterly sales figures can fluctuate by as much as 150 per cent. With such uncertainty, it is difficult to maintain R&D spending during downturns in the market. So part of Widmann's responsibility is to ensure that the SOC BU makes significant return on investments during the market upturns and does not suffer from cash flow problems during the downturns.

To deal with the challenges Widmann's team has adopted a much wider role than many controllers. 'For example, my team led a Portfolio

Management Taskforce to develop tools and processes to support top management in the SOC BU Business Board', he says. As gauging the technical risks of a project, or forecasting product sales are notoriously difficult and a single approach seldom works well, the team developed a set of tools to be used in parallel. These are based on portfolio assessment questions, market uncertainty analysis, and project scoring matrices. Communications throughout the worldwide management team have been significantly improved through the adoption of this standard set of portfolio management tools. And, to promote learning, managers' previous estimations of sales and risks are compared to actual figures and fed back to them. 'The new SOC BU Portfolio Framework has greatly helped in the way it presents the data and makes the trade-offs visible. The Management Team now has the information it requires to make fact-based decisions on which projects to back and which to kill, or postpone. We are now starting to get much better at understanding market attractiveness and risk' says Widmann.

Balancing the Portfolio

The various project evaluation methods described above help to give managers a better understanding of the potential value of individual projects. As we saw, no one method can be 100 per cent reliable, but each has its appropriate application (Figure 6.5).

A collection of projects that all represent potentially good value to the company and good use of its resources is the first aim of portfolio management. Once that has been achieved we must consider whether the portfolio represents a good balance of activities in other respects, in particular: strategic alignment; time and resources; and risk/reward profile.

Strategic Alignment

The first element of balance in a portfolio must be that of strategic alignment. For example if a company has a long-term aim to move from traditional chemistry into biotechnology, or to enter the Chinese market, a proportion of its innovation investment must be in projects directed towards that end. This priority may override most others; if so it must be injected into the portfolio management process by some 'top-down' approach. We say much more about developing an innovation strategy in Chapter 4, but from the portfolio management point of view it is clear that the strategy will be expressed by giving special emphasis to projects that express the strategic thrust of the organization, at the expense of others.

There seem to be only three generic ways in which strategic aims can feed into portfolio management. The first is by directly earmarking money for a group of projects, identified by a road-mapping process perhaps, that constitute a plan to achieve the required strategy. Road-mapping techniques are described in more detail in Chapter 4. The resources for these strategic projects must be allocated separate 'ring-fenced' funding.

The second approach is for management to declare that, as a matter of policy, a certain amount or proportion of funding will be allocated to particular types of project. This approach is known as *strategic buckets*. It may mean allocating funds to particular market sectors or product types (Figure 6.6) or to certain classes of project. The AXA insurance company,[40] which provides our main case study in Chapter 3, aims that 10 per cent of its innovation projects should be entirely novel, 10 per cent should be based on the reuse of existing ideas in new applications, 40 per cent should be incremental improvements, and 40 per cent should eliminate unnecessary functions (Figure 6.7).

Figure 6.6   Strategic alignment of projects by market served

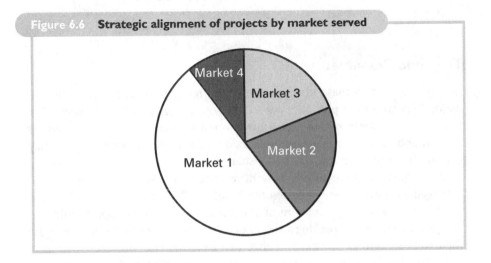

Figure 6.7   Activity allocation matrix alignment by AXA insurance

Create new customer-focused opportunities (10%)	Improve existing products, services and processes (40%)
Eliminate non-value adding activities (40%)	Re-use AXA global success stories (10%)

Source: Oke (2001).

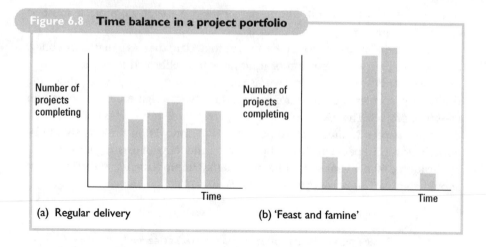

Figure 6.8 Time balance in a project portfolio

(a) Regular delivery

(b) 'Feast and famine'

Time and Resources

Clearly the need to make effective use of the resources that are available is a major constraint on a portfolio, particularly on the timing of the projects. The problem is dynamic because in innovation unexpected things are likely to happen and so as time goes on unplanned bottlenecks and opportunities may appear. If projects in the portfolio share resources of any kind (including budgets) then problems in one may have knock-on effects on the others and management must intervene to resolve them.

The projects in the portfolio must also have a balance with respect to time of completion. Generally speaking a spread of delivery dates will be desirable because there will be a limit to how much change an organization can manage at one time. A steady flow of new products is generally more motivating for the sales force and easier to handle throughout the supply chain than a glut followed by famine (Figure 6.8). On the other hand there may be good reasons to launch some innovations together to maximize their impact. For example several new products may be required together for a trade show or an exhibition. Whatever the reason, the timing of the projects in the portfolio needs separate consideration.

Risk and Reward

Another important element of balance in a portfolio is risk. Organizations may be willing to take on risky projects, but only if they have a sufficient number of low-risk projects going on at the same time to provide security. Conversely many companies worry that they are 'risk-averse'. By this they do not mean that they take too few gambles, but that they do not undertake enough of the long-term, difficult and innovative projects that have potential for generating really high returns. The *risk–reward* or *risk-impact* diagram is a convenient way to display the balance of risks among the projects and so aid decision-making. Projects are displayed on a grid where one dimension is a measure of the estimated value of the project – for example its NPV or the rating from a scoring system – while the other is a measure of the uncertainty or risk of the project.

There are several good reasons for separating perceptions of risk from perceptions of value:

☐ Risk and reward are different things and invoke different kinds of management action. In particular, risk may not be an attribute of the project itself but simply reflect a lack of knowledge. This may be readily reduced by some investigative work or experiment.

☐ Risk and reward often become entwined in our minds in unhelpful ways. We have already observed that managers often down-rate their estimates of the potential of projects as a way of accounting for the risks. Risk does not necessarily make a project less valuable; it may merely mean that work is needed to clarify the situation.

☐ When there is doubt about technical feasibility it is all too easy not to ask basic, and perhaps easily-answered, questions about value (and vice versa). We have heard managers argue: 'There's no point in worrying about the market when we don't know whether the thing will work' – and as a result much time and money has been wasted in proving the feasibility of some product that had no market potential. Separating risk and reward explicitly, as in this diagram, poses questions and prompts action on both.

Figure 6.9 is a typical risk–reward diagram. It shows the balance of the portfolio between the four quadrants, which are often named as: 'Bread and Butter' (low risk but low rewards); 'Pearls' (low risk and high rewards); 'Oysters' (high rewards but also high risk); and 'White Elephants' (high-risk, low returns – and often difficult to kill!). In this diagram the size of the circles represents the resources being used in the current phase of each project and so the diagram shows the distribution of effort at the moment. Any proposed new projects must take resources from the others, since the area of all the circles remains constant.

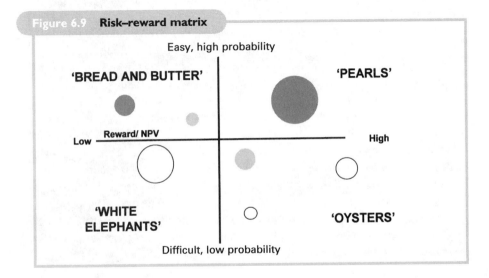

Figure 6.9 Risk–reward matrix

The shading can be used to show how near the projects are to launch, or for any other distinction; for example, to show which market sector or part of the business they relate to.

Box case 6.5   Fruit of the Loom – a portfolio of process innovations

Fruit of the Loom is an international clothing manufacturer employing over 23,000 people and based in Bowling Green, Kentucky. The business is strongly vertically integrated, spanning the complete product process from spinning the yarn and weaving and dyeing the fabric, through to creating and packaging the final garment. Consequently the company is very diverse, operating from over 50 sites around the world.

Process innovation – ranging from improvements in existing processes to the application of radically new manufacturing technology – is very important to the continuing success of the company and the target for regular significant financial investment. Management were concerned that, without some central coordination, innovation efforts might be concentrated in too few parts of the business. Moreover the best practices being developed in some parts of the business were not necessarily being shared with all the sites that could benefit. In 1998, Dr Michael Mallon, VP Manufacturing and Sourcing, set out to understand the portfolio of process innovation projects better, aiming to get better value for money and to ensure that all parts of the business were receiving appropriate attention: 'Previously, each process innovation investment had been assessed individually purely on a financial basis. There also wasn't much interaction between the different functional areas involved. We wanted to improve this process.' Mallon looked at how product portfolios were managed and started to apply these ideas to Fruit of the Loom's process innovation – probably the first company to apply this level of sophistication to process innovation projects.

A survey across all sites showed that more than 100 process innovation projects were being conducted. A portfolio bubble diagram was prepared showing the expected return on each project in one dimension and the degree of innovation in the other (Figure 6.10 – simplified to show only a few projects). Financial returns were estimated using 'Expected Manufacturing Benefit' (EMB) – a calculation based on the ideas of expected commercial value, ECV. The size of the circles on the diagram represents the level of investment. Some projects at different sites were found to be very similar; a clear waste of precious resources. So the first task was to eliminate duplication while ensuring that the experience gained from the selected projects was made fully available across the company. Once this was done attention moved to prioritizing the remaining projects. Colour-coding was added to the bubble diagram to show the stage of the manufacturing process (spinning, sewing, weaving, packaging and cutting) involved. The resulting diagram allowed managers to see the complete balance of their innovation programme on a single sheet. 'This forced all functional areas to sit down and discuss the portfolio in detail. Not only do we consider each individual project but we

Figure 6.10 Fruit of the Loom's process improvement portfolio

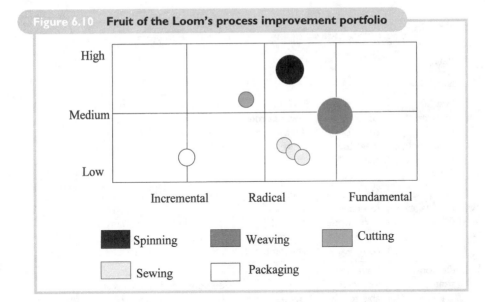

monitor whether we were innovating sufficiently at each of the process stages, such as spinning and packaging.' As the diagram indicates, the more radical innovation efforts were concentrated on the clothing stages, and packaging, a promising area for cost reduction, was being neglected.

It is now several years since Fruit of the Loom introduced process innovation bubble diagrams. However, as Mallon says, 'my colleagues still find them a highly relevant tool that creates the interaction necessary to make better investment decisions. Combined with our improved approaches to assessing technical risks, EMB, and even whether the appropriate human resources are available has helped us become much more effective at managing our manufacturing technology. Senior managers have welcomed this more formal process, as they see that it has delivered significantly superior projects than was previously the case.'

Case based on an interview with Dr Michael Mallon in December 2004, Goffin, K., Lee-Mortimer, A. and New, C., *Managing Product Innovation for Competitive Advantage* (Haymarket Business Publications, 1999), ISBN 1-902226-15-1, p. 42, and Mallon, M. J. *Manufacturing Technology Acquisition*, unpublished PhD thesis 2002, School of Engineering, Cranfield University, UK.

Scoring the Risk Dimension

It is very difficult to estimate risk, as we have emphasized earlier, but a carefully designed scoring system can take some of the subjectivity out of the process. Certainly a structured process is much superior to simply asking 'What's the probability that this project will be successful?' In Table 6.5 we give an example of such a score-sheet used by Laserco. Somewhat similar scales have been published by Davis,[41] on the basis of a survey of member companies of the

Table 6.5   Score sheet for assessing risk profile for a project

	Rating Key items	0	4	7	10	Total
'TECHNICAL'	Size of technical (in at least 1 parameter)	New concept or order of magnitude change	Step change short of order of magnitude or significant novelty of method	Less than 50% change. No major novelty	Incremental improve-ment.	
	Technical uncertainty	Many major technical uncertainties or very high complexity	Several significant technical uncertainties or high complexity	Technical solution defined but uncertainties remain	A defined and straight-forward technical task	
	Demon-strated feasibility	Have not yet been able to demonstrate feasibility	Limited demon-stration achieved. Or outline plan for cost reduction	Almost demonstrated. Full demon-stration planned. Or detailed plan for cost reduction	Full technical feasibility clearly demon-strated	
'COMMERCIAL'	Knowledge of market for this product	Pure guesswork	Rough estimate available but no specific study yet done	Specific study done but more work needed. (e.g. market known within a factor of 2)	Market size well defined. No further work needed (e.g. +/–20%)	
	Market readiness	Extensive market develop-ment required. No apparent demand	Need or benefit must be highlighted to customers	Clear relationship between product and customer need; or substitutes a competitor product	Meets a clearly expressed customer need; or substitutes one of our products	
	Channel capability	No relevant expertise or experience in our channels	Some relevant experience or expertise	Considerable relevant resources available	Leverages our existing skills and resources well	
	Comments					Total %

Industrial Research Institute. Having a check-list of factors can ensure that no major aspects of risk are forgotten; and anchoring statements help people turn information about uncertainty into a shared assessment of risk. Splitting the risk assessment into a number of components is clearly helpful (as Laserco found, see Box case 6.3) in identifying the major uncertainties that need attention.

Nevertheless the comments we made earlier in this chapter about the difficulty of making accurate probability estimates still apply. The problem is evident when we try and align the scales for the various factors: how can we be sure that a score of seven for Technical uncertainty really is equivalent to a score of seven for Market readiness? So it is important to recognize that these scores are only approximate.

The Laserco risk–reward matrix splits each dimension into only six elements. The Risk dimension is called 'Likelihood of Success' to emphasize that the scores are not supposed to be probabilities in the strict numerical sense. A high score means low risk. The assessment contains three questions about technical uncertainties and three about commercial, reflecting the experience of the company that both aspects were equally likely to be important.

Score sheets of this kind give a framework that allows managers to place projects on a risk–reward diagram in a logical way and so to assess and manage the balance of their project portfolio. The level of detail required in the assessments helps to inform and structure an open discussion. And by identifying the main sources of risk as well reward the score sheets highlight topics that need management attention.

The actions that should be considered for projects in each quadrant are shown in Figure 6.11. Only the 'White Elephant' category is intrinsically to be avoided; the status of the rest depends on other factors. 'Pearls' are the most desirable projects of all, but they may be large and long-term so a mixture of 'Bread and Butter' projects may be needed to give a background of more reliable results. These should deliver quickly and must be relatively sparing in their use of resources. The 'Oysters' form the most contentious group because their promise of high returns is linked with the chance of failure. Full-scale commitment is unlikely to be the best strategy. The pertinent question will be: what can

Figure 6.11 Appropriate actions for projects on a risk–return matrix

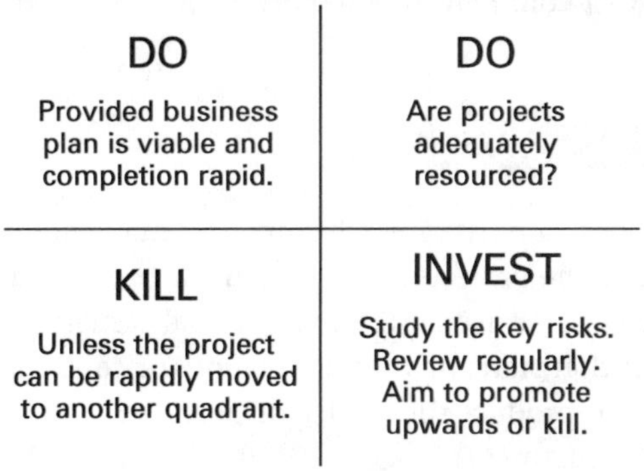

DO	DO
Provided business plan is viable and completion rapid.	Are projects adequately resourced?
KILL	INVEST
Unless the project can be rapidly moved to another quadrant.	Study the key risks. Review regularly. Aim to promote upwards or kill.

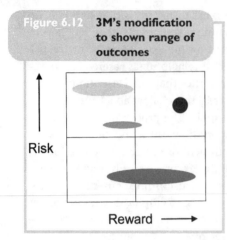

Figure 6.12 3M's modification to shown range of outcomes

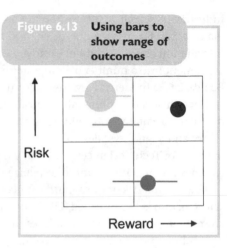

Figure 6.13 Using bars to show range of outcomes

best be done to improve understanding of the risks and so either promote the project towards 'Pearl' status or kill it off cleanly?

There need be no surprise that projects may in practice be found in any quadrant of the diagram. This would not be so in the financial world where the operation of the market ensures that low risk stocks generate a low reward and high reward goes only with high risk. The world of projects is quite different because the assets that the projects represent are not traded openly. No market mechanism operates against 'Pearls' or 'White Elephants'.

A risk–reward diagram carries a lot of useful information in a simple and accessible way. However, it shows only the most probable value of the project, which, as we have emphasized above, is a valid indicator only of the average outcome of a large number of projects. When dealing with single projects in the real world the possible upsides and downsides must be kept in mind. A modification[42] usually attributed to the 3M company shows projects as ellipses elongated to span the likely range of outcomes (Figure 6.12). The area of the ellipses no longer shows the resource levels, which is a pity. Using bars, as in Figure 6.13 includes all the information but with a certain loss of elegance.

Logically, if one uses a representation of this kind one should remove any elements of commercial uncertainty from the risk score since this is now incorporated in the range of commercial outcomes.

The Management Process

The tools and methods one uses for selecting and managing project portfolios may need to evolve as the projects mature from the broad and subjective methods in the early stages towards 'hard', financial analysis later on. For example if we imagine a project that starts in a research laboratory and makes its way eventually to a commercial product the choice of portfolio management tools may evolve as indicated in Figure 6.14.

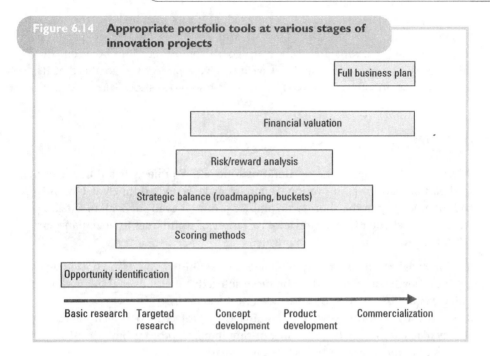

Figure 6.14   Appropriate portfolio tools at various stages of innovation projects

In the very early stages the only important thing is to identify some possibilities that excite enough interest to motivate the team. As work progresses and information accumulates it becomes appropriate to ensure that the idea fits the company's strategy. Later on, scoring methods and risk-reward assessments help to give it the right priority among all the other projects in the pipeline. As it advances further, the financial figures ought to become more believable and so should play a greater and greater part in the decision making. In the final stages most companies would expect to have a fully costed business plan in place and make decisions mostly on the basis of the figures.

It will be clear by now that we regard the management of the innovation project portfolio as a senior management responsibility. It requires a regular review of the projects that are in hand and an appraisal of:

☐   Their potential value (the business case for them).
☐   Whether they continue to fit the business strategy.
☐   The risks associated with them.
☐   Their timing.
☐   The resource requirements.

The management team that does this review must be in a position to take the necessary actions. This means that it will generally be at a divisional or corporate level in order to have the scope and power to do the job. There is, however, some debate about whether portfolio reviews should generally be conducted together with those for individual projects, or separately. Cooper[43] advocates that project reviews should be conducted at times required by the work programme and not constrained to an artificial timetable. Hence portfolio reviews should be separate. However, good communication between the processes is essential; one would not wish to give a project the go-ahead at its project review only to have it axed by the portfolio process soon after.

Summary

Selecting and managing the portfolio of innovation projects is a difficult but vital part of managing innovation. Failure to make good and timely decisions is bad for efficiency in the short term, and for profit, or even survival, in the long term. In this chapter we have reviewed a variety of techniques to help managers select the innovation projects to pursue:

- Financial methods of varying degrees of sophistication take centre-stage, but they must be backed up by more subjective methods that allow strategic and other factors to be included in the analysis.
- Particular care is necessary in valuing risky projects. Good techniques are available for a very large number of simultaneous projects but prioritizing a small number of such projects is problematic.
- Scoring systems are particularly helpful in the early stages of projects when financial information may not be reliable.
- The portfolio of projects selected must not only represent the best possible use of resources, but must also be balanced in terms of risk, timing and strategic impact.

No one set of tools suits all situations; the choice depends on the information available, the type and complexity of the projects involved and how close they are to commercialization.

Management Recommendations

- Choose project valuation tools that are appropriate for the types of project, using subjective measures such as scoring when uncertainty is high, but emphasizing financial measures more as commercialization approaches.
- Keep valuation tools simple and transparent so that the decision process remains open to debate and review, and leaves scope for management judgement.
- Treat numerical measures of risk with caution; they are always very approximate.
- Avoid point forecasts; try and understand the range of possibilities open to each project.
- Ensure that the portfolio delivers results smoothly enough over time.
- Check for strategic balance.
- Top management must be actively involved in portfolio management.

Table 6.6 Acronyms used in valuation and portfolio management

Acronym	Meaning
DCF	Discounted cash flow
DTA	Decision tree analysis
ECV	Expected commercial value
IRR	Internal rate of return
NPV	Net present value
TBE	Time to break even
BSM	Black, Scholls and Merton

Recommended Reading

(1) Bernstein, P. L., *Against the Gods: The Remarkable Story of Risk* (New York: John Wiley, 1998). An excellent and readable account of the history and ideas of risk and risk management.

(2) Boer, F. P., 'Financial Managment of R&D', *Research-Technology Management*, vol. 44, no. 4 (July 2002), pp. 23–34. Good survey of the available methods for valuing innovation projects.

(3) Cooper, R. G., Edgett, S. J. and Kleinschmidt, E. J., *Portfolio Management for New Projects*, 2nd edn (Cambridge, Mass.: Perseus Books, 2001). A complete and authoritative review of portfolio management practices, based on extensive research.

Main Case Study   Britannia Building Society – building and evolving a portfolio management process

Before reading this case study, consider the following generic innovation management issues:

□ What difficulties face a company trying to create an innovative culture?

□ Can innovation be imported into an organization from outside or must it grow from within?

□ How does innovation management differ in service and manufacturing enterprises?

□ What criteria are appropriate for evaluating projects in the service sector?

The Britannia is a building society (the British equivalent of a Mutual Fund), founded in 1856 in Staffordshire in the north of England. It provides mortgages, loans, related insurances, savings and investment products. The Society's key values of reliability, accessibility and personal service served it well, and for much of its life innovation was not high on the Society's agenda.

The 'Skunk Works'

The arrival of the internet in the 1990s caused a shift in Britannia's attitude to innovation, and in 2000 a special task force, the 'E-Business Unit', was set up to explore the opportunities and threats it posed, and to promote higher levels of innovation in general. Within this team a sub-group, called 'The Incubator' was given the task of generating new product possibilities and pushing them forward. The team operated as a 'skunk works', in a separate location, away from the day-to-day running of the business. The E-Business Unit was headed by Tim Franklin, who reported directly to the then Group Chief Executive, Graham Stow.

Mark Chizlett, the programme coordinator, approved of this organization: 'Skunk works teams are focused, fast and open to innovation. In a very disciplined, data-rational company like ours we needed a team with some independence and the ability to experiment with running new products; and with a real sense that it is OK to fail.' The Incubator team worked closely with the Board, initially in a three-month intensive strategy review, and later by regular meetings every three months to review projects and manage the portfolio.

From the start the team used a process with four gates to ensure that good ideas were selected and that the balance of projects was appropriate:

Gate 1: Presentation of ideas and decision on which to take forward
Gate 2: Review of solutions and decision whether to do a controlled pilot, 'launch and learn'
Gate 3: Decision whether to proceed to a scale implementation
Gate 4: Review of experience and decision to 'plant out' or sell off.

Review meetings started with a presentation of the existing portfolio and ended with a review of how it stood after the decisions just made. Projects that had reached a milestone were assessed and rated against a 'balanced scorecard' of criteria before being approved to move on. The criteria were different at each gate, being initially rather subjective but getting steadily more rational as the projects matured. Detailed financial analysis was not used, at least in the early phases. It was a learning experience for everyone. Chizlett says the Board were not always in their comfort zone: 'They were used to carefully-documented proposals full of data that had already been reviewed by other committees. But, with appropriate stakeholder management by Tim, they came to find the different approach refreshing and thought-provoking. And it worked: we completed six quite major new projects in the first two years'.

Britannia were well-aware of the deficiencies of running innovation teams outside the mainstream business. Chizlett commented: 'A skunk works is insulated from the day-to-day business and that means it can lose touch with the business case'. So a team of directors oversaw the activities of the

Incubator, ensuring that it focused on business results and that it had support for the new initiatives. A policy of short-term secondments to the Incubator meant that their new ideas had ready-made champions throughout the business.

One of the objectives the board gave the Incubator was to be torch-bearers for a new culture for the Society. Chizlett thinks that was probably a mistake: 'It was just too much of a cross to bear for the individuals in the team: to set up a new process and new products and change the Society's culture as well. Culture must be generated from within, not by a guerrilla group sniping from outside'.

Innovation Moves into the Main Stream

By early 2003, it was time to devolve the E-Business team. As Mark Chizlett put it 'We realized the internet is no longer something new; it's something that needs to be put back in the business. Anyway, by this time most of the team were implementing the new products and running the internet as a channel'.

But Chizlett was worried about who would now be the 'conscience for innovation': who would search actively for new opportunities? Making NPD part of the value chain rather than a separate function promised to give a clearer route to implementation; and it was felt that the new product ideas would benefit from the insights of people further upstream, who were in regular contact with customers. An NPD mission statement expressed the need very clearly:

'If we don't respond quickly to new products from the competition our members (customers) and prospective members will take their business to those that do, limiting our ability to meet targets and strategic ambitions.'

Britannia would be a fast follower in innovation, a stance driven by both their brand values and resources.

The arrival of a new Group Chief Executive , Neville Richardson, in 2003 provided a trigger for a more concerted move to change the culture of the society and to embed NPD activities more directly in the fabric of the organization. The 'Living the Values' culture-change programme was headed and driven by Richardson. All staff attended a briefing and a road-show followed by intensive training sessions, and company publications and reinforced by new personal objectives. The new culture generated several new sources of ideas: all managers now have continuous improvement goals in their objectives; the suggestions scheme was revitalized; and a route was created from the customer-care department to NPD to feed in opportunities raised by customers.

The position of New Product Development as an integral part of the company was formalized in a new management process, launched in 2003.

Figure 6.15 **Britannia's project scoring system**

Element	Weight	Manager responsible for scoring
Benefits	4	Marketing *and* Finance
Customer need	3	Customer Excellence
Strategic fit	3	Marketing
Business risk	4	Product Management
Systems and processes	3	Information Services
Operational complexity	3	Operations *and* Sales
Delivery cost	4	Finance
Dependencies	3	Information Services
Priority	3	Managing Director

The NPD manager has the job of collecting propositions and ideas from throughout the company and selecting the most promising ones. A committee, with representatives from Marketing, Treasury, IT, Administration, Finance and Sales channels helps with the selection. The managing board, chaired by Tim Franklin, now the Managing Director of the Member Business and a main board Director, reviews the chosen ideas using a balanced scorecard of nine elements, illustrated in Figure 6.15. Individual members of the board themselves provide the scores for the projects, ensuring a high level of consistency from project to project.

'I don't say that what we've done would be right for everyone but it's right for us, here and now', says Chizlett, now promoted to manage the Savings and Investments division, 'There will still be conflicts, compromises, choices. We'll start some things and have to stop and try again. But the conditions for success are all well in train.'

7 Implementation of New Products, Processes and Services

'Philosophers have only interpreted the world. The point, however, is to change it.'

(Karl Marx)

Introduction

Turning an idea for an innovation into reality is bound to be something of a unique experience that cannot usually be managed by a purely bureaucratic process. It must be treated as a project: a finite activity with its own objectives and resources, and above all its own leadership.

Successful implementation of an innovation starts with good *Project Management*, nowadays properly regarded as a professional discipline in its own right. It includes: project definition; task analysis; priority management; resource allocation; and progress monitoring. No project of any size has much of a chance without these disciplines and the leadership that goes with them. However, innovation projects also need an extra dimension of management because of the relatively high levels of uncertainty and risk that, of their very nature, they face. For this reason we stress at the outset that the effective management of innovation projects absolutely requires a clearly-identified project manager with the power to get things done and the support of higher management.

Many organizations plan for repeated innovation in some parts of their business – product development for example. The evocative term 'the design factory' has been used to describe a department devoted to innovation projects.[1] A design factory needs a process of innovation that can be used repeatedly and with some confidence. Such a process is a way of capturing the lessons the organization has learned from previous experiences and using them to guide what is done next time. A design factory also needs arrangements to cope with the difficulties of scheduling a number of unpredictable projects at a time and to continuously nurture and extend the expertise of its staff.

An innovation project is always to some extent a journey of discovery with new things being learned along the way. In this chapter we present and discuss some of the techniques available to help managers to plot their course through this uncertain terrain, when not only the path but even the destination itself may change as the route unfolds.

This chapter will describe:

▶ The basic techniques of project management.
▶ Managing the difficult early stages of projects.
▶ Risk management.
▶ Team structure and organization.
▶ The 'phase gate' management process.
▶ Managing an innovation department.

The Techniques of Project Management[2]

Projects are classically considered to have four phases: the *concept* phase in which the aims and deliverables of the project are worked out; the *design* phase in which detailed design work is done; the *planning* phase when the implementation is planned in detail; and the *implementation* phase in which the job is done. In familiar, low-risk projects, such as building a road or a hospital, the parties expect to deal quickly with the issues in the concept phase and so it may not be considered to be within the project at all. Attention concentrates mainly on design and, especially, planning and implementation. In innovation projects, on the other hand, the concept phase is not a curtain-raiser to the main action but a key part of the whole. It may last a long time and be divided into sub-phases such as research, predevelopment and concept validation; indeed the project may very well stop before it is over. In the product development literature the concept phase is often called the 'fuzzy front end'. The irreverent name is appropriate because the 'front end' is difficult to define and needs focused attention that it often does not receive. Consequently it is often ill-done and takes too long.

Ideally the concept phase ends with most of the technical and commercial uncertainties removed so that the project can proceed with little risk of failure. There is no doubt that this is the most efficient approach, but it is not always possible to eliminate all the risks early on, so a real possibility of failure may remain until near the end of the project. The management process must recognize this unpalatable fact and accommodate it.

Five elements are fundamental to the successful management of any type of innovation project:

▶ Clear and precise aims.
▶ A breakdown of the work into elements small enough to be planned and managed.
▶ A scheduling plan that ensures that the tasks are undertaken in the right order and at the right times.
▶ A resource plan to ensure that people and facilities will be available to do the tasks as required.
▶ Effective management of trade-offs.

We will consider each of these elements in more detail in the following sections.

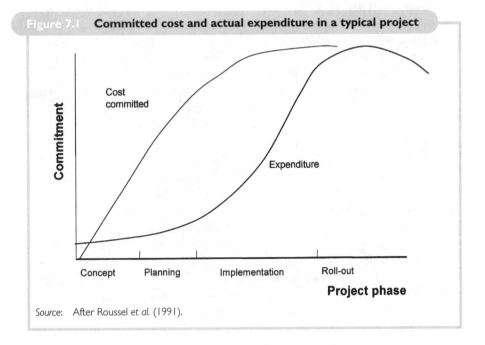

Figure 7.1   Committed cost and actual expenditure in a typical project

Source: After Roussel *et al.* (1991).

Project Aims

No project can succeed unless its aims are clear to start with. This is so obvious that it is almost embarrassing to state it, and yet ill-defined objectives – or for a product, ill-defined or ambiguous specifications – are probably responsible for more project failures than any other factor. Management must stand firm and insist that objectives and approaches are fully clarified in the concept stage. Most of the costs of any project or product are essentially committed by decisions made early on, even though they may not actually be spent until later, so this is the time when management involvement pays most dividends (Figure 7.1). In practice, however, top management attention often tends to follow the expenditure curve, so it is highest in the later stages when the activity is high, whereas it should be greatest in the early stages when crucial decisions are made.[3]

The concept phase may be lengthy and difficult because the team may be working out both what can be done and what should be done. During this phase, and perhaps beyond, management is making only interim decisions to let the project continue a bit further, not a full-scale commitment.

Box case 7.1   **The New Zealand Department of Conservation's Pest Eradication Programme – restoring the dawn chorus**[4]

Many islands in the South Pacific have been invaded by rats introduced from overseas, and these pests often wipe out indigenous species entirely. As part of its biodiversity programme, the NZ Department of Conservation (DoC) looked at the possibility of eliminating rodents entirely from some of the islands. The scientific view was that this was simply not possible, but DoC staff were not convinced: As one staff member said: 'What we were looking at, at the time, was rats invading islands and species going extinct as a conse-quence . . . The accepted wisdom was that the best you can do is to go out there and grab what you can and rescue them and take them somewhere else . . . You wouldn't have to be involved in too much work before you'd realize there's got to be a better way than that . . . Pretty soon you're going to run out of places that you can stick these things'.

The mindshift towards trying eradication took place in the early 1980s. The development of new poisons led to experiments on small islands elimi-nating only a single type of rodent, and moved on later to larger and more complex islands and multiple species. As more difficult islands were attempted, new techniques were tested and applied. Aerial application of bait was first tried in 1989 and the technique was later developed using heli-copters with specially-developed underslung baskets. When global position-ing systems (GPS) became available they were adopted to improve accuracy. By 1990, 13 species of rodent had been eradicated from 60 islands. This increased to 20 species by 2001. The biggest operation to date has been the elimination of the estimated 200,000 rats from the 11,000 hectare Campbell Island in 2001 at a cost of $2.6 million.

The vision and passion of DoC staff was one of the most important factors of the success of the pest-eradication programme. Although international experts concluded that eradication was highly unlikely, key DoC staff refused to accept this. Their refusal to give up on the vision led to experimentation and success with small projects which in turn bred the confidence to take on more ambitious ones. But the right kind of senior management support has also been very important. For example the Campbell Island project was jeopardized when a lorry full of rat poison crashed into the sea. Senior managers stepped in to deal with the consequences and protected the project manager from blame and inter-ference so that he could continue to get on with the job. A common theme in the programme was the need to have a culture of trust, forgiveness and not punishing failures. Management accepted that project teams had to experiment to find the best solutions and that some experiments would fail. Care was neces-sary to manage expectations. The Campbell Island project manager talked about his strong conviction that the organization trusted him to manage the project and to work through issues without second-guessing or unhelpful interference.

A special team, the Island Eradication Advisory Group (IEAG), consisting of administrative experts and managers from previous eradication projects played an important role in giving expert advice to project teams and ensuring that lessons were carried forward from one project to the next. The IEAG also helped with political issues, forward planning and preventing re-invasion.

Other countries are now copying the DoC's success. As Sir David Bellamy put it, 'New Zealand is the only country which has turned pest eradication into an export industry'.

Work Breakdown Structure

Successful execution of any project requires a detailed understanding of what has to be done. The starting point for this is the *work breakdown structure* which lists all the *work packages* (or, more simply, *tasks*) and the relationship between them. This step is obvious enough and yet is surprisingly often neglected. All work packages should as far as possible be self-contained entities, to be done by identified people. Most important, each must have clear and verifiable outputs, or *deliverables*. The work breakdown structure has two related purposes. The first is to determine as clearly as possible the work required and the skills and expertise needed. This allows the project manager to estimate the time, cost and staffing for the project. For innovation projects the analysis of tasks also helps uncover risks and to show where new knowledge or facilities will be required. The second purpose is to allow progress monitoring. Completed and verified deliverables from the work packages are an unambiguous measure of the progress of the project and so allow the project manager to assess progress and take corrective action when necessary. These two purposes, estimation and monitoring, define the size of the work packages. For example, if it is important to be able to track progress to within a week, then the duration of the lowest-level work packages should not be more than about a week. Excessive detail is to be avoided, however. Within these constraints the task of identifying the work packages in detail is best left to the people involved rather than imposed from above.

The Project Schedule

Once the tasks have been identified and quantified it is time to consider the order in which they are to be done. The ordering is vitally important but it is not always straightforward to work out. Some tasks may be done at almost any time between the beginning and end of the project while others cannot be started until earlier ones are complete. Most projects will contain several such sequences of tasks but there will always be one chain that is longer than the rest. This is called the *critical path*.[5] It is very important because the sum of the times required to complete all the work packages on the critical path defines the minimum length of the project. Managers will look very closely at these tasks to see if any can be avoided, rescheduled or speeded up because that is the way to reduce the time the project will take. Similarly, while the work is in progress great attention will be paid to the tasks on the critical path to try and ensure that, whatever else happens, they, at least, will be on time.

To illustrate how a scheduling diagram works, let us consider a simple project consisting of 13 work packages, labelled A to M. We will call this project Alpha. By examining each task in turn, the team can compile the *precedence list*[6] (Table 7.1) which shows which tasks must logically be completed before each one can begin.

Thus tasks B, C and E can start as soon as task A is complete (but not before).

Table 7.1   Precedence list for work packages in project Alpha

Task	Duration (days)	Tasks that must precede it
A	10	None
B	7	A
C	5	A
D	5	C
E	9	A
F	4	D
G	10	B
H	15	F, E, G
I	5	H
J	4	I
K	12	I
L	8	I
M	20	K, J, L

Task H can begin only when E, F and G (and the tasks that precede them) are all completed. With a bit of thought the precedence list can be turned into a *network diagram*[7] that shows how all the tasks are interrelated. This is shown in Figure 7.2. The amount of work, in man-days, required to complete each task is shown inside its box and we will assume for the moment that one person is available for each.

Box case 7.2   Pizza Hut – new product development

To the uninitiated, the development of a new pizza might be seen as a trivial selection of a new set of toppings. However, in the fast-food business where product consistency and fast 'roll-out' are essential, it is not that simple. Pizza Hut has a seven-stage NPD process called the FRPP – the 'Field Ready Product Process'. This process ensures that a robust product is developed, by defining the steps that are necessary to develop the recipe, select suppliers for the ingredients, test the 'manufacturability' of the product in a typical Pizza Hut restaurant, and ensure positive consumer reactions to the new product. Everything is done to ensure that no time is wasted between a product concept being selected and it being available at the majority of the chain's restaurants. Part of the FRPP ensures that the employees in the restaurants are adequately trained on the product before it is released. Increasingly, competition in the

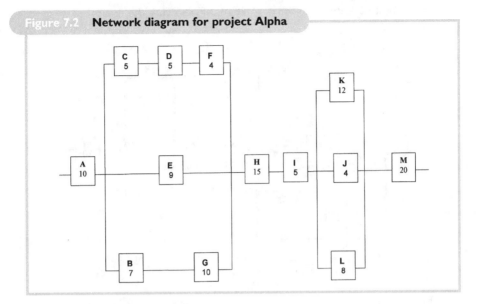

Figure 7.2 Network diagram for project Alpha

fast food industry is based on special meals that are only available for limited periods and matched to major events, such as sport championships, or film releases. In such cases, Pizza Hut has found that a reliable but flexible NPD process is essential, even if the resulting product is 'only' a pizza.

The next important step is to identify the critical path through the project. The procedure for this is very simple once the network is complete: starting at the beginning of the project one first calculates the earliest time each package could be started, and this is recorded on the left under each box as in Figure 7.3. The earliest that work can begin on task F is day 20, because it must be preceded by A, C and D, which take a total of 20 days. The final task can begin on day 59, which means that the whole project will take 79 days. The next step is to work backwards from the end, calculating the latest that each task could begin. This is recorded on the right under each box in Figure 7.3. Thus L could start as late as day 51 because it takes eight days and must be completed on day 59, and so on. Each package now has an earliest and a latest start time. If these times are different it means that there is some flexibility in when the work is done; if not then the timing is critical, and so that task is on the critical path. In this example it can be seen that the critical path runs through tasks A, B, G, H, I, K and M, shown darkened. For the other elements the difference between the earliest and latest possible start times gives the amount of slack, or *float* that is available in doing the task. Work package L, for example, has a float of four days. The flexibility that the float gives can be helpful in several ways, for example in smoothing out the workload on the people in the project, as we see in the next section.

In planning the project the next step is to examine all the work packages on

Figure 7.3 **Network diagram for project Alpha, showing the critical path**

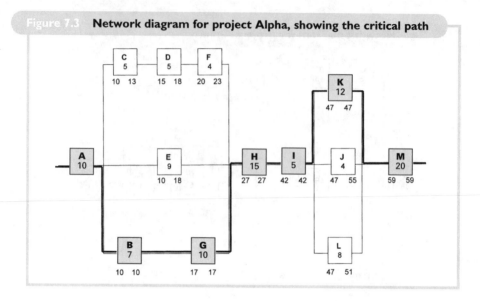

the critical path and see whether anything can be done to shorten the time they take, because this (and only this) will speed up the whole project. One question to ask is whether some parts of these tasks might in fact be done earlier or later, so reducing the length of the task on the critical path. The second question is whether any critical tasks could be accelerated by using more resources. For example if two people could work together on task G it might be done in five days, shortening the critical path and hence the whole project. Notice, however, that Figure 7.3 now shows that the upper branch, containing tasks C, D and F, becomes the critical path so not all the five days would be gained.

Nowadays a wide range of software is available to simplify the task of planning complex projects. For simpler projects the familiar bar chart, or Gantt chart,[8] is a very effective tool and it is also a convenient way to summarize the activities in a project for communication inside and outside the project team. In a Gantt chart all the project tasks are represented as bars whose length shows their duration. It shows at a glance what tasks are being done at any one time and which are to come; and by shading in the completed tasks the project manager can show clearly how the work is progressing.

The Resource Plan

The next stage in constructing a project plan is to ensure that the required resources can be made available and that they are used efficiently. Most projects will require a range of skills or resources, which may not be interchangeable, so the first thing is to analyze the requirements for different types of resource. This first analysis will usually show that the requirements vary greatly with time and that peaks occur when the plan demands more resource than is actually available

Figure 7.4 **Resource plan showing the variation of the loading of resources in a project**

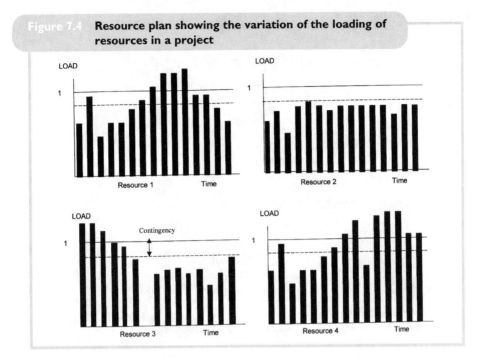

(as is the case for resources 1, 3 and 4 in Figure 7.4). This will obviously mean that some tasks may run late. If these are on the critical path the schedule for the whole project is jeopardized, but it may be possible to make adjustments to non-critical tasks to avoid the problem. For example Figure 7.3 shows tasks J, K and L being worked on simultaneously. If they all require the same resource, for example a designer, he is required full-time from day 47 to day 59 on task K, which is on the critical path, so the other tasks will run late and delay the whole project unless more resource is found. To assign two more designers to work on the other packages would certainly solve the problem but this would be inefficient because they would not both be required full-time. However, the float on these two tasks shows that there is scope to reschedule them, and in fact this allows a more efficient solution: if L is started on day 47 it will be finished by day 55 and J can then start on day 55, which is within its float. Only one extra designer is needed.

Many iterations may be needed to produce the most effective resource plan. It is best not to load any resource to its theoretical capacity, at least not for significant periods, but to leave some slack for unexpected contingencies (dotted lines in Figure 7.4).

Managing Trade-offs

A project is an activity aimed at accomplishing a task to a defined specification in a defined time and at a defined cost. Any change to the project must be

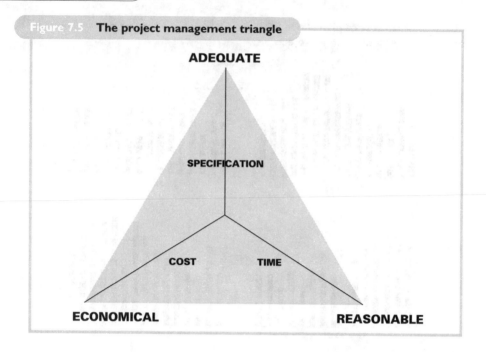

Figure 7.5 The project management triangle

expected to have an effect on one or more of them, as is illustrated in the *project management triangle* in Figure 7.5. For example, if part of the project runs significantly late, it is likely that the time can be recovered only by increasing the cost or altering the deliverables; similarly, a change to the project specification will impact either time or cost. Trade-offs cannot generally be avoided. All those with responsibility for projects should therefore decide in advance what their strategy will be in the event of difficulty, rather than to have to work it out in the heat of the moment. This is particularly prudent in projects involving innovation, where unforeseen events are especially likely.

Exploring the trade-offs between specification, cost and time is a question of running several versions of the plan using different assumptions. Cost will probably be easy to analyze but it may be more difficult to work out the impact that a late launch or a reduced specification will have on sales volume. 'Program managers who know to a penny what an additional engineer will cost and what profits will be lost if the company misses manufacturing cost targets, seldom can quantify the losses associated with a six-month slippage in the development process'.[9] However, the truth is always useful and often surprising.

Studies[10,11] have shown that the timing of a product development project often has a much greater impact on profitability that any other aspect. Several factors contribute to this; for example, a late launch reduces the total lifetime sales and also reduces the opportunities for premium pricing from a leading product in the market. The reduced sales volume also affects costs in two ways: through less-efficient use of fixed costs and the loss of 'learning-curve' efficiencies that come from accumulated operating experience. Don Reinertsen[12] of MIT

Table 7.2   Project tradeoffs

Issue	Reduction in profit
Product introduced 6 months late	31%
Quality problems reduce selling price by 10%	15%
Compatibility problems reduce sales volume by 10%	4%
10% product cost excess	4%
30% development project budget overrun	2%

Source: Based on Reinertsen (1983).

reported the figures shown in Table 7.2 for how the profitability a laser printer project by Hewlett Packard would be affected by various issues in the development process.

The message is compelling and, perhaps, surprising. These figures or *sensitivities* are often quoted to emphasize the importance of time in product development. However, they must be treated with care because they apply to a particular case: the product lifetime was five years; the market was growing at 20 per cent a year; and prices falling by 12 per cent a year. A different set of assumptions leads to quite different conclusions. For example, we calculate that a project to reduce the cost of a product by 30 per cent, in a basically static market with static pricing, shows the sensitivities shown in Table 7.3, assuming a gross margin of 50 per cent and a product lifetime of five years. In this case, the profitability of the project would be much more sensitive to product quality and cost than to the time taken. It is clearly very important to understand the actual sensitivities for each particular project.

Managers need to know the key sensitivities as early as possible because they will affect the whole conduct and emphasis of the project. In the example above the trade-off between time and development cost very much favours spending extra money to speed the project whenever the chance arises. In the second, managers will concentrate particularly on not jeopardising selling price. If time

Table 7.3   Project trade-offs on different assumptions (see text)

Issue	Reduction in profit
Product introduced 6 months late	10%
Quality problems reduce selling price by 10%	66%
Compatibility problems reduce sales volume by 10%	10%
10% product cost excess	23%
30% development project budget overrun	2%

is a key issue, it must be remembered that the clock starts ticking the moment the project is conceived so speed in decision-making at the start is just as important as speed in implementation. Time lost in the fuzzy front end is the same as time lost at the launch. Some managers find that punchy slogans such as 'every day is 20k' or 'a dollar on the cost is a million lost' help to keep the key sensitivities of a project in the minds of the team.

Box case 7.3   Organon – NPD, demand and the supply chain[13]

Organon is the human healthcare division of AkzoNobel, a Dutch multinational. Organon creates, produces and markets prescription drugs mainly for reproductive medicine, psychiatry and anaesthesia. Although the majority of its product development is concentrated in The Netherlands, the company has 10 manufacturing sites and over 12,000 employees around the globe, required to provide fast and efficient service to its geographical markets. Organon has learned to plan for demand uncertainty during NPD, to integrate the needs of its manufacturing plants into its product planning process and to design the supply chain alongside the product development.

The main risks related to the uncertain demand for pharmaceuticals are overcapacity and lost sales. It is expensive to set up pharmaceutical production facilities and, on the one hand, overcapacity must be avoided. On the other hand, a product being unavailable reduces sales and brings a loss in market share that can seldom be recovered. Consequently, Organon product launch plans include different sales scenarios: best, expected, and worst cases. Based on these sales scenarios, a number of supply-chain design options (including the suppliers to be used worldwide, the manufacturing sites to be used and its inventory strategies, and the delivery logistics selected) are prepared. Each supply-chain design option is quantitatively evaluated on five criteria: finance, risk, available resources, flexibility to scale production up and down, and (interestingly) confidence in the assumptions. 'Early in the NPD process we have added demand and supply scenario planning. We review it regularly and have increased our overall success with product innovations. It is important not only to have an excellent product but also to match it with the best supply chain design. It is not easy as you are dealing often with high uncertainties. Since we have started assessing our confidence in the forecasted figures, we have increased the quality of our decisions. As a result, we can avoid over-capacity whilst minimizing lost sales', says Erik Hoppenbrouwer, Supply Chain Director.

Managing the Early Stages

One of the most important things that distinguishes an innovation project from any other is the amount of time and effort that may be spent in the concept and design phases acquiring and organizing the information needed to do the job and deciding how to turn the customer's needs into an effective product or service. The more innovative the project, the more learning will be necessary and the more work will go into it. Ideally most of the learning is done in the early phases, but in innovation projects some key facts may only be available late in the day; and unexpected things, both good and bad may happen at any time. The planning and management of the project should not just adapt to learning distributed throughout the project but should be set up from the start to expect it.

Linking Customer Expectations to Design

Customers will usually express their needs in terms of the experience they are seeking. These may be quite different from the terms used by the supplier to describe the process of delivering it. A customer will go to a restaurant in search of a particular dining experience, perhaps a convenient or exciting or exotic one; but the chef does not cook an experience any more than the waiter lays one out on the table. The customer's experience is the result of many activities by the staff of the restaurant, some subtle such as choosing the menu and some mundane, like preparing vegetables or arranging tables. Each has to be done in a particular way to produce the desired effect – a good service product and an effective augmentation (Chapter 3). An important first step in designing an innovation is to ensure that the elements all contribute effectively to satisfying the customer. An effective tool for this is *Quality Function Deployment* (QFD).

The first step in QFD is to understand the customer's needs and desires from their point of view. Techniques such as hidden needs analysis, empathic design, repertory grids, contextual interviews and lead user consultation may be used, as described in Chapter 5. The needs elicited by these studies are summarized into simple statements in the language the customer might use. They are likely to be subjective, qualitative and non-technical. Thus the customer's perspective for a car might include 'good roadholding' and 'economical to run' but would say nothing about the engineering needed to achieve these. For an office-cleaning service the customer may require: 'always looks clean' and 'my things never disturbed' but might not say how often the cleaning would be done, how many people would be required or what training they should have.

The purpose of QFD is to ensure that it is the customer's needs (and not technical elegance, convenience, lowest price or anything else) that drive the choices that are made in the design process. These needs, and the responses of the organization to them are assembled into what is known as the *House of Quality*. In its most complete form the house can have as many as eight sections, or *rooms*, but we use only five here for the purposes of illustration (Figure 7.6). More complete treatments are to be found in the work of Don Clausing of MIT,[14] and others.[15]

The first room of the House of Quality contains the customer requirements. Taking the final stages of a postal delivery service as an example, these might be:

❑ Reliable.
❑ Daily delivery.
❑ Does not damage mail.

Figure 7.6 **The House of Quality**

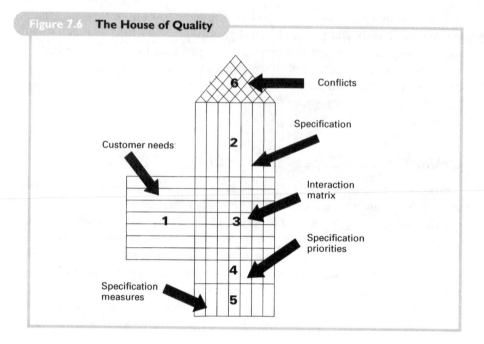

▶ Easy to divert mail when I move.

▶ Arrangements for handling parcels when nobody at home.

▶ Low cost.

These requirements are unlikely to be all equally important to the customer so it is convenient to allocate a weighting to them to express this. At this point the Kano analysis of features into basic, performance and excitement categories (see Chapter 4) is useful in deciding how important various levels of performance will be.[16]

The second room contains the key performance features of the product or process from the point of view of the organization providing it. For the postal service these might include:

▶ Local distribution points.

▶ Enough local delivery staff.

▶ Local transport.

▶ Address reading system.

▶ Sorting.

▶ Customer profile information.

The impact of each element of the product performance on the customer need is now assessed and noted in the cell of room 3 where the two intersect. It is usual to allow three levels of impact, which we represent in Figure 7.7 with one, two or three stars. Scores out of 10 are also used. This interaction matrix shows at once which features of the performance contribute most to customer satisfaction. The

Figure 7.7   Analysis of local postal delivery service

		Local distribution depots	Staff quality + incentives	Local transport	Address reading system	Sorting process	Customer profile info.	Low cost
Reliable	7	*	*		*	***		
Daily delivery	10	**		*	**			
Mail not damaged	9		***	**				
Mail can be diverted	5						***	
Low cost	6							***
Arrangements for absence	4	*	**				***	
		41	100	73	37	63	81	54
		Within 6 miles	Test score > 70%	95% availability	99.8%	99.3%	Central	

most important must be given priority in the design phase and those with low impact are candidates for elimination.

This prioritization can be made more precise by assessing the priorities of the customer needs (shown alongside them in Figure 7.7) and allocating scores for the impacts. These figures are multiplied together for each need and the results are added to give overall importance scores for the various features. It is conventional[17] to give 9 for a high impact, 3 for a medium and 1 for low in order to avoid the situation where a feature providing a very minor impact on several needs is rated more highly than one giving outstanding benefits to only one or two. In Figure 7.7 these priority scores are recorded in room 5.

The final part of the House of Quality is the sixth room or *roof*. Here any conflicts between features are recorded (Figure 7.8). For example in the postal system case it may not be possible to install address-reading equipment in local depots; and holding customer profile information may conflict with the need for low cost. These conflicts cannot be resolved within existing thinking so further innovation is needed. This part of the house points out where exploratory work may be valuable to try and resolve the conflicts.

Figure 7.8 **Conflict between features in QFD**

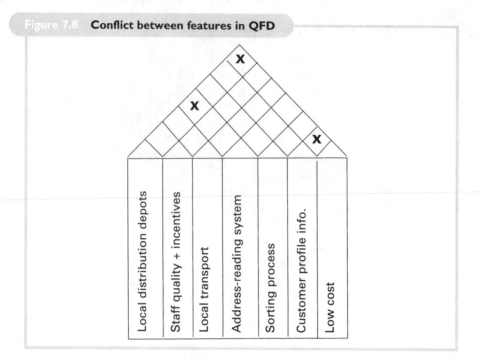

Managing Information in the Design Phase

The tasks in any project usually have to be done in some logical order, as we have already seen. What is often forgotten is that the generation of information in a project has a structure of its own, which is not necessarily the same as the structure of the tasks. The body of a car must be made, and perhaps designed, before the engine and seats that go in it, but the size and weight of the parts also affects the bodywork. Design work done at one stage may have to be adjusted in the light of decisions made later on in related parts. The Design Structure Matrix[18] (it should perhaps be called the Information Structure Matrix) is a simple and powerful tool for checking the order in which information is acquired in the course of a project and helping to minimize the amount of costly iteration that may be needed. It also, as we shall see, has something to say about team organization. As the name suggests it was invented to help in the design of hardware and software products but it applies equally well to any project where some planning or design tasks depend on information from others.

A design structure matrix shows the design tasks in a project along both axes, in the order in which it is proposed to do them, starting at the top left corner. Then on the line corresponding to each of these work packages a cross is put in any column corresponding to a package that will generate information required for successful completion of the task being considered (see Figure 7.9). Here we see that design task E requires information that will be generated by tasks B and C, while task F will require information from tasks A, C, G and H.

Figure 7.9 Schematic design structure matrix

		A	B	C	D	E	F	G	H	J
		Information required from:								
T	A	■								
	B	x	■							x
	C	x		■	x					
a	D	x	x		■					
s	E		x	x		■				
k	F	x		x			■	x	x	
	G	x			x		x	■	x	
	H				x		x	x	■	
	J		x		x		x			■

This matrix shows very quickly where the communication problems will arise in this project. Most of the work packages are correctly ordered because they require only information that comes from tasks that come before them. They have crosses below the diagonal. However, some – B, C, F and G in this example – have crosses above the diagonal, which signals that they rely on information that will be generated by packages that still have to be done. There is feedback between the tasks, which means that they may have to be revised, possibly more than once, as the facts become available. What is to be done about these? There are five possible approaches:

1 *Change the order of tasks*. The problem with task C can be overcome by simply doing it after task D, instead of beforehand. Changing the order causes no problems because D does not require information from C. However, there is no such simple solution for the information needs of tasks B and F; for them other approaches are needed.
2 *Concurrent working*. Tasks F, G and H all need information from each other and there is no ideal order in which to do them. For example, F requires information from G and H so if is done first it will have to be revised when they are done. But that revision may in turn cause changes to G and H, because they use information from F, and so on. The teams involved must work closely together exchanging information regularly as their parts of the project evolve. Ideally they would work physically together during that part of the project so that they can deal with the trade-offs and interactions quickly, face-to-face. If that is not possible then at least they must set up very close and regular communications, forming a 'virtual team', for the duration of that part of the project.

3 *Add extra, information-generating, tasks.* Task B needs information from a much later activity, J – and itself informs many later activities. It may be possible to split task J into two parts: one to be done early on, to release the information required by B, while the rest retains its natural timing. For example, suppose task J is the design of a piece of electronics and B the design of the cooling system for a product that contains it, among other items. Task B requires information about the heat generated by the electronics and this might be worked out separately before the detailed design is done. Adding this extra step removes J from above the diagonal and avoids iteration.

4 *Move staff between tasks.* An informal alternative to the last may be to second a member of the team working on task J to team B to help the them work out what cooling is needed, without making a formal task of it.

5 *Use 'working assumptions'.* As a final resort, the team working on an early task may have to make working assumptions that allow the project to continue. The assumptions may not be optimum but they can be chosen conservatively so that they will not have to be changed later. So in the above example the cooling system could be 'over-designed' so as to have enough capacity for any plausible electronics, sacrificing cost for speed of implementation. For a more closely optimised design the working assumption would have to be refined as the project goes on, requiring some degree of reworking. The project manager must make careful decisions about just how much optimization is worthwhile. Here, too, close communication throughout the team is vital.

Clearly the DSM is a more sophisticated form of the precedence list. The extra complication is worthwhile because there are much greater opportunities for optimization where the task is to generate information, than in one that produces physical results. Most of the approaches just listed (except the first) are not options when doing physical tasks.

Project Risks

The characteristic that most distinguishes innovation projects from others is their level of uncertainty, so ways of assessing and addressing risks must come high on the list of techniques for managing innovation projects.

Risk considerations enter in R&D management both in the initial selection of the project and in its subsequent management. These two aspects overlap because the resolution of the uncertainties as the project unfolds may cause reassessment of whether it is right to continue as planned. The continuing process of choosing a group of projects and reevaluating the choice – portfolio management – was covered in Chapter 6. Managing the risks within a particular project is an aspect of project management.

Early attention to risks pays dividends and 30–40 per cent reductions in costs and lead times were reported in R&D projects at Toyota.[19] Other researchers found similar results at Xerox.[20]

Project risk management occurs in four stages:[21]

1   *Appraisal.* Here the project manager and his team set out to understand the range of risks the project faces, to assess their impact, and to estimate how likely they are to come about. When this is done the team has a broad picture of the uncertainties inherent in the task and the plausible range of outcomes that they may face. The term *gross risk* is sometimes used for the downside risk at this stage.

2   *Mitigation.* Now the team makes plans to reduce or avert the more prominent risks. The plans may include 'fall-back positions': alternatives to be followed if things go wrong. Not every uncertainty can be addressed so management judgement is needed to decide priorities. The downside risk after mitigation is known as the *net risk.*

3   *Decision.* Now comes the decision whether to proceed with the project at all, in the light of the range of likely outcomes that are now apparent. At this stage the project can no longer be considered in isolation from everything else going on in the company. It is part of a portfolio of opportunities and must be compared to other projects in terms of how profitable a use it makes of scarce resources and how it advances the broader aims of the company. See Chapter 6.

4   *Review.* The previous three steps should be reviewed as the project progresses and new facts, good and bad, come to light.

Issues in Assessing Project Risks

Research shows that it is not easy to obtain a complete and objective assessment of the risks facing a project.[22] We have already observed in our discussion of portfolio management in Chapter 6 how important it is to have a carefully structured process to ensure that all possible areas of risk are addressed and that interpersonal issues do not affect objectivity. Three aspects are important:

▸   Avoid relying too much on individuals. Relevant knowledge and experience is likely to be spread among several people and much may be historic in nature. Furthermore, people differ in their tolerance of risk and their ability to estimate probabilities.[23] Therefore the best estimates are likely to come from a well-chosen group rather than an individual, however experienced. Various researchers have described how a large group is often more effective than even the most skilled individuals at estimating uncertain facts or predicting future events.[24] Intuition comes from accumulated experience; but the more novel the situation the less complete must be the experience and hence the intuition of any one person, however wise. So it is important to gather inputs from a range of people, especially of course those involved with the project.

▸   Ensure that all types of risk are considered: Technical, Operational, Commercial and Financial. Check lists can be very helpful in reminding people of problems encountered on previous projects and ensuring that all

Table 7.4   Checklist of marketing risks

Risk element	
Target market clearly defined and agreed	
Market targets based on convincing research data	
Direct feedback from key customers documented	
Specification meets consumer standards	
Fits consumer habits and/or conditions	
Non-intended use by customers adequately anticipated	
Communication about new product can be based on realistic product claims	
Target consumers' attitudes will remain stable during development period	
Product will provide easy-in-use advantages compared with the competition	
Niche marketing available if required.	

Source: After Keizer, Halman and Song (2002).

relevant areas of risk are considered. Table 7.4 gives examples of some of the topics in a check list of marketing risks used successfully in Philips and Unilever's 'Risk Diagnosing Methodology'.[25] *Anchored scales*[26] that include statements clarifying what is meant by high, medium or low risk in the various factors help align participants' approaches to scoring (see Chapter 6).

☐ Allow participants in the risk-appraisal process to raise concerns anony-mously. Many people are unwilling to express their misgivings publicly for fear of appearing to be critical of others (especially of a senior or charismatic manager) or to lack full-hearted commitment to the project. The opinion of a group may be unduly influenced by particular members who have high status, a strong personality, or who simply talk more than the others. This malign effect was well-documented in the decision-making in the Columbia space shuttle disaster.[27] Furthermore, groups of people working closely together show a tendency to seek consensus at the expense of realism. Janis[28] has termed this effect 'groupthink' and has argued that many disastrous political decisions, such as the invasion of Cuba by the USA at the Bay of Pigs, arise from the mutually-support-ive overconfidence that can arise in small, highly-motivated groups. A degree of confidentiality is therefore helpful in ensuring that everyone speaks his or her mind – for example using an independent person to collect and collate responses.[29] The 'Delphi' forecasting approach[30] has a similar emphasis on insulating individuals from the effects of group interactions.

Box case 7.4   Bank of America – testing service innovation[31]

The banking sector used to be viewed as not very innovative, but over the last decade this view has been seen to be incorrect. Following a series of mergers and acquisitions in the United States in the 1990s, banks are facing a period where growth will largely only be possible through retaining existing customers and taking them from competitors. When a new Chief Executive joined Bank of America in 1999 he recognized this and quickly formed a new Innovation and Development Team (IDT), tasked with spearheading new services and delivery mechanisms. The IDT reviewed ideas for innovations but had the foresight to realize that testing new services and delivery mechanisms is just as important as making physical prototypes is for tangible products. Initial testing was made possible by setting up a mock branch created by the IDT at headquarters. However, experimentation to determine the reaction of real customers was the next step.

Extensive testing was made possible by selecting over 20 of the Bank's branches in Atlanta as test branches. These were equipped with new systems and the staff received training on the test services that would be offered in parallel to the normal range of services. Through 'live' testing, including the careful monitoring of customers' reactions, the Bank has been able to swiftly determine the viability of new services.

The staff members at the test branches were initially highly motivated to support the development of new services. However, problems of staff motivation arose soon afterwards. Staff members are normally paid on a commission basis and so they found that their incomes were dropping significantly because of the time that they had to spend being trained on the new services being tested. This was solved by putting the staff on a fixed salary but this caused friction with staff at other branches who felt they were under more pressure on commission. It also meant that the new services under test were not linked to tellers' commission, as were all the existing products at the Bank.

Bank of America's experiences demonstrate two main tenets of new service development. Firstly, it shows the need to iron out design problems in a realistic setting off-line, before moving to interact with customers. Secondly, it shows that the motivation of employees can be a key consideration in the design of new service products.

The FMEA Process

Failure Mode and Effect Analysis (FMEA)[32] is a disciplined technique designed to produce an overall ranking of risks considering both their likelihood and their possible effects. It is most widely used for exploring the failure modes of tangible products but it can equally well be applied to a new process or service. With minor adjustments, which we consider below, it is also useful for appraising the risks to an innovation project. When it is applied to products and services, every part of the product or step in the process is assessed in detail to determine all the ways in which it might fail. (It is assumed from the outset that failure is always possible; the point is to find out which failures are severe enough and likely enough to warrant attention). Each failure mode is then ascribed a score of 1–10 according to how likely it is to happen and a further score of 1–10 according to the severity of the impact it would have if it did. A third score is often used to indicate the likelihood that the cause of failure can be detected. The product of the scores is the *Risk Priority Score*, which gives an overall indication of the risk posed by that element. An example of such an analysis is given in Table 7.5.

Once the risks have been prioritized in this way the project team puts together action plans aimed at reducing them all below an acceptable value. The same methodology can be used to appraise the risks facing a project but with one important difference. Any likely failures of a service or product must be dealt with before it is released to the customer, whereas in a project it may be quite possible to deal with problems as the work goes on. It is an entirely different thing to say (as one might in considering a product): 'there is a risk that the fuel

Table 7.5 FMEA analysis applied to a supermarket checkout point (in part)

Failure mode	Likelihood	Severity in impact	Failure to detect	Risk priority score	Action
No bar code on product	5	2	4	40	Review process. Consider reward for detection
Bar code reader fails	1	2	1	2	
Product wrongly recorded/ priced in computer system	3	8	6	144	Special project required
Item not on computer	5	2	1	10	
Assistant enters same item twice	2	8	7	112	Investigate software prompt.
Assistant fails to enter item	2	2	9	36	Training
Out of bags	4	8	1	32	Plenty of spares
Item dropped or broken	6	6	1	36	Review flooring

pipe will fracture during use' and saying (for a project) 'there is a risk that the pressure in the fuel pipe will turn out to be much higher than currently expected'. The first case is certainly a serious matter. The second may simply involve a trivial change to a stronger pipe or it may require extensive alterations to many components, which may (or may not) jeopardise the whole project. So in doing risk assessments in projects it is important to consider not only the impact of the problem and how likely it is to arise but also whether there is likely to be scope to deal with it within the project. The 'probability of detection' is appropriately replaced by 'probability that the risk can be dealt with in time'.[33]

In addressing project risks any 'show-stoppers' that might cause the total failure of the project should be tackled first (equivalent to the convention in FMEA of assigning the highest priority to safety threats). However, this is not always possible because some parts of the project cannot be tackled until others have been completed.

Box case 7.5   Fiat Iveco – testing products to the extreme

Iveco is the arm of Fiat responsible for manufacturing and marketing commercial and industrial vehicles, buses and diesel engines. The company is thirty years old and is organized around business units: light commercial vehicles, trucks, buses, powertrain and special vehicles. It was founded through the merger of various European truck manufacturers and its name is derived from *I*nternational *V*ehicle *C*ompany. In a typical year, Fiat Iveco produces 160,000 trucks across the four business units and 400,000 diesel engines are sold worldwide. The company's headquarters are in Torino and it has a number of engineering and manufacturing facilities in Europe.

Truck drivers live in their vehicles on long journeys and so part of developing a vehicle is designing a living space. Massimo Fumarola, the Platform Development Manager for trucks says, 'you just cannot understand truckers' needs from the results of a survey or focus group. These guys are demanding because their work is extremely demanding'. To really understand truck drivers' needs, Fumarola moved his whole marketing team for two weeks to a motorway truck stop just south of the Alps. His people had extensive contact with drivers all hours of the day. 'We lived with the truckers for two weeks, literally not going home at night. We accompanied drivers on journeys, ate with them, slept in trucks and collected a mountain of ideas . . . now our challenge is to find ways of incorporating these ideas into the next product'.

Trucks are used relentlessly and so the design must be robust. One of Iveco's heavy trucks was recently serviced and had an incredible 250,000 km 'on the clock' after only one year (compared to the industry average of 120,000 km per year). This vehicle is used for non-stop international runs across Western Europe with different drivers working shifts. Iveco uses such vehicles as a test-bed for ideas. Such demanding usage leads to a vast array of design requirements.

Many manufacturers design the next generation product by focusing on what the users' needs will be at the time of the product introduction. 'We have learnt to look further into the future, as our product life cycles are long. So we design products with features that will still be relevant in the market towards the end of the product life cycle, not just at the time of introduction – that can mean thinking 20 years ahead', says Fumarola. He has recently moved from trucks and is working at Iveco's Engine Business Unit but finds many of the issues similar: 'In both business units effective new product development is crucial – but the real challenge is being innovative in every-thing we do, throughout our business, and in every process'.

Team Structure and Organization

The two extreme ways of organizing an innovation project have been termed[34] the *Functional* and the *Autonomous* team structures. The first is in a sense not a team at all: the project is passed in sequence from one department to another, each manager taking responsibility for their own phase and then passing it to the next one in the chain. This is often pejoratively described as the 'over the wall' approach. The autonomous team (sometimes also called a *skunk works*[35]) is the opposite. Here a quite separate team is set up to do the job with its own management and resources and full powers to do whatever is necessary to achieve the agreed result, even including, in some cases, writing its own rule book. The working of such a team is dramatically described in Tracey Kidder's book *The Soul of the New Machine*.[36] There are several possibilities between these extremes. We discuss the advantages and disadvantages of the various types of organization in more detail in Chapter 8.

The Need for Cross-Functional Working

The 'over the wall' approach to projects impedes feedback between parts of the project and greatly hinders cooperation between people working on different aspects. This is particularly undesirable in the concept and planning phases because, as our discussion of the design structure matrix has shown, this forces teams working on the earlier phases to resort to 'working assumptions' about the needs of later ones. Such assumptions usually lead to an inefficient and unnecessarily expensive design. Furthermore, if something unexpected arises late on in the work the feedback processes are not in place to allow rapid reaction.

The solution is to accept from the start that feedback between the various parts of the project is likely and desirable, and to organize with this in mind using cross-functional teams (see Chapter 8). Such teams are particularly impor-tant in service organizations, where too many companies omit to bring all func-tional areas into the development of new products (and consequently face problems).

Box case 7.6 Cruise Liners – new service development[37]

The world cruise business is 8 million guests per year, and there are approximately 150 luxury cruise liners currently sailing the world's oceans. A typical guest invests $2,500 for seven nights and the clientele is conservative. Synthiea Kaldi is a former Guest Relations Manager with six years' experience in the industry, working for two of the most successful operators. One of these operators commissioned a new liner and Kaldi's experience on that project shows the critical importance of a cross-functional team being involved from the beginning if the service concept is to be successful. The problems encountered with the design of the new ship mean that the cruise operator involved is best left anonymous.

'What was good was that the whole service team came together to discuss the new liner as it was being built. Looking back, though, not enough time was spent to iron out problems, and discussing blueprints wasn't a very effective way to recognize the issues. We did see some things that had been forgotten such as safety deposit boxes. Fortunately these could still be installed. Other basics were also missing, such as locking cash drawers in the reception desk for the Front Desk Attendants. These were later added but they were never as secure as desired', says Kaldi. Customers also noticed the lack of drawer space leading to a regular complaint about the staterooms.

'One of the attributes of the new cruise concept was the "Food Court". This buffet restaurant was designed to give passengers fast and efficient service in pleasant surroundings. However, it was not as successful as hoped due to a number of factors. The limited number of drink stations slowed the overall service considerably. A serious issue was that the trolleys to bring the food efficiently from the galley, many decks below, did not fit in the lift'. Worse still, one of the vents into a main guest corridor captured the sewage type odour from the water processing plant many decks below. This led to guests perceiving the ship as not being as new or clean as it really was. ' "Line of sight" issues in the show lounge were identified too late, although most were remedied before the ship went into service. Again, this was not spotted from the blueprints and it cost the company hundreds of thousands of dollars as each seat had to be individually elevated and tilted to give a good view of the stage'. Once the ship was in service, it was realized that the signage for the toilets, while visible to wheelchair bound guests, was not visible to those who were standing. 'It quickly became apparent to the team that line of sight issues are nearly impossible to identify from blueprints and the ship designers should have found a better way to deal with this', states Kaldi.

Fortunately, she says, there were also some notable successes built on some good designs for the servicescape. The disco was intended to draw the younger, late-night crowd and its decoration, which was pure 1960s, was very effective at achieving this. 'And the ambience chosen for the alternative restaurant, which was only available upon reservation at an additional charge, worked so well that the guests actually felt they weren't paying enough for the experience! It really shows how getting the design right is crucial to the service concept.'

The more innovative a project is, the more it needs strong project management and dedicated teamwork. A model tending towards the Functional is fine for managing incremental improvements in processes or products where the Design Structure matrix shows that the tasks can probably mostly be done in an orderly sequence. But if many of the tasks are going to require iteration, team members will spend a lot of time working closely together, so a more tightly-knit team makes sense. More important, unexpected opportunities or setbacks may mean that tasks that could previously be done in isolation suddenly need intensive cooperation with other departments. Such changes will obviously need strong project leadership, so the more likely they are, the more autonomous the team will need to be.

Much has been written about the benefits of cross-functional teams in managing innovation projects and particularly new product introductions (the terms *concurrent engineering* and *simultaneous engineering* are used to describe the same management practice). For example, Ellis[38] states that using concurrent techniques generated improvements of 60 per cent in design lead-time, 40 per cent in manufacturing cost, 80 per cent in scrap/rework and over 90 per cent in post-launch design changes. These arise from:

▢ Avoiding changes and rework in the later stages of the project by ensuring that the ideas and contributions of everyone involved are available from the start.
▢ Avoiding delay and uncertainty as the project moves through the organization by giving all the participants the chance for full physical and psychological preparation for the parts they have to play.
▢ Making trade-offs for the benefit of the project as a whole rather than maximizing one part at the expense of another.
▢ Giving the best chance to adapt the project to unforeseen events.
▢ Maximizing the sense of commitment and ownership of all concerned.

Despite the many eulogies published in management magazines, cross-functional teams are difficult to run effectively. In Chapter 8 we will discuss ways to make them work well.

Managing an Innovation Department

Many companies rightly see innovation not as a 'one-off' event but as a continuing need and so they look for management processes designed to help them manage a stream of projects, some of them simultaneously.[39] New product introduction (NPI) is an example of such a project stream and much of the most influential work in the field has been done in the context of managing the R&D function.[40,41] The PACE process promoted by Michael McGrath[42] and the Stagegate® of Robert Cooper[43] of McMaster University have been particularly influential.

Managers should install a specific process for managing innovation projects for several reasons: as an aid to monitoring progress; to ensure that priorities are regularly reviewed (and, if necessary, changed); to improve communication; and as a vehicle for learning and improvement.

Phase Gates

The basic control and standardization in the management process is imposed through the use of milestones, or *gates*. Each gate is the occasion for a careful and formal review of the project, bringing together the experience and expertise of the organization. Phase review meetings are an important part of the innovation management process for several reasons:

1 They enable, even force, a formal and objective review of progress, which serves to identify problems and plan the next steps.
2 They give management an opportunity to update their understanding of the aims and impacts of each project.
3 They give an opportunity to review the environment of the project to check if there have been any changes that might affect its viability.
4 Finally, they are formal decision points: if all is well, formal approval is given to go on to the next phase; if not, the project is stopped, or at least delayed until the deficiencies are corrected. For this reason the process is often called a *Phase Review* or *Stage Gate*.[44]

A phase-gate process must operate over all the stages of a project, from concept to delivery. How many phases there should be depends on the needs of the organization, the speed and complexity of the projects and to some extent the strength of the project management function. Weaker project organizations can be helped by a more formal process. Clearly, more gates allow closer scrutiny but at the expense of time spent by the teams in preparing for the review meetings and by senior management attending them for every project. When adopting phase gates for the first time, companies often opt for a relatively large number; we have seen 12- or even 14-phase processes. Experience seems to lead towards simplicity, however, and a current consensus favours somewhere between four and eight phases for most purposes. Standard process designs are available in the literature with suggestions for what should be expected by each phase.[45,46] These are useful but should be used only as a framework. The formal process and the check-lists that back it up, must suit the company and, crucially, must evolve to reflect and embody the learning carried over from project to project. Figure 7.10 illustrates the phase-gate process used by one company, Domino Printing Sciences. The activities expected in each phase are summarized in the upper section, and the scope of the reviews at each gate are shown in summary below.

Management Process at the Gates

One key role of a phase-gate process is to prevent projects rolling steadily forward when they actually contain serious problems not addressed and perhaps

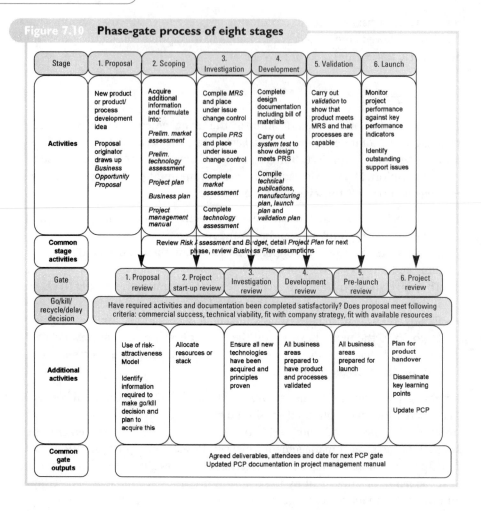

Figure 7.10 Phase-gate process of eight stages

Stage	1. Proposal	2. Scoping	3. Investigation	4. Development	5. Validation	6. Launch
Activities	New product or product/process development idea Proposal originator draws up Business Opportunity Proposal	Acquire additional information and formulate into: *Prelim. market assessment* *Prelim. technology assessment* Project plan Business plan Project management manual	Compile *MRS* and place under issue change control Compile *PRS* and place under issue change control Complete market assessment Complete technology assessment	Complete design documentation including bill of materials Carry out *system test* to show design meets PRS Compile technical publications, manufacturing plan, launch plan and validation plan	Carry out *validation* to show that product meets MRS and that processes are capable	Monitor project performance against key performance indicators Identify outstanding support issues

Common stage activities	Review *Risk assessment* and *Budget*, detail *Project Plan* for next phase, review *Business Plan* assumptions

Gate	1. Proposal review	2. Project start-up review	3. Investigation review	4. Development review	5. Pre-launch review	6. Project review

Go/kill/ recycle/delay decision	Have required activities and documentation been completed satisfactorily? Does proposal meet following criteria: commercial success, technical viability, fit with company strategy, fit with available resources

Additional activities	Use of risk-attractiveness Model Identify information required to make go/kill decision and plan to acquire this	Allocate resources or stack	Ensure all new technologies have been acquired and principles proven	All business areas prepared to have product and processes validated	All business areas prepared for launch	Plan for product handover Disseminate key learning points Update PCP

Common gate outputs	Agreed deliverables, attendees and date for next PCP gate Updated PCP documentation in project management manual

not fully acknowledged. This common problem is well-acknowledged by practitioners and requires firm management actions to control it. It is, of course, a manifestation of the tendencies such as 'groupthink' that make risk appraisal so difficult.

A powerful way to avoid overconfidence is the *peer review*. This practice, originally known as a *design review* is widely used by electronic hardware designers among others. It brings in a team of colleagues from outside the project to do an in-depth review with the aim of picking up any problems that the team may have missed, 'before', as one engineer put it, 'Mother Nature tells us herself'. Design reviews are a development of the old software engineering practice of 'code reading' in which programmers go carefully through each other's work to find the errors of logic that the writer himself may miss time after time. The members of the reviewing team do not take over, or even share, responsibility for the work. Their job is only to offer advice for the responsible team to use as it sees fit. The role of managers is to check that the reviews happen but otherwise to stand clear.

Design reviews should be built into the phase gates so they are expected as a matter of course at the critical points, not just demanded *ad hoc* when management becomes suspicious.

In addition to the results of peer reviews, other documents or evidence of progress may be required at phase gates. Test results, market survey reports, financial analyses, marketing plans and so on may be expected, and if not produced may stop the progress of the project. The formality of the occasion forces everyone to pause, take stock and to address difficult questions. Senior managers can probe for weaknesses and ask for proofs and demonstrations of key aspects of the project. In doing so they assure themselves that the project is on track; and in giving the formal go-ahead for the next phase they also assure the project team of their continuing support.

Improving and Maturing the Management Process

A well-designed phase-gate process is not only a tool for management control, but a repository of learning about managing innovation projects in the particular organization. The documents or other proofs of progress that are called for at each gate will be those relevant to the particular business. Some, such as sales forecasts, financial plans, test results and so on will be mandatory because they apply to all projects but there is also an important place in the phase-gate documentation for more informal notes that capture the experience from past projects. This kind of learning is too valuable to be left only in the memories of those who were there at the time, but too detailed to appear on the agenda of a formal review with the CEO. An advisory check-list or an advice file is the way to capture it and to ensure that learning from the past is really carried forward. Hewlett-Packard uses video to capture interviews with project managers who have experiences, good or bad, that may help managers of projects arriving at a particular gate. We cover the subject of learning from projects in more depth in Chapter 9.

A good innovation management process may be written down very readily but it needs steady effort and improvement[47,48] for it to become fully embedded in the organization. 'Every company that really improves the new product development process goes through evolutionary stages'.[49] Table 7.6 shows the kind of maturity process that may be expected.[50]

A more detailed analysis of how the component parts of the process may mature is to be found in McGrath 1996.[52]

Managing Collaborations

As technology and business processes become more sophisticated, companies are driven to concentrate on their core competences and to outsource an increasing range of activities.[53] In the words of Frank Corrubba, chief technology officer of Philips: 'In this wonderful world of short lifecycles, eroding margins, dynamic economies and competitors coming out of the woodwork . . . no one company

Table 7.6   **Maturity of a product development process[51]**

Stage	Characteristics
1	No formal NPI process – Resource conflicts across projects – No documented procedure – Successful outcomes due to heroics and individual skill – Frequent time-cost overruns and rework
2	A process exists, but – It is not respected and is used inconsistently – It is often ignored by project teams – It is over-bureaucratic and seen as a burden not an aid – Still frequent overruns and rework
3	Process used and understood – Clear roles and responsibilities – Process moderately well understood by all – It is not bureaucratic – It supports consistent new product innovation
4	Continuous process improvement – Metrics exist for performance of products and process – Regular process reviews – Learning stimulated at all stages of development and disseminated to other teams – Process is culturally ingrained and understood across the business

can have all the core competencies necessary to introduce new products in a timely way'.[54] William Joy of Sun Microsystems says simply 'Not all the smart people work for Sun'.[55] The ability to manage alliances is an increasingly important competence for companies to acquire.[56] The possibilities for collaboration range from simple subcontract, through joint development projects and licensing, to joint ventures, equity participation and acquisition.[57]

Strategic issues

Clearly there can be great advantages in incorporating the cutting-edge capabilities of other organizations into one's service or product offering (indeed there may be little choice). However, the loss of control that this implies may be a problem in the longer run. IBM's decision to outsource most of the components of its PC was hailed at the time as an object lesson in distributed innovation, and it certainly enabled them to move quickly into a market they had previously neglected. In the long run, however, it meant that they lost control of the design and they are now no longer a dominant player. Clearly it is important to have a robust strategy for collaboration and outsourcing.[58] Henry Chesbrough and David Teece of the University of California at Berkeley

Figure 7.11 **Choice of outsourcing strategy for different types of innovation**

	Systemic innovation	Autonomous innovation
Competences already exist outside	**DANGER** Allies are required, but beware loss of control	**OUTSOURCE** unless it is a key competitive element in which you have special competence
New competences must be created	**DO IN-HOUSE** if possible but beware emergence of alternative dominant design	**CREATE IN-HOUSE** if there is possibility of long-term competitive advantage. Otherwise ALLY

Source: Derived from Chesborough and Teece (1996).

make a distinction between *autonomous* innovations that affect only part of the product and *systemic* innovations that affect several parts of the design simultaneously.[59] Autonomous innovations can usually be safely and efficiently outsourced – the lamps on a car or the parking arrangements for a supermarket are examples. Systemic innovations on the other hand require coordination among several suppliers and so need to be directed by a single player, who in effect has control of the product itself. The logistics system of a supermarket and the power train of a car are examples. In general this implies that autonomous innovations may be outsourced but systemic ones should be kept in-house if possible. There are caveats however. A company may not wish to relinquish control of an autonomous innovation if it is a particularly important competitive feature and the company has a special competence in it. On the other hand control of systemic innovations is valuable only as long as the underlying design has a chance of emerging as a dominant design (see Chapter 4). Unlike IBM, Apple Computers retained control of the architecture of their product but lost out to the PC standard nevertheless. See Figure 7.11.

Management issues

Collaboration with other organizations in innovation projects is not easy. The problems of choosing partners, partitioning the work between them and managing the relationship are added to the usual issues of innovation management. Pete Fraser, Clare Farrukh and Mike Gregory of Cambridge University list[60] seven key process areas that are important for success in collaboration projects, and at least five of them represent major additional tasks beyond those normally required in innovation projects. Organizations cannot expect to become excellent at all of these at once and there is typically a steady maturing of competence with experience, as we noted above for in-house processes. Table 7.7 shows the seven processes with summary statements indicating typical stages of maturity.

Clear contractual relationships are important in managing collaborations but there are limits to what can be written into a contract to ensure success, especially when there is an element of discovery in the work. Alliances typically fail because operating managers do not make them work, not because contracts are poorly written.[61] For this reason care is needed to ensure that there is a climate of trust and confidence between the partners, that communication is open and frequent, and that the arrangement is clearly understood to be a 'win–win' situation.[62]

Managing Simultaneous Projects

Any project organization other than the independent autonomous team is likely to require some members of staff to work on more than one project at a time. An obvious problem that this raises is that it is easy for individuals to become overloaded if they work for more than one boss, and this is likely to mean that one or more projects will slip. This is not the end of the story, however, as there are two factors that mean that a department, or even an individual, working on many projects tends to be less efficient than expected.

The first factor is the inefficiency that comes from changing from one job to another. Every change needs a period of readjustment, and of 'getting up to speed' with the new task. This may be no more than recalling the details of the new job, but it may involve meetings, visits, even relocation. All this is time wasted. Wheelwright and Clark report[63] their experience that for engineering work the wastage is such that working on four jobs simultaneously halves effectiveness. Their results are shown in detail in Figure 7.12.

Interestingly, the optimum is not necessarily to work on only one project. This is because a person working on a single job may have periods of waiting time if the flow of work is not perfectly scheduled, as is quite likely. However, these figures generally support the intuitive feeling that it is usually better to get on with one task and finish it off than to try and keep lots of balls in the air at the same time.

The other inefficiency that arises from working on multiple projects is more subtle and less well-recognized. It is the time that is wasted in waiting and queuing due to variations in scheduling. This problem would not arise if all the projects were perfectly scheduled so that each individual or department receives a new task at the precise moment when they complete the previous one. But in reality this seldom happens, even if the project plan says it should. Few tasks ever take exactly their allotted time. In a chain of tasks performed one after the

Table 7.7   Maturity stages for the key processes of NPI collaboration

	Level 1	Level 2	Level 3	Level 4
Collaboration strategy	(Not) invented here	Occasional *ad hoc* partnering	Some established partners	Regular review of joint competencies
Structured NPI process	No formal NPI process	A process exists, but not well-used or appreciated	Process used and understood	Continuous NPI process improvement
Task partitioning	Interfaces not well-defined	Modularity considered intuitively	Formal configuration planning	Conscious simultaneous design
Partner selection	Cross fingers and hope. Little structured assessment	Based on word-of-mouth reputation	Good review of technical capabilities	Broad assessment of capabilities
Getting started	Work starts before agreements in place or IPR ownership clear	Contract, but without full buy-in. Problems with resourcing	Agreement in place	All ground rules agreed. Clear role definition. Resources agreed
Partnership management	Misunderstandings. Changes come as an unpleasant surprise. Specs too loose or too constraining	Managed but not championed. Normal project management but no more	Collaboration champions on both sides	Frequent and open communication
Partnership development	'Them and us' attitude. New skills jealously protected	Little effort to improve, but cost of changing partner considered too great	Growing trust and confidence	Mutual trust. Clear sense of 'win–win'. Combined effort to develop joint capabilities

Source: After Fraser *et al.* 2003.

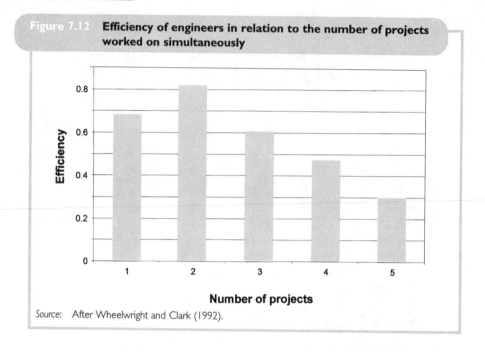

Figure 7.12   **Efficiency of engineers in relation to the number of projects worked on simultaneously**

Source: After Wheelwright and Clark (1992).

other, these uncertainties quickly add up so that in the later part of the chain the actual times have a large random element even though the *average* rate of arrival of tasks may be as planned. The result is that the individual or department experiences periods without work followed by a time of overload. Queues build up and tasks are delayed. This situation is familiar to anyone who has ever queued in a shop or at a motorway toll station. The problem is not a shortage of capacity to deal with customers, on average, but the irregularity with which they arrive.

Service companies seldom have an R&D department and so their problem is that employees responsible for innovation often have to do this in parallel to their normal activities, which tend to take precedence, adding a further random element. The result is that neither the normal operational, nor the longer-term innovation, work is done on time. Service managers need to ensure that sufficient capacity is available and reserved for innovation activities.

Randomness in scheduling means that queues will occasionally form and cause delays even if the flow of work is quite low. In fact there is a trade-off between the length of the queue and the utilization of the worker. In project management terms this means a trade-off between delay to the project and utilization of the time of the people working on it. Maybe the effect is not surprising; but what may come as a shock is just how strong the trade-off is. Figure 7.13 shows that a single person dealing with a stream of tasks arriving at random intervals causes a waiting time equal to the length of each task if she is busy on average 50 per cent of the time, if the tasks also have random lengths. To get the queuing time below 10 per cent, the worker must be prepared to be idle 80 per cent of the time! The delays reduce substantially if

Figure 7.13 **The relationship between the utilization of the server and the delay caused by queuing. The jobs arrive at the server at random intervals (Poisson distribution)**

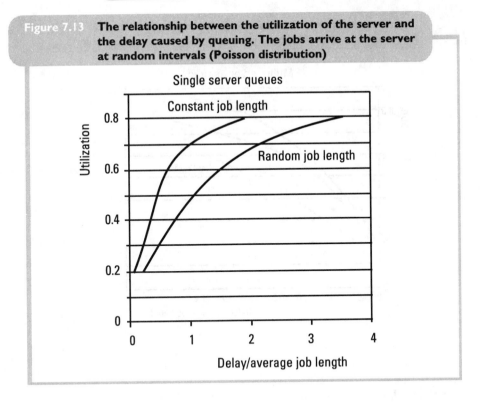

the task lengths are constant so that the only random element is in the scheduling.

There are four things managers can do to reduce scheduling inefficiencies in managing innovation projects:

1   As already discussed, avoid working on too many projects at once. Better to complete one job and move on than to juggle several, with the increased randomness that results (on top of the inefficiency of switching, already noted).

2   Reduce the variability of the duration of jobs as far as possible by detailed planning and preparation and by learning and using the lessons of past projects.[64]

3   Arrange flexibility of capacity, for example by arranging for temporary contract staff to be available when necessary to cover transient peaks.

4   Arrange to share work among members of the project team. Transient loads on any one person can be accommodated without queues and without engaging extra staff if another team member is also able to do the same work. The chance of both people being overloaded simultaneously is less than for either one alone, and with more people the efficiency builds up rapidly as is shown in Figure 7.14. The flexibility allows a much higher utilisation of the team's capacity without introducing delays.

Figure 7.14 **Improvement in utilization by sharing peaks among a number of staff (random job lengths, random scheduling)**

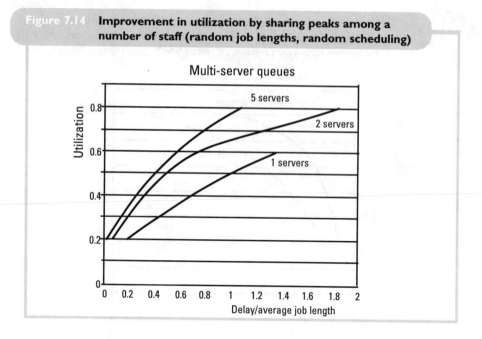

Multi-server queues

Summary

The key points covered in this chapter were:

- Managing the implementation of innovations requires all the normal techniques of effective project management augmented with some specialist processes to control the high levels of uncertainty often encountered.
- The most important of these are the adequate appraisal and treatment of risk and ensuring that the needs of the customer are fully reflected in the design.
- A disciplined management process with clear review points not only helps control and monitoring of progress but facilitates learning so that competence in innovation management can mature over time.
- Managing multiple projects simultaneously demands extra care, especially to avoid queuing.
- Increasingly, innovation projects involve collaboration with others and organizations need to develop competence in doing so effectively while not jeopardizing their strategic position.

Management Recommendations

- Ensure that strong project management processes are in place.
- Set up an appropriate team organization.
- Appraise and manage risk.

- Handle trade-offs when unexpected events occur.
- Manage the flow of information and avoiding unnecessary iterations.
- Install control processes such as the Phase Gate that allow clear management, and facilitate the transfer of learning from one project to another.
- Avoid queues and delays when managing a number of projects simultaneously.
- Develop a competence in managing collaborations with others.

Recommended Reading

(1) Wheelwright, S. C. and Clarke, K. B., *Revolutionizing Product Development* (New York: The Free Press, 1992). Authoritative and readable introduction to the subject.

(2) Cooper, R. G., 'Third-Generation New Product Processes', *Journal of Product Innovation Management*, vol. 11, no. 1, January (1994) pp. 3–14. Summary of the stage-gate process pioneered by Cooper and his co-workers.

(3) Cooper, R. G., 'From Experience. The Invisible Success Factors in Product Innovation', *Journal of Product Innovation Management*, vol. 16 (1999) pp. 115–33. Excellent and practical survey of do's and don'ts in managing innovation projects.

(4) Keizer, J. A., Halman, J. I. M. and Song, M. 'From Experience: Applying the Risk Diagnosing Methodology', *Journal of Product Innovation Management*, vol. 19 (2002) pp. 213–232. Detailed description of a successful process for identifying and managing risks in innovation projects.

Main Case Study   Wipro Techologies, India – optimizing NPD

Before reading this case, consider the following generic innovation management issues:

- What are the issues when new product development is conducted at multiple sites? How can these issues be addressed?
- How can the product development process be optimized through learning from each project?
- What should companies do to stimulate learning that is not just related to specific new product development projects?

Wipro Technologies is a world leader in IT services with global revenues of $1.2 billion. Moreover, it is the world's largest provider of R&D services, with annual revenues of over US$270 million and employing nearly 8,000 engineers in this domain. Founded over 20 years ago, it has eight development centres, including a major facility in Bangalore, India. It provides offshore product engineering for a wide range of companies in both the electronics and service sectors. The industries where it is active include automotive electronics, medical devices, telecommunications, computing (hardware and software), consumer electronics and industrial automation. The company has an approach that it calls 'Extended Engineering', whereby clients can outsource any part of the value chain, including complete product development, product sustenance and support. The demand for cost-effective product development is high, as companies attempt to design products with faster time-to-market and lower costs.

The Problem

The downturn in the world economy has limited the amount of money that companies can invest in their portfolio of innovation projects, and heightened the interest in offshore engineering. Advances in information technology have made it easier to co-ordinate outsourced activities and the number of companies taking this approach has increased significantly. Sachin Mulay, Strategic Marketing Manager for the Embedded and Product Engineering Group, says there are a number of factors driving companies towards offshore engineering. 'Initially, it was the cost advantage that caught people's attention. That is still important, but now there is recognition that offshore engineering can also improve speed to market, and the quality of the finished product can also benefit'.

Cost, Quality, Time – Extended Engineering

It has long been recognized that co-location makes NPD teamwork easier. However, as an offshore R&D service provider, Wipro always has to deal effectively with multiple-site work and a global delivery model. A. Vasudevan is the Vice President of VLSI & System Design and manages over 600 engineers working on clients' projects. He has clear views on the challenges in new product development and says, 'We must excel at running multiple-site projects. To achieve this, we put a lot of emphasis on defining roles and responsibilities at the beginning of projects. We also have a 'handshake' concept, where we put milestones into the schedule where we deliberately check that both parties are 100 per cent satisfied with both progress and communications.' Wipro engineers are not only technical experts but also they are highly trained in project management. 'As part of our "Talent Transformation" programme, engineers receive intensive coaching in cross-cultural issues, project management techniques, optimizing communications, and negotiation', says Vasudevan.

A recent Wipro project was to develop a human–machine interface for IxFin Magnetti Marelli. This company is the second largest European automotive supplier of what are called 'instrument cluster' products – the instruments and related electronics located around the dashboard, including the entertainment system, air conditioning and the like. IxFin Magnetti Marelli were looking to position themselves as the technology leader in their market, offering automotive manufacturers a fully integrated 'infotainment system': an in-car multimedia system with GPS navigation, telephone connections, links to service centres for breakdown and emergency calls, and voice recognition controls for functions such as air conditioning. One challenge was that IxFin Magnetti Marelli had no previous experience of offshore projects. However, extensive communications allowed the transfer of key knowledge to the Wipro team and the timely delivery of a system that was needed for the launch of a new model from Fiat. In fact, in one year of the project only two person months out of 105 person months of engineering effort were 'on-shore'.

Wipro's expertise was initially seen by clients to be purely technical. That meant that clients' projects were run largely following their own NPD processes. 'Increasingly, however, clients are recognizing our process expertise and are interested in us helping them speed-up their own processes. We conduct over 500 projects per year and so Wipro has a greater opportunity to learn about the strengths and weaknesses of the product development process than companies working only on their own limited number of projects', says Vasudevan. 'After every project we analyse what the technical and managerial lessons are, and in the VLSI/Design space we have defined our design methodology called "EagleWision" ' (the name alluding to the clarity of an eagle's vision). Effective reuse and automation are the basic tenets of this design methodology.

Service Sector

Although Wipro is very active in electronics and manufacturing, it also has a rich history of working in the service sector, particularly financial services. These clients are served by a specific organization that has gained significant expertise in the different field of supporting new service development.

Prudential is a leading life and pensions supplier in the United Kingdom, with a customer base of around 7 million. The company had numerous call centres spread across diverse locations in UK, with each call centre dedicated to handle customer enquiries related to a single product line. This meant that customers had separate numbers for each of their products, and the call-centre consultant had to sometimes transfer them to a different department for each product. As a strategic IT partner, Wipro rationalized Prudential's product categories and business processes, and provided an integrated view of transactions across products. The most important initiative was the integration of multiple front-end customer services applications into a single consolidated system. This will give Prudential's customer service agents a consolidated view of the customer allowing them to deal with a significantly larger number of transactions. Prudential will be able to deliver on the brand promise of 'one operation', reducing costs and delivering even better customer service.

The Innovation Council and the Future

One of the potential dangers of R&D service consultancy work is that all of the innovation at Wipro could be solely in response to clients' specific requirements. Management recognized that innovation should not only be project-driven, and three years ago formed the 'Innovation Council'. 'We recognized that we consistently need to push forward our own expertise. Through our own knowledge of a wide range of technologies, we saw that we could identify opportunities', says Mulay. The Council evaluates technology development proposals and provides internal funding for the best ones. The resulting projects develop intellectual property that can be licensed to customers and integrated into their products. 'Such projects demonstrate our ability to offer leading edge technology to our customers. They see a roadmap of the components and technologies we are planning and know that it is not just a single product development project where we can serve them but really in the long-term', says Vasudevan.

The Innovation Council is made up of senior managers but the ideas are gathered 'bottom-up'. 'It is our engineers and project managers who are immersed in the technical issues who have the creative long-term ideas. Management's job is to choose the best ones, based on our analysis of how the resulting technologies and components will, in turn, both increase the quality and speed of NPD for our customers' says Vasudevan, 'and, for example, we have recently developed some key technology for wireless networking'.

Although Wipro Technologies was founded as a provider of contract R&D, it has come a long way. It has become a leader by not only developing technological know-how, but also by developing expertise in NPD processes, excelling at communications, becoming adept at spotting technological opportunities, and managing innovation in general. It is a hotbed of NPD learning that is likely to provide a lot of managerial lessons for the future.

8 People, Organization and Innovation

'Ordinary people cannot be innovative all of the time. However, if somebody gives them a target.'

(Akio Morita, Sony)

Introduction

The fifth and final element of the Pentathlon concerns people and organization. In many ways the fifth element is the foundation stone of innovation, as without motivated, skilled employees and a suitable organization with a creative atmosphere, companies will not be innovative. Finding effective ways to manage people, culture, teams and organization is one of the most challenging aspects of innovation management.

Figure 8.1 illustrates how people and organization underpin all of the other elements of the Pentathlon. Firstly, innovation strategy is critically dependent on leadership, achieving a culture of innovation often requires change management approaches, and alliances and joint ventures need co-ordination of people management issues. Secondly, creativity and ideas depend on the right atmosphere and rewards. In start-ups, understanding the role of culture can help entrepreneurs create a more appropriate atmosphere from the beginning, through instigating suitable reward mechanisms. Thirdly, people issues impact the prioritization of projects. Employees' willingness to take risks very much depends on the existence of a 'no-blame' culture. Which projects can be attempted in parallel is contingent upon the availability of good team leaders and team members for the types of innovations planned. Finally, successful implementation builds on cross-functional relationships, charismatic innovation champions, and project-to-project organizational learning.

This chapter covers how organizational culture, teamwork and people management relate to all other aspects of innovation, in particular:

▶ How organizational culture should promote innovation.
▶ The effective management of teams for innovation projects.
▶ Recruiting, motivating and rewarding individual employees to make significant contributions to innovation.

The majority of organizations have a personnel department or human resource management function. Such a function needs to play a proactive role in innovation management as people can be thought of as the 'building blocks' of an innovative organization. In the literature such an approach is referred to as

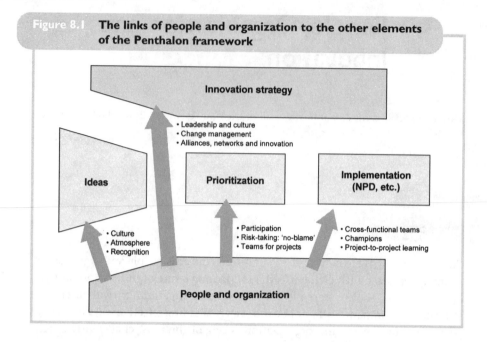

Figure 8.1 The links of people and organization to the other elements of the Penthalon framework

strategic human resource management. (In contrast to a reactive role, where a personnel department is only involved with administering hiring, pay and conditions.) As Figure 8.1 shows, the influence of people and organization is fundamental to innovation and so a strategic view of human resources is essential.

Organizational Culture and Innovation

Organizations can have very different cultures and the characteristics of these cultures impact innovation levels. Culture has been defined as: 'the set of values, understandings and ways of thinking that is shared by the majority of members of a work organization, and that is taught to new employees as correct'.[1] Some companies have proudly built a culture of innovation and gone out of their way to allow employees a level of freedom to support this. For example, the Sony Corporation has become an icon for innovative products but culture alone does not guarantee performance – as the quote at the beginning of this chapter shows, clear goals and targets are a necessary precursor for employees to be constantly innovative. The first step in creating an appropriate culture is to understand how culture relates to innovation.

Understanding and Assessing Culture

Although the widespread opinion is that it is difficult to manage culture, it is by no means impossible.[2] Much of the research in organizational theory has

Figure 8.2 The cultural web[5]

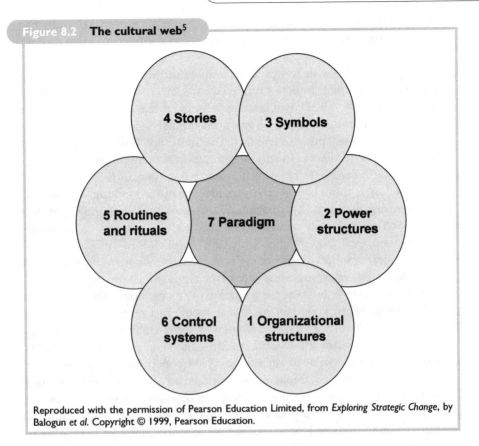

Reproduced with the permission of Pearson Education Limited, from *Exploring Strategic Change*, by Balogun *et al.* Copyright © 1999, Pearson Education.

considered culture and many of today's ideas stem from the ground-breaking work of Edgar Schein at the MIT Sloan School of Management.[3] He was the first researcher to identify the different levels of culture, from the visible aspects (for example, the formal organization), to the values and basic assumptions within an organization. Schein's work led directly to practical ideas on how managers can detect, interpret, and work with culture.

A simple and effective tool for assessment is the *cultural web* from Gerry Johnson of Strathclyde University in Scotland.[4] It was developed from empirical studies of organizations and identifies six partially overlapping aspects of culture, as illustrated by Figure 8.2. It can be seen that the middle of the web is the so-called *central paradigm* of the organization. The web identifies both tangible manifestations of culture like the formal organization as well as the 'taken-for-granted', intangible characteristics. The diagram helps to make the different levels of culture cogent and acts as a management tool for 'diagnosing' culture and understanding how it can be positively influenced.

The key aspects of culture as captured by the web are:

1 *Organizational structures.* The formal organization is the most tangible aspect of culture. Formal structures are normally related to what is important in an organization, and it is also the aspect of culture that is most often changed

by management. This misses the opportunity to address the other aspects of culture – organizational changes need to be viewed within the wider context of the web.

2 *Power structures.* These are related to the formal structure of an organization but not easily recognizable from organization charts. The power in an organization might lie more with R&D than marketing, although the two departments and their managers are at equivalent levels in the formal organization. In a service organization the real power might lie in the back office. Power structures often reflect the central beliefs of the organization and, for example, Hewlett-Packard was famous in the 1980s for being 'an engineering company'.

3 *Symbols.* Just as tribes have symbols that represent their culture, so it is with business organizations. These symbols include advertising and logos, the style of offices, company cars, titles and dress codes. The language and terminology used, especially acronyms, strongly reflect culture.

4 *Stories.* Every organization has stories that capture the essence of key events and share 'folklore'. Such stories are told to new recruits and visitors and act to reinforce behaviours.[6] Federal Express tells a story of an employee who organized a helicopter to get an important package to a customer on time. Although the cost was exorbitantly high, the employee was not disciplined because management was impressed by the dedication to the customer that it demonstrated and recognized the potential of such a story. 3M concentrate on stories about mavericks that pushed through the development of what eventually have become successful products, despite the initial opposition of management.

5 *Routines and rituals.* Routines are the ways employees in an organization learn to act towards each other and to process work. Such routines enable an organization to run smoothly. In addition to formal processes, organizations develop what become 'taken-for-granted' approaches to particular issues. This, for instance, could be an unwritten rule about how different departments interact during the innovation process. The routines underlying interaction can mean that formal processes are applied very differently from how they are described on paper. Routines can be difficult to change because they are often based on tacit knowledge and may strongly support the overall paradigm of the organization. Organizations have *rituals*, such as neophyte programmes, meetings, promotion criteria and appraisals, all of which indicate to employees what is valued in the organization.

6 *Control systems.* These include formal processes, measurement systems, and reward and recognition systems. All of these show what the organization values and help to set the focus of attention. Considering innovation, the most important control systems are those used to generate ideas, select the best ones, and implement them efficiently (this corresponds to the middle slice of the Pentathlon). Control systems, as shown in Figure 8.2, overlap with routines and rituals, and organizational structures.

7 *Paradigm.* Reflecting back to the definition of culture given above, the central paradigm is expressed as a statement summarizing the main points about how an organization 'thinks' and 'acts'. It is the distillation of the points from the six surrounding circles, as we will see in an example very soon.

Applying the Cultural Web

Overall, there are three steps to using the web in an innovation context:

1 Determine the current cultural web – how well does the existing culture support innovation?
2 Identify a 'desired' cultural web that supports innovation more effectively.
3 Determine the changes necessary and how they can be achieved.

To determine the cultural web, it is normal for outsiders (consultants or researchers) to talk to a representative sample of members of the organization, taking into account different functions and the hierarchy. Once the elements of the cultural web have been explained, simple open questions can be used to gather each individual's opinions on the web.[7] A workshop with employees is very useful for extracting the central paradigm from the six indicators of culture. The cultural web is very effective at identifying aspects of culture that can hinder the further development of an organization. For example, Hay Management Consultants, the well-known international human resources consultancy, recognized from their cultural web that they were too narrowly focused on 'job-evaluation' services (analysis of remuneration), whereas the market required a broader mix of consultancy services.[8]

To understand the utility of the cultural web in an innovation management context, we will discuss one example in detail.

Determining the Current Web

Figure 8.3 shows the cultural web derived for a multinational manufacturer of building materials, which we will refer to as 'BuildCo'.[9] Information was gathered in 36 one-to-one interviews and a workshop with employees from five departments. Employees were asked in the workshop to individually identify aspects of the cultural web and discussions were used to define the paradigm. A strong degree of alignment was found between the individuals' views on the current culture:

1 *Organizational structures.* The formal organization had recently been changed to link it with a new Stage-Gate product development process and several employees said words to the effect that 'this has been interpreted by the Process Managers as [a licence to] "command and control" '. In addition, a strong functional orientation in the organization hindered the use of cross-functional teams for new product development. Certain individuals such as the Head of Business Development and Process Managers had a very heavy influence. Specifically, the Process Managers were seen as championing their processes rather than adding real value to actual projects.
2 *Power structures* were seen as rigid and centralized and this led to conflicts for the business units. One manager said, 'the parent company's over-riding philosophy of being a low-cost commodity . . . company is at odds with a business unit which seeks to add value through the application of technical and market knowledge'.

Figure 8.3 The current cultural web for a manufacturer of building material: BuildCo

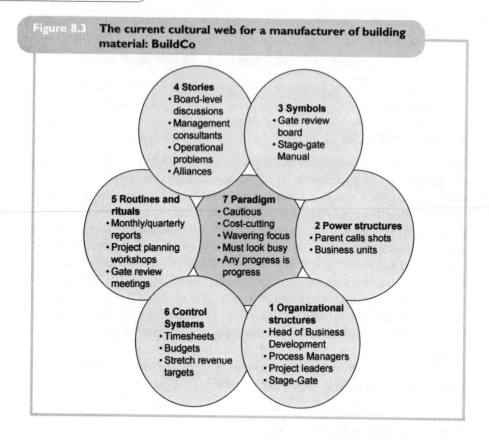

3 *Symbols.* Although it was relatively new, the Gate Review Board (responsible for assessing the progress of all new product development projects) had already achieved a symbolic status; it represented how BuildCo was extending its predisposition for tight controls into the area of innovation. Moreover, the Stage-Gate manual had quickly become identified as symbolic of an organization with what employees termed 'a reliance on paperwork and red tape'.

4 *Stories.* In order to improve their new product development, the company had recently implemented the recommendations of a large management consultancy firm (including the Stage-Gate NPD process). One of the common stories was about the modus operandi of the consultants and their influence on top management. Other commonly related stories berated the way the board made all of the key decisions. This was reflected in the power structure, which was concentrated at the centre; employees said the 'parent calls [the] shots'. Although BuildCo was profitable, operational problems were frequent and almost seen as inevitable in the way they were presented in common anecdotes. Finally, the story of an unsuccessful alliance reinforced the view that such ventures are risky and therefore undesirable.

5 *Routines and rituals.* The most important routines and rituals were identified as the monthly and quarterly reporting, and project planning meetings.

6   *Control systems*. Matching the power and the organization, the building materials company had many control mechanisms, from timesheets that individual employees were required to submit, to budget reports at the department level, and challenging revenue targets for the business units. Overall, BuildCo was tightly controlled and hierarchical.

7   *Paradigm*. The workshop participants described the central paradigm under five headings: including 'cautious', 'cost cutting', and '. . . with a varying focus'. Such a paradigm was perceived as incongruous for a company with the aim of being more innovative.

Identifying a 'Desired' Web

The second stage of applying the cultural web to innovation management is to identify an appropriate culture of innovation for an organization. To achieve this, BuildCo ran a second workshop. Firstly, participants (a range of employees) were asked to define a desirable and achievable new paradigm. Secondly, they were required to look at the six aspects of culture that would reflect this central paradigm. The overall result is shown in Figure 8.4. It can be seen that to achieve the central paradigm of an 'innovative, entrepreneurial, responsive and goal-orientated' company, many changes were deemed necessary.

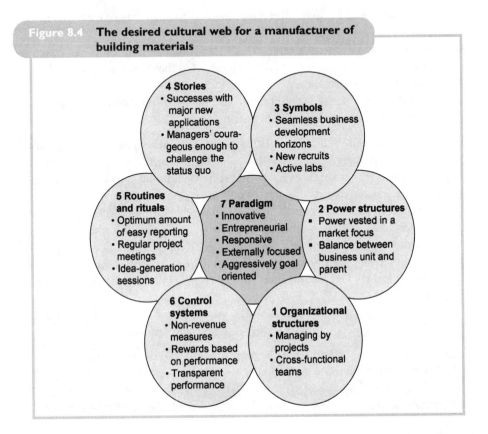

Figure 8.4   The desired cultural web for a manufacturer of building materials

4 Stories
- Successes with major new applications
- Managers' courageous enough to challenge the status quo

3 Symbols
- Seamless business development horizons
- New recruits
- Active labs

5 Routines and rituals
- Optimum amount of easy reporting
- Regular project meetings
- Idea-generation sessions

7 Paradigm
- Innovative
- Entrepreneurial
- Responsive
- Externally focused
- Aggressively goal oriented

2 Power structures
- Power vested in a market focus
- Balance between business unit and parent

6 Control systems
- Non-revenue measures
- Rewards based on performance
- Transparent performance

1 Organizational structures
- Managing by projects
- Cross-functional teams

To become more innovative, there was a perception that the formal and informal power structures at BuildCo must become decentralized. Participants had widely differing views on the most feasible organizational changes and discussions were lively. Market-focused projects and cross-functional teams were seen as the way to start. Connected to this, new symbols of innovation were needed, such as new recruits bringing a fresh wind, seamless business development (across the functions) and more dynamic laboratories (R&D). Stories that would communicate the paradigm would concern 'successful innovations', or 'managers having the courage to challenge the status quo'. Just as stories were needed in the new culture, so were new routines, rituals, and less control would be needed to reflect easier reporting, more positive project meetings and sessions to generate innovative ideas.

Effecting the Change

The final step in using the cultural web for innovation purposes is to gather ideas on how culture can be modified to the desired state. The main ideas that emerged within BuildCo were:

☐ Management led by the CEO should communicate a clear innovation strategy, and give autonomy to the business units to develop new products and markets.

☐ Reporting would be streamlined and aligned to the goals of each business unit.

☐ Cross-functional teams would become an integral part of development projects and project managers would be selected that had the ability to drive these projects appropriately.

☐ The Process Managers should be moved directly into project management, where they could make a direct contribution.

As management realized from the results of the cultural web exercise, BuildCo's initial culture was inappropriate and hindered innovation. The cultural web was a shock but sometimes this is exactly what is needed. BuildCo has made a range of changes to move towards the desired culture.

One aspect of using the cultural web for change – stories – is often perceived by managers to be open to manipulation. Here we stress that it is management's role to create the atmosphere and opportunities for top performance to be possible so that success stories arise, rather than 'making up' stories. An innovative organization creates success and is able to learn from failures. Managers need to highlight this.

Box case 8.1   United Parcel Service – culture and innovation[10]

UPS is one of only 16 Fortune 100 companies from 1900 that have survived and it attributes much of its success to its strong company culture. At UPS culture is perceived as 'myths, rituals, language, ideas, goals, and values'[11] that are shared by the company's 350,000 employees. Some of the aspects of the culture are tangible. For example, the *Policy Book* and *Code of Business Conduct* give specific advice on dealing with customers and conflicts. Employees receive detailed feedback annually in their Quality Performance Review, in which managers, peers and team members contribute to the evaluation. Promotions are largely internal. Regular communications are key and most departments use the Prework Communications Meeting approach, where employees informally update each other of the current issues at the start of their shift.

Less tangible are the drivers of technical innovation at UPS. These can be traced back to the founder, Jim Casey, who was the first to modify the Model-T Ford for parcel deliveries, the first to utilize conveyer belts for parcel sorting, and also led UPS to be the first logistics company to experiment with air freight (in 1925). UPS is still clear that being at the forefront of technology is important and has recently made significant investments in the development of databases.

All of the company's routines, rituals and control systems focused on being a provider of cost-effective package shipping (rather than premium priced fast delivery). A strong culture can, of course, have its disadvantages and UPS was relatively slow to react when Federal Express launched its next-day service. This shows that, just as formal organizational structures need to be reviewed regularly, so does culture. Corporate culture should not be left in abeyance. The culture at UPS now focuses on offering customers a choice of services (options on delivery and price), and optimizing the coordinated flow of goods, data and funds through advanced information technology.

Studies of Innovation Culture

Research can give us ideas on how to make organizations more innovative, but these ideas need to be adapted for particular contexts – there are no universal solutions. We should bear in mind that many studies have been conducted in famous organizations that have particular characteristics, such as 3M, Hewlett-Packard, Toshiba and Texas Instruments. The ideas and recommendations from such studies must be adapted specifically to the organization whose innovation performance we are trying to improve. We will discuss three major studies.

Two US scholars of organizational behaviour, Mariann Jelinek (College of William and Mary, Virginia) and Claudia Schoonhoven (University of California), conducted a major longitudinal study of culture and innovation.[12] They spent eight years investigating five successful electronics firms in the USA: Intel, Hewlett-Packard, National Semiconductor, Texas Instruments, and Motorola. The main source of data was in-depth interviews with senior managers covering: strategic planning, idea generation, project management, and company organization (and re-organization). Their results show that routines and rituals underpin formal processes and, 'a strategy of innovation is contained not in "plans", but in the pattern of commitments, decisions, approaches and persistent behaviours that facilitate doing new things'.[13]

Jelinek and Schoonhoven show that sustained innovation is possible in a large organization but is dependent on several factors. Firstly, the innovation strategy needs to be relevant and understood throughout the organization. It is important to create relatively small business units, as these will be more focused and communication will be easier. Frequent re-organizations help to keep a company closely aligned to its markets and to keep employees flexible and positively disposed towards change. A strong company culture can help in periods of market turmoil. But strong culture fosters innovation only if it is built on norms such as accepting failure, questioning decisions and conclusions, and so on. The limitations of strong cultures are that they can suppress new ideas (by causing everyone to think in a certain, unquestioning way – *groupthink*) and companies can become slow to recognize opportunities (see box case on United Parcel Service). Jelinek and Schoonhoven found that managing culture and organizational change requires significant amounts of top managers' time.

In another study, Charles O'Reilly of Stanford and Michael Tushman of Harvard conducted 200 in-depth interviews with managers in Silicon Valley, in order to determine views on the aspects of culture that promote innovation. They structured their research around their belief that 'two component processes underlie all innovation: *creativity* . . . and *implementation*'.[14] Best practices identified included people challenging the status quo, reward and recognition for risk taking, and a positive management attitude even when problems arise. Furthermore a tolerance of mistakes was identified as essential. The norms that promote efficient implementation are teams with the authority to make quick decisions, and open sharing of information between functions.

The third study we will look at is from two researchers employed by the Polaroid Corporation, Karen Zien and Sheldon Buckler.[15] They used in-depth video interviews, analyzed by anthropologists, to examine the culture of eleven innovative companies in Asia, Europe and the USA. The research elicited seven principles of culture that were apparent across all companies. The first common trait was that the companies were staunchly proud of their reputation for innovativeness. A willingness to experiment and the development of an excellent working relationship between marketing and R&D also stood out as key. The fourth and fifth principles were a real understanding of the customer, and the engagement of the whole organization. All of the companies studied focused on tapping both individuals' and the organization's capacity to innovate. Finally, stories appeared also to act as a *leitmotif* for innovation.

Best-Practice Ideas for Innovation Culture

There are many parallels between the three studies. To put them in a useful form for practitioners, Table 8.1 summarizes ideas for establishing an innovation culture based on best practice:

1 *Organizational structures*. Four different best practices can be identified for organizational structures to promote innovation: market-orientation; frequent re-organizations; teams; and 'innovation managers'. Aligning

organizations to markets is a common and effective practice, provided it is matched with the delegation of authority to these units. In large organizations, the role of the CEO is that of an 'organizational architect' who needs to find the best way to match the organization to constantly changing markets – frequent re-organizations are an important approach.[16] Autonomous teams can be the best way of dealing with radical innovations, which cannot efficiently be developed within the existing organization and processes. One new approach that has not yet received much coverage in the management literature is the creation of specific positions for 'innovation managers'. Having this role creates a figurehead for innovation improvement programmes. For example, GlaxoSmithKline and Zurich financial services have innovation managers responsible for improving innovation processes throughout their organizations. Procter & Gamble have a manager who is responsible for sourcing external ideas.[17]

2   *Power structures.* Both researchers[18] and practitioners have recognized the value of cross-functional awareness. ShinEtsu is a Japanese-owned manufacturer of polished silicon wafers and has customers such as Intel and Samsung. In their Malaysian operation, part of the culture is a very strong relationship between the R&D and manufacturing departments. This is fostered through routines which lead to a balance of power. A 'freshman's programme' for new R&D engineers requires them to learn how to operate manufacturing equipment and actively participate in *kaizen* teams, constructive criticism is actively encouraged and sometimes whole teams will transfer from R&D into manufacturing in a 'cradle to maturity' approach to responsibility (rather than the 'over the wall' *de facto* approach of many companies).[19]

3   *Symbols.* Three sorts of best practice can be identified. Communication, both internal and external needs to have an innovation focus and, for example, Hewlett-Packard recently adopted the 'HP Invent' slogan in all of their advertising. As an internal communication tool, the AXA Quadrant has been very successful and is a symbol of their new understanding of innovation (see main case at the end of Chapter 3). Displays of product and process innovations can and should inspire and Unilever make innovation highly visible in their facilities. Ideo, the Californian innovation consultancy, have dozens of gadgets around the workplace to trigger ideas and experimentation (and even have 'librarians' responsible for collecting artefacts).[20] Outstanding individual contributions can be recognized through plaques and certificates that are visible in the workplace and act as symbols of innovation.

4   *Stories.* Talented managers can develop an ability to use stories effectively.[21] Zien and Buckler developed a typology of management styles related to the use of organizational culture. Some managers use no stories, focus entirely on figures and thus miss the opportunity to promote innovation. Others relate anecdotes from the 'good old days', which alienates and places innovation in the past. 'Innovative leaders' reshape old stories and inspire the future. The research indicates that managers can be 'transformational leaders' if they develop and constantly tell enlightening stories in staff meetings, interviews and outside speeches.

Table 8.1 Best practices for achieving a 'culture of innovation'

Aspects of culture/best practices	Companies examples
1 Organizational structures ▲ Market-oriented structures ▲ Frequent re-organizations ▲ Teams ▲ 'Innovation managers'	▲ Market-oriented organizations engender focus and urgency. Monsanto and a myriad of other companies have such changes to enhance innovation. ▲ Large organizations can stay more adaptable through re-organizations (Motorola; Hewlett-Packard). ▲ Creating autonomous teams for new ventures (for example, IBM, DuPont, and Rank-Xerox). ▲ Formally appointing an innovation manager gives focus to performance improvements (GlaxoSmithKline; AXA; Bank of America); To tap outside resources more effectively, Proctor and Gamble recently created the post of 'Director of External Innovation'
2 Power structures ▲ Training ▲ Cross-functional rotation	▲ ShinEtsu promote excellent R&D and manufacturing relationships through their 'freshman's program'. 3M trained their top manager's to 'let go' and delegate authority more effectively. ▲ Sony managers place particular emphasis on managing cross-functional boundaries.
3 Symbols ▲ Communication ▲ Displays of innovation successes and other artefacts ▲ Symbolic recognition and awards	▲ Company logos and slogans are a symbol and some companies update them regularly to ensure the typeface and style is modern. Hewlett Packard recently added a focus on invention with the line 'HP Invent'; AXA have developed the 'Innovation Quadrant', which has become both an internal symbol of innovation (for example, as a screen-saver) and a tool for communicating the meaning of innovation. ▲ The workplace and the reception area should celebrate innovation by displaying relevant product and process innovations: 'artefacts'. Unilever has interesting displays of not only their product innovations but also their process improvements (see main case study at the end of this chapter). Artefacts are used to encourage experimentation at Ideo. Axa have an 'innovation corridor' (outside the staff canteen). ▲ Plaques, certificates and other recognition for innovative employees can become symbols. When Hewlett-Packard introduced a new reporting metrics for NPD[27] and every division manager trained in the approach received a Perspex desk block with a diagram of the metrics.

4	Stories	▶ 3M 'mavericks'; Sony Corporation's Walkman. Managers can compare their style to Zien and Buckler's typology, in order to learn how to use stories more effectively.
5	Routines and rituals ▶ Promoting new ideas for products and process improvements	▶ 'Fresh Eyes' Joie de Vivre; 'tinker time' at 3M; NIH at Texas Instruments (see Box case in this chapter). Giving a sufficient challenge to employees is essential (Hamilton Acorn). ▶ *Internal venture management*: making finance available for funding entrepreneurial ideas and opportunities.
	▶ Tolerating mistakes	▶ 'Failure is our most important product' Johnson and Johnson; Dupont 'good try' language; 'Bury the dead' party HP (now Philips).
6	Control systems ▶ Processes	▶ Most companies have introduced Stage-Gate or other formal NPD processes. Leading organizations have moved more to having a flexible process for the whole of innovation. Systems and processes to promote entrepreneurial thinking (for example, Richardsons: see main case in Chapter 2).
	▶ Metrics	▶ Company goals and metrics are 'cascaded to all levels' (Schefenacker is particularly good at this). Canon set notoriously tough NPD goals.
	▶ Reward and recognition	▶ Rewards and recognition are linked to innovation closely, including employee performance appraisals (Fischer GmbH have an interesting approach described later in this chapter).

Source: Based on the literature, supplemented with further examples collected by the authors.

5   *Routines and rituals* can be used to support innovation. Two categories of best practice are shown: promoting new ideas and tolerating mistakes. A leading innovator in the US hospitality sector, Joie de Vivre, has an interesting routine.[22] The 'Fresh Eyes' programme takes advantage of the different perspectives that new employees have of the business. In most service companies, new employees have a top-down performance evaluation after 30 days. The roles are reversed at Joie de Vivre and new employees are encouraged to challenge complacency by asking questions such as: 'why is it done this way?' and giving their evaluation of what they have seen. Motivating employees by giving them more interesting tasks is central to the philosophy of Hamilton Acorn, an award-winning UK manufacturer of professional quality paintbrushes. For example, production engineers are encouraged to design and build complex production equipment and not just focus on running the existing production lines.[23] Making the funding available for new ideas within organizations is a key step in encouraging people to recognize commercial opportunities. Tolerance of mistakes is part of the culture at Johnson and Johnson and enshrined in the founder's maxim that failure is an important 'product'. Other approaches that promote tolerance and creativity include: Dupont's use of the phrase 'it was a good try' to avoid negative criticism and; the symbolic burying in the woods of a prototype scanner that was a market failure (this allowed the engineers to vent their frustration) for Hewlett-Packard Medical.

6   *Control systems* should give direction, and processes for portfolio management and NPD are key. Metrics can be used to measure and promote innovation throughout an organization and Schafenacker, a supplier of automotive mirror systems, excels at this by 'cascading' management goals all the way to the level of the individual employee.[24] Later in this chapter we will discuss reward and recognition for individuals.

Best practices in people management are particularly difficult to transfer because how they are viewed and accepted is subjective. Consultants recommended that EvotecOAI, a German-owned chemical research services company, adopt 3M's 'rule' that every researcher is free to spend 10–15 per cent of their time to work on their own projects. The CEO was sceptical that such an approach would bring a return on what he saw as a large investment of time for a small organization. Therefore, the idea was modified and top performers, selected by their peers, were allowed 10 per cent free time for a period of one year. This focused programme was very effective at spurring on researchers to achieve peer recognition. Additionally, the work of the top performers in the 10 per cent of their time dedicated to 'personal projects' turned into ideas that were very profitable for the company.[25]

In using Table 8.1, managers should choose the ideas which appear most relevant to their own situation and think 'context, context, and context'. Overall, a combination of changes will be necessary to move towards the desired culture. Best practices in human resource management and culture provide useful starting ideas; managers must find ways to 'fit' them into the context of their own organization.[26] Changes to the culture should be integrated with the other actions to increase innovation and how this is best done is the subject of Chapter 9: Boosting Innovation Performance.

Table 8.1 shows that most of the examples in the literature come from manufacturing as service sector research is rare. Bearing in mind the contrasting nature of service companies (Chapter 3), creating a culture of innovation in services includes stimulating more ideas on the service augmentation, and making innovation processes more tangible but not bureaucratic),

---

Box case 8.2   Texas Instruments – realigning R&D culture

Some organizations are focused on being first-to-market and so the ability to invent is essential. This said, there can be a downside to inventiveness if it becomes the strongest component of R&D culture – it can lead to the proverbial reinvention of the wheel. In dealing with technical issues, solutions to similar problems are often known and so R&D engineers do not need to start from scratch. Unfortunately the *not invented here* (NIH) syndrome, where researchers do not adopt or adapt existing ideas, instead insisting on developing their own original solutions, wastes resources. Research-intensive companies, including ABB, Aerospatiale, Audi, BASF, BMW, BT, Nestlé, Nokia, Phillips, Renault, Royal Dutch Shell, Siemens and 3M, have recognized NIH as a common problem.[28]

Texas Instruments (TI), the developer and manufacturer of integrated circuits, has taken steps to avoid NIH as part of their 'Vision 2005' initiative. This includes an annual 'NIHBWDIA prize' for the R&D employee who takes an idea from somewhere else and makes a significant contribution to product or process innovation.[29] The 'not invented here but we did it anyway prize' has been instrumental in making an important improvement to the culture of innovation at TI.

Promoting Entrepreneurial Spirit

The main aim of innovation is to gain a commercial advantage, and so many organizations hope to instil an entrepreneurial spirit amongst their employees. Certainly, entrepreneurs have a particular way of viewing business, from which we can learn.

The first characteristic of successful entrepreneurs is that they generate many business ideas, a trait that is useful to every organization. Entrepreneurs also quickly screen-out those ideas that do not look promising and have the drive to push their ideas forward. The methods that entrepreneurs use for screening ideas are less structured that those discussed in Chapter 6 on Prioritization. Studies of entrepreneurs show that they make quick assessments, which can be in stark contrast to the slow-moving decision process in large organizations. It is a matter of applying an appropriate, generally simple, level of analysis.

Research[30] has shown that entrepreneurs focus on three areas in their assessment of potential businesses. Firstly, the scope of the venture is important, as the resources (including finance) required can be vastly different, depending on the market to be served. (For example, the founder of Federal Express needed a dedicated fleet of aircraft and over $90m investment before opening for business.) Secondly, entrepreneurs are talented at spotting external changes that leverage the demand for new products and services. Often these new services do not need to be radical breakthroughs because superior execution can lead to superior customer satisfaction (see Box case on Japanese Barbershops). Entrepreneurial thinking focuses on developing new products or services to solve problems faced (but not necessarily articulated) by customers.[31] Thirdly, entrepreneurs intuitively know that for survival they need to raise the barriers to their competitors.

Over 70 per cent of successful entrepreneurs 'replicated or modified an idea encountered through previous employment'.[32] It is also interesting to note that employees that are frustrated with the working atmosphere at established companies create most entrepreneurial ventures.[33] This means that established companies have to find ways to encourage entrepreneurial spirit (entrepreneurship in existing organizations is often referred to as *intrepreneurship*). Peter Drucker has said 'it takes special effort for the existing business to become entrepreneurial and innovative'. Mechanisms that can help are initiatives where employees can propose innovations and quickly receive special funding for such projects – this is normally referred to as *internal venture management*. Management needs to be willing to constantly try out new products and services and focus on recognizing opportunities. Once such opportunities are seen, clear and separate entrepreneurial organizations need to be created and these need to be staffed with people with the right personality.[34]

Not surprisingly, the common personality traits of entrepreneurs have been studied. From this work it can be concluded that there is no blueprint for a successful entrepreneur. Generally it is perceived that entrepreneurs will have a propensity for taking the responsibility for solving problems, set themselves challenging but achievable goals, have a tolerance for risk and uncertainty, and prefer direct feedback on their performance.

Box case 8.3   QB Net Japanese Barbershops – entrepreneurial thinking[35]

QB Net is the largest chain of barbers in Japan and the brainchild of entrepreneur Kuniyoshi Konishi, who was dissatisfied with the expensive and time-consuming traditional hairdressers in Japan. Konishi-san's hunch was that Japanese businesspeople just did not want to lose an hour for a haircut and did not value the hot towels and other aspects of the traditional approach. A simple market survey showed that 30 per cent of respondents said they were interested in a fast, low-price alternative, and this led him to open his first QB Barbershop in Tokyo in 1996. Now he runs over 200 outlets in Japan, with revenues of over $14m and plans to expand throughout Asia.

The QB Net approach is systematic and high-tech. Each and every opportunity is used to save time and reduce costs, and achieve the target of a haircut in 10 minutes, for 1,000 yen. Locations are chosen directly in business districts. Customers can tell the waiting time from green, yellow and red indicator lights mounted outside every shop. The stylish layout of salons has also been linked to speeding the process of haircutting and special chairs with sensors are used to determine the waiting time. A contribution to both lowering costs and accelerating the process is that customers must buy a ticket from a vending machine, thus eliminating the need for a cash register. Customers sit in a small cabin for their haircut (a 'QB Shell'), which has a seat, a sliding door, mirror and just those utensils needed by the hairdresser for fast and efficient hairdressing. For example, a vacuum 'airwash' tube mounted from the ceiling is used to clean the customer's neck and clothes of loose hair (and eliminate the need for a time-consuming hair wash). QB Shells have even been installed directly on railway platforms in Japan.

The basis of Konishi-san's hugely successful business was recognizing a problem faced by a large number of people: lack of time. What is impressive is the way in which he systematically analysed the process flow in a barbershop and developed the optimal solution.

Counter-Culture of Innovation

All too easily a culture can emerge that stifles innovation. Uncertainty, strong hierarchical control, lack of recognition, and simply not making it clear to employees that innovation is the responsibility of everyone are common faults. Organizational change, with reduction in employee numbers – downsizing in the vernacular – is probably the most destructive. Research has shown that the uncertainty surrounding such re-organizations, which has been termed *anticipated downsizing*, is worse in lowering creativity levels than *actual downsizing*.[36] Negative impacts can persist for a long time after actual downsizing, and these are the result of the depressed atmosphere in the workplace directly lowering creativity, and, secondly, those employees who are still creative keeping their ideas to themselves (for personal advantage). For managers the messages are clear: if downsizing is necessary, then the process needs to be completed as fast as possible to minimize the uncertainty; and active steps to prevent a negative culture arising are necessary.

It should be recognized that companies that most need cultural change often have the least time and money to go through all the necessary steps: identifying the problems, selecting champions, building commitment to change, auditing progress, rewarding intended outcomes, and so on. Companies operating in highly volatile contexts, but with bureaucratic mentalities and structures, tend to tighten up even further (seeking stronger hierarchical control). That may lead to short-term success (for example, saving money), but limits their long-term adaptability even further. And such companies do not have the time and resources to improve their adaptability through building a culture of innovation.[37] What they should do instead under 'conditions of stress' is experiment with new ideas, and create new structures that support innovation.[38]

Managing Innovation Teams

How successfully an organization can implement its innovation projects depends significantly on how efficient it is at selecting appropriate team structures and developing the necessary leadership skills within the organization. The human resource function of an organization should take a leadership role in driving this.

Team Structures

Most of the studies of project teams have focused on their use in new product development but the findings are also relevant to new services and process innovations. Innovation requires a mix of skills and viewpoints and so the utility of cross-functional teamwork has long been established in the manufacturing sector. In new service product development, the recognition of the importance of cross-functional teamwork is still emerging. Process improvements can often be assigned to the manufacturing function alone (in the manufacturing sector) or the operations groups (in the service sector). In other cases, though, it is the mix and even clash of different functional perspectives that can generate really good ideas and prevent implementation problems.

There are different types of project team structure. Each has advantages and limitations, which means that it is important at the beginning of every innovation project to consider what is most appropriate. This consideration should also take account of the culture of the organization; it is not realistic to try to move 'overnight' from a strong functional approach to a more autonomous approach. We will discuss five types of teams that are relevant for innovation projects, as shown by the work of researchers such as Michael Martin[39] (Dalhousie University, USA) in the late 1980s and Steven Wheelwright and Kim Clark at Harvard in the 1990s:[40]

- Functional teams.
- Cross-Functional teams.
- Heavyweight (cross-functional) teams.
- Autonomous teams.
- Virtual teams.

Functional Teams

It is possible that members of only one function are needed for some innovation projects – *functional teams*. Figure 8.5 shows the organization of a typical business unit, with R&D, operations, marketing and finance. A functional team might be formed in any of the functional areas. Normally functional teams are used for simple innovation projects and perhaps the best example is the continuous improvement (*kaizen*) team working together to optimize a manufacturing process. In the service sector, groups of operations employees may also work

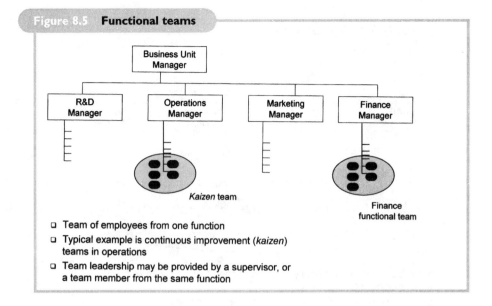

Figure 8.5 Functional teams

- ❑ Team of employees from one function
- ❑ Typical example is continuous improvement (*kaizen*) teams in operations
- ❑ Team leadership may be provided by a supervisor, or a team member from the same function

together on improving a process in a function: AXA insurance have a 'Taskmasters' programme to encourage teams of employees from operations to identify where they can eliminate non-value-adding steps in key processes.

A functional team has the advantage that its members all have similar goals and so little management time will be required to set up the team. Often the team itself can nominate a team leader and so functional teams do not tie up precious project management talent. Incremental innovation projects are an example of where functional teams may be the best approach. They can be highly motivating for participants, provided that the team members have been given the necessary training in teamwork. The disadvantages of functional teams are the perspectives and range of skills included may be too narrow for complex projects, or a suitable team leader may not be available. In this case, a moderator could be assigned from another function.

Cross-Functional Teams

It is not feasible to rely on inputs from only one functional area for the majority of innovation projects. Therefore, cross-functional teams are needed, in which each functional area assigns people to the innovation project. As shown in Figure 8.6, the project manager is normally from one of the functional areas and reports to their normal manager (in the Figure, the project manager is shown as having been assigned from R&D).

The biggest advantage of a cross-functional team is that it combines experience from every function and so it is less likely that a key point will be forgotten. For example team members from operations will start discussions about how a product or service product will be prepared and delivered. The

Figure 8.6 **A cross-functional team**

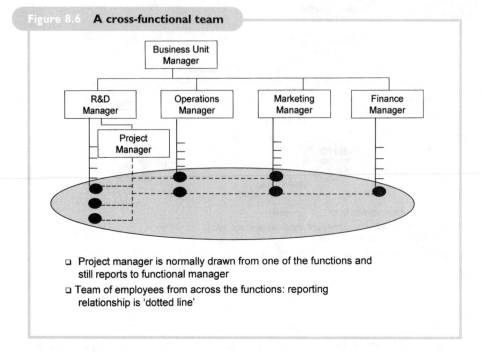

- Project manager is normally drawn from one of the functions and still reports to functional manager
- Team of employees from across the functions: reporting relationship is 'dotted line'

disadvantages of cross-functional teams are that they need management attention to make them work (conflicts of interest often arise between the functions represented), and the project manager does not have direct authority over the team members (normally it is a 'dotted line' reporting relationship). This can mean that it is hard to gain the full commitment of team members, who still report to their functional managers. Consequently, the project manager may not have access to the appropriate level of resources. Unfortunately, some companies assign their employees to several cross-functional projects in parallel and this exacerbates the problem.

Box case 8.4   3M – myth, or motivation and mentality?

In the extensive management literature there is one company that stands out in terms of innovation culture; 3M has been regularly discussed and both its practices and products eulogized (including the ubiquitous 'Post-it'). So much has been said about 3M that there is almost a myth surrounding the way the company manages its people and its innovation. Looking at it objectively, there are three levels at which 3M has taken steps to stimulate more innovation: at the company, team and individual level.

In the early 1990s, 3M's performance was stagnant. Few enhancements were being made to the massive portfolio of 60,000 products, and to combat this the new CEO, L.D. 'Desi' DeSimone, introduced a set of measures of innovation performance at the company level.[41] These goals were 30 per cent of revenues must be from products less than four years old, and 10 per cent from products less than one year old. To support this, the 'Challenge 95' programme provided extra funding, fast-track management decisions on innovative projects, and encouragement to combine ideas across the company's wide range of businesses. These steps invigorated innovation in the company and many new products were launched. However, many of these innovations were only incremental products (such as variations on the Post-it theme) that did not have the desired market impact. In driving for more radical innovations, various steps were taken. Firstly, the internal view of what constitutes a 'new product' was revised in order to swing the focus away from incremental projects. Secondly, it was perceived that customers may not recognize their needs or be able to articulate them, and the lead-user approach (see Chapter 5) was adopted throughout 3M to generate more radical ideas.[42] Thirdly, 3M management stressed that they were expecting innovation in all areas of the business, from the R&D laboratories, to marketing and sales, and after-care.

Although company measures are essential, it is at the team level that projects are conducted and projects in aggregate constitute company performance. Therefore 'Action Teams' were introduced for NPD.[43] Management recognized the dichotomy that a tight organization could lead to process efficiency but a looser process would devolve authority and be more effective. 3M found that not only the Action Teams needed training but also top management needed coaching to 'back off' and really empower the team.

At the individual level, 3M have taken steps to promote and reward innovation. In hiring, 3M look for people that are creative, have broad interests, are self-motivated, energetic, have a strong work ethic, and are resourceful. During the interview process, applicants' problem-solving ability is tested thoroughly in group exercises. A range of approaches promotes innovative ideas from employees. The rule that development people can spend up to 15 per cent of their time on investigating their personal ideas is almost as famous as the Post-it. 'Genesis grants' are available to fund the first investigations of personal ideas. Taking promising ideas further is supported by the 'Pacing Plus' scheme, which motivates by what 3M term the 'Pinball Effect' (success gives you the chance to play again); and the Carlton Award is 3M's 'highest recognition, their 'Nobel Prize'.[44]

Heavyweight Cross-Functional Teams

The main limitations of cross-functional teams relate to the conflicts of interest that may arise. If the project manager does not have a high degree of personal charisma or negotiation skills, the fact that they do not have formal authority over team members can be a problem. As the formal reporting of team members to the project leader is a 'dotted line', employees may give more weight to their functional allegiance than to the project.

Therefore, the formal organization is often modified to give a stronger reporting relationship. Figure 8.7 shows that a *heavyweight project manager* is designated

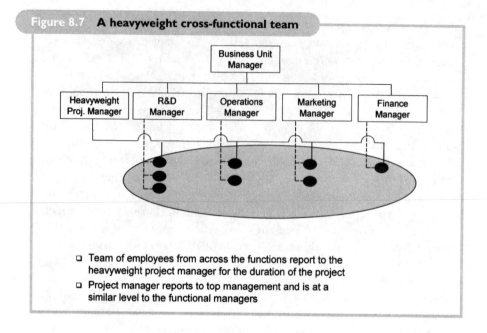

Figure 8.7 A heavyweight cross-functional team

☐ Team of employees from across the functions report to the heavyweight project manager for the duration of the project

☐ Project manager reports to top management and is at a similar level to the functional managers

to lead the team and, to give this manager the necessary authority, they are at the same hierarchical level as the functional managers.

The heavyweight cross-functional team has similar advantages to a normal cross-functional team. In addition, the project manager has direct authority and can be forthright in driving a project. One disadvantage of heavyweight cross-functional teams is the scarcity of suitable project managers to lead them. Therefore, such teams are not a panacea. Also, an influential heavyweight team manager can tend to divert resources from cross-functional teams led by more junior project managers. Consequently, it is essential that the allocation of resources is linked appropriately to project selection. It is important to consider project leadership requirements as part of portfolio management.

Autonomous Teams

In the *autonomous* team shown in Figure 8.8, an entrepreneurial project manager (*new venture manager*) is selected and assigned a small team. Many of the 'rules' of start-up ventures apply to the design of an autonomous team. It is crucial to have people experienced in certain functions. A small number of participants is ideal and they need to define a simple but effective process for driving an idea to market. A wide number of companies, including IBM and DuPont, have used autonomous teams and these are also called *skunk works* (see box case). Provisional studies[45] have shown the importance of the team being placed in a separate location and being led by a high-level manager, freed from bureaucracy.

Autonomous teams have the advantage that they can adopt different ways of working and do not have to fit within the same cost structures. There are several

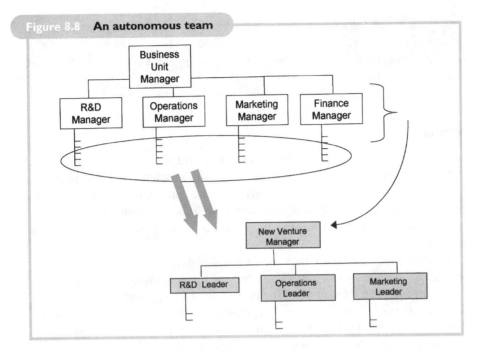

Figure 8.8 **An autonomous team**

limitations. They require an entrepreneurial style of management and finding suitable candidates to lead autonomous teams may be difficult. (Some multinationals have recognized this and have linked their management development programmes to the provision of suitable managers.) The projects allocated to autonomous teams are normally challenging and inherently risky. Consequently, the first project may not be successful but in this case the idea of using such teams should not be rejected. An issue for the parent organization is that the autonomous team will quickly develop a sub-culture that may challenge many of the values of the parent. Top management need to be prepared for this and to find ways in which to channel this energy positively.

Box case 8.5   Lockheed – the original skunk works[46]

Sometimes large organizations can stifle innovation through their control systems and routines. The approaches that help make innovation more effective, for example formal NPD processes, can sometimes be too constraining. More often, it is the overhead structure of the parent organization that can prevent innovation and so mimicking the advantages of a small start-up is a popular approach that is normally referred to as starting a *skunk works*.

The original skunk works was created to accelerate the design of a new jet fighter in 1943. Lockheed assigned a team of 23 engineers to the project and freed them from bureaucracy and the official R&D process. The team was located in a separate building. The name skunk works was coined by a team member (from a cartoon strip featuring an illicit brewery with the same name) and was not so-called because the 'new organization stinks' (as many people have subsequently assumed). The results for Lockheed were dramatic; the 'Shooting Star' jet was designed in 43 days and was the first American-designed aircraft to exceed 500 miles per hour.

Virtual Teams

In all of the types of teams discussed up to now, there may be links to outside suppliers (although these have been omitted from the diagrams). In many industries suppliers make major contributions to innovation projects. Sourcing expertise for innovation from outside is increasingly important and when resources from a number of different organizations are brought together, a *virtual team* is formed.

Figure 8.9 shows a virtual team where the different competencies needed are sourced from a variety of organizations but the project management is provided by the organization that launches the project. Increasingly, virtual teams, drawn from a mixture of organizations, run innovation projects. Essentially virtual teams are very fast for the development of innovations that are not dependent on an organization's other products, processes and services.[47] The advantages of such teams are that they can bring together expertise, which is not available in a single organization, and can be fast and entrepreneurial in nature. On the downside, they are not co-located and communications can be difficult and the cost of the external resources can be very high (although cheaper in the long-term than developing internal expertise). An example of a virtual team that

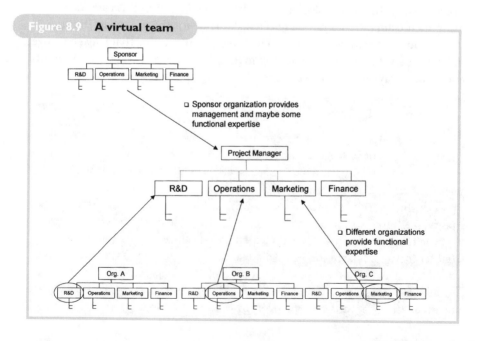

Figure 8.9 A virtual team

achieved excellent results is the Wingspan internet bank development team. This pulled together experts from a number of information technology companies and launched an online bank within 90 days.[48] The basis of this success included a clear definition of the responsibilities of each of the suppliers, an 'immersion day' to launch the project, in which all contributors met and focused on defining the interfaces between their work and others. Regular videoconferences were also held to keep the whole of the virtual team informed of progress and to identify problems.

Making Project Teams Work

The portfolio of innovation projects needs to be matched with a suitable set of project teams. When empowered teams are working effectively they can reduce the information overload on top management and improve the quality of decisions as these are made at a lower but more appropriate level in the organization. Ensuring that innovation project teams work effectively involves:

- Selecting the most appropriate team structure.
- Assigning team members.
- Creating a team and managing cross-functional relationships.
- Using project champions.
- Co- and virtual location.
- Project leaders and champions.
- Dealing with project failure.

Choosing the Appropriate Team Structure

In the hype that often gathers around new management ideas, the cross-functional team became the panacea for all of the problems of new product development in the late 1980s. Since that time, however, both researchers and practitioners have seen that cross-functional teams should not be used for every type of innovation project. Therefore, management should make a careful choice of the most appropriate type of team for a particular project. In Chapter 6 on portfolio management, we discussed the significance of having the right 'balance' of innovation projects in the portfolio. By balance we indicated the mix of innovation projects by their dimensions (product, service and process); degree (incremental and radical); risks; and returns. The right balance should also match the innovation strategy with the resources available and one of the scarcest resources is an excellent project manager. It takes time to develop good project managers and so organizations do not have the luxury of being able to assign a top project manager to every project.[49]

The size of the *core team* for an innovation project (responsible for representing the different functional interests and for driving the project) should be kept manageable, and research shows that about eight team members is the maximum.[50] A small core team makes the number of communication channels manageable and therefore speeds the decision-making process, for all those decisions that can be made at the team level (obviously some decisions require management involvement).

Table 8.2 summarizes the advantages and limitations of the five types of innovation project teams discussed and can be used as a tool for deciding which type of team is most appropriate for a particular project.

Selecting Team Members

Selection of the team members is nearly always a compromise. Whilst it is not difficult to ensure that all the relevant functions (or skills sets) are represented in the core team, having the best people from each function will not be possible. Top people are always in demand so, in practice, the project team will consist of people with different levels of team working skills. In choosing the team members, both functional expertise and team working ability are key and the latter consists of a person's commitment to team goals, being able to get along with others (particularly when under pressure), and their ability to listen and make constructive criticism.[51]

It is important to consider the type of innovation project being attempted. Higher risk, radical innovations require the highest level of team skills. In choosing a team, it can be useful to consider personality traits, as these have an influence on team working. Various tests have been developed, such as the Myers-Briggs test[52] or that developed by R. Meredith Belbin's work at Henley Management College in the UK. Essentially all such tests look at how the traits of the individuals in a team 'cover' the range of skills needed in an ideal team. There is no generally acknowledged 'best' test and so, in the absence of good comparative empirical data, we have selected the Belbin test to describe in detail, as it is easy to apply to innovation teams and provides a categorization.[53] Belbin defined *team role* as a 'tendency to behave, contribute and interrelate with others in a particular way'. Table 8.3 shows that there are eight roles in a team. A *co-ordinator* tends to focus on ensuring that the objectives are clear, how responsibilities are allocated and on summarizing team conclusions. Belbin's research with managers also identified the characteristics of typical coordinators, as shown in the table. Each of the eight roles, with their particular characteristics, brings particular strengths to a team.[54] For example, the *implementer* pushes strongly for action, whereas the *team worker* is very supportive. Typically, individuals have a tendency to a particular team role, although this may change according to the circumstances.

Belbin's work helps both in choosing and forming teams. A simple questionnaire allows individuals' roles to be determined and a balanced team can then be chosen. Often the ideal team members are not available, and in this case, the Belbin methodology can form the basis of a team 'kick-off' workshop. In this workshop, a moderator explains the method, uses the questionnaire and then creates an open atmosphere in which the team members discuss their individual roles and how, together, the team can best function. For example, if there are no obvious implementers in the team, how this deficit can be addressed. It should be stressed that the moderator must set an appropriate atmosphere in the workshop,

Table 8.2 Choosing the right type of team

	Functional teams	Cross-functional teams	Heavyweight cross-functional teams	Autonomous teams	Virtual teams
Advantages	□ Simple to organize. Do not monopolize management time. □ Ideal for 'tactical' improvements to the day-to-day processes within a function.	□ Bring together knowledge and responsibilities of functions. □ Work well for projects where something similar has already been successfully completed. □ Require relatively low management commitment.	□ Due to an experienced manager taking responsibility for the heavyweight team, it has more influence. □ Can use existing processes and resources.	□ Autonomous teams are freed of the bureaucracy and overheads of the parent organization. □ Separate location reinforces the independence of the team. □ The team spirit will quickly encourage entrepreneurship.	□ Brings together levels of expertise not available in a single organization. □ Can be much faster moving than projects resourced internally. □ Such teams are entrepreneurial in nature.
Limitations	□ Team may miss opportunities, as they have a narrow perspective. □ Team learning is not applicable to cross-functional projects.	□ Project manager has little formal power and so may not be able to control cross-functional differences. □ In competition for resources, are likely to lose out to heavyweight teams.	□ Require a very experienced manager to lead the project. □ May require significant amounts of management time. □ May not work well for new ventures, as they are too closely tied to the parent organization.	□ Radical approaches will test the capacity of the parent organization to accept change. □ Entrepreneurial management talent is hard to find.	□ Are not co-located. □ Need good communication and a simple, effective innovation process. □ Sourcing outside expertise can be very expensive. □ Intellectual property rights (IPR) need to be carefully managed.
Recommended applications(s)	□ Kaizen projects in all functions. □ Developing a process orientation within the functions.	□ Incremental innovation projects. □ More complex kaizen projects, where a cross-functional view may add a better understanding.	□ Radical innovation projects (not recommended for low complexity projects. Heavyweight teams offer a good training ground for managers with top potential.	□ New ventures: new products in new markets. □ Dealing with disruptive technology.	□ 'Fast-track' projects. □ Development of new technology, where the internal competence does not exist.

Table 8.3   Team roles

Role designations	Characteristics	Typical focus
Coordinator	Positive-minded, self-confident and impartial individual; often of average intellect	Clarifies objectives, helps allocate responsibilities, articulates team conclusions and seeks consensus
Shaper	Often an over-achiever who is impatient, provocative, emotional and outgoing	Articulates the findings in group discussions, presses for agreement and decision-making in their own way
Plant	Intellectual and knowledgeable. Individualistic and unorthodox	Makes proposals, generates new ideas.
Monitor/evaluator	Sanguine, cool-headed and clever	Analyses problems and issues, evaluates others' contributions
Implementer	Tough, pragmatic, conscientious	Wants to turn talk into action and effective implementation
Team worker	Team-oriented, gregarious, may be indecisive	Gives personal support to others
Resource investigator	Inquisitive, innovative and communicative	Brings in new ideas, negotiates with outsiders
Completer-finisher	Attention to detail, conscientious perfectionist	Emphasizes the importance of meeting schedules and achieving goals.

Source: Adapted from Belbin (1981).

as some individuals may otherwise object to being 'tested' and having the results openly discussed. If it is applied sensitively, Belbin is a valuable tool for launching and managing teams.

Creating a Team and Managing Relationships

One of the most important aspects of project team management, irrespective of whether the team is working on a product, service or process innovation, is establishing effective relationships within the team from the beginning. These consist of the individual interactions but also cross-functional issues.

Early research on team working by Bruce Tuckman from the Ohio State University showed that newly created teams typically progress through a number of phases.[55] This is often presented as the *teamwork wheel*, as shown in Figure 8.10. Initially, in the *forming* phase, members tend to be guarded, polite and the way the team works together develops. Next, as the first tasks are tackled,

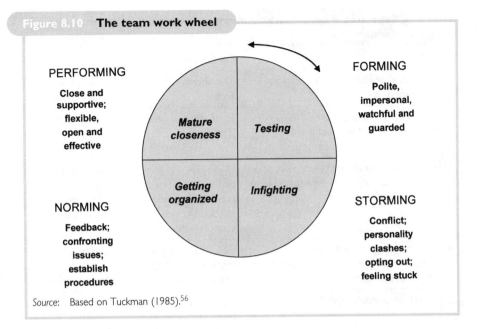

Figure 8.10   The team work wheel

PERFORMING

Close and
supportive;
flexible,
open and
effective

Mature closeness   *Testing*

Getting organized   *Infighting*

FORMING

Polite,
impersonal,
watchful and
guarded

NORMING

Feedback;
confronting
issues;
establish
procedures

STORMING

Conflict;
personality
clashes;
opting out;
feeling stuck

Source: Based on Tuckman (1985).[56]

conflicts or personality clashes may occur, or even fundamental disagreements because of different functional backgrounds – this is the *storming* phase. Some of the clashes can be healthy and bring better ideas or identify problems. The team will then move into a phase of *norming*, where it addresses the conflicts and develops rules or ways of effectively working together. Lastly, teams should move to and remain in the *performing* quadrant. Sometimes, new conflicts can move the team back into storming but good team management should move the group quickly back to performing. As discusses earlier, with suitable moderation Belbin testing can be made a useful part of forming an innovation team.

The teamwork wheel can be used to support teams in their own development, and it is particularly useful for newly formed innovation teams at their inception. It can help such teams develop their own 'teamwork rules', to govern for example how to deal with disagreements across functional boundaries. Developing such rules early on can minimize the negative aspects of storming and accelerate the transition to performing. Table 8.4 shows a number of suggested rules (this is based on our work with product development teams and is an area where empirical research is needed).

Functional and Other Interfaces

One of the most talked about aspects of innovation teamwork, particularly in NPD is the relationship between R&D and marketing. Many researchers have investigated the 'wall' that often exists between these two functions. It appears to be a perennial issue. In a major study of nearly 300 projects at 50 companies, frequent conflicts were identified and a taxonomy of relationships developed.[57]

Table 8.4 **Suggested rules of working in cross-functional innovation teams**

	Rule	Comments
1	Respect all teams members' opinions and expertise	This should help to avoid cross-functional friction
2	Customer-focus and quality should not be compromised, without a team decision	Stops internal views or technology push dominating
3	Deliver your work on time or warn the team in advance, if you expect problems	Underlines the importance of everyone delivering on-time, in order for the whole project not to experience delays; also encourages individuals to ask the team for support before it is too late
4	Communicate efficiently and always consider how your work can impact others in the team	Too often the interfaces between those responsible for different work packages or functions, are not sufficiently considered
5	Question, question, question . . .	Helps teams 'keep an open mind' and be more innovative in their approaches
6	Assess risk but expect the unexpected	Should allow some problems to be anticipated, the unexpected should be dealt with quickly as some resources are 'reserved' foe unseen problems
7	Make it a winning team	All individuals should focus on making the project team something special and achieving extraordinary results

These include *severe dissatisfaction, mild dissatisfaction,* and *harmony.* What is particularly interesting is that advantages and disadvantages to each of these categories were identified. In the former, distrust leads marketing and R&D to mutual disrespect and poor consolidation of market and technical ideas. Such friction can often result from personality conflicts and the fact that employees 'never see any signs from management that collaboration is desired'.[58] Management needs to lead by example in demonstrating the value of both functions and, particularly, the value of collaboration. Mild dissatisfaction can be the result of too few meetings between the functions and even R&D and marketing being 'too good friends'. This can stifle healthy professional disagreements (that often can lead to excellent ideas). Finally full harmony, where each function are equal partners can be positive for incremental projects but the 'give and take' attitude may lack the fire that sometimes is necessary to make innovation breakthroughs.

Although the R&D to marketing interface is the most commonly discussed, it is not the only one that managers should consider. An emerging issue is the interface between R&D and the financial controlling function.[59] Complex R&D

projects, particularly technology development, require good risk assessment. However, the adequate assessment of risks necessitates both technical and financial aspects to be considered and this requires excellent working relationships between finance experts and R&D leaders. The interface between these two functions has a significant influence on the effectiveness of portfolio management and is increasingly an area where organizations need to concentrate.

Cross-functional boundaries have been widely recognized as problematic. In addition, the different approaches typically taken and 'language' used by management, engineers and operators mean that these groups often do not communicate effectively.[60] Bringing together these different views and opinions is important for innovation projects.

Co- and Virtual Locations

Co-location is an important mechanism for innovation projects. If all team members can be brought together, then both communications and team spirit improve dramatically. Open-plan offices where furniture is on wheels make the bringing together of project teams much easier. Email is no substitute for bringing marketing, R&D and operations within speaking distance. Where co-location is not possible, extra effort must be made to coordinate and integrate the efforts of the various members of the team. Modern video-conferencing technology certainly makes the management of virtual teams easier (although it is still not a direct replacement for face-to-face contact).

Different physical locations and locations in different time zones make communication more difficult but they can bring some advantages. For example, 21Torr is a German marketing and internet consultancy company that has used separate location to its advantage. Customers in California have found it useful to choose 21Torr as a service provider, which because of the time difference can implement site modifications 'overnight'.

Project Leaders and Champions

The role of the innovation project manager should not be underestimated and depends on the degree of innovation in the project.[61] In more simple, incremental projects the leader must act as a communicator, a climate-setter, planner, and interface. However, for radical innovations the team leader must act as a real *champion*, pushing the cause when the project requires more support or encounters resistance. Research has shown that wider skills and the ability to identify and adopt unconventional approaches are essential for radical projects.[62]

As good project leaders are rare, organizations need to take active steps to ensure that they assign their best managers to the more complex projects. Development of skilled champions takes time and direct coaching of junior colleagues by experienced managers helps but, it should be noted, individual personality also plays a role. Not everyone has the passion and energy that is required to be an effective champion. To avoid key employees who are effective champions being lost, special rewards and recognitions may be necessary.

Dealing with Failure – Project Termination

Although success is the aim of every team, this can be elusive. Studies have shown that many NPD projects fail to meet their stated goals, and many products fail in the market. Many process innovations are also not successful.

Empirical evidence confirms that few organizations are efficient at determining when projects should be terminated and often such projects continue unabated. Too many organizations do not have clear termination criteria and so do not act at an appropriate time.[63] This results in wasted resources and, too often, significant de-motivation.[64] Members of teams responsible for projects that are not successful, particularly those where the failure was perceived in advance to be inevitable, are likely to be hugely de-motivated. Too often personal careers can be damaged by association with a failure, even though in NPD, for instance, research tells us that not every project will reach its goals. Just as projects can be a proving ground for new business leaders, without careful people management projects can also act as a career graveyard. Certainly, if a project leader was incompetent, then there is no point in giving them another chance. However, even on unsuccessful projects there are many team members that will have made significant contributions.

Terminations should be carried out as early as possible and the team members need to be reassigned very quickly, in order to prevent high levels of de-motivation. There is much that can be learnt from projects that are not successful and researchers have found evidence that companies that were good at this were able to 'build on this failure' to be successful on subsequent projects.[65]

Managing People for Innovation

The final level of human resource management (HRM) that we will consider in this chapter is the individual. Attracting, recruiting, motivating, rewarding and developing individuals form the backbone of effective innovation management. Many companies do not recognize the strategic importance of linking people management to innovation strategy, partly because of its complexity and often because the personnel department adopts solely an administrative role. Managing human resources *strategically* means aligning people management to the innovation strategy. It has several main components, all of which influence innovation performance.[66] These are:

- Recruitment and assigning jobs.
- Managing performance.
- Motivation, rewards and recognition.
- Employee development.

Recruiting and Job Assignment

Organizations that have the need and the financial resources to hire new staff have an ideal opportunity to look for people who will introduce more innovation. In hiring new employees selection criteria need to be matched to the innovation strategy. The technology roadmap presented in Chapter 4 prompts organizations to think how their innovation strategies create needs for competencies, either from outside or to be developed internally. A strategic approach to human resource management will include a regular check on how the changes in innovation strategy create the need to build or strengthen competencies.

Innovation strategy can create needs for certain 'technical' knowledge (for example, on a particular technology, or market), or it can mean that a natural ability to drive innovation is required. In the latter case, it is difficult to assess how innovative a particular candidate will be. Their track record, a willingness to take risks, and competence at problem solving are useful indicators. The interview and selection process should be enhanced to assess the innovation capabilities of candidates. The use of psychometric tests has increased over the last ten years and specific tests have been developed to identify if an applicant is innovative. One test for example measures adaptability, motivation towards change, work style, and challenging the status quo.[67] Such tests should be used as part of the overall interviewing process and HRM specialists warn against relying on the results of tests alone.[68]

Four factors should be considered in assigning employees to particular roles: their 'technical' expertise (for example, technical or market knowledge); cross-functional team skills; their ability to champion innovative ideas; and their motivation. Technical expertise is probably the easiest to assess. The assessment of cross-functional skills and the ability to champion ideas needs to be an integral part of the appraisal and development systems, which we will discuss soon. If the appraisal system does not look at these factors, then employees will be assigned to roles without good, objective information on their capabilities being available. The earlier section on innovation project teams indicated that some of these teams require particular competencies in the team members.

In job assignment, account should be taken of employees' job tenure, as it has been found that this has an influence on motivation and innovation.[69] An employee's perspective goes through three phases. Firstly, *socialization* is the phase where an employee is new to their position and is learning their responsibilities and the supervisor's expectations, making social contacts for the role and gaining acceptance. This phase is relatively short and for the employee is primarily concerned with proving their competence and gaining acceptance. The next phase is called *innovation* (an unfortunately confusing label in a book about innovation management) and starts when an employee feels secure in their new position. They look for particularly challenging work and so seek to enlarge their contribution to their department's work. Hard work at this stage can enhance visibility and promotion potential. When employees work in the same position for a substantial time, they transition to *stabilization*, where their focus can move to preserving their autonomy and minimizing vulnerability. This means that their openness to innovation can drop significantly. The rate at which an employee moves between the phases depends on both their personality and contextual issues. What is pertinent from an innovation perspective, is that employees who have been in their jobs for a long time tend to become less creative in their approach to problem-solving because they are more rigid in their thinking, and are committed to established processes ('we have always done it that way'). Job rotation and bringing in new team members can help counter the potential problems of job longevity (and links to the ideas about sources of creativity that we discussed in Chapter 5).

Managing Performance

Managing performance is essential but it is complex and the theories that have been developed to explain *motivation* in the workplace are inconclusive. It has been said that whilst the various theories are inconclusive, they provide a framework for managers to draw upon in work situations.[70]

Work performance is a function of an employee's ability and motivation. Two categories of theories of motivation have developed: *content* theories and *process* theories. Content theories concentrate on the factors that motivate people. Process theories stress the process by which motivation is achieved.

Content theories include the well-known work of Maslow and Hertzberg. Maslow's greatest insight was that individuals' needs form a hierarchy, and once needs such as pay and job security are satisfied, motivation will be dependent on factors such as esteem (for example, status) and self-actualization (for example, advancement). Hertzberg's work essentially extends Maslow's ideas. It divides motivating factors into *hygiene factors* (which lead to dissatisfaction if missing) and *motivators*, which when present lead to motivation and job satisfaction. The empirical evidence on these theories is inconclusive but both have been widely applied by practitioners. For example, they help managers to realize the role of non-monetary rewards.

Process theories look at the dynamic relationships between the variables responsible for motivation. *Equity theory* identifies the importance of employees' feelings; if they do not feel that they are being fairly treated compared to their colleagues, their motivation will drop. Objective systems for reward and recognition are therefore essential. The concept of the *psychological contract* – the two-way exchange of perceived promises and obligations between an employee and an organization[71] – is useful because it reminds organizations that the relationship with their employees is governed by mutual perceptions and not just formal contracts. *Expectancy theory* states that 'employees will direct their work effort towards behaviours that they believe will lead to desired outcomes'.[72] It stresses the importance of clear links between effort and performance, performance and rewards, and rewards and goals. Managers are responsible for clarifying these links, and showing employees how different efforts will lead to different performance, and so on.

There are a number of points that managers can take from the above discussion. It is important to understand the nature of individuals' needs and provide the possibility of them being met. As the 'lower level' needs are met, other factors such as recognition and responsibility will be more important. The process by which employees become more motivated depends on their perceptions of the psychological contract between them and the organization. Meeting expectations and demonstrating objectiveness are important and transparency – clarifying goals and potential rewards – is the next step.

It is useful to *cascade* the top-level innovation goals down the organization, to each and every employee. Figure 8.11 illustrates this, showing that high-level goals like revenues from new products can be linked to a project team's goals and in turn to the goals of each member of the team. In cascading goals it is important to check that the goals at each level are specific, measurable, achievable, relevant and timed (as represented by the mnemonic SMART).

At the employee level, goals need to link to the work of peers, to promote teamwork. This is particularly important in fast-track breakthrough projects, which require particular commitment from team members and cannot afford to have individuals focus on their personal goals to the detriment of the team's. In Figure 8.11, therefore, individual A is tasked with not only writing a particular software module but also with ensuring that this links to module B and incorporates manufacturing test routines. Clear links to rewards at the team and individual levels are also useful in cascading.

Goals should be clear and measurable. Table 8.5 suggests a number of possible goals that can be used to promote innovation. These include goals directly related to performance but should also cover the acquisition of new skills required.

Appraisals

There are two key aspects of appraisal from an innovation perspective: the topics to be covered and who conducts the appraisal.[73] Although most organizations perceive the importance of innovation, research has shown that few include innovation as a criterion in their annual appraisal systems.[74] It can be an advantage to

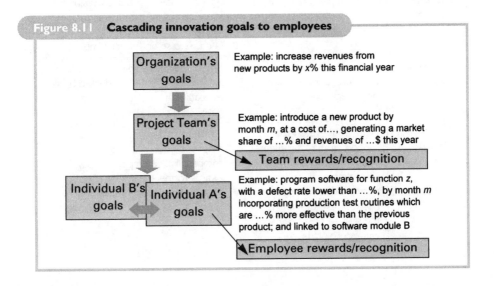

Figure 8.11   Cascading innovation goals to employees

Organization's goals — Example: increase revenues from new products by x% this financial year

Project Team's goals — Example: introduce a new product by month m, at a cost of…, generating a market share of …% and revenues of …$ this year

Team rewards/recognition

Individual B's goals

Individual A's goals — Example: program software for function z, with a defect rate lower than …%, by month m incorporating production test routines which are …% more effective than the previous product; and linked to software module B

Employee rewards/recognition

Table 8.5 **Employee-level innovation metrics**

Metrics	Details	Notes on usage
Scientific publications	Number published in last x years	❑ Objective measure but only applicable to R&D engineers and scientists ❑ Does not show the real value to the firm
Patents	Number granted in last x years	❑ Objective measure but only applicable to R&D engineers and scientists ❑ Does not show the real value to the firm
Ideas generated	Suggestions submitted, etc.	❑ Does not show the real value to the firm; better to use measures of the ideas implemented and the advantages they brought
Cost savings	Transactional savings	❑ Largely one-off savings
Project goals	Specific time, quality and cost project goals that can be cascaded to the individual	❑ As shown in Figure 8.10, a project's key goals should link to individual's goals
Process innovation	Removal of non-value adding stages from common business processes (for example euros saved per year)	❑ Objective measure, easy to link to reward and recognition
Service innovation	Enhancement of the interaction with customers during the service delivery	❑ Can be linked to customer satisfaction metrics; should cover all aspects of the service augmentation (Chapter 3)
Innovation performance rating	For example, a rating on the scale of 1 ('excellent') to 5 ('poor')	❑ Rating is subjective but discussion is more important than the actual rating ❑ See Box case on Fischer GmbH
Teamwork	Encourages individuals to focus on achieving team or project goals	Is best to link the goal for individuals to be team-oriented by evaluating them directly on team goals
Competencies gained	Helps employees focus on supporting the attainment of the organization's innovation goals and personal development (for example developing the skills to be a heavy-weight project leader)	❑ See main case at the end of this chapter on Lever Fabergé; this company linked employees' pay awards to the attainment of both business 'work targets' and 'personal goals'

change this, as including innovation as a criterion will certainly put more focus on it within the organization (see Box case on Fischer GmbH). Innovation can be included in the appraisal by looking at reviewing actual performance versus the agreed goals, using the type of metrics given in Table 8.5.

There are several possibilities on whom to involve in the appraisal. The assessment can be conducted solely by the employee's direct manager, or by their manager's manager. Alternatively, it can be run by the personnel department, through self-appraisal, or be based on assessments by peers, subordinates or customers. A combination is also possible and the so-called *360-degree assessments* take inputs from above, from peers and from subordinates. Assessing an employee's contribution to innovation is not always easy, and so one advantage of using 360-degree assessments is that a broader view can be obtained. Also by collecting inputs from multiple sources, it forces a number of managers and peers to think about an individual's contribution to innovation and this tends to increase an organization's focus. In service companies, the assessment can be used to increase focus on, for example, improved augmentation.

Box case 8.6   Fischer GmbH – motivating employees to innovate

Many companies want to become more innovative but do not effectively communicate this message to their employees. Fischer, a manufacturer of industrial fixing devices based in southern Germany, takes a different approach. The company has a tradition of innovation – it has filed hundreds of patents – and so there has always been a strong focus on R&D generating ideas for new products. However, Managing Director Klaus Fischer has attempted to extend the generation of new ideas across all functions because, he says, 'when we're not innovative across the whole company, then we haven't a chance'. Employees' contributions to innovation are assessed in annual appraisals in different ways. R&D engineers are measured on the number of patents and the speed and effectiveness with which these are converted into products. All employees are assessed on contributions to process innovation – improvements and cost reductions in manufacturing and business processes. In every appraisal a rating on a 1–5 scale is used to summarize an employee's overall contribution to innovation. Although the rating is subjective, it stimulates discussion between employees and management about innovation. The company has found that the process has been an effective catalyst in increasing overall performance.

Fischer perceives his role in promoting innovation to be central and therefore takes personal responsibility for driving the company's suggestions scheme and maintaining an effective bonus scheme linked to this.

Motivation, Rewards and Recognition

Reward and recognition systems should emphasize attitudes and behaviours that support innovation; provide timely feedback from supervisors, managers and peers; encourage teamwork; and publicly signal the importance of innovation.

In the human resource management literature, there is strong recognition of the importance of rewards and recognition in supporting the achievement of strategic goals.[75] Therefore, reward and recognition are tools to support the achievement of innovation strategy. There are several decisions to be made concerning reward and recognition: the amount of reward and recognition planned; the performance and sort of behaviour to be targeted; the types of reward and recognition that will be offered; and when to inform employees of new rewards and recognition. Expectancy theory tells us that impossible goals will lead to frustration, unrewarded goals will not be taken seriously, and good performers will only be motivated by rewards that they value.[76]

The overall level of the monetary rewards available is normally driven by profitability. From this, a particular sum may be reserved for overall pay increases (for example, cost-of-living related increases) with the remaining sum available for all of the performance-related increases. In creating a focus on innovation, organizations may decide to reserve and label some amount for particular innovation projects and individuals that have been particularly innovative. The types of reward and recognition that are most normally used are listed in Table 8.6. These are, it can be noted, no different to the general types of rewards and recognition used by organizations. In shaping a culture of innovation, it is useful to reassess how motivation can be focused towards

Table 8.6   Example of rewards and recognition that can be used to promote innovation

Categories	Examples	Comments
Rewards	☐ Pay increase ☐ Bonus payments ☐ Stock options ☐ 'Project equity' ☐ Time and resources for 'personal projects' ☐ Extra holiday ☐ Company cars ☐ Paid training ☐ Paid education (for example MBAs) ☐ Promotions ☐ Dual ladder schemes	Rewards should always be considered in light of the theories of motivation and the state of the business environment. They can have certain disadvantages. For example, stock options have little value in low growth periods and can, when allocated to small numbers of employees lead to equity issues. Equity theory prompts managers to consider how rewards and recognition are allocated. Peer review schemes can be very effective at both demonstrating objectivity and raising team motivation
Recognition	☐ Praise from management ☐ Publicity ☐ Plaques and certificates ☐ Peer recognition ☐ What top performers themselves value (for example, development opportunities)	Content theory shows the importance of not only providing hygiene factors but also motivators, such as esteem

innovation by launching schemes specifically linked to innovation. Here we can learn from expectancy theory and investigate the sort of recognition that good performers themselves value.

A key decision is which reward and recognition schemes are targeted at the individual and which should be targeted at encouraging teamwork. Individuals are unlikely to take on unfamiliar tasks in cross-functional teamwork unless it is rewarded.[77] One of the rewards for good performance is obviously promotion. However, not every employee has the aptitude to become a good manager and so the *dual-ladder* approach recognizes that some employees can have excellent skills within their function (for example, an engineer may be a expert in particular technologies) but may not have the competences, potential or desire to develop as a manager. Dual-ladder salary schemes at large companies provide motivation for employees to develop their technical competencies.

The level of most innovation rewards and recognition tend to be known *after the event*, in that they are announced after projects are finished. In some circumstances it may be beneficial to define and publish the levels of rewards available in advance. Zenith Electronics in the USA decided that rewards needed to be known *before the event*, to motivate the team on a particularly challenging project (see Zenith's 'Project Equity' Scheme). Rank-Xerox has a management reward scheme dependent on company, division, and individual performance.[78]

A clear link between goals and rewards is important. Such *transparency* can lead to open discussions on how goals can best be achieved and the appropriate rewards. Saab Training Systems, the Swedish defence contractor, found it useful to change the reward structure to put more emphasis on teamwork.[79] To fully support innovation, reward and recognition should not only focus on the achievement of business goals but also on encouraging individuals to increase their expertise. For example, few people have the necessary skills to manage a skunk works. Reward and recognition can be geared to encourage individuals with the necessary potential to acquire these skills and thus increase the innovation potential of the organization. The main case study for this chapter, on Lever Faberge, demonstrates how monetary rewards can be directly linked to personal learning goals.

Overall, reward and recognition systems need to be suitably maintained and sufficient management time needs to be reserved for this. Top management need to invest sufficient time in people issues to ensure that all of the other elements in the Pentathlon are positively supported. Without an appropriate culture and supportive people management policies, innovation performance cannot be boosted.

Box case 8.7 Zenith Electronics – 'project equity' scheme[80]

The US-based Zenith Electronics Corporation has used various approaches in providing rewards to employees involved in innovation projects. These were normally 'after the event' awards, given to teams or individuals for top performance. However, a multi-million dollar contract with a heavy delivery time penalty clause led Zenith to realize that a new approach was essential. This realization was also influenced by the recognition that the project was also considered to be technically high-risk.

It was decided to create a 'share scheme' for the project with a sum of several hundred thousand dollars reserved for rewarding the large team of over 25 dedicated members and 40 part-time members. At the start all dedicated team members were allocated 200 shares and part-timers received 50. The initial value of the shares was zero, but the successful achievement of each milestone and quality target, led to set increases in the share value, whereas each day of delay would lead to a defined loss in share value. The rules for calculating the value of shares were all defined up-front and were transparent to the whole team – so it was clear that, if everything went to plan, a dedicated team member could earn upwards of $15,000 bonus. Discretionary shares were also reserved for allocation to those employees that made extraordinary contributions.

Although the scheme required careful up-front definition and explanation, it shows that in forming innovation project teams the issue of reward and recognition needs to be considered. Special projects may require special schemes. Zenith was successful at developing the high-risk technology exactly on time – it was for use in digital television – and was convinced that the adoption of a new reward and recognition scheme contributed to the achievement of all of the milestones and quality goals. Zenith has also recognized the need to regularly update their reward system.

Development of Employees

As mentioned in the above sections, employees need to develop new skills that will contribute to innovation. The innovation strategy should define some of the new skills that are needed in an organization and these should be apparent from the technology roadmap (Chapter 4). These requirements can then be compared to existing skills and, where gaps exist, either hiring or employee development can be selected. Technological and specific market knowledge are clear skills that may need to be developed but also cross-functional team working skills and particularly project team leadership skills need to be constantly targeted for development. In the service sector, the ability to design an effective service augmentation is an area where employees may need to be developed, through specific training if available, or maybe through education.

Future skill requirements should be one driver of the development of employees. However, of equal importance is the link between individual development and motivation. Developing employees' skills in areas where they are not currently directly applicable can bring dividends in terms of motivation and creativity.

Summary

This chapter has covered the fifth and final element of the Pentathlon – people and organization, including cultural and team issues. It has stressed the strategic importance of the management of human resources. Three levels of analysis were presented: the organization level; innovation project teams; and the employee level. Overall the chapter has:

❑ Explained the research on management culture and how this can be used to help develop a 'culture of innovation'.

❑ Summarized best practices for creating an innovative working environment, while cautioning that people management practices are context dependent and are therefore difficult to transfer.

❑ Described the advantages and limitations of the five main types of teams that can be used to manage innovation projects.

❑ Explained the steps required to form and successfully run innovation teams, including selecting team members and managing the functional interfaces.

❑ Covered the main aspects of managing individual employees, from their recruitment, to their appraisal, and the recognition of their performance. It also showed the complexity facing managers in their need to encourage motivation.

Illustrating the above points, this chapter's main case study is about Unilever's Lever Fabergé plant and the way employees' performance and development were directly linked to their remuneration.

This and the previous four chapters have proposed a wide range of tools and techniques for innovation management, relating to each of the elements of the Pentathlon. The management challenge is to boost innovation performance by coordinating the improvements in each element of the Pentathlon and is the subject of the next chapter.

Management Recommendations

❑ Use the cultural web as a diagnosis tool and apply ideas from best practice to create a real 'culture of innovation'.

❑ Choose a suitable mix of different types of project teams.

❑ Manage innovation project teams not only to obtain the maximum returns from projects but also to develop sufficient talent for driving such projects.

❑ Link innovation strategy to the development of employees and support this with appropriate reward systems.

Recommended Reading

(1) Bratton, J. and Gold, J., *Human Resource Management: Theory and Practice* (Basingstoke UK: Palgrave Macmillan, 2003), ISBN 0-333-99326-8. Comprehensive text covering all aspects of HRM.

(2) Tushman, M.L. and Anderson, P. (eds), *Managing Strategic Innovation and Change* (Oxford: Oxford University Press, 1997), ISBN 0-19-510011-5. Useful readings on how change management can be used to support innovation. A classic.

(3) Jelinek, M. and Schoonhoven, C.B., *The Innovation Marathon: Lessons from High Technology Firms* (Oxford, UK: Basil Blackwell, 1990), ISBN 0-631-15392-6. Insights into the cultures of leading innovative companies.

Main Case Study   Lever Fabergé, Unilever – encouraging innovation[81]

Before reading this case, consider the following generic innovation management issues:

- How can a culture of innovation be introduced?
- How can the message be communicated to staff effectively?
- How can reward and recognition stimulate both the achievement of both business goals and the development of new skills?
- What levels of innovation can result?

Unilever's Lever Fabergé plant in Leeds, UK, is a showpiece factory and in 2000 it won the 'factory of the year' prize in the demanding Management Today/Cranfield School of Management Best Factory Awards. Lever Fabergé's approach clearly demonstrates how good people management can be an enabler of excellent manufacturing processes. The factory's mission is to produce Unilever's range of personal care products. 'It's the largest aerosol factory in the world, producing 300 million aerosols a year', says Gary Calveley, works director at the time of the award, and now Unilever Home and Personal Care Europe (HPCE) logistics director. While half the factory produces deodorants in aerosol form, the other half produces personal care products in a wide range of packaging variants, such as: sticks, roll-ons, creams and liquids – examples of which are found on virtually every bathroom shelf in Europe. The personal care products market is highly competitive and consequently the Leeds factory's performance must constantly improve.

All of the plant's products are produced in high volumes and the quality, cost-efficiency and dependability of the operation has been based on a number of manufacturing process improvement initiatives. A programme for reducing the cost of non-quality succeeded in cutting it by a factor of eight in three years. Autonomous maintenance has passed the responsibility for maintaining production line equipment to operators and reduced 'down-time' to insignificant levels. Productivity improvements, set-up time reductions, and workplace management have all met exacting targets. Management has played a significant role in starting such operations initiatives but it is the drive of the operators on the factory floor that is the key to Lever Fabergé's success.

The Way Forward

When Calverley arrived in 1997, the Leeds factory had several particular characteristics. Firstly, the workforce was 75 per cent female, many of whom had started their careers working 'part-time' shifts of five hours to fit in with their domestic obligations. It was a unionized plant with 'good but not exceptional' industrial relations. Thirdly, the factory had experimented with many of the new approaches that swept through British manufacturing industry in the 1980s and 1990s (most of which originated from Japan) but the results had been decidedly average.

Yet management knew that success could be achieved because many of the manufacturing practices being considered were already successfully in operation in the Unilever Cartersville plant in Georgia, USA. In teamwork, for example, Cartersville was recognized as probably the best Unilever factory worldwide. However, the best way forward for Leeds was far from clear.

Recognizing this, Calverley put together a formal proposal to senior Unilever executives within HPCE, to invest in a 'manufacturing change programme'. Its objective: to transform the plant into something resembling (and hopefully surpassing) Cartersville. With senior management signed-up, Calverley's next action was to appoint Eugene Toner, a 22-year Unilever veteran to spearhead the transformation on a day-to-day basis. Together, Toner, human resources manager John Clayton and senior union convenor Malcolm Colbeck were to prove highly instrumental in the journey ahead. 'Although Malcolm and I perform very different roles, we're actually quite similar', is how Clayton puts it. 'We've both been here a long time, are passionate about the business, and are desperate to see it succeed'.

Toner and Clayton took Colbeck and two other union representatives to Cartersville. An outcome of this visit was the decision to closely emulate the way in which Cartersville had used a joint management-union working party and a series of small ad-hoc groups with individual tasks in achieving its transformation. One task that was urgent was to spread the vision. Unusually, to achieve this, Toner hired a small theatre company to spend a few days working in the factory and to then write and stage a play about their experiences. A redundant building was turned into a temporary theatre, and HPCE divisional board members were invited along for the opening night.

It was, says Toner, something of a gamble but one that paid off brilliantly. In three performances, viewed by over 600 employees, the theatre group vividly portrayed the factory's past, present and future. The working practices of the 1960s and 1970s were contrasted with those of the mid-1990s – and again with those of the post-change programme future; when empowered, autonomous teams would pervade the factory. After each performance of the play, employees were asked to challenge and modify the vision – the principal feedback was along the lines of 'Great. But when is it going to happen?'

Before it could happen, several crucial changes had to be made to the way that people were motivated, developed and rewarded within the plant. 'Being willing to work in a new way . . . is one thing,' says Clayton. 'Having the relevant confidence and competencies is quite another.' This became very apparent when employee focus groups determined the skills and competencies needed for autonomous teams. The gulf between employees' actual abilities and the required levels was huge.

Coaching the Change

Based on what he had seen at Cartersville, Calveley sought the authority to recruit a team of full-time 'coaches' to work alongside the factory's employees, developing their skills and competencies. Four of the dozen who were eventually hired came from within the factory and the remainder came from backgrounds such as the air force, the police, fitness instruction and teaching. Their first few weeks were rocky and the coaches wondered what they had let themselves in for. 'Looking back, there was a great deal of misunderstanding, doubt and confusion', says coach Nigel Spencer. Nevertheless, the scope for improvement was very obvious: Spencer vividly recalls working with one production team for a week, fine-tuning the running of their line to a state of perfection, only to come in on the following Monday morning to find that weekend maintenance had disrupted all the settings and put the line back to where it was a week before.

Two developments were to give focus to the work of the coaches. The first was the emerging understanding of precisely which skills and competencies contributed to successful performance in particular jobs within the factory. A listing, the 'competencies framework', proved particularly useful, in tackling areas such as communication, safe working, and teamwork.

The second development concerned pay. For many years, pay had been based upon the results of an annual round of negotiation between management and the union. Calveley and his team recognized that a mechanism was needed to positively reinforce the messages that they were trying to get across. This, says Clayton, was a huge leap – not just for the factory's union representatives but also for the workforce. It also took a great deal of midnight oil, invested by both management and union to develop a mutually acceptable mechanism.

'Right from the start, we knew that we wanted to reward people for exceptional effort – and not reward people who were just coasting along', Clayton says. As the work of the coaches gradually produced results, it was a philosophy with which more and more of the workforce were in agreement. 'We began to get a lot of feedback saying: "Thank God you're doing this – because I'm sick of working hard to just carry other people",' he says. 'Now, every single person on site is paid according to their achievement of personal objectives', observes Calverley.

Despite its apparent complexities, the new system was really fairly

Main Case Study *continued*

straightforward to administer. In effect it put an incentive on two dimensions: specific 'work targets', and 'personal goals' – the acquisition of new 'skills and competencies'. Typically, each year individuals were given three work targets to achieve, and three enabling skills and competencies to acquire. The work targets were not simply output- or productivity-based, but focused on achieving specific parts of the factory's transformation – for example implementing autonomous maintenance on a specific line. The second dimension can be explained as follows: 'skills' are learning how to carry out a specific job in the factory, and 'competencies' are behaviours, such as communication and taking the initiative.

Employees' performance on these two dimensions was determined in appraisals by line managers using a matrix (Figure 8.12), guided by observations from the coaches and regular feedback. 'The idea is that at the end of the year, there shouldn't be any surprises', says Spencer, who, in his role as a coach, often facilitates interim appraisals. To determine the appropriate payment, a scoring system is used. First, each individual's performance against their personal goals is classified into four categories. These are: 'none achieved', '1 achieved', '2 achieved', '3 achieved' or 'over-achieved'. The work target classifications are: 'hardly/none', 'partial', 'full', and 'exceptional'. Each individual's position in the matrix is determined and this determines the level of pay award that they are to receive. It does so in the form of a multiplying factor based on the 'standard' increase, which is linked to the overall achievements of the factory's

Figure 8.12   Lever Fabergé's achievements and rewards matrix

Pay Awards Through The Integrated Approach

Achievement of Personal Goals

		Achievement of Personal Goals				
		None Achieved	1 Achieved	2 Achieved	3 Achieved	Over Achieved
Work Target Achievement	Hardly/None	6	6	6	6	6
	Partial	6	5	5	4	3
	Full	6	5	1	3	2
	Exceptional	6	4	3	2	1

Individual performance pay

1 standardx4   4 0.5 standard

2 standardx2   5 None

3 standard   6 None

objectives. The individual's position in the matrix gives a 'score' (for example, 'over-achieved' personal goals and 'full' achievement of work targets leads to a '2'), which in turn leads to a pay increase of 'standard ×2'. Employees who over achieve on both dimensions receive a score of '1' and an increase of 'standard ×4'. Underachievement on either dimension reduces pay increases or, for poor performance in both dimensions gives no increase.

How important has the scheme been in bringing about the factory's manufacturing excellence? It is hard to overstate its value, say managers such as Toner and Clayton who have now seen it in operation for four years. Not everybody happily signs up to the principle, adds Spencer, but they do at least recognize that by not doing so, they are influencing their salary level, particularly when increases are compounded over several years. What is more, adds Calveley, the approach has leveraged top-level objectives, by linking them directly to individuals' targets and pay. This supports constant process innovation.

People Make Processes Work

The top-level results achieved speak for the value of the pay system. Targets and visual communications abound in the factory – notice boards containing breathtaking detail on the initiatives that have led to significant performance improvements. Clear links to the management metrics can be found in the performance measures used on the lines. Next to every production line is a wealth of data; statistics on yield, set-up time, maintenance, and so on – up to 30 graphs which the operators take a pride in explaining both to colleagues and visitors.

Matching the thoroughness of the communications, Fabergé's housekeeping programmes have been meticulously implemented. Operators have clearly specified procedures and prepared problem-recording charts. These are backed by maintenance trolleys with colour-coded lubricants and cleaners, glass inserts let into machinery so that belt drives, relays and actuators can be inspected without removing the covers, superb workshops . . . the list goes on. Even routine cleaning is embraced. Purpose-built cleaning trolleys are placed in strategic positions, and contain everything needed to support housekeeping and cleaning activities: buckets, mops, brushes, spades, cleaning materials and solutions, gloves, wipes and so forth. Standard operating procedures, checklists, 'lock-off' boards and schematic diagrams of each cell – as well as ample provision of the tools and materials required for each task. Quite simply, the factory is superbly well-organized, and clean well-laid-out factories pay dividends in terms of product quality and efficiency.

The factory has made huge strides with workplace practice. Rightly, the emphasis on innovation at Fabergé has been on the human resources practices that have brought about the extraordinary change in a short time. Coaches, a vision play, genuine empowerment, and a payment scheme that combines skills acquisition with the achievement of objectives – these are the people management approaches that have brought extraordinary process innovations.

9 Boosting Innovation Performance

'There are risks and costs to a program of action, but they are far less than the long range risks and costs of comfortable inactions.'

(John F. Kennedy)

Introduction

The Pentathlon framework reminds us of the need to consider each of the elements of innovation management and not to focus on one area alone. In the previous five chapters we have looked at each of the elements and presented key tools and techniques to maximize performance. However, exemplary performance in one area of the Pentathlon alone is not enough and it is necessary to 'step back' and assess the overall effectiveness of an organization's innovativeness. It is important to determine priorities and start appropriate improvement efforts. The five elements of the Pentathlon are not independent and so steps taken to improve, say, portfolio management will impact other areas, and vice versa. Interactions should be managed to reinforce overall performance but the relationships between the different areas are complex and interactions cannot be predicted with certainty. Inaction is not an option and managers must be proactive in attempting to master something to which many organizations aspire but which few actually achieve – continuously high levels of innovation.

This chapter covers the main aspects of this challenge giving:

▸ An overview of how to improve innovation performance.
▸ Suggestions on how to choose suitable performance measures and determine the priorities for improving innovation management.
▸ A discussion of the linkages between the different elements of innovation management.
▸ Ideas on how to improve overall performance such as developing learning loops from innovation projects and using change management techniques focused on innovation.
▸ A case study on an automotive supplier that has consistently achieved high levels of innovation despite its limited resources – Sidler GmbH and Co.

Figure 9.1 Improving innovation performance

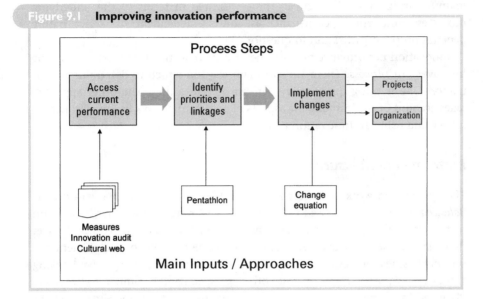

Performance Improvement

Figure 9.1 shows a suggested process for improving innovation performance. We deliberately say 'suggested', as this flow diagram is a simplification of a methodology that is very dependent on the individual circumstances facing a company, its processes, and its culture of innovation. The diagram could leave the impression that we are being overly deterministic and the steps required are clear-cut; this is not the case. Variations on the approach and multiple iterations are likely to be necessary for any one organization to achieve significant improvements.

The diagram shows that there are three main components to improving performance, each of which will be discussed in this chapter:

◻ Assessing current performance. As shown in Figure 9.1, the areas for improvement can be identified using performance measures, the cultural web (Chapter 8), and what is called an *innovation audit*.

◻ Identifying priorities and linkages between the different elements of the Pentathlon.

◻ Implementing changes to improve performance (at both the project and organizational levels).

Assessing Current Performance

In this chapter we will use the term *innovation performance*. By this, we mean the total innovation produced by an organization, in terms of the generation and commercialization of ideas for new products, new services, new or improved manufacturing or service delivery processes, *and* in terms of the underlying processes. Innovation performance is context dependent; its exact nature depends on the organization in question.

Innovation performance needs to be measured, as this is the first part of the improvement process. There are two main ways in which to determine performance. One is using quantitative performance measures. The other approach takes account of the less tangible aspects of an organization's innovation performance and using an innovation audit.

Performance Measures

The well-known work of Robert Kaplan and David Norton of Harvard on the *Balanced Scorecard* has stressed the need to have a range of measures in addition to the classical financial ones. The measures in the balanced scorecard cover financial aspects, the customer perspective, the perspective of the efficiency of internal business processes, and an innovation and learning perspective.[1] Taking a broad view, with financial and other perspectives, is similar to what we discussed in Chapter 6 – where we recommended that portfolio management should be based on a mixture of financial and non-financial approaches. Kaplan and Norton stress the importance of innovation saying 'we came to realize that innovation was a *critical* internal process' (their italics).[2]

The performance of an organization in terms of innovation is not easy to determine, and our own case study research has shown that managers recognize the difficulties they have with measurement.[3] Work with their clients has also led the McKinsey consultancy company to state that performance measures are one of the main challenges of innovation management.[4] Recognizing that there are different types of measures is the first step in developing an appropriate measurement system.

Types of Performance Measures

The topic of performance measurement has been studied in-depth, by operations management researchers. A fundamental approach in this discipline is to view all management processes as having inputs and outputs.[5] Figure 9.2 shows this *input–output model* view of innovation. *Inputs* are the time and resources required, such as people or information technology. Innovation is largely a knowledge-based process and ideas are transformed by the work of employees into services and products that can be sold to customers. The resources required are the time and investments made, the people working on the innovation projects, information technology and can also include equipment, such as that used in service or manufacturing production and delivery processes.

Applying the input–output model to innovation helps us to recognize that there are three types of measure. *Input measures*, such as the percentage of revenues invested in R&D, are useful benchmarks but they do not gauge how effective a company is at turning R&D capacity into commercial success. *Process*

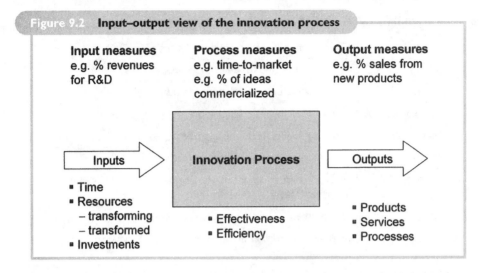

Figure 9.2   Input–output view of the innovation process

Input measures
e.g. % revenues
for R&D

Process measures
e.g. time-to-market
e.g. % of ideas
commercialized

Output measures
e.g. % sales from
new products

Inputs

Innovation Process

Outputs

- Time
- Resources
  - transforming
  - transformed
- Investments

- Effectiveness
- Efficiency

- Products
- Services
- Processes

measures are indicators of the efficiency of the innovation process within an organization, for instance of the time required to bring an innovation to the market. Similarly, the percentage of ideas that are commercialized is a useful indicator of both how relevant the ideas generated are, and also how efficient the process to implement them is. *Output measures* are directly related to the commercial impact of innovations – such as revenues generated by a new service product, or cost savings through a more efficient service augmentation. Patents are a popular measure of innovation but it should be noted that this is not an output measure. Inventions described in patents need to be commercialized, either by being directly applied in products, services or processes, or through licensing. The number of patents generated is a measure of the innovation process within the company. An output measure related to patents is earnings from patent licensing.

Organizations need to choose measures in each of the three categories. Using input measures alone neglects the commercial side of innovation. Taking only output measures can make an organization commercially aware but the process itself needs to be monitored, if it is to be improved. Measures of the efficiency of 'the innovation process' (that is, the various sub-processes, such as NPD and ideation, that make up the way an organization approaches innovation) are needed.

Selecting Performance Measures

Research on performance measures shows that organizations typically measure too much. Complex measurement systems can cloud priorities. Bearing in mind that only a few measures should be used, measures need to be selected that are appropriate. Table 9.1 gives a set of questions that should be asked to determine appropriateness. These questions help managers choose individual measures

	Table 9.1	Points to consider in choosing performance measures

	Aspect	Questions to ask about the potential measure
1	Strategy	Is it directly related to the intended innovation strategy?
2	Simplicity	Is it simple to understand (and communicate)?
3	Action ability	Can and will the it be acted upon?
4	Appropriateness	Does it provide timely and appropriate feedback?
5	Validity	Does it reliably measure what it is meant to?
6	Reliability	Is it consistent, irrelevant of when or by whom is the measure-ment was made?
7	Clarity	Is interpretation of the measurement unambiguous?
8	Behaviour	Will the introduction of the measure have any adverse behavioural affects?
9	Cost-effectiveness	Is it worth the cost of collecting and analyzing the data?

Source: Based on Neely et al. (1997).[6]

that can be easily understood, effectively linked to strategy (and therefore support the implementation of strategy), can be trusted (because they are reliable), and are appropriate (for example, actionable).

Table 9.2 lists possible input, output and process measures for innovation, from which suitable ones should be selected. It covers the different perspectives recommended by Kaplan and Norton. Performance measures are context-dependent – they should relate to organization's business and the priorities for improvement. However, some general guidelines can be given. A range of measures should be selected that covers inputs, outputs, and process (to monitor and to learn how to improve the process itself). Ratio measures are often useful, as they are easier to compare than absolute measures. An example of this would be taking the innovation rate as the number of new products ('new' is normally defined as less than three years old) compared to the number in the existing portfolio, rather than just the number of new products developed. Overall, the number of measures used must be appropriate because, as noted earlier, having too many measures wastes management time.

The measures given in Table 9.2 on pp. 318–19 can be applied in both service and manufacturing organizations. In service, particular care should be taken to ensure that innovation performance measures adequately cover not only service products but also service augmentation. Table 9.2 includes a number of specific measures recommended for service organizations[10] but which are also relevant to the many manufacturing organizations that deliver services as well. It should also be recognized that certain measures commonly used for innovation, such as patents and the percentage of revenues invested in R&D are less useful in service companies as benchmarking data are less likely to be available or reliable.[11]

Using Performance Measures

Measures can be used to decide whether:

▢ The input resources are suitable, sufficient and are efficiently used to produce significant commercial innovations.

▢ The innovation process in the company is effective at producing innovations that have a commercial impact.

▢ Current innovation output is sufficient, compared to the strongest competitors and leading companies in other fields, benchmarking figures from competitors can provide useful comparisons.

▢ The innovation strategy is being successfully implemented.

The visual display of innovation data is useful as it allows past data to be compared to current values, or to the estimated values for competitors. Prominent visual displays of innovation data can act as powerful communication and motivation tools in organizations (for example, AXA Ireland have an 'innovation corridor' (see Chapter 3 main case study).

The Innovation Audit

The fact that it is difficult to create valid and reliable measures for all aspects of innovation has led to the innovation audit concept. Innovations 'audits' are different to financial audits, which are based on quantitative measures of financial performance (that is, output measures of past performance). Innovation audits look at not only performance (an output measure) but also how this performance was achieved (a process measure). This is because 'measuring performance is helpful, but it's only part of the story. To learn from our past successes and failures, we need to understand how they came about'.[12]

The concept of an innovation audit is not new. One early audit developed in the 1980s focused mainly on creativity and took a functional perspective, with audit questions to be answered by production, marketing, R&D, personnel, and so on.[13] Later audit tools have looked at all aspects of innovation management and their use has increased. New product development and innovation management consultants Arthur D. Little strongly recommend innovation audits.[14] The European Union has given substantial financial support for companies to have innovation audits conducted by consultants – over 760 organizations in 18 countries have benefited from this.[15] The British Standard on innovation management also emphasizes the need to audit innovation by looking at both the organizational aspects (16 questions) and product and service issues (seven questions).[16] Table 9.3 shows a number of the questions from the British Standard and it can be seen that many of them (for example, no. 6 on the 'innovative attitude') are hard to answer based on facts and so employees and managers will give their opinions. Although in many cases opinions are collected, the consensus of these can help to identify the strengths and weaknesses of an organization.

Table 9.2   Example input, process and output measures

Input measures	Process measures	Output measures
Financial	**Financial**	**Financial**
□ Per cent of revenues invested in product R&D	□ Average project costs	□ Per cent of sales revenues from new products/enhancements
□ Per cent of revenues invested in process R&D	□ Costs off/savings through outsourcing	□ Per cent of sales revenues from new services
□ Per cent of revenues invested in technology acquisition	**Process Efficiency**	□ Per cent cost savings/revenues from process innovation
□ Per cent of projects delayed or cancelled due to lack of funding	□ Average break-even-time	□ Quality improvements from process innovation
Customer Perspective	□ Average time-to-market	□ Return on innovation investment
□ Per cent mix of projects by their strategic drivers (for example meeting customer needs, reactions to competition; technology-driven; based on internal ideas; etc.)	□ Hours worked per project	□ Profitability of the new product programme
	□ Average time for a specific task (for example, initial design)	□ Earnings from patent licensing
Resources	□ Per cent time spent on project-related tasks	**Customer Perspective**
□ Per cent of total employees involved in innovation projects	□ Per cent time spent on non-project tasks (administrative and support) tasks.	□ Innovation rate (number of new products compared to total number of product in the portfolio)
□ Per cent of personnel trained in creativity and problem-solving techniques	□ Number of patents received/number commercialized	□ Number of new products compared to competitors
	□ Per cent mix of product/process /service/business process innovation projects	□ Number of new services compared to competitors
	□ Per cent usage of appropriate tools and techniques (for example advanced market research projects; computer-aided design; computer-integrated manufacturing, and so on)	□ Number of enhancements to service augmentations

- Per cent of personnel who have worked in two or more functions
- Number of ideas per source (for example ideas from employees, ideas from customers)
- Number of ideas generated per year for development into new products, services & processes
- Number of ideas considered per year for new products, services & processes
- Efficiency of links to external organizations
- Per cent of projects delayed or cancelled because of lack of human resources

- Per cent of projects that entered development and were ultimately considered commercial successes
- Per cent of projects killed too late (that is after significant expenditure)
- Per cent of employees actively contributing to innovation

Learning

- Per cent of projects where post-project reviews are conducted
- Number of improvements to innovation processes

Specific Service Measures

- Customer throughput time
- Complaints: number and type
- Staff satisfaction
- Efficiency of innovations in products and service augmentations
- Cost per customer
- Profit per customer
- Retention rates

- Number of process innovations (number of innovations per year compared to the total number of major processes used in operations)
- Per cent mix of first-to-market, fast follower, and me-too products
- Market share growth due to new products/ enhancements
- Market share growth due to new services
- Strike rate (ratio of orders to enquiries or quotations)
- Per cent of orders delivered on time
- Customer satisfaction indices

Source: Based on Goffin (2001), Neely *et al.* (1997) and Johnston and Clark (2001).[7,8,9]

Table 9.3   **Example innovation audit questions from the British Standard**

Number	Question
1	What types of innovation do you have in your organization?
2	Does your organization have a procedure for developing third-generation products and services?
3	Is this process documented?
4	How does your enterprise use its long-term vision of the future to inform and influence present activities?
5	What is your organization's budget for new product development?
6	Does an innovative attitude pervade your organization?
7	Is this innovation attitude communicated internally and externally?
8	Does your organization have a skills audit?
9	Is your organization involved in any alliances?
10	What mechanism does your organization have to react fast to threats or surprises from the competition?
11	How does your organization protect its intellectual property?
12	How does your organization learn from failures?

Innovation audits are just as useful for the service sector as for manufacturing. A concise set of questions recommended for service companies is given in Table 9.4. This can be used to make a fast assessment of innovation performance and such approaches normally use scoring, to capture perceptions in a quantitative form that can easily be summarized using descriptive statistics.

Conducting Innovation Audits

Innovation audits collect a variety of quantitative and qualitative data through survey techniques, and are normally conducted by outsiders (who are neutral) interviewing a representative sample of employees, managers and, possibly, customers. Interpreting answers to many of the questions requires experience and so this is an important reason for using an outside consultant to conduct the audit.

Many aspects of innovation cannot be expressed in figures and so qualitative data on an organization's performance is collected, or managers' views on performance levels are captured on perceptual scales. Audits gauge the innovation performance of individual organizations and data from different organizations are not directly comparable. The cultural web discussed in Chapter 8 can be used in conjunction with an innovation audit to collect information on how the culture of an organization impacts its innovation.

Table 9.4	Innovation audit questions recommended for the service sector[17]	

Number	Question
1	Is innovation stated as part of your corporate objectives and business plan?
2	Do you have at least two experiments or pilots of new service concepts being conducted at any one time?
3	Do you regularly review your portfolio of service offerings to make sure that they are balanced in terms of novelty/innovation and risk?
4	Is your objective to be the market leader by exceeding the value added of your main competitor?
5	Does your financial reporting system reflect innovation as an investment rather than as a cost?
6	Are you attracted by new technologies and considering how to apply them to your business?
7	Do you provide support to staff who try out new ideas even if the ideas fail?
8	Do you have a procedure for having staff 'mystery-shop' the competition and report back?
9	Do you provide training for staff in innovation-related skills?
10	Do you expect to get at least 5 per cent of export revenues from innovative services?

In conducting an innovation audit, the aims are:

☐ To identify an organization's strengths and weaknesses from an innovation perspective, through gaining the views of a representative sample of managers and employees.
☐ To collect ideas on how to make improvements.

The scope of the audit needs to be decided in advance, in terms of the number of people to be surveyed and also in terms of the breadth of questions to be used. Normally there are two levels of audit: a simple, fast version to obtain an initial idea of strengths and weaknesses, and a version that probes more deeply. Figure 9.3 shows a 'fast' version, in which the audit questions have been grouped using the Pentathlon framework in order to determine in which of the five areas a company is stronger or weaker. The fast audit can be completed in a workshop with managers, where their initial ideas for improvements and their views on the cultural web can also be collected. However, considering only the views of the management team is not sufficient (and can give a biased view) and so a representative sample from the whole organization should be surveyed. This is more revealing, as individual employees will give creative ideas for improving innovation. For example, the

Figure 9.3 'Fast innovation audit' questions[18]

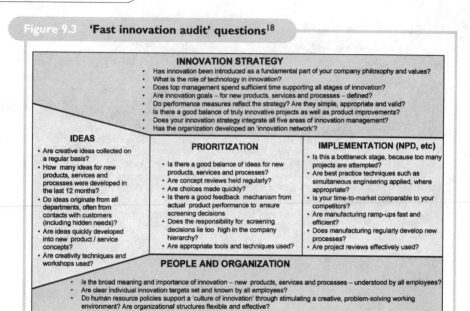

INNOVATION STRATEGY
- Has innovation been introduced as a fundamental part of your company philosophy and values?
- What is the role of technology in innovation?
- Does top management spend sufficient time supporting all stages of innovation?
- Are innovation goals – for new products, services and processes – defined?
- Do performance measures reflect the strategy? Are they simple, appropriate and valid?
- Is there a good balance of truly innovative projects as well as product improvements?
- Does your innovation strategy integrate all five areas of innovation management?
- Has the organization developed an 'innovation network'?

IDEAS
- Are creative ideas collected on a regular basis?
- How many ideas for new products, services and processes were developed in the last 12 months?
- Do ideas originate from all departments, often from contacts with customers (including hidden needs)?
- Are ideas quickly developed into new product / service concepts?
- Are creativity techniques and workshops used?

PRIORITIZATION
- Is there a good balance of ideas for new products, services and processes?
- Are concept reviews held regularly?
- Are choices made quickly?
- Is there a good feedback mechanism from actual product performance to ensure screening decisions?
- Does the responsibility for screening decisions lie too high in the company hierarchy?
- Are appropriate tools and techniques used?

IMPLEMENTATION (NPD, etc)
- Is this a bottleneck stage, because too many projects are attempted?
- Are best practice techniques such as simultaneous engineering applied, where appropriate?
- Is your time-to-market comparable to your competitors?
- Are manufacturing ramp-ups fast and efficient?
- Does manufacturing regularly develop new processes?
- Are project reviews effectively used?

PEOPLE AND ORGANIZATION
- Is the broad meaning and importance of innovation – new products, services and processes – understood by all employees?
- Are clear individual innovation targets set and known by all employees?
- Do human resource policies support a 'culture of innovation' through stimulating a creative, problem-solving working environment? Are organizational structures flexible and effective?
- Is innovation covered by employees' appraisals?

consulting company Synectics always focuses on obtaining the views of a wide range of employees in its efforts to enhance organizations' innovation performance. Direct interviews are more effective than distributing audit questionnaires, as in the discussion vital information about the organization's workings can emerge.

A representative survey should use a more comprehensive set of questions than the fast version. A widely used innovation audit was developed by a team from London Business School (LBS) and called a 'technical innovation audit'. It has questions covering both innovation processes (for example, concept generation; NPD; process innovation; and technology acquisition) and their 'enablers' (such as human resource practices and leadership from top management).[19] Managers are required to rate their company's performance in various areas on a scale of 1 ('poor') to 5 ('world class'). Such an audit forces managers and employees to review all aspects of their innovation management and this automatically stimulates thinking on ways of improving performance.[20] In the appendix we give a suggested 'in-depth' innovation audit, based on the LBS version, enhanced by questions from a number of other sources.

The cultural web and the innovation audit provide pointers on the current performance of an organization. The discussions with employees will also generate a wealth of ideas on how to improve performance. The next step is determining the priorities and considering the linkages.

Box case 9.1   Evotec OAI – using an innovation audit

Evotec OAI is a leading provider of biological, chemical, and screening services, which help pharmaceutical companies accelerate the discovery and development process, manage risk, and reduce the time and cost of bringing new drugs to the market. The company has over 600 employees, many of whom are PhD scientists, based in Hamburg and in the UK arm, which was formerly Oxford Asymmetry International (OAI). Evotec OAI has an impressive set of clients, which reads like a who's who of the chemical and pharmaceutical industries and includes BASF, GlaxoSmithKline, Pfizer and Roche.

Five years ago OAI used a team of consultants to conduct an innovation audit. Interviews were held with a sample of staff, covering all functions and levels and using a comprehensive set of audit questions. The results were revealing: staff rated OAI relatively low on creativity; innovation was not perceived as sufficiently customer-led; knowledge was not optimally applied in the company; there was not enough communication between the two divisions (discovery and development); and clearer rewards and recognition were needed. Some of the management team were disappointed with the results of the audit and expressed the opinion that it did not reflect the OAI they knew and the market view that OAI was already very innovative. Nevertheless, the audit seemed to show that management and employees viewed the potential for more innovation differently and the management team quickly set about making some significant changes.

The changes included major efforts to become more creative. For example, a knowledge management system was implemented to capture and share much of the expertise of individual OAI scientists. This made the solution of clients' problems more efficient and helped identify innovations that would most impact the customer. OAI managers also worked on both the formal and informal communication. The bringing together of the two divisions in a new building made a big impact, as did a range of new reward and recognition schemes that spurred innovation. The President of Evotec OAI's Chemical and Pharmaceutical Development Division, and then Chief Operating Officer of OAI, Dr Mario Polywka, sees the innovation audit as an important catalyst, 'we probably would have made a lot of the changes such as implementing a knowledge management system anyway. However, the innovation audit helped galvanize our actions. We have seen a lot of returns on the investments we have made in our people, knowledge management, and communications. What is more, our customers have also seen many tangible benefits in both the range and speed of services we offer to support drug discovery and development. For me, the biggest steps we have made are firstly that our employees now realise that being a service company involves significant technical creativity, but that also the way we do business, commercially and financially, is innovative in itself'.

Priorities and Linkages

Priority Areas

An innovation audit identifies the areas of the Pentathlon in which an organization is strong and those in which it is weak. Normally through having collected the views of a significant number of employees, a picture emerges of how an organization's approach to innovation. Quickly it becomes clear, for example, whether a broad number of sources contribute to the generation of product ideas. Similarly, employees' views on how well innovations are implemented will provide insights into how effective new product development and related processes are. A typical result would be that the implementation processes (based on Stage-Gate methodology) are very efficient but that the front end fails to generate really innovative ideas. When related back to the Pentathlon framework, most organizations perceive they are good in one or two areas and need to improve in at least three others.

The summarized results of the audit should be fed back to the organization, and sometimes it can be a surprise to management to learn how employees perceive weaknesses in the organization's overall innovation processes. Further short workshops with management can be used to define priorities for improvement. Identifying linkages can help to generate more effective improvement plans.

Considering Linkages

In Chapter 2 we looked at the literature on innovation and saw that it could be categorized by the level at which innovation was analysed. The numerous economic studies have looked mainly at the impact of innovation on markets and economies – the macro level. These studies should remind us that not only the linkages between the elements of the Pentathlon are important, but also the linkages beyond the elements – for instance the linkages between an organization and its external environment.

At the other end of the research spectrum, a plethora of studies have investigated the factors that influence the effectiveness of new product development. Between these two bodies of literature, there has been far less research conducted at the organizational level: 'the vast majority of previous research is project-based and lacks the general perspective of executive-level managers'.[21] However, it is this company-level perspective that is the most relevant to senior managers.

Several themes about the linkages between aspects of innovation management can be extracted from the latest literature. Table 9.5 shows how selected papers have identified these emerging themes. The academic and practitioner papers that have discussed the latest thinking on innovation management at the organizational level cover four topics:

Table 9.5　Emerging issues – linkages – in innovation management

Main topics	Borins (2001)[22]	British Standard (1999)[16]	Calantone et al. (1995)[23]	Chambers & Boghani (1998)[38]	Day et al. (1994)[39]	Karol et al. (2002)[36]	Linder (2003)[30]	McGourty et al. (1996)[24]	Sakkab (2002)[34]	Smith et al. (1999)[41]	Thamhain (1990)[25]	Webber & LaBarre (2001)[44]
1 Innovation leadership	√	√	√					√			√	
2 Creating knowledge networks	√	√		√	√	√	√		√			√
3 Linking idea generation to the NPD process				√	√	√				√		
4 Change management approach needed	√							√			√	√

☐   The type of leadership required to drive innovation.

☐   Creating knowledge networks inside and outside the organization.

☐   How idea generation needs to be integrated with new product development.

☐   The need to manage change to achieve innovation.

We will consider each of these in more detail.

Innovation Leadership

The role of senior managers and product champions in innovation is central. Leadership and commitment appear to be absolutely necessary to drive the successful implementation of innovation strategy.[22] Attributes of leadership in the context of innovation include providing a vision and a role model, instilling a culture in which innovation is visible and widely communicated[23] and rewarded,[24] and having the ability to understand the multiple disciplines, processes, and projects in an organization.[25] Leadership appears to be fundamentally important in pulling all the strands of innovation together as, 'an organization's capacity to innovate is affected far more by *those* who set the environment in which innovation is to occur and manage innovative activities than those who undertake the creative work' (our emphasis).[26] The particular attributes required to lead innovation appear to be rare and so there is a need to link innovation strategy with people development programmes that ensure the availability of entrepreneurially-thinking managers for innovation projects.

Management leadership in the context of innovation is particularly importance as both the nature of innovation and how it can be achieved is not as clear as, for example, more developed management disciplines such as total quality management. This means that top management will need to reserve sufficient time to communicate, communicate and communicate again the role and goals of innovation.

Creating Knowledge Networks

Improving the process by which ideas are generated for all types of innovation is widely recognized as a way of gaining a competitive advantage. Ideas should come from multiple sources, both internal and increasingly external,[27, 28, 29, 30] as unexpected links often produce the best ideas.[31] Bringing people together from different backgrounds and functions – generating cross-boundary ideas – is particularly effective. (For example, external R&D can create real value, as can buying the rights to others' intellectual property.[32]) Knowledge management techniques, such as systems for storing and sharing ideas can be effective.[33] The Procter & Gamble company uses an 'Innovation Net' system to communicate ideas between employees worldwide and also has run an 'Innovation Expo' to make connections between employees from different organizations.[34] In services, employees with direct customer interaction need to be more effectively used in gathering ideas from customers.[35] DuPont is also active in looking for external sources of innovation.[36]

More network connections bring the potential for more ideas but they also have an 'overhead' – managers need to find ways to manage the interfaces and sources of innovation effectively (see also Box case: Fiat Iveco). Clearly ideation is becoming more dependent on creating linkages across departmental and organizational boundaries and managers need to take a lead here.

Linking Idea Generation to NPD

Although new product development is an important part of innovation management, it is by no means the only part. From the late 1980s there was a strong emphasis on defining effective NPD processes, many of which were based on the Stage-Gate ideas of Cooper and Kleinschmidt.[37] Nowadays, most companies have efficient product development processes and so it is hard to compete on the basis of a NPD process alone.[38,39,40] What is needed is an overall faster way of creating innovative ideas, rapidly dropping those that are less attractive, and implementing the remaining ones quick;y. Leading companies such as AlliedSignal and Alcoa in the USA have focused on making such links tangible through what they have termed the 'Front-end Innovation Process'. This is based on the philosophy that, 'the faster that ideas can be evaluated and the earlier flawed ideas terminated, the more productive the pipeline becomes . . .'.[41] AlliedSignal and Alcoa use fast evaluation based on an integrated assessment of the technologies and market attributes of potential projects.

For managers the message is clear: new product development, ideation and portfolio management are very closely linked. Management actions to make improvements in any one area will impact the other two; all three should be considered in unison.

Box case 9.2   Cobra, Thailand – leadership and windsurf boards[42]

Based in Chonburi in Thailand, Cobra International was founded in 1985 and is a manufacturer of windsurf and surfboards and a range of other items for recreational sports. Cobra's strategy has always focused on quality, technology, and a strong customer orientation.

Cobra uses professional quality management techniques, focuses on quality consistency, and is the only manufacturer in the industry with ISO 9001:2000 certification. This is one of the reasons that it has become a world leader, with over 50 per cent market share today as an original equipment manufacturer (OEM) supplying the top brands. Windsurf boards must withstand tremendous loads, as top windsurfers can launch their boards up to seven meters off rolling surf. Making boards that can withstand such a buffeting requires not only good manufacturing but also an intimate knowledge of the leading technologies – fibre-reinforced composites. Cobra is constantly developing the 'combination of methodologies and materials' says Pierre Olivier Schnerb, Vice President of Technology. 'For example, Cobra Tuflite® technology applies techniques learnt from windsurfing to surfing'.

The third element of strategy has come from the employees' intimate knowledge of the sports for which they manufacture equipment. Kym Thompson, an Australian, has been a champion surfer for over 30 years. In addition, for 30 years he has been professionally pushing forward the quality standards of surfboard manufacturing and is Cobra's manager of surfboard production. Many other employees are active sportspeople and bring product and design ideas into the company. Being users themselves has helped Cobra develop top designs and enabled them to build very close relationships with nearly all of the top brands.

Vorapant Chotikapanich, the founder and current President, thinks innovation is absolutely essential for the company's competitiveness. In order to stimulate innovation, he gives employees the power to create, experiment and decide. 'I ensure that they get adequate top management support but I also drive for hot ideas to be implemented quickly', says Chotikapanich. Additionally, he perceives organizational innovation as key, 'we are currently organized according to technology rather than industry. So, for example, the Thermo Compression Molding Division manufactures everything from windsurf boards, surfboards, wakeboards to kiteboards. It is important to apply our technical expertise across all of our products. We also supplement our own competencies with those from a network of customers, suppliers, and designers'.

Managing Change

To improve innovation performance requires the management of a wide range of issues, from ideas, to technologies, to culture, to organizational change. How changing conditions and changing customer requirements can best be met requires managers to positively oriented towards change.[43, 44] To be effective at driving changes needed to support innovation, managers will need to be effective at identifying and dealing with barriers. Barriers to innovation, particularly internal political ones, need to be effectively addressed by managers.[45] Organizational practices will need to be changed to match the strategic direction.[46] Therefore, in giving leadership to an organization, it is importance to use change management techniques and these will be discussed in depth in a later section.

Box case 9.3   Fiat Iveco – identifying innovation challenges[47]

Iveco is the arm of Fiat responsible for manufacturing and marketing commercial and industrial vehicles, buses and diesel engines. Massimo Fumarola has worked as Platform Development Manager in the heavy vehicles division and as Business Development Manager in the Engine Business Unit. In both roles he has been closely involved with considering how Iveco can increase overall innovation performance. He says, 'in my opinion there are three challenges in managing innovation. The most important one has to do with the organization and here there is a dilemma. On the one hand we want employees to work in structured, methodical ways to produce products in a timely, in fact a very disciplined way. On the other hand, we want people to challenge the established ways of thinking and working. This is a big problem and the only way to solve it is sometimes to take suitable people and break them out from the parent organization and give them freedom not just to act but also to think innovation.'

'Getting enough people with the right experience is something we need to work on. We have great functional specialists but not enough people that have worked in several functions and have a deep understanding of the interfaces [between functions]. Unfortunately, in this industry and other ones I talk to, not enough people want to become what I'll call "cross-functional boundary managers". It takes time to find, encourage and develop such people' says Fumarola.

'Thirdly, it's about getting everyone involved. It's not just the voice of the customer. You also need to involve the truck operators, the suppliers, the regulatory agencies, and all the other stakeholders right from the beginning. Interfaces, not functions, generate most of the problems and we're getting more interfaces to consider. I think that the best managers of tomorrow will be the ones that can maximize innovation performance by minimizing the interface issues'.

In a topic as complex as innovation management, the relationships between different elements of the Pentathlon may not be obvious. It is useful to at least try and predict what they might be, before launching improvement initiatives. A common problem can otherwise arise. Anecdotal evidence shows that companies that take steps to boost the number of innovative ideas being generated within their organizations, without considering the impact on new product development, often end up outing more ideas into the pipeline and slowing the output. Managers need to carefully consider how linkages can be turned to advantage (and researchers urgently need to investigate how companies attempt to boost innovation).

Actions to Boost Performance

Actions to improve innovation can be aimed at both the project and organizational levels (as shown in Figure 9.1). The sum of the results of individual innovation projects constitutes the total output of an organization and so it is important to learn from both successes and failures. Therefore, each individual innovation project should generate learning on both how the project itself was conducted and on the underlying innovation process.

Project-to-Project Learning

The ability to learn from each and every innovation project is essential.[48] One way of improving the performance in subsequent projects is to conduct *post-project reviews* (PPRs) – in which project team members discuss how projects were conducted and what could have been improved. Such reviews can generate knowledge that can lead to competitive advantage and consequently, the importance of PPRs is widely recognized. Using PPRs can be understood as adding a learning loop to the Pentathlon. There is a need to learn how implementation can be better managed but learning can focus on improving other areas as well.

Although the idea that PPRs can be a valuable approach is established, research shows that most companies do not use them and therefore miss a learning opportunity.[49] There are a number of key points to consider when organizing PPRs:[50]

☐ *Timing.* It is important that reviews are held relatively soon after the innovation project has been completed, otherwise the availability of the key players is likely to prove difficult and also their interest and memories of the project will be less reliable.

☐ *Scope, atmosphere and moderation.* The PPR meeting needs to be effective at uncovering issues and so may need to enter the 'zone of uncomfortable debate'. This normally requires a 'no-blame' atmosphere and a skilled *PPR moderator*. The moderator should normally be from outside the project team and have prior experience of leading probing debate.

☐ *Learning from failures.* Just as successful innovation projects should be used to gather learning, PPRs should also be conducted for failed projects.

☐ *Learning at different levels.* It is important to take the opportunity to learn at different levels. Technical problem solving is an obvious area but probably more important lessons can be derived about the process used for the project. Such learning can help management make better estimates of project quality, time and costs for future projects.

☐ *Dissemination of the results.* The time and effort invested in running a review is wasted unless the key findings are efficiently disseminated and are available when they are relevant to other projects. The impact of key messages is often lost if they are simply documented in (yet another) report that is distributed to other project managers. Recipients may underestimate the importance of what is covered in a report, or the key messages are lost in the deluge of information that project managers receive. To combat the poor leverage of written reports, leading companies have adopted other approaches. Hewlett-Packard has recorded short 'what I learnt from this project' video interviews with project managers and made these available on their intranet. Others have recognized that the results of post-project reviews should be discussed at the start of new projects, or should be a focus for mentoring schemes for project managers. A salient point is to make sure that the PPR learning is applied to future actions and senior managers should promote this.

☐ *Linking the learning to actions.* Recent research shows that disseminating the knowledge effectively requires a *project knowledge broker*, whose role is to concentrate on the transfer of learning between project teams.[51] In particular this broker is tasked with ensuring that new projects have specific actions linked to the learning from previous projects, in order to avoid repeating mistakes. One useful approach is to identify how each learning point can be built into the stages and gates of all current projects.

PPRs should not only generate ideas on how to improve current and future projects but also where processes can be optimized. Senior management are the custodians of the innovation processes within their organization and need to drive the improvements.

Change Management and Innovation

Learning from projects and using this knowledge to improve innovation processes is important. However, research has shown that there are two major forms of change in organizations: either *convergent* (or *incremental*) change or *frame-breaking* change.[52] Project-to-project learning and improving processes can be seen as incremental change and so organizations that want to achieve significant improvements in innovation performance will need to do more. Market discontinuities, shifts in product life cycles and even internal company dynamics all have major consequences in the way in which a company should be organized.[53]

Performance measures, the innovation audit, and the cultural web all help to diagnose weaknesses from an innovation perspective. The tripartite approach also provides rich information on how employees perceive innovation performance can be enhanced. Innovation has an inherent ability to excite people. However, managers should not underestimate the time and energy that needs to be invested by management to successfully boost innovation. In particular, changes to organizational culture require much management effort; much more than the superficial attempts usually made to manage culture.[54] Companies with a human resource management function need to utilize this to support the process of change management (and Section 5.0 of the innovation audit in the Appendix includes several questions to gauge whether the HR function has a strategic role). Managers may need to make radical changes in the way an organization approaches innovation, in its culture, or in the way it is formally organized. Individual employees can be reluctant to change and so an organization can have an in-built inertia. Change management techniques are useful to moderate resistance to change in innovation management and there are some diagnostic and implementation tools that are essential to managers, which we will discuss.[55]

A useful way of looking at change is to consider what factors are necessary to overcome the organizational resistance to change. Researchers who have made major contributions to the understanding of change management, such as Michael Tushman at Harvard, have found that different components are necessary. These are:

❑ Dissatisfaction.
❑ A vision.
❑ A process for change.

It is often the case in management situations that one of these three factors is missing and so the change management fails. Each factor is necessary but not sufficient for change. A memorable 'shorthand' is to express the relationship between these factors mathematically. The three factors are linked in the *change equation* (which should be read as 'the product of D, V and P needs to exceed C'):[56]

$$DVP > C \qquad\qquad (9.1)$$

where D = dissatisfaction; V = vision; P = process; C = perceived cost of change.

This equation demonstrates that there is a perceived cost to change and that the three factors must each contribute to overcoming inertia. Note also that change management experts stress that it is essential to address all three factors. If any of them is neglected, no matter how well the other two are addressed, then the change management initiative will fail. Equation 9.1 shows this in that the three factors D, V and P are multiplied and so if dissatisfaction, vision, or the process is not clear (that is, equivalent to zero), then the product of all three will be zero. To demonstrate the application of the change equation to an innovation management situation, we will take an actual example.

A business division of a major international bank chose to focus on innovation three years ago. For reasons of confidentiality, we will refer to this organization as 'BankCorp'. The Managing Director (MD) of this division became interested in innovation, having read of the successes of various manufacturers in boosting their output of new products. Having decided that his organization needed to become more innovative, the MD who is a dynamic person developed the vision of an organization that would compete by being first-to-market with new banking products. A consultant was hired to support the development and implementation of this vision. However, as discussed above, a vision is not sufficient for successful change and this was the case for BankCorp, as we will see as we discuss each of the factors of the change equation.

Identifying Dissatisfaction

In overcoming the inertia to change inherent in every individual and organization, dissatisfaction plays a key role. The reluctance to change must be overcome by galvanizing opinion on the role of innovation. This might be obvious to managers; so obvious in fact that they cannot understand why it is not seen as a priority by everyone in the organization. Change management experts often say that a *burning platform* issue is required. (The term comes from the Piper Alpha oilrig disaster in the North Sea. As the platform burned, workers were forced to jump from the inferno into a sea of burning oil. Fortunately, some of the workers who made this split second decision survived.) A burning issue in change management terms is an issue that readily motivates the majority to action, even if this involves difficult decisions.

In communicating the need to become more innovative, it is useful to consider:

- Financial and market arguments.
- Customers' views on innovation. These can identify end-users frustrations and the need for all types of innovation.
- Employees' views. People in organizations that are not particularly innovative normally recognize this and the levels of internal dissatisfaction can be high (consider the results of BuildCo's cultural webs discussed in Chapter 8).
- Where problems resulting from a lack of innovation affect different functions, as 'shared dissatisfaction' will help overcome inertia.

Referring to the situation at BankCorp, an innovation audit was conducted by the consultant hired to support the company. In discussions with employees from across the functions and levels of the division, a high level of dissatisfaction on two points emerged. Firstly, both employees and middle management were totally sceptical about the MD's vision, as it was clear that the bank had not been first-to-market with a financial product in the previous five years and was seldom even a fast-follower ('we are a slow-follower . . .' said several staff in answer the innovation audit questions on strategy). This surfaced significant dissatisfaction with the status and also showed the vision of being first-to-market was unrealistic. Secondly, one of the reasons why the division was not fast was due to its high levels of bureaucracy and slow decision-making (for example, changes to product advertising required nearly 20 sign-offs). Both these points led the top management team to work on creating a new vision.

Creating the Vision

Every innovation management program needs a vision, which should be not only inspiring but also realistic. 'When a vision is clear, consistently articulated, and widely shared, decisions throughout the organization can be made in a more consistent, directed way', however, research shows that management often communicates only a vague vision.[57] There are several key questions to ask. What are you trying to achieve and how will this impact customers? What will more innovation mean (internally and externally)? Where could innovation make a real breakthrough for your company? Overall the innovation vision should address some or all of the following issues:

- How customers will directly benefit from the improved products, services and processes that will result from greater innovation performance.
- How quickly innovations are currently developed (Is the organization first-to-market, or a follower? Should it be faster to market?).
- The ways in which innovation will make significant improvements to an organization's competitive position.

Management at BankCorp realized that the vision they had originally selected for the innovation programme was inappropriate. Since the company had not been first-to-market in the past, and employees were not satisfied that this would be possible, the focus was changed to becoming a fast-follower that would learn from the first-mover's mistakes and capitalize on these. The new vision capitalized on the dissatisfaction within the organization and was quickly and widely supported by employees.

Box case 9.4 Synectics – driving clients' innovation products and processes

Synectics is a leading innovation management consultancy. George Prince and William J.J. Gordon, who both had extensive experience in helping companies develop new product concepts, founded the company in 1960. Fascinated by the dynamics in meetings held to develop new product ideas, Gordon and Prince taped thousands of hours of such meetings in order to study how people interacted. Analysis of the tapes showed significant differences in the flow of meetings that were successful at generating breakthrough ideas, compared to meetings that failed to do so. Using these observations, proprietary tools and techniques were developed for generating creative product ideas – including 'springboards', 'excursions', and 'itemized response'. Springboards are a way of generating thoughts that lead to new thinking. They focus on wishes, challenges to constraints on a problem, feelings, gut-level reactions, or apparently conflicting points of view. Excursions are a process to enable the power of the subconscious to be released onto a problem. The problem is put aside and thinking focused elsewhere; thinking about different worlds, objects, art, and so on. Such stimuli firstly generate seemingly irrelevant material. Links are then 'forced back' to the original problem. Itemized response is a process for protecting ideas, which are all too easily destroyed during the process of idea evaluation. The process of itemised response focuses first on identifying the positive aspects about an idea, in order to strengthen it. Next, areas of concern with the idea are identified and answers to these sought.

The three techniques have been applied by Synectics in a diverse range of companies from both service and manufacturing. Key successes include helping Liptons turn iced tea from a summer product to a popular year-round drink, improving the logistics processes for a major shipping line Neptune Orient Lines, and even turning a struggling Gaelic football team into champions.

Although Synectics has always been very successful in the area of creativity, it has deliberately developed a broad portfolio of services to support clients in the areas of innovation strategy, product development, marketing, and critical process optimization. Trudy Lloyd is a Partner in the London office of Synectics and perceives three key issues in the management of innovation. 'Innovation is a challenge for the leaders in many organizations. The very characteristics that help them manage organizations successfully, such as decisiveness, analytical rigour, and practicality, can impact negatively on creativity. To be creative in business there is a need to suspend judgement, tolerate ambiguity and put aside practical considerations, albeit temporarily to generate a suitable stream of ideas.' Secondly, 'organizations that identify breakthrough ideas select them exactly because they are new and fresh. Then they find ways to build feasibility into the idea. At Synectics we believe you cannot do the reverse . . . build newness into a feasible idea.'

Finally, 'it's important that everyone in an organization understands their role in the innovation process'. Lloyd insists that the innovators as not just the people in the project teams coming up with new product and process ideas. 'There comes a stage when any new concept has to be operationalized and this involves everyone. Innovations present staff with challenges that are different from those of running the current business . . .' says Lloyd, 'and businesses that innovate successfully have a culture where the whole organization is enthused and committed to making new initiatives work'.

Developing the Change Process

Achieving high performance in innovation does not normally happen overnight. Managers need to recognize that there are three key stages; moving from the *current* to the *desired* state, via a *transition* state.[58] Individuals and organizations can enter a state of shock during change. Research has shown that being to articulate a clear link of how to move from the current to the future state is an attribute of good leadership.[59]

The starting point of the change process is crucial. Often an innovation performance improvement programme is best linked to a particular project, the success of which should act as a signal and can fire the whole organization. A project that is so large that it is very high risk should not be selected; the project chosen should present a reasonable challenge. Change management experts talk of the importance of looking for the 'low-hanging fruit', which are projects where success quickly brings considerable returns.

Just as a new product development project is dependent on a product champion, so change management is dependent on an effective *change agent*. In selecting the path forward the change agent needs to be particularly careful to avoid trying to simply adopt best practice.[60] It is far better to consider the context of the organization in which change is deemed necessary and adapt ideas rather than simply adopting them. The way in which an organization can best be changed depends on identifying those in favour of change and those against. For members of both of these groups plans should be made to make best use of allies and change potential adversaries into allies. The change agent has a wide range of choices on how to go about change and needs to answer a number of questions. Do we need radical and fast change? Should it be organized to cascade down from senior management? Should external consultants be used to promote the changes? The answers to these questions flow into the plan for change. Performance measures should form an integral part of the change process, as they allow both challenging but realistic goals to be set and progress monitored.

The process of change at BankCorp was based on an analysis of the competencies necessary to be a fast-follower. For example, product managers were given resources and clear responsibilities to collect more competitive data and internal product development processes were streamlined. A twice-yearly 'Innovation Fair' was introduced, at which teams of employees present their ideas for more competitive products (using role plays of sales discussions as a way of 'prototyping' product concepts). Employees appreciated the freedom to be more innovative and welcomed the changes. Middle management was initially shocked and needed to be convinced to delegate many of their responsibilities, and therefore reduce the number of approvals required for product innovations. Known process bottlenecks, such as information technology resources were also better managed. Three years on, BankCorp has consistently achieved its target of being a fast-follower that introduces new products copied from the ideas of competitors, but with differentiating factors to make them more competitive than the incumbent's products.

Making a Breakthrough

If an organization decides to focus on innovation then it is worth taking the time and effort to make a breakthrough in performance. Incremental improvements can help but management should set the organization's sites high. The aim should not be to just improve innovation performance but really boost it. To achieve a sustainable boost, as opposed to a short-term improvement and the generation of a few innovative ideas, all aspects of innovation management need to be considered. No single element of the Pentathlon should be considered in isolation and similarly, the organization should not be considered in isolation from its business context. Management teams must also push to overcome their own limitations, as 'there may be a lack of imagination that starts right at the top'.[61]

Some companies will turn to innovation as a solution to difficult times. This is perfectly valid and, sometimes business problems bring an urgency and therefore openness to new ways of doing things. In such conditions, though, managers will need to be particularly effective as 'one of the crucial functions of leadership is to provide guidance at precisely those times when habitual ways of doing things no longer work, or when a dramatic change in the environment requires new responses'.[62]

Boosting innovation performance is the goal of many managers with which we come in contact. They urgently are looking for better ways top achieve this goal and this is an area where we hope that researchers will provide insights very soon. Currently, too little is known.

Summary

This chapter has suggested a scheme for determining ways to change innovation performance, whilst stressing that individual organizations will need to find their own particular way of achieving better performance. It has covered:

- The suggested approach with its four main steps: from assessing performance to determining actions to improve performance.
- Suggestions on how to choose suitable performance measures and conduct an innovation audit.
- A discussion of emerging evidence on the critical linkages in innovation management.
- Ideas on how to improve performance at both the project and organizational levels, including applying change management techniques to innovation.

This chapter's case study describes a small automotive supplier, Sidler, that has consistently achieved high levels of innovation despite its limited resources, through creative management of outside linkages.

Management Recommendations

- Select and use performance measures to understand and help communicate the innovation performance of your organization.
- Use an innovation audit to determine the strengths and weaknesses of your organization in innovation management. Determine the priorities.
- Develop an action plan to improve performance at both the project and organizational levels. Reserve enough top management time to take an active part in leading the implementation.
- Use change management techniques to gain acceptance for your plan.
- Be aware that there is no 'silver bullet' for improving innovation performance and it is management's responsibility to explore the best ways of achieving it in their own organizations.

Recommended Reading

(1) Balogun, J., Hope Hailey, V. with Johnson, G. and Scholes, K., *Exploring Strategic Change* (London: Financial Times – Prentice Hall, 2nd edn, 2003), ISBN 0273683276. Not specifically aimed at innovation management issues, but very useful coverage of change management tools and techniques.

(2) British Standard. *Design Management Systems – Part 1: Guide to Managing Innovation*. British Standard BS7000-1:1999 (London: British Standards Institution, 1999). Interesting document based on the results of intensive workshops including managers, academics, and professional associations. Somewhat deterministic in its style with a 'complete innovation management framework' but well worth consulting.

Sidler GmbH & Co – sourcing innovation[63]

Before reading this case, consider the following generic innovation management issues:

▢   What role can outsourcing play in a company's innovation strategy?
▢   How can companies access and exploit external expert knowledge?
▢   What criteria should be used for selecting partners?
▢   How can confidentiality be managed for innovation projects involving interorganizational collaborations?

All companies need a vision. For Sidler, a German automotive component manufacturer, it is to supply 'a Sidler component in every car world-wide'. Although it is an ambitious target, the company, which specialises in the design, development and manufacturer of car interior lighting systems and interior trim, already supplies many of the major manufacturers. These include Volkswagen, the Fiat company, along with the American giants Ford and General Motors, and a number of the Japanese assemblers. In the competitive and technology-driven field of car interior lighting systems, Sidler is market leader in Europe (with a 35 per cent share) and worldwide has a 12 per cent share. Sidler managers say 'innovation has to be a way of life to stay competitive. However, with limited resources we cannot do everything ourselves'.

Originally founded in 1925 to make metal parts, the company moved into the design, development and manufacture of synthetic parts – mainly interior lighting components – for the automotive industry during the 1970s. Over recent years the market for its primary product has changed significantly. Customers – car manufacturers – are no longer simply looking for a supplier to produce parts to their specifications. Instead, the market has changed to one in which complete lighting systems are designed, developed and manufactured by suppliers. In total Sidler employs 650 people and has a turnover of over 90 million euros, of which over 40 per cent is generated from worldwide exports.

A major part of the company's success is down to its research and development capability, in particular the development of tooling and injection moulding technology. This is used to produce interior lighting with specific surfaces, e.g. rhomboid line structures, which give plastic car interior light covers the characteristics of lenses (focusing light to the required area of a car). However, unlike many of the giants that it supplies, the company is not big enough to maintain a large in-house R&D facility. Instead, the company has developed a policy of leveraging the best knowledge available through outsourcing a significant proportion of its R&D work. This includes a whole range of approaches: using universities for specialist long term research; technology centres in Austria and Germany for undertaking materials analysis; and establishing joint projects with other companies for developing specialist products.

'For instance', explains Herr Dr. Helmut Rapp, the company's managing director, 'Our in-house technology monitoring recognized that a university was working on laser holographic lenses. We need lenses, and so after assessing their initial research, we have given them a project to specifically look at whether the technology they are developing can be used in our products. If this project proves that their technology is relevant, then we will give them the task of industrializing it.'

'In fact, outsourcing is often much more efficient than trying to do everything in-house. Universities often have the equipment and the expert research staff, that most companies – including ourselves – cannot afford. They are also often looking for funding and support. Similarly, other research organizations have the staff and the dedicated processes that ensure that they can do specific jobs, such as materials testing and analysis, better and often cheaper than we could if we tried to do it in-house. Therefore, a whole range of research activities is not considered by us to be core activities. Where we can find an external source who is capable, we outsource the work', states Rapp.

Managing Risk and Intellectual Property

Admittedly there are risks involved with this outsourcing approach, and one that many companies fear is the loss of competencies and lack of control over intellectual property. Since Sidler understands this concern, it balances the risks by taking steps to maintain control over outsourced development.

As Rapp notes 'when it comes to R&D for smaller companies, such as ourselves, the simple choice is between the risk of losing a lot of money if you invest in developing a technology in-house that ultimately doesn't work, or the risk of losing a bit of know-how if an outside organization develops it and it does work. Anyway, there are ways to maintain some control over the process, and what we always try to do when more than one area of research is involved – which is quite often – is that we do not bring all the experts together. We coordinate the development, and so in this way it is our coordinators who communicate with all the experts involved and pull all the possible different strands of a research project together . . . we actually develop the overall expertise, the competency that is most appropriate to Sidler.'

A prime example of managed outsourcing is a testing programme undertaken in cooperation between Sidler and another manufacturing company. Together, the two companies have developed a new process (not previously technically possible), which enables laser etching on pale coloured paints. However, rather than invest in in-house testing facilities, both Sidler and their partner decided to outsource the testing to a specialist paint shop and a separate laser etching business. This network of companies was used to solve the application problems, but with the work co-ordinated and project managed by Sidler technologists. While this meant that the external testers developed certain knowledge, it was the Sidler engineers who effectively controlled all the pieces of the jigsaw. After a two-year effort, the process was perfected and now the partners are making a 1.5 million Euro investment in the special painting and laser etching process. And, because they now can offer this specific technical solution, Sidler has achieved 'sole supplier status' with a major German motor manufacturer.

In many companies technical outsourcing is often hindered by an internal culture that refuses to accept the need for such an approach. Engineers in particular are susceptible to the desire to do all the new development themselves, and this often permeates throughout R&D, where something not developed by the group is frowned upon. Sidler managers say they are not completely immune from the 'not invented here' syndrome. To ensure that this negative influence is minimized, Sidler always ensures that people know what is going on and why, and always assigns someone from R&D to oversee an outside project. So while they may not be doing the research themselves, they are actually project managing the effort.

Another problem that many companies perceive with outsourcing is confidentiality. But this is not a factor as far as Sidler is concerned. This is for two reasons. One is that Sidler's research co-ordinators control all the pieces of the puzzle that is important to them, including the industrial application of the research. The other reason is that rapid implementation cycles do not give anyone the chance to break any confidences.

'So far we've never made confidentiality agreements', says Rapp. 'It's not worth the paperwork. You create it, you sign it and you file it. Who is really going to do the follow up? It's a waste of time. The important thing is to work with those external experts to get the problem solved, to get the process going, and then to go rapidly into industrial application with that process. You only have to be slightly in front at this stage, because within the industrial application you gain experience day by day, and it is this unique application knowledge that provides the real competitive advantage.' But such approaches mean that selecting partners is a key process.

Selecting Partners

The first step in effective use of outside research agencies is to identify opportunities. At Sidler, the internal R&D team has the brief to monitor technological developments in many areas. As well as reading journals, at least one member of the team visits relevant conferences and exhibitions and reports back. If anything of interest is seen, such as a new high pressure moulding process, this is followed up through investigations to evaluate its usefulness. This typically includes team members visiting the company or research institute that has developed the technology. If it is an existing technology and it seems applicable, then Sidler simply test it. If it is just a research idea, then the head of the R&D team will initially visit the outside organization, to instigate discussion on a possible collaboration project.

There is also the issue of finding the right outsourcing partners. According to Rapp, 'If we are looking to become part of a long-term research project, it is not just a matter of finding a relevant project, as there are often a number of different organizations working along the same lines. The decision to work with an external research organization is as much about that organization's style and approach – and how they fit with our non-bureaucratic style of working – as it is about its project and competency. We also do not put too much emphasis on performance and time schedules as we recognize that these projects need time to find the answers we want'. 'Whereas', he adds, 'when we're working with companies who do all our materials testing and analysis, we are looking primarily for on-time performance and professionalism. If we send a sample out and request an answer within two days, we expect it within two days. If we get it in three weeks, that's no good.'

University-Based Research

An example of where Sidler's approach to outsourcing has helped solve one of its 'long-term' technical problems is its current work with a German university. Sidler's internal R&D team had already developed, through a combination of specialist tooling, material additives, control techniques and the usual trial and error, a special purpose machine for producing high quality 'in-mould decorated' parts. While many companies can do in-mould decoration (the process is used extensively by the furniture trade to produce fake wood panelling and doors), Sidler is the only company who can at present meet the quality standards required by the automotive industry. As a result, the company is now building up a factory in the UK, which will start with 10 million euros turnover, of which 80 per cent is based on orders for in-mould decorated parts for the automotive industry.

However, the existing manufacturing process requires all parameters to be tightly controlled in order to be stable. While this means it is hard for competitors to copy, it also means that it requires very skilled operators. In looking for ways to overcome this operator dependence, the company came across a university project to create an intelligent moulding process. In this, the injection moulding machine's control system gets feedback about the pressure and temperature in the tool, and then automatically makes the necessary process changes.

'Our in-mould decoration process ideally needs a self-regulating feedback system which we do not have yet. But our internal technology monitoring highlighted the university research and having looked at the work they are doing we decided to join the project', explains Rapp.

Sidler has provided the university with moulding equipment, into which the researchers will be putting the in-tool measurement devices. Also, one member of the company's R&D team is working on the project. In return, Sidler will gain the knowledge it needs to improve its own processes and an added benefit. As Rapp concludes, 'there is now a young engineer who is doing his PhD on this project – and I know where this guy is going to work when he has finished his studies!'

10 The Future of Innovation Management

'The commanding General is well aware that the weather forecasts are no good. However, he needs them for planning purposes.'[1]

Introduction

In this final chapter we allow ourselves the luxury of looking forward to what the future may hold for managers of innovation. To provide a structure for this we return to the first topic of Chapter 1, the drivers of innovation, and consider what trends for the future are discernible in each of the four main factors that we discussed there. For each one we will indicate what we believe are the challenges for managers to address. As so often in discussions of innovation, a formal structure helps to ensure that nothing important is overlooked, but few topics fit neatly into their allotted place.

The drivers we consider are:

▶ Customers.
▶ Technology.
▶ Competition.
▶ The business climate.

Customers

Customers throughout the world are generally becoming older, wealthier and more urban, as well as more numerous, and these trends will affect the kind of innovation needed to serve them. In Western Europe and Japan the average age of the population is creeping steadily upwards because people are living longer and having fewer children. The same thing is happening in China as a result of the 'single-child' policy.[2] Older people use more personal services (not only medical) and they have particular needs in relation to physical products. We have already noted in Chapter 5 that the Ford motor company designed their Focus model with the older market in mind and had their designers wear special clothing and glasses to give them some empathy for this customer segment.

A continuation of economic growth seems likely for many years yet and prospects appear particularly hopeful in India and China, a combined market of over two billion people. These markets have very different requirements to

Western ones, so companies will need to 'design for culture' – taking steps to ensure that their product and service offerings are fully appropriate to local needs. Increasing wealth does not appear to satiate demand for new possessions and experiences; if it were so people in the wealthier countries would already be choosing to work shorter hours or saving, rather than spending, their money. There is no sign of either of these. Nevertheless as people become richer they show one very clear pattern of behaviour that has implications for the type of innovation we may expect in the future. This is highlighted by the move from agriculture to industry and then to services, a trend that, as we discussed in Chapter 1, has been observed in every major country over the last 300 years.

The underlying cause of the trend stems from what is usually known as Maslow's Hierarchy of Needs. This framework is not based on solid empirical evidence, although it is intuitively appealing and frequently quoted. Maslow[3] suggested that human needs may be thought of as extending along a spectrum, which starts from the most basic physical ones such as food, warmth and shelter and extends through social needs such as sex, love, companionship and status to more personal strivings for meaning, spirituality and self-fulfilment. Maslow's original list is shown in Figure 10.1, though it has been extended and reinterpreted many times by other authors. There is much room for discussion about exactly where a particular need fits in the hierarchy, but two aspects of the list hold broadly true. First, the most basic needs are the most urgent and until they are adequately taken care of people generally have less concern for the rest. Second, the basic needs are quite easy to define and straightforward to satisfy, while the social and self-fulfilment needs are subtle and difficult to define – and apparently insatiable.

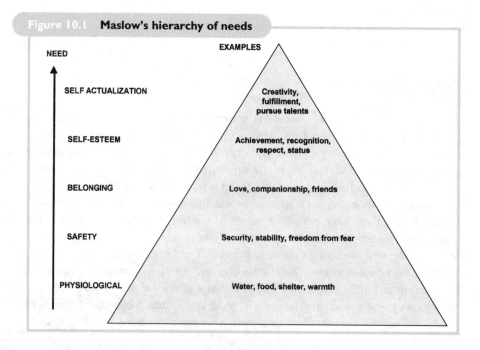

Figure 10.1   Maslow's hierarchy of needs

NEED

EXAMPLES

SELF ACTUALIZATION — Creativity, fulfillment, pursue talents

SELF-ESTEEM — Achievement, recognition, respect, status

BELONGING — Love, companionship, friends

SAFETY — Security, stability, freedom from fear

PHYSIOLOGICAL — Water, food, shelter, warmth

It is also true to say that the most basic needs are to a large extent absolute in nature: one is either hungry, or cold, or one is not. Social needs, such as status or well-being are often relative, in that standards move constantly according to how everybody else is doing.

It is not surprising that the proportion of the world's economy devoted to agriculture declines as productivity improves, because the demand for food (as well as the land available to grow it on) is fundamentally limited. Similarly, the other more basic needs of shelter, warmth and even mobility use relatively less and less resources as time goes on. Quite clearly much of the industrial effort and most of the service sector in the developed world are now targeted at social and personal needs that are right at the other end of the Maslow hierarchy. The effects of this on innovation are clear: although the demand for innovation in goods and services apparently has (as yet) no bound, that demand is likely to become more elusive, unstable and subject to the whims of fashion as the innovation caters to more subtle needs.

In such conditions companies will find it increasingly difficult to predict in advance how successful a new product will be. The old paradigm: write the specification, build the product and then go out and sell it, no longer works. Anthropological studies and empathic design will be increasingly needed to uncover and define customers' subtle needs. However, these techniques are not yet well-developed, so until they become more reliable, companies must increasingly be prepared to go through a process of experimentation, trying out new products or services with potential customers and then modifying them, perhaps through several iterations,[4] until a satisfactory result is achieved. The same pressures will make the demand for new services or products more volatile and unpredictable which in turn will make all aspects of the supply chain more difficult to manage. In the fashion industry (surely the exemplar of the top end of the Maslow hierarchy), Zara have shown that great cost and sales advantages can be gained from a very short and flexible supply chain, that enables it to respond rapidly to new trends, even though it increases the cost of manufacture (see Box case 6.2). This allows them both to get new products into the shops very rapidly and to withdraw them if they are not successful (or have run their course) without penalty.

Box case 10.1 Automotive – is the assembly line bunk?

In 2004 the *Financial Times*[5] and the *New York Times* reported a proposal by Martin Leach, former head of Ford Europe for a new approach to vehicle manufacturing. This would entirely alter the relationship between manufacturing, sales, service and the after-market. The concept is to assemble cars in retail parks from kits shipped in from low-cost manufacturers in India or China. By using plastic panels the company would be able to customize the vehicles to a high degree so as to be able to follow fashions and persuade customers to upgrade frequently. Crucially, the vehicles would be leased, not sold, so that returned cars could be refurbished and leased again at a reduced rate. Since there would be no second-hand market, theft would be little or no problem (why would you steal a car that cannot be resold?) so insurance would be cheap. R&D costs would also be low or zero because the product would not be differentiated by having the most up-to-date performance. The manufacturer would now participate in finance, spares and the rest of the aftermarket. The customer would get a new approach to vehicle ownership that emphasized customization, cost and convenience instead of performance.

This concept still has to be tested in the marketplace but it is an interesting example of a new approach to an established industry, offering a disruptive combination of a new business concept and an alternative value proposition.

Technology

Herman Kahn became famous in the 1960s for leading a think-tank that dared to debate seriously about the possibility of waging and surviving a nuclear war. He became notorious for his use of the 'megadeath' as a suitable unit for measuring casualties in a global nuclear conflict. Later he turned his attention to predicting the future of science and technology with his famous book, *The Year 2000, A Framework for Speculation on the next Thirty-Three Years*, written in 1967 with Anthony Wiener. In their book, Kahn and Wiener ventured a list of 'One hundred technical innovations very likely in the last third of the twentieth century'.[6] When the new millennium arrived, several commentators reviewed Kahn's predictions and tried to judge how accurate they were. Opinions varied from 15 to 50 per cent – not surprisingly perhaps as some of the predictions were rather vague. However, one report,[7] based on the views of a panel of eight experts, found that Kahn and Wiener's predictions in one particular class were as much as 80 per cent accurate. These were the ones about (or derived directly from) developments in computers and communication. They were based on the assumption of a steady improvement in the technology of integrated circuits;[8] a trend that was already established at the time and has indeed continued relentlessly to this day. The predictions that did not have an underlying rationale of this kind were noticeably less successful – perhaps they were little more than wishful thinking. We will therefore not speculate about whether entirely new technologies may emerge but confine ourselves to trends that are already discernible.

A good place to start is with electronics and computing because a period of spectacular improvement must be approaching its end. The underlying driver of this, as already mentioned in Chapter 4, is Moore's law: that the number of transistors that can be fabricated on a single chip would double every 1½–2 years. This has been well borne out in practice, and the number has actually grown a million-fold since the 1960s. But this cannot go on indefinitely. The origin of the improvement has been the steady reduction in the size of the circuit elements and this is now pressing on some fundamental limits. By 2009 the smallest parts of the circuits will be only 50 atoms across. By 2020 this should be 10 atoms.[9] Moore's law may already be slowing,[10] and it seems very likely that the industry will face fundamental limits within the next 10 or 15 years. If so, we will see the end of the era of apparently endless cost reduction in the hardware of electronics and computing, which has made possible so much innovation in many industries: banking; financial services; audio and video recording; logistics; mobile communications; photography; automation and so on. When it falters, as it assuredly will, it will have a profound impact in many industries. However the time is not quite yet, and no doubt this great summer of progress will be followed by an autumn in which we can continue to harvest benefits for some time.

Perhaps quantum computing will provide a new revolution? Perhaps; but history tells us that real revolutions in technology take time. It took over 100 years for photography to move from being a scientific curiosity to a usable product. Arguably[11] telephony took over 50 years, and radio 35. Controlled fusion power is not yet a reality more than 50 years since the first hydrogen bomb, and genetic engineering is only recently producing serious results nearly 50 years since the discovery of the structure of DNA.

Innovation in the technology of materials seems certain. Whether there will be breakthrough to room-temperature superconductors is anyone's guess, but the steady progress (and considerable investment) in nanotechnology will surely produce radically new materials (see Box case 10.2) and new opportunities. The trends in biotechnology are now well enough established for it to be clear that understanding of the way genetics shapes living things at the most fundamental level is set to accelerate rapidly. Serious impacts on the treatment of disease must follow but perhaps the greatest influence will be in engineering microbes to produce useful chemicals more efficiently than before. If the efficient conversion of plant material into useable fuel can be achieved it will reduce the world's reliance on oil and coal and so simultaneously remove the greatest sources of political instability and environmental pollution.

Box case 10.2   The Lotus Effect – technology cross-over[12]

Biologists from the University of Bonn in Germany investigated the 'lotus effect' – the apparently smooth leaves of this plant repel water and almost all dirt and grime. Microscopically, the surface of lotus leaves showed itself to have a particular undulating pattern of what looked like higher and lower 'mountains'. Nanotechnology has now enabled this surface to be mimicked and 'easy-to-clean' products are now entering the marketplace. These include coatings for bathroom ceramics, paint for walls, and coatings for surgical devices. Easy-to-clean technology promises to save not only time by minimizing the need for cleaning, but also cleaning materials.

Nanotechnology and biotechnology will be revolutionary in their own ways but we would doubt that their impact on the process of innovation will be as profound as the electronics and communication revolution has been. This has transformed not so much our ability to manipulate the world but our ability to manipulate knowledge itself and to communicate the results to each other. This has accelerated innovation in every part of human activity, not only in electronics, because it has affected the very material of innovation itself. The next revolution to affect innovation itself will not be until there is real progress in artificial intelligence, or until we countenance altering our own genetic makeup or directly manipulating the workings of the brain.

Competition

It is estimated that by 2025 the number of people educated to graduate level will be greater than the total world population in 1900.[13] China and India with their huge, well-educated populations, totalling more than a third of mankind, no longer provide only low-cost manufacturing but are beginning to emerge as centres of innovation in their own right. Bangalore in India has more IT professionals than the whole of Silicon Valley, and is home to Wipro, now the largest R&D services company in the world with a turnover of a billion dollars (see the main case study in Chapter 7). Texas Instruments' Indian branch has filed over 200 patents, and Intel's filed 63 in 2003 alone.[14] These figures by no means rival the output of western R&D laboratories, but they surely signal the emergence of these economies, based as they are on old and sophisticated civilizations, as centres of innovation. The globalization of business and the spread of IT mean that these potential powerhouses of innovation will link quickly into world markets, just as Korea, Taiwan and others have before them. It was recently reported that there are over 400 companies making DVD players in China alone.[15]

Not only are there powerful new sources of competition, but competition itself is becoming more efficient. Although the GATT talks are stalled at the time of writing, tariff barriers continue to be reduced through the expansion of trading blocks such as the EC and Mercosur. Cheaper air and sea transport help the flow of goods between countries. Perhaps most important for innovation, IT and the internet are having a dramatic effect on the free flow of information, aided by the increasing use of English as the international language for business. The British Council recently estimated that half the world's population will speak at least basic English by 2015. These factors sharpen competition by giving customers better access than ever before to competing products and more opportunity to compare them. Competition will become clearer. Well-informed customers lead to tighter competition and better products. Yet few people can navigate confidently through the billions of pages of information available to us, and search engines are clearly only in their infancy. There is much more improvement still to come.

The lessons for innovation managers are not comforting but they are exciting. Whatever business you are in, expect more competition. It may not be local, though it will increasingly speak your language. Only those providing localized services will be exempt. Customers will be better informed, but they will also be more numerous so good companies can expect to prosper as never before. The successful companies will be those able to respond quickly to new practices and ideas, and to search constantly for new opportunities.

Box case 10.3 Vodafone Group Plc – future innovation[16]

Vodafone Group Plc provides an extensive range of mobile telecommunications services, and is the world's largest mobile telecommunications company with a staggering 146 million customers worldwide. As market leader and with such a large customer base, Vodafone has found it essential to constantly identify opportunities for technological and service innovation and this is the responsibility of Group R&D.

Group R&D consists of 7 research & development centres round the world. In Germany, Group R&D–D is officially known as Vodafone Pilotentwicklung GmbH, which has 34 permanent employees, 20 contract staff and 20 students from universities, all with a wide range of backgrounds. Its role is to analyse trends and new technologies, build future visions, monitor 'players' (organizations associated with the market), and track the business environment to derive ideas for tomorrow's competitive products and services. Their work prepares the ground for specific R&D projects by prototyping possible future products and services. To achieve this they have established a structured approach to identify, evaluate, and utilize opportunities. This structure relies on effective use of tools and techniques, networking and communication.

Vodafone Group R&D–D uses various tools and techniques. For analysing technologies and markets, employees can choose from a range of individual methods in the 'Group R&D–D toolkit'. For example, this collection includes several scenario planning methods. No individual employee is experienced in the use of all tools and techniques but new employees are trained on the basic methods. Since the toolkit is summarized as a single sheet mind map, it is easy to identify where alternatives to the basic methods may be appropriate and to contact experienced colleagues. Dr Christiane Hipp, who drives the innovation process in Group R&D–D, says: 'In dealing with the future we have found it better not to rely on just one or two analysis methods as most other companies do. As we have a portfolio of techniques available, this means that we can look for the best tool for the job. It also provides variety which is important in maintaining a fresh and energetic feel to our work.'

Vodafone has a philosophy of keeping individual R&D sites small, with typically around 15 to 80 permanent employees. This means that Group R&D–D employees need to communicate and network effectively with both their internal and external contacts. Torsten Herzberg, a Group R&D–D freelancer, says: 'Innovation is often the result of communication between people who do not have homogeneous ideas and so we need to stimulate constant dialogue – internally and externally.' This communication takes various forms.

The Group R&D–D office in Munich is largely open plan and was designed together with the well-known architect Professor Gunther Henn using his 'programming concept'. In this the architecture of the office supports the way employees work with, for example, several 'marketplaces' – open areas where all employees can meet regularly and discuss their work. In addition to doing everything to create an informal 'culture of communication', Group R&D–D has regular short meetings where employees present their work, bounce ideas around and discuss 'lessons learned' from previous projects.

Group R&D–D is also experimenting with bringing artists together with their technical employees, to help stimulate creativity. They have found that mixing artistic and technical thinking supports the creation of radically new visions and ideas for their implementation. A symbol of the use of artistic thinking is the traditional red English telephone box, which was installed in the roof garden as part of a current project, where artists and technical employees are investigating the role of 'private' areas for mobile phone calls in today's increasingly open-plan office environment.

To stimulate communication across the whole Vodafone organization, Group R&D–D organizes both internal and external marketing, including the Annual Conference. This is a two-day event where the whole of Group R&D present new ideas and innovative projects. Around 150 Chief Technology Officers and Strategy Directors from the Vodafone companies worldwide attend the conference. There are various presentation sessions and an 'Innovation Zone' with live demonstrations of the latest prototypes of new products and services. 'Piloting and prototyping everything in a professional and innovative way makes it possible not only for visitors to be able quickly to understand the ideas but also to be able to give constructive feedback. It requires a lot of effort but the conference has been hugely influential in optimizing communication inside Group R&D, and between Group R&D and Vodafone operations', says Eva Weber, responsible for innovation marketing and communication at Group R&D–D.

The Business Climate

The economic growth of China, India and other Asian countries and the opening up of the countries of the former USSR increases global competition, as we have just discussed, but also opens up huge new business opportunities. The growing middle classes in these new markets will be purchasers of many of the goods and services already sold in developed markets. But in addition the poorer consumers, by their very numbers, provide new opportunities. The success of 'micro credit' schemes is an example. These give small loans, without collateral, to start new enterprises based on a purchase of something as small as a goat or a single mobile phone. The rates of interest are relatively high but the micro-entrepreneurs, usually women who previously had no access to capital at all, use it very efficiently; and the default rate on the loans is very low. Many companies are finding that producing less-sophisticated versions of existing ideas can open new markets (such as Whirlpool's 'Ideale' washing machine, mentioned in Chapter 1 and the 'Jaipur Foot' Box case 10.4).

Box case 10.4   The Jaipur Foot – Indian low-tech

What is the appropriate level of technology? This is a question that should be asked by product design teams constantly, as the customers and end-users of products and services will seldom be persuaded to adopt a higher level of technology than is appropriate. A clear example of this is the 'Jaipur Foot', which has become a household name in the war zones of the world.

Bio-medical engineers have long studied the workings of the body and designed artificial limbs, some of which incorporate microprocessor control and feedback systems. Unfortunately, the demand for prostheses is heavy; a direct result of the millions of anti-personnel mines that have been laid during wars over the last fifty years. Mines are cheap and easy to produce, simple to lay and extremely difficult, dangerous and time-consuming to clear. The civilian populations in the war zones pay a heavy price and many people in countries such as Afghanistan have lost and continue to lose limbs as they return to their villages and agricultural fields following conflicts. It is estimated that 500 people are killed or maimed by landmines every week. Injured civilians often do not have the money or access to the high-tech devices found in the bio-medical engineering laboratories of the West. Enter the Jaipur Foot.

It was not only the cost of conventional artificial limbs that acted against them being adopted, it was also that their design did not fit with the lifestyle of people in Asia, where many people squat, eat and sleep on the floor. The Jaipur Foot is the solution and it is made of simple materials – rubber, wood and aluminium – which are not only readily available but also can be worked by local craftsmen. Typically it takes 45 minutes to build, lasts five years and costs about $30.

Collaborative Innovation

As we discussed in Chapter 7, companies are increasingly teaming up with others to introduce new products to the market faster and more reliably. Instead of expecting to control all aspects of a new product, they use a network of collaborators who work with them as partners, rather than merely as subcontractors.

This has long been the pattern in industries where a dominant design has emerged (see Chapter 4). In the automotive sector, for example, manufacturers habitually source complete electronics or hydraulic systems, or even engines, from third parties who take responsibility for all aspects of design and innovation. However the complexity of products and the need for rapid introduction has pushed many companies into collaborative ventures even when the product is still relatively immature. Box case 10.5 is an example of how Microsoft became a high-volume maker of games consoles. The company did this by using a mixture of subcontractors and partners to design and supply all the cutting-edge hardware components, manufacture the product and, crucially, design most of the games. Even Microsoft could not expect to maintain cutting-edge capabilities on all of these in such a fast-moving industry. Their contribution was the product concept and some core software, their brand name, and a great deal of finance and organizational muscle.

Box case 10.5   Microsoft – distributed innovation for the X Box[17]

Microsoft started work on the X Box games console in early 1999. The project was a combination of top-down direction from Bill Gates and his team, and a bottom-up initiative from games enthusiasts in the company. Microsoft faced a strategic threat that the TV would acquire processing and communications capabilities and eventually displace the PC and with it Microsoft's flagship, the 'Windows' operating system. Gates later said that in the strategic picture Microsoft needed twin pillars, with 'a PC in the den and an X Box in the living room'.[18]

But Microsoft had little competence in the design of many of the key elements that go to make up a games console, such as the audio and graphics chips that deliver the realistic pictures and sound on which the game depended. Nor did they have much experience in designing and manufacturing electronics hardware. Finally, Microsoft already had a games division but they could expect to supply only a fraction (albeit a profitable one) of the games for the console. So for a successful entry into this established and competitive market Microsoft would have to assemble a coalition of suppliers, whose work would make or break the project. In such a fast-changing market the chosen partners would have to be able to drive performance up and price down very aggressively. Sony had already shown the way: they forced the cost of their PlayStation down from $450 to $80 over five years by combining components and simplifying the design as technology progressed. And when the PlayStation 2 was launched its graphics were 600 times better than those of its predecessor. Microsoft's job would not be easy.

Microsoft had one technical card to play: a suite of software called Direct X that made it easy to write games and other software for PCs. PCs come in a wide range of configurations with different processor speeds, memory sizes and peripherals. Direct X took care of the interfaces between the software and whatever hardware there was, and 'allowed game developers to make use of all the add-on gear that computers had gained without worrying about the particular mix'.[19] Games developers would not have to learn a new set of programming techniques for each new generation of machine – as was the case, for example, with the PlayStation.

Microsoft's team approached all the major suppliers of PCs one by one, proposing they join the project as partners and handle the hardware. None found the business attractive because traditionally games consoles are sold at a loss and all the money is made on the games. So Microsoft now had to take full responsibility for the hardware; but they chose to subcontract the complete manufacturing task to an established contract manufacturer,

Flextronics of Singapore who proposed to build two new factories to make the X Box, one in Mexico and one in Hungary.

The support of games designers inside and outside Microsoft was crucial for the success of the project. Even the choice of Nvidia as the maker of the vital graphics chip was heavily influenced by their preferences.

The launch date for the X Box was originally set for late in 2000, but it became clear that the performance that could be achieved at that time would not provide the impact that Microsoft, as a newcomer to the market, required. So it was decided to delay the project by a year to allow the use of Nvidia's next generation graphics chips and larger storage capacity.

Microsoft now provides only the business and design concept, the finance, the styling, and the core operating software (not Windows, as it turned out). All the key components and the manufacturing were subcontracted. Microsoft would sell the hardware at a significant loss and generate income from its own games, and from a $7 licence fee that it collects on games from third parties. The business plan forecasted a loss of $900 million, even if all went well, a price the company was prepared to pay to open up a new business area.

The X Box was launched in November 2001, 18 months after Sony's PlayStation 2 and six months after Nintendo launched their GameCube. By mid-2004 they had sold 14 million units, somewhat more than Nintendo's 13 million but well-behind the 80 million sales of PlayStation 2.

The next-round generation of games consoles looks like being a two-horse race between the X Box 2 and the PlayStation 3. It is predicted that Microsoft will aim to sell a higher proportion of their own games next time and that they may design their own graphics chip, giving them greater control of this critical element.[20]

Dominant design is a familiar kind of standardization that facilitates cooperative innovation. But another kind of standardization is emerging whose scope is much broader and goes far beyond its origins in the electronics industry. It derives from three sources: digitization; integration; and interconnection standards. Digitization is the trend to encode signals as numbers that can be represented by sequences of zeros and ones. These signals can be stored, processed and reproduced with effectively perfect accuracy and so although digital circuits are often immensely complicated they are utterly reproducible. So a circuit made by one manufacturer can be replaced with an equivalent from another with complete confidence. The manufacture of digital circuit chips is now so reliable that few companies bother to make their own; they just send the designs to a 'silicon foundry', probably on the other side of the world. Few people pause to think what an extraordinary change to manufacturing methods this is.

There are many different types of electronic function, so most pieces of electronics are still made up of many separate components. However, a collection of standards have evolved to govern how these parts interconnect. Using these standards an equipment maker can assemble a collection of complex components from diverse sources and be confident they will work together. The impact on equipment design has been dramatic. Much more important, though, this combination of digitization with interconnection standards is at the heart of the communications revolution. It is what allows an agent in India to handle an insurance claim from England; a salesman in Turkey to check progress of his order in the USA; the sale of an item from a supermarket in France to trigger immediate re-supply from Spain; or a traveller from China to view and then book a hotel room in Australia.

The combination of digitization, integration and interconnection standards has an effect rather like that of a dominant design in that it allows very complicated functions to be independently developed by different companies and yet linked reliably together. These can range from a keyboard or display to a complete library or logistics system.

Distributed innovation allows the resources of many companies to be brought together to design a new product using the most up-to-date of components. Such innovation can be very fast because each supplier drives its own part forward independently and brings the most up-to-date version to each new project.

The Dangers of Distributed Innovation

The danger for the lead company is that the technical ownership and intellectual property increasingly lies with the suppliers and their own contribution (the product concept and the integration of the resources to bring it into being) may prove difficult to defend. Certainly the barriers to new entrants in such a market are much lower than in the days when large, vertically integrated manufacturers retained control of most of their product. Such a pattern has recently emerged in the mobile telephone market. In the past the industry was dominated by large vertically-integrated firms such as Motorola, Ericsson, and Nokia. The technology was so complicated that each company needed to have command of all aspects of the design, from the radio chips to the audio circuits. Fitting all this into a tiny, carefully-styled case and then manufacturing it in high volume itself required unique expertise. Now, however, the design has stabilized and all the core radio components, as well the displays, processors, cameras and so on, can be bought from suppliers who design and make modules for the whole industry. Some will even design and supply the complete product. These Original Design Manufacturers are now selling their own products directly into some markets. As a result the lead companies are reducing subcontracts and concentrating some of the key design skills back in the main company so as not to lose control of the product.[21]

In the automotive field, on the other hand, the main suppliers retain major collateral assets in their assembly expertise, distribution and brand name, which are important enough to allow them to defend themselves against competition from their suppliers (though even this could be threatened by alternative business models, as Box case 10.1 shows).

In a world in which companies must collaborate with others for some of the most innovative parts of their products or services, innovation strategy becomes vital. Today's valued partners can become tomorrow's competition. Managers must be sure that they understand the sources of their competitive advantage in the long term and develop strategies to keep control of them.

Managing Innovation

Throughout this book we have focused on presenting tools and techniques for managing innovation, which appear from research to be both practical and reliable. However, as we said in Chapter 1, the management of innovation is a developing area and nothing like as mature as the field of quality management. Although we are not saying that innovation, with its inherent risk and uncertainty, will lend itself to anything like the highly structured approach of Six Sigma quality management, we do believe that there will be significant advances. For example, much of the research has concentrated on new product development projects: 'the vast majority of previous research is project-based and lacks the general perspective of executive-level managers'.[22] There is much to be learnt about service innovation, which is particularly important as the service sector now dominates in many countries and, as Tom Peters says, 'Great service is the greatest innovation'.[23] For senior managers, topics such as how to create a culture of innovation are paramount and hopefully research will provide new insights.

From research and practice we expect new frameworks to emerge which will help innovation managers deal more effectively with the risk and uncertainty they face. However, we do not expect that predictive models will make inroads into innovation management, as it is so often context dependent. The test of time will show whether we are right and, in addition, whether our own framework – the Pentathlon – is an enduring and useful tool for managers.

Summary

In this chapter we have reviewed trends for the future in the four main drivers of innovation: customers, technology, competition and the business environment. We suggest that the need and opportunities for innovation will continue unabated, but the next wave of technology will not further accelerate the rate of change. However, new services and products will be targeted at more subtle needs than before, and so it will be more difficult to define products in advance. Organizations will have to be prepared to experiment more in the marketplace and to accept that demand will be more difficult to predict, so supply chains must be more flexible. And all this in a context of better informed customers and more competitors, speaking our language and brought literally and metaphorically to our doorsteps by improved travel and information technology. There are exciting times ahead!

Management Recommendations

- Explore ways to understand your customers' hidden needs but know that this is an imperfect science.
- Be prepared to experiment with new services and products and change them as you learn.
- Expect higher levels of competition.
- Accept that more of your innovation will come from outside the organization.
- Embrace collaboration with other companies but ensure that you know and can defend your competitive position.

Main Case Study   Hewlett-Packard BITS[24]

Before reading this case, consider the following generic innovation management issues:

- What will be the challenges in the future in managing innovation?
- Which aspects of the customer relationship are essential to a business model?
- What are the key differences between managing innovation in small and large organizations?

Innovation Consultancy

Business Innovation and Transformation Services (BITS) is an internal consulting group serving the Hewlett-Packard Corporation (HP). BITS concentrates on sharing best practice amongst HP's business units, using knowledge transfer to improve the performance of business teams, and 'accelerating' business results.

The origins of BITS lie in the late 1980s when Hewlett-Packard began its transition from being a hardware engineering company to one that predominantly develops products based on software. The company, with its long-standing commitment to retaining employees, determined that it would be necessary to train many of its hardware-focused R&D engineers in software. A Software Initiative group was created to design training courses and improve the overall management of software projects. Meanwhile, other internal groups such as Corporate Product Marketing (responsible for product definition and market research), Corporate Quality (tasked with developing metrics and customer centered design), and Strategic Change Services (in charge of organizational design, governance, and group decision making), were gathering and generating the approaches that later formed the basis for many of BITS's methodologies. Each of the corporate groups developed a number of company-wide programs that focused on improving particular functional processes. In contrast, BITS was formed in 1999 to provide integrative, cross-functional services to HP's many business units.

Main Case Study *continued*

True Cross-Functional Thinking

The early recognition that a cross-functional approach was essential to business performance was central in guiding the services that BITS would offer. Although engineering has often been a driving force within HP, the BITS team was assembled with an eye for creating a business melting pot. The 25 individuals in BITS have diverse backgrounds: including engineering PhDs, marketers, anthropologists, business analysts and medical technologists. Mike Northcott, who manages the BITS group says, 'business problems are rarely if ever singularly focused; they are not just about customers, or investments or change management. The diversity of BITS helps us put together consulting teams that come at the problem from different angles. Furthermore, we understand the culture and language of the company's different functions'. BITS encourages business units to take a 'horizontal view' across the functions. 'You have to understand the needs of your customers through all of the interactions they have with your business, from awareness, through support, to repurchase. Only then can you develop innovations that create exceptional customer loyalty', emphasizes Northcott.

Three Teams, Three Domains

Currently, BITS is active in providing business support in three domains: 'acceleration services', 'business strategy services', and 'customer strategy services'.

Acceleration services are based on the recognition that the speed at which strategic business decisions are made has a strong influence on a business unit's competitiveness. Fast but effective decision-making is supported through two types of 'event'. The first is known as 'GarageWorks' and consists of facilitated meetings with 15–30 people, designed to creatively identify breakthrough ideas or new concepts. The second type involves helping large groups quickly reach shared decisions; these are known as 'Decision Accelerators' and have 30–200 participants. In addition to running events, the acceleration services team consults on change management, corporate and business governance modelling, and team and leadership development.

Business strategy services work with HP's businesses on developing strategic plans. This team's assignments run the gamut from identifying new business opportunities and business model design, all the way through strategic portfolio analysis.

The customer strategy services team specializes in understanding the 'customer experience', uncovering latent user needs through ethnographic, empathic design, and other techniques. Their work also includes the development of value delivery systems 'maps', which help focus businesses on the operational investments that will yield the greatest returns.

Working with HP's divisions (and those of Compaq since the 2002 merger), BITS needs to not only spread innovation best practices, but also to plot the future of innovation management at HP. Focusing on the three domains will not be sufficient for much longer. Consequently, Northcott is looking at how his group needs to change. 'BITS is a service operation working within what was originally a pure R&D and manufacturing company. However, HP is moving towards a services-led business model and, to remain relevant, my team needs to evolve ahead of the businesses' needs. We have to harness innovative consulting services ourselves, bring these into the company, and make them relevant to HP's problems. Unlike many external consulting services, we measure our value by our ability to improve HP's capabilities. If we don't generate extraordinary and sustaining value, then HP would be better off outsourcing our services', he says.

Changing Nature of Innovation

In developing ideas for new approaches, Northcott also works closely with William Pipkin, a 21-year HP veteran who now runs his own innovation management consultancy, specializing in advising start-ups how they can commercialize their technology. 'William brings the urgency and critical perspective of a small start-up into our discussions, matched with an awareness of the full implications of what he is saying for a large company like HP. Sometimes the 'small company view' is painful but it certainly helps us to look at innovation differently', says Northcott.

Invention and technology have always played a leading role in innovation at HP and the garage in California where the founders set up the company is not only an icon within the firm but is also a protected historic building (hence the name GarageWorks for new business workshops). However, more than technology is needed because, 'today's latest technology is tomorrow's commodity', says Northcott, 'so we must concentrate on designing innovative business processes'. For example, although HP has a history of excellent manufacturing, outsourcing is now used extensively. Managing the interfaces between the key organizations along the value chain is where the real value can be captured. Northcott says, 'it is now a case of finding how to positively control the customer experience without having to own all the assets. It's a case of bringing customer-oriented insights into what would otherwise be standardized business processes. Like in a small company, everyone has to be engaged in customer dialogue to generate these insights'.

Pipkin and Northcott identify two main challenges for both large and small organizations that want to become more innovative. These are: expanding the skills of their employees, and understanding and meeting the transforming needs of customers.

Much has been written about pulling together the skill base required for innovative project teams. 'However, while many people are excellent at the technology, or the finance, or marketing, few if any are excellent at all three.

Hardly any people have the skills needed to pull it all together and, without such people you are progressively more likely to fail', says Pipkin. Although a large company has functional expertise, Northcott perceives the need for HP to develop more individuals with 'multi-functional and entrepreneurial skills'. He thinks it is the ability to drive processes that cut across the traditional boundaries 'that are going to be critical in the future'. Pipkin identifies some major changes in the general nature of customers' needs. 'As our society continues to develop, so our needs climb up Maslow's Triangle. We are no longer hunter-gatherers. Previously, companies could focus on basic needs, but now it's all about experiential requirements; needs that are not easy to identify or satisfy', he says. Northcott has a similar view: 'it is not only getting harder to identify customers' real needs, but these are becoming more personal'. Both believe that businesses will need to deliver a consistently excellent 'experience' for customers with every interaction they have with the company. The challenge will be to identify the internal process changes that must occur to achieve this, and to do so ahead of the demand curve. As Northcott puts it, 'providing innovations to customers who will increasingly defy the rules of market segmentation is going to require radically different leadership skills'.

Appendix: Innovation Auditing

Introductions

The following set of innovation audit questions is based on six main references, adapted to match the Pentathlon Framework. One of the problems with innovation audits is that are various sets of recommended questions but which are the most appropriate ones for a particular context is not well understood. Additionally, the various sets of questions available have not been previously collated. Therefore, here we have indicated the source of each question by superscripts, referring to the numbers (below) of the references. Redundant questions have been eliminated. *Italics* indicate where original questions have been (slightly) modified. Questions in *italics* without superscript numbers are new and have been developed by the authors to cover areas such as project prioritization, where insufficient questions were previously available.

References on Innovation Audits

(1) Anonymous, 'Managing Change in Your Organization' *International Trade Forum*, Issue 2/2000, pp. 26–8.

(2) British Standard, *Design Management System – Part 1: Guide to Managing Innovation.* British Standard BS7000–1, British Standards Institution: London, 1999.

(3) Goffin, K. and Pfeiffer, R., *Innovation Management in UK and German Manufacturing Companies.* Anglo–German Foundation Report Series, London December 1999, ISBN 1–900834–17–0.

(4) Majaro, S., *The Creative Marketer* (Oxford: Butterworth-Heinemann, 1991), ISBN 0–7506–1706–X.

(5) Tidd, J., Bessant, J. and Pavitt, K., *Managing Innovation: Integrating Technological, Market and Organizational Change*, 2nd edn (Chichester: Wiley, 2001), ISBN 0–471–49615–4.

(6) Voss, C. A., Chiesa, V. and Coughlan, P., *Innovation – Your Move, Self-Assessment Guide and Workbook*, (London: UK Department of Trade and Industry, 1993).

Applying the Innovation Audit

Chapter 9 explains how the innovation audit can be used to better understand the innovation performance of an organization, in conjunction with other tools such as the cultural web. In using the audit two main points much be considered:

1 The results cannot be directly compared from one organization to another.
2 Collecting and analyzing the extensive data is best conducted by an external consultant with direct experience of innovation audits, rather than someone from within the organization to be audited.
3 The audit needs preparation for the specific context in which it will be used.

These points need some explanation.

The question in some innovation audits are designed to be answered on a numeric scale (for example, Majaro, 1991). However, it should be remembered that although the answers are quantitative, they are only based on managers' opinions. Therefore, we caution readers against assuming that the results can be directly compared from company to company, as the scales are not absolute. Many aspects of innovation management are too complex to allow all of the inputs, processes and innovation outputs to be represented by a single number. This means that it is difficult to 'benchmark' more than a few aspects of innovation performance, such as the revenues generated by new products, or the percentage of revenues invested in R&D. Even time-to-market figures, which apparently should be comparable, are notoriously difficult to compare reliably.

Although we present a comprehensive set of innovation audit questions in this appendix, we do not recommend that a company should attempt to apply it themselves. It is worth investing in having the audit conducted by external consultants, who should have experience in innovation auditing. Outsiders are more likely to be able to encourage employees to make a candid assessment of company performance, to objectively interpret the results, draw comparisons to other organizations, and support the process of boosting innovation performance. In conducting interviews, the consultants will need to gain the confidence of employees and so it is best for anonymity to be promised. In our own experience of conducting innovation audits, we have found that contextual issues play an important role. Therefore, the questions selected need to match the organization and the business environment being investigated.

Some questions will not be applicable to the context of the organization being investigated and will need to be dropped. For example, some of the technology management questions might not be applicable to a service sector company. Also the number of questions needs to be manageable and the full set needs to be reduced appropriately. This is best done through a number of pilot interviews, where the external investigators learn about the organization to be audited. The audit questionnaire used should also give the interviewee adequate opportunity to suggest ways in which the innovation performance of the organization can be improved.

After the pioneering work of Majaro (the first version of his audit was published in 1988) and the widely applied audit developed by Voss *et al.* (1991), the area of innovation auditing has been somewhat ignored by researchers. This is certainly partly due to the difficulties of validating the effectiveness of innovation audits in complex contexts. Nonetheless, the need for innovation audits as a tool has if anything increased over the last few years. We have collated all the audit questions from the above-mentioned sources, in order to give a comprehensive list of questions that will cover all eventualities.

From our own experience in conducting innovation audits, we have seen that organizations have a far greater need for support in gauging performance that can be satisfied using the current tools and techniques. Much remains to be done by researchers to take with work further and develop a precise tool for practitioners.

Innovation Audit Questions

Organization .... Interviewer ....
Interviewee .... Date ....

1.0 Innovation Strategy

1.1 Management Leadership

1 Is innovation a fundamental part of the organization's philosophy and values?[3]
2 What types of innovation do you have in your organization?[2]
3 Does top management spend significant time supporting all forms of innovation?[3]
4 How does innovation strategy link formally to corporate strategy?[5]
5 *Is there a* high level of market orientation in the strategy and planning process? *Is there* continuous monitoring of progress and strong internal commitment to change?[6]
6 Does your innovation strategy integrate all five areas of innovation management?[3]
7 What is the organization's main innovation strategy (for example, first-to-market, or fast follower)?[3]
8 How well is the innovation strategy communicated?[5]
9 Is there a clear shared sense of strategic vision and ownership of the business plan?[5]
10 How are innovation goals and priorities set and incorporated into the organization's mission, plans and strategies? How *does the organization* ensure that innovation is a key activity throughout the business?[6]
11 How does *the organization* use its long-term vision of the future to inform and influence present activities?[2]

1.2 Market and Competitor Analysis

1 How does the organization monitor its operating environment to identify key trends and market drivers (for example legislation, changing needs, new technology, etc.)?[6]
2 Do links with government provide early warning of relevant regulation and promotion and mechanisms for responding and communicating?[5]
3 *Does the organization* use explanatory techniques such as Delphi and Scenarios to help to identify future trends?[5]
4 What potential innovative advantages (disadvantages) derive from the national (local) environment?[5]

5   What action is being taken to benefit from foreign systems of innovation?[5]

6   Does the organization monitor the market continuously to identify competitive strengths and weaknesses from a customer viewpoint? How is this done?[6]

7   *How does the* organization react fast to threats or surprises from the competition?[2]

8   Are customer surveys carried out to refine strategy and tactics? What form do these take? *Does the organization* get feedback from sale, service, after-sales staff?[6]

9   How *does the organization* compare to the competition in product, price, quality, delivery, level and composition of R&D, patents and publications, other benchmarks?[5]

10 Does the organization monitor its *competitors' technical capabilities*?[6]

11 Is there systematic product benchmarking (of competitors' products)?[6]

1.3   Funding of Innovation

1   *Does the organization's* financial reporting system reflect innovation as an investment rather than as a cost?[1]

2   What are the policies for funding R&D, *innovation* and other technology acquisition?[6]

3   What are the policies for funding product and process development?[6]

4   What is *the* organization's budget for new product development?[2]

5   How much of this budget is set aside for 3rd generation products?[2]

6   In R&D *and innovation* spend protected and related to potential business contribution over the short- and long-term?[6]

7   Is there flexibility to *fund* innovative ideas that arise outside core development programmes?[6]

8   How are R&D *and innovation* expenditures evaluated?[5]

1.4   Innovation Performance Measures

1   How does management measure innovation performance?[6]

2   What targets are set for innovation? How is this does?[6]

   –   For the organization as a whole?[6]
   –   For individual departments and/or processes?[6]

3   Are these targets communicated to, and understood by, all employees? How is this ensured?[6]

4   Do performance measures reflect the strategy? Are they simple, appropriate and valid?[6]

1.5 Innovation Performance (Results)

On the performance measures currently used . . .

5 What are the trends and current levels of:

 – Product and process innovation performance?[6]
 – Customer satisfaction/dissatisfaction indicators?[6]

6 How do current performance levels compare with those of your main competitors?[6]

1 Are there any improvements in the organization's competitiveness, market share and profitability, which can be attributed to better innovation performance?[6]

1.6 Innovation Networking

1 Is *the* organization involved in any alliances?[2]

2 *Does the organization* include all relevant individuals and organizations in *an innovation* network?[5]

3 *Does the organization* seek to develop and maintain formal and informal knowledge networks?[5]

4 *From which external sources is the organization currently actively learning? Are these links being sufficiently utilized?*

5 *Does the organization* have clear criteria for identifying and selecting potential alliance partners?[5]

6 *Does the organization* segment and manage suppliers according to its objectives?[5]

7 *Does the organization* have clear policies for outsourcing, licensing-in & licensing-out technology?[5]

8 Are relationships with customers suppliers useful for technology planning?[6]

1.7 Technology Management

1 What are our technological competencies and where are they located in the firm?[5] Are they effectively linked to each other, and to other corporate functions?[5]

2 Does the organization understand its core competencies in technology and innovation and have policies for allocating resources to build and strengthen them?[6]

3 Do organizational practices reinforce the exploitation of technological opportunities?[5]

4 What are the potential opportunities and threats emerging from advances in key technologies?[5] What are the implications for corporate skills, markets and organizational practices?[5]

5 Are emerging technologies and technologies likely to give future competitive advantage identified?[6]

6 *Does the organization* have explicit policies for sourcing technologies, including in-house R&D, licensing in and out, partnerships and external linkages?[6]

7 Is the organization getting satisfactory benefits from the application of new technology *(to products, services, and the service augmentation)*?[4]

8 Does the *operations function* have a record of recommending and adopting methods associated with new technology?[4]

9 Does the *operations function* understand and learn from the practices of its competitors, with respect to new technology?[4]

10 *Are technology roadmaps used to summarize and communicate the links between innovation strategy and required resources?*

11 *Does the organization consider* how to apply *new technologies to the service business?*[1]

1.8 Market Planning and Review

1 *Does the marketing plan link directly to the innovation strategy?*

2 What are the mechanisms within the organization to ensure that the marketing strategy and plan are continuously reviewed and changed where appropriate?[6]

3 How often is the marketing plan reviewed and changed?[6]

4 What measures are used to set targets and monitor performance against plan (for example sales by major customer/segment, numbers of new customers, market share, etc.)? How often are these comparisons made and how does the organization react to the results?[6]

2.0 Ideas: Managing Creativity and Knowledge

2.1 Culture of Creativity and Innovation

1 Is the general climate within all the *organization's departments and functions* supportive of the process of generating ideas?[4]

2 Does the organization undertake regular training or idea-generating exercises in order to stimulate the overall climate for creativity?[4]

3 Is top management involved and actively interested in the process of generating ideas?[4]

2 Does a communication system exist for 'marketing' the corporate approach to creativity and innovation?[4]

3 *Is support provided* to staff who try out new ideas even if the ideas fail?[1]

4 Does the *management of all of the organization's departments and functions* take an active interest in idea-generation, as opposed to just sitting back and waiting for others to come up with ideas?[4]

5 *Do all departments'* objectives mention 'creativity' or 'innovation', or both?[4]

6 Do people in *all departments* talk about 'creativity', 'ideas' and 'innovation'?[4]

7 Is the *management of all departments* approachable and receptive to ideas?[4]
8 Do people in *all departments* know how and to whom they can submit their ideas?[4]
9 Does a system exist for screening and evaluating ideas in every department?[4]
10 Does the organization actively encourage communication and cross-fertilisation of ideas:

  – between different levels of the organization?
  – between different functions?
  – between different operating units?
  – between different international markets?[4]

1 How are teams used to develop new product concepts and product enhancements?[6]
2 How are *creative ideas* matched with technological capabilities to generate new product and service concepts and enhancements of existing products?[6]
3 *Does the organization* have at least two experiments or pilots of new service concepts being conducted at any one time?[1]

2.2 Use of Creativity Tools, Approaches

1 *Do all departments* undertake regular training or use 'idea generating' exercises in order to solve problems and/or identify opportunities?[4]
2 *Are* brainstorming *and* structured problem solving *approaches* used?[6]
3 *Are left–right brain alternatives (or similar approaches) used to ensure that ideas are generated for improving the service augmentation?*
4 *Is there* a procedure for having staff 'mystery shop' the competition and report back?[1]
5 *Is attribute analysis used to generate ideas for novel new products, services, and service augmentations?*

2.3 Knowledge Management

1 Are there formal mechanisms in place to capture and share learning?[5] How do they operate?[5]
2 how far do we seek to learn from the experiences of others in managing innovation?[5] Within our sector?[5] Outside our sector?[5]
3 How well *does the organization* keep up with new thinking and concepts in innovation management?[5]
4 How do we capture learning from projects and feed it into future practice?[5]
5 How well is knowledge shared across the organization?[5] How often do we reinvent the wheel or repeat the same mistakes?[5]
6 *Does the organization* take the opportunity to learn from the share experiences with other organizations?[5]
7 *Does the organization* seek to help develop learning in our supply chain?[5]
8 *Is team learning promoted?*

9 *Are post-project reviews used to stimulate and capture the learning from innova-tion projects?*

10 *Does the organization understand the role of tacit knowledge and manage the learning from innovation projects accordingly?*

2.4 Use of Enhanced Market Research Methods

1 *Is there a* company-wide focus on customer needs?[6]
2 *Is detailed* market research and analysis undertaken regularly?[6]
3 *Is the concept of hidden needs analysis understood and applied by using a range of suitable enhanced methods for market research?*
4 How *does the organization* ensure that new product concepts are market led?[6]
5 Does the organization build and maintain relationships with customers as a specific means of getting information on needs and opportunities?[6]
6 How are groups used to get data (for example, customer product groups, *lead users*)?[6]
7 Is feedback from functions such as field service used to gain customer input?[6]
1 *Is a* broad range of functions involved in concept development and evalu-ation?[6]
2 Is an analysis made of the customer-product experience cycle?[2]

2.5 Creativity Levels in the Organization

3 What is the overall level of creativity in the organization?[4]
4 Is the level of creativity and innovation in the following functional areas satisfactory:

- – Marketing?
- – *Operations?*
- – Personnel?
- – Research and Development?
- – Finance?
- – Central Administration/Services?[4]

5 How does *the organization* protect its intellectual property?[2]

- – *Through patents?*
- – *Through other means?*

3.0 Prioritization: Selecting & Managing the Portfolio

3.1 Prioritization Process

1 Is there a system (as opposed to ad-hoc arrangements) for screening and evaluating ideas in the organization?[4]

2   *Does the portfolio prioritization process clearly link the choice of projects to inno-*
    vation strategy?

3   *Does the organization* regularly review *the* portfolio of service offerings to
    make sure that they are balanced in terms of novelty/innovation and risk?[1]

4   How is product development prioritized in the face of multiple opportuni-
    ties, customer demands for variety and product improvement and limited
    resources?[6]

5   How are choices made between different opportunities for new and
    enhanced products?[6]

6   If the organization conducts R&D or funds outside development, what are
    the procedures for project selection, risk analysis and resource allocation?[6]

7   How are R&D projects selected/generated and how are external sources and
    relationships used for technology acquisition and building technical
    alliances?[6]

8   Is funding available for unplanned development projects?[6]

9   Are members of the finance function involved, on their own initiative, as
    members of multi-disciplinary project-appraisal teams?[4]

4   In general are members of the *controlling and finance* department viewed by
    other departments as creative contributors to the success of the business (as
    opposed to being 'score-keepers')?[4]

5   Are explicit choices made to decide between in-house R&D, licensing, part-
    nership and external linkages?6 How are these choices made?[6]

6   *Does the organization consider the availability of good project managers in its*
    portfolio management process?

7   *Is the portfolio of process innovation projects known and adequately managed?*

3.2   Analysis Tools and Approaches

10 *Are both financial and scoring methods effectively and efficiently applied to eval-*
    uate projects?

11 *Is the concept of risk adequately understood in the organization? Does this allow*
    projects to be objectively analyzed?

12 *Does the organization* identify the desired balance of risk, returns and
    timescales, and identify the appropriate mix of basic research and develop-
    ment?[6]

13 *Does the organization* systematically search for new product opportunities?[5]
    How is product innovation planning linked to the overall business strategy?[5]

14 *Does the organization* have a system for selecting product innovations in the
    face of competition alternatives?[5] Is this a formal or informal process?[5]

15 *Are all the organization's* financial stakeholders involved in major new
    programmes to promote their understanding?[5]

3.3   Current Portfolio

1   Is the number of innovations produced by the organization considered to
    be satisfactory?[4]

2 Is the organization's record of new product/service development satisfactory when compared with its main competitors?[4]

3 Is there a good balance of truly innovative projects as well as product improvements?[3]

4 *Does the current portfolio meet the principles of a good portfolio (that is, each project is good value; the collection of projects makes the most efficient use of resources; risk is balanced; there is a match to strategy)?*

5 *Is there* long-term planning *of* three or more generations of products?[6]

6 Is the success rate of new products or services satisfactory?[4]

7 What are *the organization's* weaknesses in long-term conceptualization and development?[2]

4.0 Implementation

4.1 The Management Process

1 How does management ensure that suitable procedures are in place to bring innovative products to the market?[6]

2 Is there a systematic product development process?[6]

3 Is there a formal procedure for reviewing progress against a series of 'stage gates'?[5] Is this used in practice or are there alternative 'short cuts'?[5]

4 Are there measures to show that each stage of the process has been completed and done thoroughly (for example design review criteria)?[6]

5 Are there means to ensure that customer and end user input is used throughout the process?[6]

6 *Are there* established procedures and objectives with flexibility to allow small *and priority* projects to move through quickly? Parallel and integrated activities?[6]

7 What is management's role in, and responsibility for, ensuring that there are best practice processes for bringing innovative new and enhanced products to the market?[6]

1 What are the procedures for taking a new product from concept to launch?[6]

2 What is the process; its scope; the phases, milestones, reviews and sign-off procedures?[6]

2 How do you minimise the development lead time for new products?[6]

3 To what extent are the steps integrated. Doe activities take place in parallel with each other?[6]

1 How *does the organization* ensure that sufficient capacity is available in manufacturing, suppliers and support functions to allow fast and effective product development?[6]

4.2 Structure and Organization

1 *Does the organization* have dedicated product development teams?[6]

2 Are they multi-disciplinary?[6]

3 To what extent are the teams and their leaders fully responsible for the product from start to finish?[6]

4 What decision-making authority do they have?[6]

5 How early are the teams set up?[6] Are suppliers involved?[5]

- *Is there* strong team leadership and both team and leaders empowered to make decisions?[6]
- *Is there a* long-term champion for *each* new product?[2]
- Apart from the product champion, who else will be involved in the 3rd generation product conceptualization and development?[2]
- Is there early involvement and concurrent working within the product development system?[5]
- *Does the organization* use different project management structures for different projects (functional, matrix, heavyweight team, etc.?[5]
- *Does the organization* invest in team development?[5]
- Is communication effective?[5] Does it operate vertically and horizontally and in two-way mode?[5]

4.3 Industrial Design

1 Are industrial designers involved throughout the product development process?[6]

2 How is industrial (aesthetic and ergonomic) design built into the innovation process *for both products and services*?[6]

3 Are internal experts and external design groups used to ensure high quality industrial design?[6]

4 How *does the organization* ensure that the industrial design of the product is tested with end users?[6]

4.3 Transfer to Operations

- How strong are the links between design and manufacturing?[6]
- What process is used to ensure the successful transfer from design into operations and subsequent distribution to the customer?[6]
- How good is the capability of operations to tests prototypes; identify key risks and problems; give rapid feedback to design; ramp-up new products into full-scale production; take the product into the field?[6]
- What are the procedures for handling product *design* changes?[6] How effective are they?[6]
- Is there a mechanism for feedback from manufacturing and field service to design on quality, manufacturability, etc.?[6]

1 Has the organization been able to improve the quality and/or reduce the cost of logistics in recent years?[4]

4.3 Marketing and Distribution

1 *Have* innovative approaches to distribution and marketing been developed and implemented?[6]

2 *Are* all elements of the marketing mix continuously monitored in comparison with own and competitor's performance?[6]

3 Has the organization evaluated alternative methods of selling and distribution to assess the most cost-effective routes to the market?[6]

4 How does the organization communicate with its customers and prospects? How are sales leads generated? Has the organization experimented with different proportional methods and measured the results?[6]

5 How does the organization measure customer satisfaction?[6]

6 How often do staff outside the sales function talk to customers?[6]

7 Are there mechanisms to allow feedback of customer views into the innovation process? What are these mechanisms?[6]

1 Has the organization been able to improve the loyalty of its intermediaries and improve service to customers in recent years?[4]

2 Does the marketing team involve the channel intermediaries in the process of idea-generation and/or strategy planning?[4]

3 Is the organization's distribution sufficiently creative compared with that of its main competitors?[4]

4 Does the marketing management monitor the costs and benefits of data collection and input, and seek to improve their pay-off value?[4]

5 Are the relative costs of in-house marketing research and fees to an outside agency for comparable work known and acted upon?[4]

6 Is the organization's record of new product/service development satisfactory when compared with its main competitors?[4]

7 Is the speed at which ideas are converted into practical innovations improving?[4]

8 Has the marketing team overcome pricing problems by using creating 'non-price' strategies?[4]

9 Is pricing used creatively to give the organization a distinctive position in the market, as opposed to being merely the application of a formula?[4]

10 Does the marketing department observe the practices other companies in order to help solve difficult pricing problems?[4]

4.4 Promotional mix

11 Has the level of creativity demonstrated in the promotional mix over the last few years been high?[4]

12 Has the cost – benefit ratio of promotional campaigns improved in recent years?[4]

13 How does the organization distribute and sell its products? What promotional methods are used to raise awareness and generate enquiries?[6]

14 Does the organization develop its own promotional ideas, as opposed to relying on outside agencies to do the creative thinking?[4]

15 Does the organization experiment with new communication ideas (such as new technology) on a fairly regular basis?[4]

16 Does the marketing management effectively scan and identify good ideas used in its own or other markets?[4]

4.4 Tools for Innovation

8 *Is there* widespread use of appropriate tools to capture customer needs and to ensure the effectiveness of product and process design? Established protocols such as design for manufacture, design for test, design for customer use?[6]

1 Does the organization use information systems to promote information exchange in support of the innovation process?[6]

2 *Does the organization make full use* of systems such as CAD, CAD/CAM, CIM, product data management systems and process simulation?[6]

3 Are *tools* used to accelerate product development and improve design effectiveness? How is this achieved?[6]

4 How does the use of tools contribute to achieving faster and more effective product development?[6]

5 What techniques are used for product and process design?[6] For example:

- quality function deployment *(QFD)*?[6]
- Design to Cost?[6]
- Design for Customer Use?[6]
- Design for Test (DFT)?[6]
- rapid prototyping?[6]
- Design for Manufacture (DFM)?[6]
- experimental design methods including Taguchi?[6]
- statistical process control (SPC)?[6]
- failure mode and effect analysis (FMEA)?[6]
- *Design for Supportability (DFS)?*

4.3 Process Innovation

1 *Are there* strong links between product, *service* and process development?[6] *Are these used to generate sustainable competitive advantage?*

2 How are new *operational* processes conceived and developed?[6]

3 Is there a formal *operations* strategy? Is it market led? Does this define the need for new *operational* capabilities and processes?[6]

4 *Is* information on new process technology actively sought and *are* new processes tested to gain experience?[6]

5 What is the process for ensuring effective implementation of new process technology?[6]

6 Does the organization run a continuous improvement programme on *all operational processes including* customer service, delivery performance, etc.?[6]

7   How is process improvement integrated with day-to-day quality control and quality assurance? Are work teams encouraged to identify opportunities for process improvement?[6]

8   Is internal data from techniques such as statistical process control and external data such as customer feedback, competitive benchmarks and product performance used to improve process performance? How is this done?[6]

9   How does the organization keep informed of sources of new process technology and test new processes?[6]

10 How *does the organization* determine when existing processes need to be upgraded?[6]

11 *Do* implementation teams stay together into full production to ensure learning and improvement? *Is there* active involvement of suppliers?[6]

12 What is the organization for implementation of new processes?[6]

13 Are the resources, skills and flexibility available to support new product testing and ramp-up?[6]

14 Is the choice of new process technology matched to the resources available for its operation?[6]

15 *Is a* TQM programme in place including a focus on achieving improved innovation performance?[6]

16 How is quality assured in the design process and what methods are used to analyse and improve the quality of innovation processes?[6]

17 How is quality assurance used to ensure that customer requirements are identified and incorporated into products and processes?[6]

18 Is ISO 9000 used in product development and *operations*?[6]

19 Does the *operations* department make creative contributions to methods of inventory control, cost control and so on?[4]

20 Does the *operations* department take steps to improve the productivity of its own personnel through simpler systems, reduced paperwork, better used of existing data and the like?[4]

21 Can the *operations* department demonstrate examples of creative improvements in quality?[4]

1   Are 'quality circles' used as a way of solving quality problems?[4]

2   Are *operations* personnel encouraged to discover and analyse the quality-control procedures of competitors?[4]

3   Have investigations been carried out to check whether customers are happy with the quality improvements introduced (i.e. are improvements customer-orientated)?[4]

5.0   People and Organization

5.1   *Innovation Culture*

11 Does the organization's mission statement mention 'creativity', 'innovative' or both as being part of the corporate ethos?[4]

12 How does management create and sustain an innovative climate?[6]

13 How involved are senior managers in promoting innovation; ensuring that the climate encourages development of new ideas, risk taking and entrepreneurship?[6]

14 To what extent do people in the organization understand how innovation helps it compete?[5]

15 Is there top management commitment and support for innovation?[5] How is it expressed?[5]

16 Are key individuals recognized and supported in *the* organization?[5]

17 Is employees' innovative and entrepreneurial behaviour is encouraged and rewarded?[6]

18 Are there adequate communications procedures to explain and encourage innovation? Is the innovation policy understood and supported throughout the organization?[6]

19 Does an innovative attitude pervade *the* organization?[2]

20 Is this innovation attitude communicated internally and externally?[2]

21 Is there any evidence of creativity or innovation in the general appearance of the reception area?[4]

22 Is there any evidence of creativity or innovation in the landscaping or general external appearance of the premises (especially the areas that make an impact on visitors)?[4]

23 Does the organizational structure support or inhibit innovation?[5]

24 *Does the organization* have a supportive climate for new ideas – or do people have to leave in order to carry them forward?[5]

25 *Does the organization have* effective teamwork?[5]

26 *Does the organization* invest in team-building?[5]

27 Are there adequate rewards and recognition for innovation?[5]

28 How far is the workforce involved in innovation?[5] Are there formal mechanisms for finding and solving problems which people use?[5] Are these linked to monitoring and measurement systems to guide improvement?[5]

29 Is there a framework for monitoring and measuring how well innovation projects run? How often is it reviewed?[5]

30 How does *the* organization learn from failures?[2]

5.2 Recruiting and Job Assignment

1 How are the people needs for innovation identified? How are these needs translated into recruitment, training and development?[6]

2 How does the organization plan the level of resources needed?[6]

3 Does *the* organization have a skills audit?[2]

4 Has the HR department been proactive in identifying factors such as skill shortages, which would reduce organizational efficiency?[4]

5 What procedures are used for recruiting, developing, evaluating and rewarding the human resources required for innovation?[6]

1 How does the organization manage human resource development:

   – technical staff career planning?[6]
   – cross-functional development?[6]

2 Does the HR department demonstrate creativity in assessing the number
   and needs of managers in the future?[4]
3 Has HR department been innovative in the field of recruitment and selection procedures?[4]
4 Is the cost of recruitment known and are steps being taken to reduce it, or
   improve its effectiveness?[4]
5 Have creative ideas been used in communicating company information to
   prospective recruits and/or new employees?[4]

5.5 Managing Performance

1 In general, are existing incentive packages innovative?[4] Has the *HR* department recommended creative non financial components in the total
   employee 'remuneration package'?[4]
6 Has the personnel department experimented with new and better ways to
   motivate all company employees?[4]

   ☐ Are creative steps taken to improve or maintain morale throughout the
      organizations?[4]
   ☐ Are there formal procedures to help people find and solve problems
      and record the results of their improvement activities?[5]

5.4 Development of Employees

   ☐ *Does the organization* provide training for staff in innovation-related
      skills?[1]
   ☐ Is training and development a priority issue?[5] How well does it
      compare with the sectoral average?[5]
   ☐ *Have all departments* taken steps to improve *levels* of productivity?
   ☐ *Does the HR* department made a creative contribution to improvements
      in the productivity of other departments?[4]
   ☐ Have the organization's management-development and training
      systems benefited from innovative thinking?[4]
   ☐ *Is there sufficient focus on the development of good project managers and
      product champions?*
   ☐ Has the *HR* department taken steps to motivate managers to pursue
      programmes of self-development?[4]
   ☐ Has the *HR* department been creative in selecting and working with
      outside training agencies?[4]
   ☐ Has the *HR* department been successful in facilitating the return to
      work of managers who have been on courses, so that they can put their
      new learning into practice?[4]
   ☐ Is the training and development of managers being achieved in a
      better, more cost-effective way than previously?[4]

5.5 Organizational Structure

6   Is team problem solving encouraged and, if so, how?[6]

7   *Do the organization's* career structures support innovation through development of people across different functions?[6]

8   What status, influence and responsibilities do *project managers* have in the organization (for example spending authority, leadership, budgetary control, conflict resolution, team selection, input to performance reviews, dedicated to part-time)?[6]

9   What is the use and composition of development teams? How does their use ensure effective communication and problem solving during development, and that product concepts are properly defined prior to the start of development?[6]

10   *Is the HR function active in supporting the management of change within the organization?*

Notes and References

Chapter I The Role of Innovation

1   Drucker, P. F., 'The Discipline of Innovation', *Harvard Business Review*, vol. 76, no. 6 (November–December 1998), pp. 149–57.

2   Sheth, J. N. and Ram, R., *Bringing Innovation to Market: How to Break Corporate and Customer Barriers* (New York: Wiley, 1987) ISBN 0-47184-977-4.

3   Feige, A. and Crooker, R., 'Innovationen als Medizin gegen Arbeitslosigkeit und Mittelmass', *Frankfurter Allgemeine Zeitung* (7 December 1998).

4   Taylor, E., 'Super Market', *The Wall Street Journal Europe* (Friday/Saturday/Sunday 5–7 December 2003), p. R4.

5   www.future-store.org, accessed in January 2004.

6   Jordan, M. and Karp, J., 'Whirlpool Launches Affordable Washer in Brazil and China', *The Wall Street Journal Europe* (Tuesday, 9 December 2003), p. A8.

7   De Meyer, A. and Pycke, B., 'Falling Behind in Innovation: The 1996 Report on the European Manufacturing Futures Survey', *INSEAD Working Paper Series*, no. 96/95/TM (1996).

8   Tether, B. and Miles, I., 'Surveying Innovation in Services – Measurement and Policy Interpretation Issues', in B. Thuriaux, E. Arnold and C. Couchot (eds), *Innovation and Enterprise Creation: Statistics and Indicators* (European Communities, 2001), ISBN 92-894-1576-2, pp. 77–87.

9   Watson, P., 'It's Innovation, Stupid – Britain must Learn to Manage Better the Exploitation of its Inventions', *Financial Times* (22 March 1996), p. 101.

10 Houlder, V., 'Technology: Quiet Revolution', *Financial Times* (26 March 1996), p. 143.

11 Anonymous, 'Produktoffensive soll Vorwerk Umsatz bringen. Hohe Investitionen in die Entwicklung/Bekenntnis zum Standort Deutschland', *Frankfurter Allgemeine Zeitung* (3 May 1997).

12 Anonymous, 'Wirtschaft: Rasanz bei neuer Autotechnik: DaimlerChrysler will Innovationen schneller zum Kunden bringen', *Sueddeutsche Zeitung* (23 September 1998).

13 Majaro, S., *The Creative Gap* (London: Longman, 1988), ISBN 0-851-21196-8.

14 Schumpeter, J. A., *The Theory of Economic Development* (Boston, USA: Harvard University Press, 1934).

15 Porter, M. E., *The Competitive Advantage of Nations* (London: Macmillan, now Palgrave, 1990), ISBN 0-333-73642-7.

16 Priessl, B., 'Service Innovation: What Makes it Different? Empirical Evidence from Germany', in Metcalf, J.S. and Miles, I., *Innovation Systems in the Service Economy: Measurement and Case Study Analysis* (Norwell, Massachusetts: Kluwer Academic Publishers, 2000), ISBN 0-7923-7730-3.

17 Djellal, F. and Gallouj, F., 'Innovation Surveys for Service Industries: A Review', in Thuriaux, B., Arnold, E. and Couchot, C. (eds), *Innovation and Enterprise Creation: Statistics and Indicators* (European Communities, 2001), ISBN 92-894-1576-2, pp. 70–6.

18 OECD, 'The Measurement of Scientific and Technical Activities' (Paris: OECD, 1981).

19 West, M. A. and Farr, J. L., 'Innovation at Work', in M. A. West and J. L. Farr (eds), *Innovation and Creativity at Work: Psychological and Organizational Strategies* (Chichester, England: Wiley, 1990), ISBN 0-47-192655-8, p. 9.

20 Pisano, G. P. and Wheelwright, S. C., 'The New Logic of High-Tech R&D', *Harvard Business Review*, vol. 73, no. 5 (September–October 1995), pp. 93–105.

21 *cambridge-consultants.com* website accessed June 2001.

22 Based on unpublished research by Goffin.

23 Sekhar, A., 'At Your Service: Your Wish is Their Command at Les Concierges', *Asian Business*, vol. 37, no. 5 (May 2001), pp. 48–9.

24 Kim, W. C. and Mauborgne, R., 'Value Innovation: The Strategic Logic of High Growth', *Harvard Business Review*, vol. 75, no. 1 (January–February 1997), pp. 103–12.

25 Booz-Allen and Hamilton, *New Products Management for the 1980s* (New York: Booz-Allen and Hamilton Inc., 1982).

26 Wind, Y. and Mahajan, V., 'New Product Development Process: A Perspective for Reexamination', *Journal of Product Innovation Management*, vol. 5, no. 4 (December 1988), pp. 304–10.

27 The idea to compare the phases of an innovation to a funnel goes back to at least to Majaro, S. *The Creative Gap* (London: Longman, 1988), ISBN 0-85121-196-8.

28 Wheelwright, S. C. and Clark, K., *Revolutionizing Product Development: Quantum Leaps in Speed, Efficiency, and Quality* (New York: The Free Press, 1992), ISBN 0-02-905515-6.

29 Mansfield, E., *Economics: Principles, Problems, Decisions* (New York: Norton, 5th edn 1986), ISBN 0-393-95475-7.

30 Goffin, K. 'Enhancing Innovation Performance', *Management Quarterly* (The Institute of Chartered Accountants in England and Wales, Part 13 October 2001), pp. 18–26.

31 Griffin, A. and Hauser, J. R., 'Integrating R&D and Marketing: A Review and Analysis of the Literature', *Journal of Product Innovation Management*, vol. 13, no. 3 (May 1996), pp. 191–215.

32 Quote from Morita, A., 'The UK Innovation Lecture' (UK: Department of Trade and Industry, 6 February 1992), Video Number INDY J1800NJ, 5/92.

33 Geroski, P., *Market Structure, Corporate Performance, and Innovative Activity* (Oxford: Clarendon Press, 1994), ISBN 0-19-828855-7.

34 Schumpeter, J. A., *Capitalism, Socialism and Democracy* (New York: Harper & Row, 3rd edn 1950), ISBN 0-06-133008-6.

35 Ali, A., 'Pioneering Versus Incremental Innovation: Review and Research Propositions', *Journal of Product Innovation Management*, vol. 11, no. 1 (January 1994), pp. 46–61.

36 Cowan, R. and van de Paal, G., *Innovation Policy in a Knowledge-Based Economy* (Luxembourg: European Commission, June 2000) Publication no. 17023.

37 Rogers, E. M., *Diffusions of Innovations* (New York: The Free Press, 1995), ISBN 0-02-926671-8.

38 Rosegger, G., *The Economics of Production and Innovation* (Oxford: Butterworth-Heinemann, 3rd edn 1996), ISBN 0080339581.

39 Ali, *op. cit.*

40 Johne, F. A. and Snelson, P. A., 'Success Factors in Product Innovation: Selective Review of the Literature', *Journal of Product Innovation Management*, vol. 5, no. 2 (June 1988), pp. 114–28.

41 Nonaka, I. and Kenney, M., 'Towards a New Theory of Innovation Management', *European Management Review* (Summer 1995), pp. 2–9.

42 Nevens, M. T., Summe, G. L. and Uttal, B., 'Commercializing Technology: What the Best Companies Do', *Harvard Business Review*, vol. 68, no. 3 (May–June 1990), pp. 154–63.

43 Balachandra, R. and Friar, J. H., 'Factors for Success in R&D Projects and New Product Innovation: A Contextual Framework', *IEEE Trans. on Engineering Management*, vol. 44, no. 3 (August 1997), pp. 6–287.

44 Chan Kim, W. and Mauborgne, R., 'Value Innovation: The Strategic Logic of High Growth', *Harvard Business Review*, vol. 75, no. 1 (January–February 1997), pp. 103–12.

45 Burgelman, R. A. and Rosenbloom, R. S., 'Technology Strategy: An Evolutionary Process Perspective', in Tushman, M. L. and Anderson, P. (eds), *Managing Strategic Innovation and Change: A Collection of Readings* (New York: Oxford University Press, 1997).

46 Clark, K. B., 'What Strategy Can Do for Technology', *Harvard Business Review*, vol. 67, no. 6 (November–December 1989), pp. 94–8.

47 Brown, J. S., 'Research that Reinvents the Corporation', *Harvard Business Review*, vol. 69, no. 1 (January–February 1991), pp. 102–11.

48 Tushman, M. L. and Anderson, P. (eds), *Managing Strategic Innovation and Change: A Collection of Readings* (New York: Oxford University Press, 1997).

49 Jelinek, M. and Schoonhoven, C. B., *The Innovation Marathon: Lessons from High technology Firms* (Oxford: Basil Blackwell, 1990), ISBN 0-631-15392-6.

50 *Ibid.*

51 Cimento, A. P. and Knister, R. J., 'The High-Productivity Electronics Company', *The McKinsey Quarterly*, no. 1 (1994), pp. 21–32.

52 Pisano, G. P. and Wheelwright, S. C., 'The New Logic of High-Tech R&D', *Harvard Business Review*, vol. 73, no. 5 (September–October 1995), pp. 93–105.

53 Cooper, R. G. and Kleinschmidt, E. J., 'Major New Products: What Distinguishes the Winners in the Chemical Industry?', *Journal of Product Innovation Management*, vol. 10, no. 2 (March 1993), pp. 90–111.

54 Gobelli, D. H. and Brown, D. J., 'Improving the Process of Product Innovation', *Research Technology Management*, vol. 36, no. 2 (1993), pp. 38–44.

55 Cooper, R. G. and Kleinschmidt, E. J., 'Determinants of Timeliness in Product Development', *Journal of Product Innovation Management*, vol. 11, no. 5 (November 1994), pp. 381–96.

56 Datar, S., Jordan, C. C., Kekre, S., Rajiv, S. and Srinivasan, K., 'Advantages of Time-Based New Product Development in a Fast-Cycle Industry', *Journal of Marketing Research*, vol. XXXIV, no. 1 (February 1997), pp. 36–49.

57 Cooper, R. G., 'Third-Generation New Product Processes', *Journal of Product Innovation Management*, vol. 11, no. 1 (January 1994), pp. 3–14.

58 Boag, D. A. and Rinholm, B. L., 'New Product Management Practices of Small High Technology Firms', *Journal of Product Innovation Management*, vol. 6, no. 2 (June 1989), pp. 109–22.

59 Adler, P. S., Mandelbaum, A., Nguyen, V. and Schwerer, E., 'Getting the Most out of Your Product Development Process', *Harvard Business Review*, vol. 74, no. 2 (March–April 1996), pp. 4–15.

60 Bowen, H. K., Clark, K. B., Holloway, C. A. and Wheelwright, S. C., 'Make Projects the School for Leaders', *Harvard Business Review*, vol. 72, no. 5 (September–October 1994), pp. 131–40.

61 Griffin, A., 'The Effect of Project and Process Characteristics on Product Development Cycle Time', *Journal of Marketing Research*, vol. XXXIV, no. 1 (February 1997), pp. 24–35.

62 Lievens, A. and Moenert, R. K., 'New Service Teams as Information-Processing Systems', *Journal of Service Research*, vol. 3, no. 1 (August 2000), pp. 46–65.

63 Cooper, R. G., 'Developing New Products On Time, In Time', *Research Technology Management*, vol. 38, no. 5 (September–October 1995), pp. 49–57.

64 Griffin, A., 'Evaluating QFD's Use in US Firms as a Process for Developing Products', *Journal of Product Innovation Management*, vol. 9, no. 2 (June 1992), pp. 171–87

65 Zirger, B. J. and Hartley, J. L., 'A Conceptual Model of Product Development Cycle Time', *Journal of Engineering and Technology Management.*, vol. 11, no. 3/4 (1994), pp. 229–51.

66 Griffin, A., 'Metrics for Measuring Product Development Cycle Time', *Journal of Product Innovation Management*, vol. 10, no. 2 (March 1993), pp. 112–25.

67 Ittner, C. D. and Larcker, D. F., 'Product Development Cycle Time and Organizational Performance', *Journal of Marketing Research*, vol. XXXIV, no. 1 (February 1997), pp. 13–23.

68 de Brentani, U., 'Success and Failure in New Industrial Services', *Journal of Product Innovation Management*, vol. 6, no. 4 (December 1989), pp. 239–58.

69 Hipp, C., Tether, B. S. and Miles, I., 'The Incidence and Effects of Innovation in Services: Evidence from Germany', *International Journal of Innovation Management*, vol. 4, no. 4 (December 2000), pp. 417–53.

70 Djellal, F. and Gallouj, F., 'Innovation Surveys for Service Industries: A Review', In Thuriaux, B., Arnold, E. and Couchot, C. (eds), *Innovation and Enterprise Creation: Statistics and Indicators* (European Communities, 2001), ISBN 92-894-1576-2, pp. 70–6.

71 Johne, A. and Storey, C., 'New Service Development: A Review of the Literature and Annotated Bibliography', *City University Business School, Management Working Paper* B97/2 (April 1997).

72 Ramaswamy, K. and Modi, M., 'Singapore International Airlines: Service with a Smile', Thunderbird: *The American Graduate School of International Management, Case Study* A07-01-0012, 2001.

73 Gavin, D. A., *Managing Quality: The Strategic and Competitive Edge* (New York: The Free Press, 1988), ISBN 0-02-911380-6.

74 Russell, R. S. and Taylor III, B. W., *Operations Management: Focusing on Quality and Competitiveness* (London, UK: Prentice-Hall International, 1998), ISBN 0-13-896119-0, p. 74–5.

75 Goffin, K. and Pfeiffer, R., *Innovation Management in UK and German Manufacturing Companies* (London: Anglo-German Foundation Report Series, December 1999), ISBN 1-900834-17-0.

76 Jelinek, M. and Schoonhoven, C. B., *The Innovation Marathon* (Oxford: Basil Blackwell, 1990), ISBN 0-631-15392-6.

77 Case based on interviews with Daniel Scuka, co-founder and business manager at Wireless Watch Japan (www.wirelesswatch.jp) and John Lagerling of the DoCoMo i-mode Global Strategy Department in Tokyo; company documentation on the Internet, several company reports as cited separately, and Hunter, J.,

Chan Kim, W. and Mauborgne, R., 'NTT DoCoMo I-mode: Value Innovation at DoCoMo', *INSEAD-EAC Case Study*, no. 303-04301 (Fontainebleau, France, 2003).

78 NTT DoCoMo, 'DoCoMo Initiatives to Develop Energy-Efficient Mobile Phones', *NTT DoCoMo Report* (December 2002), p. 9.

79 NTT DoCoMo, 'The Use of Cell Phones / PHS Phones in Everyday Urban Life', *NTT DoCoMo Report* (November 2000).

80 NTT DoCoMo, 'Current Trends in Mobile Phone Usage Among Adolescents', *NTT DoCoMo Report* (March 2001).

81 Adapted from: www.nttdocomo.com/corebiz/imode/why/strategy.html, used with permission.

Chapter 2 Innovation and Economics

1   Shionoya, Y. and Perlman, M. (eds), *Schumpeter in the History of Ideas* (USA: The University of Michigan Press, 1994), ISBN 0-472-10548-5.

2   Schumpeter, J. A., *The Theory of Economic Development* (Boston, USA: Harvard University Press, 1934).

3   Rosegger, G., *The Economics of Production and Innovation* (Oxford: Butterworth-Heinemann, 3rd edn 1996), ISBN: 0-080-42407-4, p. 10.

4   Geroski, P. A., *Market Structure, Corporate Performance and Innovative Activity* (Oxford: Clarendon Press, 1994), ISBN 0-198-28855-7.

5   Iansiti, M. and West, J., 'Technology Integration: Turning Great Research into Great Products', *Harvard Business Review*, vol. 75, no. 3 (May–June 1997), pp. 69–79.

6   Schumpeter, J. A., *Capitalism, Socialism and Democracy* (New York: Harper & Row, 3rd edn 1950).

7   See for example Bound, J., Cummins, C., Griliches, Z., Hall, B. H. and Jaffe A., 'Who Does R&D and Who Patents?' in Griliches, Z. (ed.), *R&D, Patents and Productivity* (Chicago: University of Chicago Press, 1984), pp. 21–54; and Klette, T. J. and Griliches, Z., 'Empirical Patterns of Firm Growth and R&D Investment: A Quality Ladder Model Interpretation', The Institute for Fiscal Studies London, Working Paper no. 25 (1999).

8   Hanson, J. A., 'Innovation, Firm Size and Age', *Small Business Economics*, vol. 4 (1992), pp. 37–44.

9   Wakasugi, R. and Koyata, F., 'R&D, Firm Size and Innovation Outputs: Are Japanese Firms Efficient in Product Development?', *Journal of Product Innovation Management*, vol. 14, no. 3 (May 1997), pp. 383–92.

10 Bertschek, I. and Entorf, H., 'On Non-Parametric Estimation of the Schumpetrian Link between Innovation and Firm Size', *Empirical Economics*, no. 21 (1996), pp. 401–26.

11 Audretsch, D. and Vivarelli, M., 'Firm Size and R&D Spillovers', *Small Business Economics*, no. 8 (1996), pp. 249–58.

12 Geroski, *op. cit.*

13 Cohen, W. and Klepper, S., 'A Reprise of Size and R&D', *The Economic Journal*, no. 106 (1996), pp. 925–51.

14 Brynjolfsson, E. and Kahin, B. (eds), *Understanding the Digital Economy: Data, Tools and Research* (Cambridge, Massachusetts: The MIT Press, 2000), ISBN 0-262-02474-8.

15   Salvatore, D., *Managerial Economics in a Global Economy* (Fort Worth, Philadephia Harcourt College Publishers (2000), ISBN 0-03-031158-6.

16   Brynjolfsson, E. and Kahin, B. (eds), *Understanding the Digital Economy: Data, Tools and Research* (Cambridge, Massachusetts: The MIT Press, 2000), ISBN 0-262-02474-8.

17   Based on data from: Anonymous, *The 2001 R&D Scoreboard: Commentary and Analysis* (Department of Trade and Industry, UK, DTI Publication no. 5676/5K/9/01/NP URN 01/31, September 2001) and Anonymous, *The 2001 Capex Scoreboard* (Department of Trade and Industry, UK, DTI Publication no. 58103/3K/12/01/NP URN 01/191, December 2001).

18   Gwynne, P., 'As R&D Penetrates the Service Sector, Researchers Must Fashion New Methods of Innovation Management', *Research-Technology Management*, vol. 41, no. 5 (September–October 1998), pp. 2–4.

19   Djellal, F. and Gallouj, F., 'Innovation Surveys for Service Industries: A Review', in B. Thuriaux, E. Arnold and C. Couchot (eds), *Innovation and Enterprise Creation: Statistics and Indicators* (European Communities, 2001), ISBN 92-894-1576-2, pp. 70–6.

20   Koenig, H., Buscher, H. S. and Licht, G., 'Employment, Investment and Innovation at Firm Level', in *OECD, The OECD Jobs Study – Investment Productivity and Employment* (Paris: Organization for Economic Cooperation and Development, OECD, 1995).

21   See for example: *OECD Science, Technology and Industry Outlook 2000* (Paris: Organization for Economic Cooperation and Development, OECD, 2000), pp. 161–83.

22   Cowan, R. and van de Paal, G., *Innovation Policy in a Knowledge-Based Economy* (Luxembourg: European Commission, Publication no. 17023, June 2000).

23   *Ibid.*

24   ESN, Brussels, *European Trend Chart on Innovation* (Brussels: European Commission, ESN, 2000).

25   Yamashina, H., 'Japanese Manufacturing Strategy – Competing with the Tigers', *Business Strategy Review*, vol. 7, no. 2 (Summer 1996), pp. 23–36.

26   www.archi.net.au, accessed in February 2004.

27   Archibugi, D. and Iammarino, S., 'The policy implications of the globalisation of innovation', in Archibugi, D., Howells, J. and Michie J. (eds), *Innovation Policy in a Global Economy* (Cambridge, UK: Cambridge University Press, 1999), ISBN 0-521-63361-3.

28   'Innovation Policy in Europe 2001', *European Commision, Innovation Papers*, no. 17, ISBN 92-894-1786-2.

29   Kuntze, U., 'Research and Technology Policies and Sustainable Development – the Situation in the USA, Japan, Sweden and The Netherlands', in Meyer-Krahmer, F. (ed.), *Innovation and Sustainable Development – Lessons for Innovation Policies* (Heidelberg, Germany: Physica Verlag, 1998), ISBN 3-790-81038-X, pp. 187–202.

30   See for example: Roper, S., Ashcroft, B., Love, J. H., Dunlop, S., Hofmann, H. and Vogler-Ludwig, K., *Product Innovation and Development in UK, German and Irish Manufacturing* (Belfast: Northern Ireland Economic Research Centre – The Queens University of Belfast, and Glasgow: Fraser of Allander Institute – University of Strathclyde (March 1996), ISBN: 1-871753-244.

31   European Commission, Luxembourg, *Entrepreneurial Innovation in Europe* (Report EUR 17051, 2003) ISBN: 92-894-4448-7.

32 ESN, Brussels, *European Trend Chart on Innovation* (Brussels: European Commision, 2000).

33 Burda, M. and Wyplosz, C., *Macroeconomics: A European Text* (Oxford: Oxford University Press, 2001), ISBN 0-19-877650-0.

34 Based on teaching material prepared by Professor Dr. Harald Hagemann, University of Hohenheim, Germany (2001). Used with permission.

35 Gordon, R. J., 'Does the "New Economy" Measure up to the Great Inventions of the Past?', *Journal of Economic Perspectives*, vol. 14, no. 4 (2000), pp. 49–74.

36 *Ibid.*

37 Burda, M. and Wyplosz, C., *Macroeconomics: A European Text* (Oxford: Oxford University Press, 2001), ISBN 0-19-877650-0.

38 Arena, R. and Dangel-Hagnauer, C. (eds), *The Contribution of Joseph Schumpeter to Economics* (London: Routledge, 2002), ISBN 0-415-22824-7.

39 McGuigan, J. R., Moyer, R. C. and Harris, F. H. D., *Managerial Economics: Applications, Strategy and Tactics* (Cincinnati, USA: South Western – Thompson Learning, 2002), ISBN 0-324-05881-0.

40 Based on an MBA presentation prepared by Gamarci, R. (February 2003). Used with permission.

41 Grossmann, G.M. and Helpmann, E., *Innovation and Growth in the Global Economy* (The MIT Press, 1991), ISBN 0262071363.

42 The importance of SMEs has been identified in many publications. See, for example: Thuriaux, B., Arnold, E. and Couchot, C. (eds), *Innovation and Enterprise Creation: Statistics and Indicators* (Brussels: European Commission, 2001), Publication no. 17038, ISBN 92-894-1576-2.

43 Tether, B. and Massini, S., 'Employment Creation in Small Technological and Design Innovators in the UK During the 1980's', *Small Business Economics*, vol. 11, no. 4 (1998), pp. 353–70.

44 Cooper, R. G. and Kleinschmidt, E. J., 'Stage Gate Systems for New Product Success', *Marketing Management*, vol. 1, no. 4 (1992), pp. 20–9.

45 Roper, S., Ashcroft, B., Love, J. H., Dunlop, S., Hofmann, H. and Vogler-Ludwig, K., *Product Innovation and Development in UK, German and Irish Manufacturing* (Belfast: Northern Ireland Economic Research Centre – The Queens University of Belfast, and Glasgow: Fraser of Allander Institute – University of Strathclyde (March 1996), ISBN: 1-871753-244.

46 De Meyer, A. and Pycke, B., 'Falling Behind in Innovation: The 1996 Report on the European Manufacturing Futures Survey', *INSEAD Working Paper Series*, no. 96/95/TM (1996).

47 Chan, A., Go, F. M. and Pine, R., 'Service Innovation in Hong Kong: Attitudes and Practice', *Service Industries Journal*, vol. 18, no. 2 (April 1998), pp. 112–24.

48 Kulicke, M., Broß, U., Gudrum, U., Hudetz, K. and Hemer, J., 'Innovationsdarlehen als Instrument zur Förderung kleiner und mittlerer Unternehmen', *Mitteilungen Fraunhofer Institut für Systemtechnik und Innovationsforschung*, 9/97.

49 Ali, A., 'Pioneering Versus Incremental Innovation: Review and Research Propositions', *Journal of Product Innovation Management*, vol. 11, no. 1 (January 1994), pp. 46–61.

50 Loch, C., Stein, L. and Terwiesch, C., 'Measuring Development Performance in the Electronics Industry', *Journal of Product Innovation Management*, vol. 13, no. 1 (January 1996), pp. 3–20.

51 Based on an MBA assignment by Dannenhauer, M. (February 2003) and information from www.extricom.de. Used with permission.

52 Rogers, E. M., *Diffusion of Innovations* (New York: The Free Press, 1995), ISBN 0-02-926671-8.

53 Based on *ibid*.

54 Case adapted with permission from Goffin, K., Lee-Mortimer, A. and New, C., *Managing Product Innovation for Competitive Advantage* (London: Haymarket Publications, 1999), ISBN 1-902226-15-1.

Chapter 3 Contrasting Services with Manufacturing

1 Storey, C. and Easingwood, C. J., 'The Augmented Service Offering: A Conceptualization and Study of Its Impact on New Service Success', *Journal of Product Innovation Management*, vol. 15, no. 4 (1998), pp. 335–51.

2 Griffin, A., Gleason, G., Preiss, R. and Shevenaugh, D., 'Best Practice for Customer Satisfaction in Manufacturing Firms', *Sloan Management Review*, vol. 36, no. 2 (Winter 1995), pp. 87–98.

3 Djellal, F. and Gallouj, F., 'Innovation Surveys for Service Industries: A Review', in Thuriaux, B., Arnold, E. and Couchot, C. (eds), *Innovation and Enterprise Creation: Statistics and Indicators* (European Communities, 2001), ISBN 92-894-1576-2, pp. 77–87.

4 *Ibid.*

5 Sheram, K. and Soubbotina, T. P. *Beyond Economic Growth: Meeting the Challenges of Global Development* (New York: World Bank Publications, 2000), ISBN 0-8213-4853-1.

6 Based on the *CIA World Factbook 2002*, accessed under http://www.cia.gov/cia/publications/factbook/index.html (June 2003). The statistics are mainly for 2002 but some are 1999–2001 (refer to website for the latest estimates).

7 Based on: Tether, B. and Miles, I., 'Surveying Innovation in Services – Measurement and Policy Interpretation Issues', in Thuriaux, B., Arnold, E. and Couchot, C. (eds), *Innovation and Enterprise Creation: Statistics and Indicators* (European Communities, 2001), ISBN 92-894-1576-2, pp. 77–87. Supplemented from the internet.

8 Gwynne, P., 'As R&D Penetrates the Service Sector, Researchers Must Fashion New Methods of Innovation Management', *Research-Technology Management*, vol. 41, no. 5 (September–October 1998), pp. 2–4.

9 Steele, J. and Murray, M. A. P., 'The Application of Structured Exploration to Develop a Culture of Innovation', Chartered Institute of Building Engineers – National Conference 2001, UK.

10 Gwynne, P., 'As R&D Penetrates the Service Sector, Researchers Must Fashion New Methods of Innovation Management', *Research-Technology Management*, vol. 41, no. 5 (September–October 1998), pp. 2–4.

11 Based on data from: Anonymous, *The 2001 R&D Scoreboard: Commentary and Analysis* (UK: Department of Trade and Industry, September 2001), DTI Publication no. 5676/5K/9/01/NP URN 01/31. Supplemented with individual company data from the internet.

12 Chan Kim, W. and Mauborgne, R., 'Value Innovation: The Strategic Logic of High Growth', *Harvard Business Review*, vol. 75, no. 1 (January–February 1997), pp. 103–12.

13 Horovitz, J., 'Core Competences and Service Firms', *Financial Times*, Mastering Management Series Part 17(2) (1 March 1996), Q1:553.

14 Knecht, T., Lezinski, R. and Weber, F. A., 'Making Profits After the Sale', *The McKinsey Quarterly*, no. 4 (1993), pp. 79–86.

15 Goffin, K. and New, C., 'Customer Support and New Product Development – An Exploratory Study', *International Journal of Operations & Production Management*, vol. 21, no. 3 (2001), pp. 275–301.

16 United Nations, *Manual on Statistics of International Trade in Services* (New York, US: United Nations Publications, 2002), ISBN 92-1-161448-1, p. 7.

17 *Ibid.*

18 Storey, C. and Easingwood, C. J., 'The Augmented Service Offering: A Conceptualization and Study of Its Impact on New Service Success', *Journal of Product Innovation Management*, vol. 15, no. 4 (1998), pp. 335–51.

19 Johne, A. and Storey, C., 'New Service Development: A Review of the Literature and Annotated Bibliography', City University Business School, *Management Working Paper* B97/2 (April 1997).

20 Bitner, M. J., 'Servicescapes: The Impact of Physical Surroundings on Customers and Employees', *Journal of Marketing*, vol. 56 (April 1992), pp. 57–71.

21 Bennett, D. J. and Bennett, J. D., 'Making the Scene', in Stone, G. and Farberman (eds), *Social Psychology through Symbolic Interactionism* (Waltham Mass.: Ginn-Blaisdell, 1970, 2nd edn New York: Wiley, 1981), ISBN 002417890X, pp. 190–6.

22 Lunsford, J. L. and Michaels, D., 'Aircraft Designers are Masters of Illusion', *The Wall Street Journal Europe* (Monday, November 25, 2002), p. A5.

23 Lunsford, J. L., 'Boeing "Dreamliner" Sets Ambitious Course', *The Wall Street Journal Europe* (Tuesday, November 18, 2003), p. A10.

24 Based partly on Russell, R. S. and Taylor III, B. W., *Operations Management: Focusing on Quality and Competitiveness* (London, UK; Prentice-Hall International 1998), ISBN 0-13-896119-0, pp. 212–15.

25 Verma, R., 'An Empirical Analysis of Management Challenges in Service Factories, Service Shops, Mass Services and Professional Services', *International Journal of Service Industry Management*, vol. 11, no. 1 (2000), pp. 8–25.

26 Tether, B. and Miles, I., 'Surveying Innovation in Services – Measurement and Policy Interpretation Issues', in Thuriaux, B., Arnold, E. and Couchot, C. (eds), *Innovation and Enterprise Creation: Statistics and Indicators* (European Communities, 2001), ISBN 92-894-1576-2, pp. 77–87.

27 Adapted from Slack, N., Chambers, S. and Johnston, B., *Operations Management*, 2nd edn (London: Pitman, 2003), ISBN 0-273-62688-4, p. 640.

28 Van Dyke, T. P., Prybutpk, V. R. and Kappelman, L. A., 'Cautions on the Use of the SERVQUAL Measure to Access the Quality of Information Systems Services', *Decision Sciences*, vol. 30, no. 3 (Summer 1999), pp. 1–15.

29 Khan, A., 'Perceived Service Quality in the Air Freight Industry', *Ph.D. Thesis*, Cranfield School of Management (1993).

30 de Brentani, U., 'Success and Failure in New Industrial Services', *Journal of Product Innovation Management*, vol. 6, no. 4 (December 1989), pp. 239–58.

31 Johne, A. and Storey, C., 'New Service Development: A Review of the Literature and Annotated Bibliography', City University Business School, *Management Working Paper* B97/2 (April 1997).

32 Metters, R., King-Metters, K. and Pullman, M., *Successful Service Operations Management* (Ohio, USA: Thompson South-Western, 2003), ISBN 0-324-13556-4.

33 Storey, C. and Easingwood, C. J., 'The Augmented Service Offering: A Conceptualization and Study of Its Impact on New Service Success', *Journal of Product Innovation Management*, vol. 15, no. 4 (1998), pp. 335–51.

34 Hipp, C., Tether, B. S. and Miles, I., 'The Incidence and Effects of Innovation in Services: Evidence from Germany', *International Journal of Innovation Management*, vol. 4, no. 4 (December 2000), pp. 417–53.

35 Magnusson, P. R., Matthing, J. and Kristensson, P. 'Involvement in Service Innovation: Experiments with Innovating End Users'. *Journal of Service Research*, vol. 6, no. 2 (November 2003), pp. 111–24.

36 Christensen, C. M. and Tedlow, R., 'Patterns of Disruption in Retailing', *Harvard Business Review*, vol. 78, no. 1 (January–February 2000), pp. 42–5.

37 Lievens, A. and Moenert, R. K., 'New Service Teams as Information-Processing Systems', *Journal of Service Research*, vol. 3, no. 1 (August 2000), pp. 46–65.

38 Rich, M., 'Hospital Design Is Tied to Health', *The Wall Street Journal Europe* (Thursday, November 28, 2002), p. A8.

39 Froehle, C. M., Roth, A. V., Chase, R. B. and Voss, C. A., 'Antecedents of New Service Development Effectiveness: An Exploratory Examination of Strategic Operations Choices', *Journal of Service Research*, vol. 3, no. 1 (August 2000), p. 3–17.

40 Metters, *et al.*, *op. cit.*

41 Tether and Miles, *op. cit.*

42 Johne, A. and Storey, C., 'New Service Development: A Review of the Literature and Annotated Bibliography', City University Business School, *Management Working Paper* B97/2 (April 1997).

43 *Ibid.*

44 Based on an unpublished case: Oke, A. and Goffin, K., 'Innovation Management at AXA-Ireland', Cranfield School of Management 2001 and company information gathered in interviews and from the Internet.

Chapter 4   Developing an Innovation Strategy

1 Johnson, G. and Scoles, K., *Exploring Corporate Strategy* (Prentice Hall Europe, 1999).

2 Takahashi, D. 2002, *Opening the X Box* (California: Prima Publishing, Roseville, 2004).

3 www.foresight.gov.uk

4 Porter, M. *Competitive Advantage* (New York: Free Press, 1985).

5 Case based on an interview with Klaus Stemig; articles in the press such as Martens, H. 'Sprung ins Dunkle', *Der Spiegel*, no. 27, 2004, p. 97; and internal documentation from Allianz and Mondial.

6 Kano, N., Saraku, N., Takahashi, F. and Tsuji, S., 'Attractive Quality and Must-be Quality', in J. Hromi, (ed.), *The Best on Quality*, vol. 7, ch. 10, (ASQC, Milwaukee, 1996), pp. 165–86.

7 Matzler, K. and Hinterhuber, H., 'How to make product development projects more successful by integrating Kano's model of customer satisfaction into quality function deployment', *Technovation*, vol. 18 (1998), pp. 25–38.

8 Burchill, *Concept Engineering: An Investigation of Time vs Market Orientation in Product Concept Development'* (MIT, 1993).

9 Adapted from 'Value Innovation: The Strategic Logic of High Growth' by W. C. Kim and R. Mauborgne, *Harvard Business Review*, Jan.–Feb. 1997, pp. 103–12

10 Foster, R., *Innovation: The Attacker's Advantage* (New York: Summit Books, 1986).

11 Roussel, P. A., Saad, K. N. and Erickson, T. J., *Third Generation R and D. Managing the Link to Corporate Strategy* (Arthur D. Little, 1991).

12 Foster, *op. cit.* p. 27.

13 *Ibid.*, pp. 118, 183.

14 Cusumano, M. A., Mylonadis, Y. and Rosenbloom, R., 'Strategic Maneuvering and Mass-Market Dynamics: The Triumph of VHS over Beta', in M. L. Tushman and P. Anderson (eds), *Managing Strategic Innovation and Change* (New York: Oxford University Press 1997), ch. 6 (Reprinted from *Business History Review*, Spring 1992).

15 Utterback, J. M., *Mastering the Dynamics of Innovation* (Boston, Mass.: Harvard Business School Press, 1996).

16 Albright, R. E., 'What can past technology forecasts tell us about the future?', *Technological Forecasting and Social Change*, June 2002, vol. 69. no. 5, pp. 443–64.

17 Martin, M. J. C., *Managing Innovation and Entrepreneurship in Technology Based Firms* (New York: John Wiley, 1994).

18 Moore, G., 'Cramming more components onto integrated circuits'. *Electronics*, vol. 38 (1965).

19 Data kindly provided by Dr C Cunningham of the Royal Observatory, Edinburgh and Roberto Gilmozzi of the European Southern Observatory.

20 J. J. Lew Cambridge University: unpublished.

21 J. J. Lew, Cambridge University, personal communication.

22 Adapted from a presentation by A. Sherrif, Director of Product Development, Fiat, May 1998.

23 Abernathy., W. J. and Utterback, J., 'Patterns of Industrial Innovation', *Technology Review* (1978), pp. 40–7.

24 Conway Morris, S., *Life's Solution: inevitable humans in a lonely universe* (Cambridge: Cambridge University Press, 2003).

25 Rogers, E. M., *Diffusion of Innovations,* 4th edn. (New York: The Free Press, 1995), p. 8.

26 Gould, S. J., 'The Panda's Thumb of Technology', in M. L. Tushman and P. Anderson (ed.), *Managing Strategic Innovation and Change* (New York: Oxford University Press, 1997), ch 5 (Reprinted from *Natural History*, Jan 1987).

27 Gladwell, M., *The Tipping Point* (London: Little, Brown, 2000).

28 Nayak, P. R. and Ketteringham J. M., *Breakthoughs!* (New York: Rawson Associates, 1986).

29 Cusumano *op. cit.*

30 Christensen, C. M., *The Innovator's Dilemma* (Boston, Mass.: Harvard Business School Press, 1997).

31 Bower, J. L. and Christensen, C. M., 'Disruptive Technologies: Catching the Wave'. *Harvard Business Review* (Jan.–Feb. 1995).

32 Gilbert, C., 'The Disruption Opportunity', *Sloan Management Review* (Summer, 2003), pp. 27–32.

33 Charitou, C. D. and Markides, C. C., 'Responses to disruptive strategic innovation', *Sloan Management Review* (Winter, 2003), pp. 55–63.

34 *Ibid.*

35 Schnaars, S. P., *Managing imitation strategies: How late entrants seize markets from pioneers* (New York: Free Press, 1994).

36 Tellis, G. J. and Golder, P. N., *Will and Vision: How latecomers grow to dominate markets.* (New York: McGraw-Hill, 2001).

37 Rogers, *op. cit.*, ch. 10.

38 *Ibid.*, ch. 7.

39 Teece, D. J., 'Profiting from Technological Innovation: Implications for integration, collaboration, licensing and public policy', *Research Policy*, vol. 15 (1986), pp. 285–305.

40 *Ibid.*

41 Courtney, H., Kirkland, J. and Viguerie, P., 'Strategy under uncertainty', *Harvard Business Review* (Nov.–Dec. 1997), pp. 67–79.

42 Diagram courtesy of Dr R. Phaal, Cambridge University.

43 McMillan, A., 'Roadmapping-Agent of Change'. *Research-Technology Management* (2003), pp. 40–7.

44 Willyard, C. H. and McClees., C. W., 'Motorola's Technology Roadmap Process', *Research Management* (1987), pp. 13–19.

45 Groeneveld, P., 'Roadmapping Integrates Business and Technology', *Research-Technology Management* (1997), pp. 48–55.

46 Barker, D. and Smith, D. J. H., 'Technology foresight using roadmaps'. *Long Range Planning*, vol. 28 (1995), pp. 21–8.

47 http://www.public.itrs.net.

48 www.foresightvehicle.org.uk.

49 Courtesy of Dr Rob Phaal of Cambridge University.

50 Phaal, R., Farrukh, C. J. P. and Probert, D. R., *T-Plan: the fast-start to technology roadmapping – planning your route to success* (Cambridge: Institute for Manufacturing, University of Cambridge, 2001).

51 Phaal, R., Farrukh, C., Mitchell, R. and Probert, D., 'Starting-up Roadmapping Fast', *Research-Technology Management* (2003), pp. 52–28.

52 Albright, R. E. and Kappel, T.A., 'Roadmapping in the corporation', *Research-Technology Management* (2003), pp. 31–40.

53 Van der Hijden, K., *Scenarios, The Art of Strategic Conversation* (John Wiley, 1996).

54 Schwarz, P., *The Art of the Long View* (Doubleday, 1991).

55 Ringland, G., *Scenario Planning. Managing for the Future* (John Wiley, Chichester, 1998).

56 *Ibid.*

57 Utterback, *op. cit.*

58 Henderson, R. M. and Clark, K. B., 'Architectural Innovation: The Reconfiguration of Existing Product Technologies and the Failure of Established Firms', *Administrative Science Quarterly*, vol. 35 (1990), pp. 9–30.

59 Cooper, A. C. and Smith, C. G., 'How established firms respond to threatening technologies', *Academy of Management Executive*, vol. 6 (1992), pp. 55–70.

60 Loutfy, R. and Belkhir, L., 'Managing R and D at Xerox', *Research-Technology Management*, vol. 44 (2001), pp. 15–24.

61 Gilbert, *op. cit.*

62 Utterback, *op. cit.*

Chapter 5   Ideas: Managing Creativity and Knowledge

1   Donkin, R., 'Recruitment: Men in the Empty Suits – Management Hierarchies and Concerns May be Stifling Innovation', *Financial Times*, 6 December, 1995, p. 202.

2   Amabile, T.M., 'How to Kill Creativity', *Harvard Business Review*, vol. 76, no. 5, September–October 1998, pp. 77–87.

3   Thomke, S. and Fujimoto, T., 'The Effect of "Front-Loading" Problem-Solving on Product Development Performance', *Journal of Product Innovation Management*, vol. 17, no. 2 (March 2000), pp. 128–42.

4   Couger, J. D., *Creative Problem Solving and Opportunity Finding*, Boyd and Fraser (1995), ISBN 0-87709-752-6.

5   Hargadon, A. and Sutton, R. I., 'Building an Innovation Factory', *Harvard Business Review*, vol. 78, no. 3 (May–June 2000), p. 157.

6   Csikszentmihalyi, M., *Creativity: Flow and the Psychology of Discovery and Invention* (New York: HarperCollins, 1996), ISBN 0-06-017133-2.

7   Amabile, T. M., Hadley, C. N. and Kramer, S. J., 'Creativity Under the Gun', *Harvard Business Review*, vol. 80, no. 8 (August 2002), pp. 52–61.

8   Amabile, T. M., 'Minding the Muse', *Working Knowledge – A Quarterly Report on Research at Harvard Business School*, vol. IV, no. 1 (1999).

9   Based on presentations by Fisher, J. H. at Cranfield School of Management in 1996 and 1997.

10   Nemeth, C. J., 'Managing Innovation: When Less is More', *California Management Review*, vol. 40, no. 1 (Fall 1997), pp. 59–74.

11   Hayes, N., *Managing Teams: A Strategy for Success* (London: Thompson Learning, 2002), ISBN 1-86152-782-9.

12   Couger, J. D., *Creative Problem Solving and Opportunity Finding* (Boyd and Fraser, 1995), ISBN 0-87709-752-6.

13   Koestler, A., *The Act of Creation* (London: Hutchinson, 1964).

14   Goldenberg, J. and Mazursky, D., *Creativity in Product Innovation* (Cambridge: Cambridge University Press, 2002), ISBN 0-521-80089-7.

15   Goldenberg, J., Horowitz, R., Levav, A. and Mazursky, D., 'Finding Your Innovation Sweet Spot', *Harvard Business Review*, vol. 81, no. 3 (March 2003), pp. 3–11.

16   Altschuler, G., *And Suddenly the Inventor Appeared* (Worchester, MA: Technical Innovation Center Inc, 1996).

17   Ambrosini, V. and Bowman, C., 'Tacit Knowledge: Some Suggestions for Operationalization', *Journal of Management Studies*, vol. 38, no. 6 (September 2001), pp. 811–29.

18   Nonaka, I., Toyama, R. and Byosiere, P., 'A Theory of Organizational Knowledge Creation: Understanding the Dynamic Process of Creating Knowledge', in Dierkes, M., Berthoin Antal, A., Child, J. and Nonaka, I., *Handbook of Organizational Learning and Knowledge* (Oxford, UK: Oxford University Press, 2001), ISBN 0-19-829583-9, pp. 491–517.

19   Hargadon and Sutton, *op cit.*

20   *Ibid.*

21   Saban, K., Lanasa, J., Lackman, C. and Peace, G., 'Organizational Learning: A Critical Component to New Product Development', *Journal of Product and Brand Management*, vol. 9, no. 2 (2000), p. 101.

22   Senge, P. M., *The Fifth Discipline: The Art and Practice of the Learning Organization* (Century Business Press, 1990).

23   Brailsford, T. W., 'Building a Knowledge Community at Hallmark Cards', *Research-Technology Management*, vol. 44, no. 5 (September–October 2001), pp. 18–25.

24   Herstatt, C. and Sander, J. G. (eds), *Produktentwicklung mit virtuellen Communities* (Product Development with Virtual Communities) (Wiesbaden: Gabler, 2004), ISBN 3-409-12476-4.

25   Balachandra, R., and Friar, J. H., 'Factors for Success in R&D Projects and New Product Innovation: A Contextual Framework', *IEEE Trans. on Engineering Management*, vol. 44, no. 3 (August 1997), pp. 276–87.

26   Cooper, R. G. and Kleinschmidt, E. J., 'Major New Products: What Distinguishes the Winners in the Chemical Industry?', *Journal of Product Innovation Management*, vol. 10, no. 2 (March 1993), pp. 90–111.

27   Heygate, R., 'Why are we Bungling Process Innovation?', *The McKinsey Quarterly* (1996) no. 2, pp. 130–41.

28   Athaide, G. A., Meyers, P. W. and Wilemon, D. L., 'Seller–Buyer Interactions During the Commercialization of Technological Process Innovations', *Journal of Product Innovation Management*, vol. 13, no. 5 (September 1996), pp. 406–21.

29   Oppenheim, A. N., *Questionnaire Design, Interviewing and Attitude Measurement* (London: Printer, 2nd edn 1992).

30   Dillman, D. A., *Mail and Internet Surveys – The Tailored Design Method* (New York: John Wiley, 2nd edn 2002).

31   Green, P. E., Tull, D. S. and Albaum, G., *Research for Marketing Decisions* (London, UK: Prentice-Hall International, 1988), ISBN 0-13-774217-7.

32   Sandberg, K. D., 'Focus on the Benefits', *Harvard Management Communication Newsletter*, vol. 5, no. 4 (2002), pp. 3–4.

33   Magnusson, P. R., Matthing, J. and Kristensson, P. 'Managing Service Involvement in Service Innovation: Experiments with Innovating End Users', *Journal of Service Research*, vol. 6, no. 2 (November 2003), pp. 111–24.

34   Kärkkainen, H., Piippo, P., Puumalainen, K. and Tuominen, M., 'Assessment of Hidden and Future Customer Needs in Finnish Business-to-Business Companies', *R&D Management*, vol. 31, no. 4 (2001), pp. 391–407.

35   Goffin, K., 'Repertory Grid Technique' in Partington, D. (ed.) *Essential Skills for Management Research* (London: SAGE Publications, 2002), ISBN 0-7619-7008-8.

36   Goffin, K., 'Understanding Customers' Views: A Practical Example of the Use of Repertory Grid Technique', *Management Research News*, vol. 17, no. 7/8 (1994), pp. 17–28.

37   Leonard-Barton, D., *Wellsprings of Knowledge: Building and Sustaining the Sources of Innovation* (Boston: Harvard Business School Press, 1995), p. 194.

38   Leonard-Barton, D. and Rayport, J. F., 'Spark Innovation through Empathic Design', *Harvard Business Review*, vol. 75, no. 6 (November–December, 1997), pp. 102–13.

39   Robson, C., *Real World Research* (Oxford, UK: Blackwell, 1993), ISBN 0-631-17689-6.

40   Burns, A., Barrett, R., Evans, S. and Johansson, C., 'Delighting Customers through Empathic Design', 6th International Product Development Management Conference (July 5–6 1999), pp. 157–71.

41   Rosier, B., 'From the Dreams of Children to the Future of Technology', *The Independent on Sunday* (UK) (15 July 2001), p. 8.

42 Based discussions with Chris Towns of Clarks and Towns, C. and Humphries, D., 'Breaking New Ground in Customer Behavioural Research: Experience from Clarks/PDD', *Product Development Management Association UK & Ireland Conference*, London (November, 2001).

43 Herstatt, C., 'Search Fields for Radical Innovations involving Market Research', Technical University of Hamburg-Harburg, Germany, Working Paper no. 10 (2001).

44 Herstatt, C. and von Hippel E., 'Developing New Product Concepts Via the Lead User Method: A Case Study in a "Low-Tech" Field', *Journal of Product Innovation Management*, vol. 9, no. 3 (September 1992), pp. 213–21.

45 von Hippel, E., Thomke, S. and Sonnack, M., 'Creating Breakthroughs at 3M', *Harvard Business Review*, vol. 77, no. 5 (September–October 1999), pp. 47–57.

46 Thomke, S. and von Hippel, E., 'Customers as Innovators: A New Way to Create Value', *Harvard Business Review*, vol. 80, no. 2 (March–April 2002), p. 74–81.

47 Caroll, J. D., Green, P. E. and Charturvedi, A., *Mathematical Tools for Applied Multivariate Analysis* (Oxford, UK: Academic Press, 1997) ISBN 0121609553.

48 Gustafsson, A., Herrman, A. and Huber, F., *Conjoint Measurement: Methods and Applications* (Berlin, Germany: Springer-Verlag, 2nd edn 2001), ISBN 3-540-42323-0.

49 Burda, M. and Wyplosz, C., *Macroeconomics: A European Text* (Oxford, UK: Oxford University Press, 2001, ISBN 0-19-877650-0, p. 446.

50 UK Trade Marks Act 1994, ISBN 0-10-542694-6.

51 Prystay, C. 'Crocodile Battle Over Chinese Turf'. *The Wall Street Journal Europe* (Friday/Saturday/Sunday, April 2–4, 2004), pA7.

52 Aeppel, T., 'Brothers of Invention', *The Wall Street Journal Europe* (Tuesday April 20, 2004), p. A12.

53 Kingston, W., *Enforcing Small Firms' Patent Rights* (Luxembourg: European Commission, 2000).

54 *Ibid.*

55 Pisano, G. P. and Wheelwright, S. C., 'The New Logic of High-Tech R&D', *Harvard Business Review*, vol. 73, no. 5 (September–October 1995), pp. 93–105.

56 Case based on a telephone interviews with Wim Obouter and Seth Bishop. For further details of the Micro products see: www.micro-mobility.com.

57 Case based on personal interviews with senior Texas instruments managers in April 2003 by K. Goffin and the following published material:

    – Parks, A., Edwards, C., Reinhardt, A. and Kunii, I. M., 'Dawn of the Superchip', *Business Week* (November 4, 2002), pp. 128A–128B.
    – http://www.ti.com/corp/docs/company/index.htm.
    – Texas Instruments Incorporated 2002 Annual Report.
    – http://www.ti.com/corp/docs/company/2000/c00061.shtml.
    – Buchanan, M., 'Make Room for More Laws, Gordon', Electronic News (October 28, 2002), p. 19.

Chapter 6   Prioritization: Selecting and Managing the Portfolio

1 Chapman Wood, R. and Hamel, G., 'The World Bank's Innovation Market', *Harvard Business Review*, vol. 80, no. 11 (November 2002), pp. 104–12.

2 Cooper, R. G., Edgett, S. J. and Kleinschmidt, E. J., *Portfolio Management for New Products* (Cambridge, Mass.: Perseus Books, 2nd edn, 2001), ISBN 0-7382-0514-1.

3 Ryan, G. and Ryan, P., 'Capital Budgetting Practices of the Fortune 1000: How have things changed?' *Journal of Business and Management* (2002) pp. 1–10.

4 Brigham, E. F. and Erhardt, M. C., *Financial Management, Theory and Practice*, 10th edn (Thomson Learning, 2002), p. 509.

5 Brealey, R. A. and Myers, S. C., *Principles of Corporate Finance* (New York: McGraw-Hill, 1996).

6 Perdue, R., 'Valuation of R&D Projects Using Options Pricing and Decision Analysis Models', *Interfaces*, vol. 29 (1999), pp. 57–74.

7 Dixit, A. K. and Pindyck, R. S., *Investment Under Uncertainty* (Princeton: Princeton University Press, 1994), p. 109.

8 Ryan and Ryan, *op. cit.*

9 Brigham and Erhardt, *op. cit.*

10 *Ibid.*

11 Bernstein, P. L., *Against the Gods: The Remarkable Story of Risk* (New York: John Wiley, 1998).

12 Hacking, I., *The Emergence of Probability: A Philosophical Study of Early Ideas* (London: Cambridge University Press, 1975).

13 Bernstein, *op. cit.*

14 Fleming, M. C., Nellis, J. G., *Principles of Applied Statistics* (Thomson Learning, 2000), Ch. 11.

15 Arrow, K. J., 'I Know a Hawk from a Handsaw', in Szenberg, M. (ed.), *Eminent Economists: Their Life and Philosophies* (Cambridge and New York: Cambridge University Press, 1992), pp. 42–50.

16 Antikarov, V. and Copeland, T., *Real Options: A Practitioner's Guide* (New York: Texere, 2001) p. 24.

17 Hayes, R. H. and Abernathy, W. J., 'Managing Our Way to Economic Decline' *Harvard Business Review* (1980), pp. 67–77.

18 Boer, F. P., 'Risk-Adjusted Valuation of R&D Projects', *Research-Technology Management*, vol. 46, (Sept–Oct 2003), pp. 50–8.

19 Brealey and Myers, *op. cit.*

20 Razgaitis, R., *Dealmaking Using Real Options and Monte-Carlo Analysis* (Hoboken New Jersey: John Wiley, 2003).

21 For example 'Crystal Ball' from Decisioneering (Denver Colorado), www.crystal-ball.com.

22 Dembo, R. and Freeman, A., *Seeing Tomorrow: Rewriting the Rules of Risk* (New York: John Wiley, 1998).

23 See, for example Angelis, D. I., 'Capturing the Option Value of R&D', *Research-Technology Management*, vol. 43, no. 4 (2000), pp. 32–4. or Boer, F. P., 'Valuation of Technology using "Real Options" ', *Research-Technology Management*, vol. 43, no. 4 (2000), pp. 26–30.

24 For example two papers by T. A. Luehrman: 'Investment Opportunities as Real Options: Getting Started on the Numbers', *Harvard Business Review* (July–Aug. 1998), pp. 51–67, and 'Strategy as a Portfolio of Real Options', *Harvard Business Review* (Sept.–Oct. 1998), pp. 89–99.

25 Two useful books on the subject are: Razgaitis (*op. cit.*) and Howell, S., Stark, A., Newton, D., Paxson, D., Cavus, M., Pereira, J. and Patel, K., *Real Options. Evaluating Corporate Investment Options in a Dynamic World* (Harlow, England: Pearson Education, 2001). See also Perdue (1999), *op. cit.* Boer, F. P., 'Valuation of

Technology Using "Real Options" ', *Research-Technology Management* vol. 43 (2000), pp. 26–30. and Bowman, E. H. and Moskowitz, G. T., 'Real Options Analysis and Strategic Decision Making', *Innovation Science*, vol. 12, no. 6 (2001), pp. 772–7.

26   MacMillan, I. C. and McGrath, R. G., 'Crafting R&D Project Portfolios', *Research-Technology Management*, vol. 45, no. 5 (2002), pp. 48–59.

27   Luenberger, D. G., *Investment Science* (New York: Oxford University Press, 1998).

28   Perlitz, M., Peske, T. and Schrank, R., 'Real Options Valuation: The New Frontier in R&D Project Evaluation?', *R&D Management*, vol. 29, no. 3 (1999), pp. 255–69.

29   Luenberger, 1998, *op. cit.*

30   Boer, 2003, *op. cit.*

31   Cooper, R. G., Edgett, S. J. and Kleinschmidt, E. J., 'Portfolio Management in New Product Development: Lessons from the Leaders – 1', *Research-Technology Management*, vol. 40 (Sept.–Oct. 1997), pp. 18–29.

32   Kaplan, R. S. and Norton, D. P., *The Balanced Scorecard: Translating Strategy into Action* (Harvard: Harvard Business School Press, 1996).

33   Cooper, Edgett and Kleinschmidt 1997, *op. cit.*

34   Roussel, P. A., Saad, K. N. and Erickson, T. J., *Third Generation R&D. Managing the Link to Corporate Strategy* (Arthur D. Little, 1991).

35   Quoted in Cooper Edgett and Kleinschmidt. 2001 *op. cit.* p. 53.

36   See in particular Cooper, R. G., Edgett, S. J. and Kleinschmidt (1997 and 2001), *op. cit.* and other publications by the same authors. Also Davis, C., 'Calculated Risk. A Framework for Evaluating Product Development', *Sloan Management Review* (Summer 2000), pp. 71–7. and Davis, J., Fusfield, A., Scriven, E. and Tritle, G., 'Determining a Project's Probability of Success', *Research-Technology Management*, vol. 44 (May–June 2001), pp. 51–7.

37   Surowiecki, J., *The Wisdom of Crowds* (London: Little, Brown, 2004), ch. 9.

38   Makridakis, S., Wheelwright, S. C. and Hyndman, R. J., *Forecasting: Methods and Applications* (New York: John Wiley, 1998).

39   Graves, S. B., Ringuest, J. L. and Case, R. H., 'Formulating Optimal R&D Portfolios', *Research-Technology Management*, vol. 43, no. 3 (2000), pp. 47–51.

40   Oke, A., 'Making It Happen: How to Improve the Innovative Capability of a Service Company', *Journal of Change Management*, vol. 2, no. 3, pp. 272–81.

41   Davis, J., Fusfield, A., Scriven, E. and Tritle, G., 'Determining a Project's Probability of Success', *Research-Technology Management*, vol. 44 (May–June 2001), pp. 51–7.

42   Tritle, G. L., Scriven, F. V. and Fusfeld, A. R., 'Resolving Uncertainty in R&D Portfolios', *Research-Technology Management*, vol. 43, no. 6 (2000), pp. 47–55.

43   Cooper, Edgett and Kleinschmidt, 2001 *op. cit.*

Chapter 7   Implementation

1   Reinertsen, D., 'Managing the Design Factory: a product developer's toolkit' (New York, London: The Free Press, 1997), ISBN 0684839911.

2   There are many good books on project management techniques. For example: Maylor, H., *Project Management* (Harlow, UK: Pearson Education, 2003), 3rd edn. ISBN 0-273-65541-8; Baguley, P., *Managing Successful Projects. A Guide for Every Manager* (London: Pitman, 1995), ISBN 0-273-61344 (paperback); Reiss, G., *Project Management Demystified* (London: E. & F. N. Spon, an imprint of Chapman and Hall, 1995), 2nd edn., ISBN 0-419-20750-3.

3   Roussel, P. A., Saad, K. N. and Erickson, T. J., *Third Generation R and D* (Boston: Harvard Business School Press, 1991) ISBN 0-87584-252-6, p. 85.

4   Adapted with permission from 'Getting results. Case Studies of Innovation in the Public Service', by Alicia Wright and Virginia de Joux (Amherst Group Ltd).

5   Maylor, 2003, *op. cit.* p. 199.

6   Lockyer, K. and Gordon, J., *Project Management and Project Network Techniques* (London: Pitman Publishing, 1996), 6th edn, ISBN 0-273-61454-1.

7   *Ibid.*, also see Maylor, 2003, *op. cit.* p. 197.

8   Maylor, 2003, *op. cit.*, p. 106

9   Nevens, T. M., Summe, G. L. and Uttal, B., 'Commercializing Technology: What the Best Companies Do', *Harvard Business Review*, May–June 1990, pp. 154–62.

10 Datar, S., Jordan, C. C., Kekre, S., Rajiv, S. and Srinivasan, K., 'Advantages of Time-Based New Product Development in a Fast-Cycle Industry', *Journal of Marketing Research*, vol. 34, no. 1, February 1997, pp. 36–49.

11 Smith, P. G. and Reinertsen, D. G., *Developing Products in Half the Time* (New York: Van Nostrand Reinhold, 1991), ch. 2.

12 Reinertsen, D. G., 'Whodunnit? The Search for New Product Killers', *Electronic Business*, July 1983, pp. 62–6.

13 Case based on material from Organon and an interview with Erik Hoppenbrouwer in October 2004.

14 Clausing D., *Total Quality Development* (New York: ASME Press, 1994).

15 Cohen, L., *Quality Function Deployment* (Reading, Mass: Addison-Wesley 1995), ISBN 0-201-63339-2.

16 Matzler K. and Hinterhuber, H. H., 'How to make product development projects more successful by integrating Kano's model of customer satisfaction into quality function deployment', *Technovation*, vol. 18, no. 1 (1998), pp. 25–38.

17 Clausing, 1994 *op. cit.*, p. 133.

18 Eppinger S. D., 'Innovation at the Speed of Information', *Harvard Business Review* (January, 2001) pp. 149–58.

19 Thomke, S., 'Enlightened Experimentation. The New Imperative for Innovation', *Harvard Business Review* (2001) February, pp. 67–75.

20 Hartman, G. C. and Lakatos, A. I., 'Assessing Technology Risk: A Case Study' *Research-Technology Management* (1998) (March–April) pp. 32–8.

21 Keizer, J. A., Halman, J. I. M. and Song, M., 'From experience: applying the risk diagnosing methodology', *Journal of Product Innovation Management* (2002) vol. 19, pp. 213–32.

22 Bazerman, M. H., *Judgements in managerial decision-making* (New York: John Wiley, 1990).

23 Kahneman, D. and Tversky, A., 'Prospect theory: an analysis of decision under risk', *Econometrica* (1979) vol. 47, pp. 263–91.

24 Surowiecki, J., *The Wisdom of Crowds* (London: Little, Brown, 2004).

25 Kaiser, *et al.*, 2002, *op. cit.*

26 Davis, J., Fusfield, A., Scriven, E. and Tritle, G., 'Determining a project's probability of success', *Research-Technology Management* (2001) May–June pp. 51–7.

27 Surowiecki, *op. cit.*, ch. 9.

28 Janis, I. L., *Groupthink* (Boston: Houghton-Mifflin, 1972).

29 See Keizer, *et al.*, 2002, *op. cit.*

30 Makridakis, S., Wheelwright, S. C. and Hyndman, R. J., *Forecasting: Methods and Applications* (New York: John Wiley, 1998).

31 Thomke, S., 'R&D Comes to Services', *Harvard Business Review*, vol. 81, no. 4, 2003, pp. 71–9.

32 See Baxter, M., *Product Design: practical methods for the systematic development of new products* (Stanley Thornes, 1999) or any of the project management texts.

33 Keizer, *et al.*, 2002, *op. cit.*

34 See the section on team structure in Chapter 8.

35 Gwynne, P., 'Skunk Works, 1990s-Style'. *Research-Technology Management*, vol. 40, no. 4 (July–August 1997), pp. 18–23.

36 Kidder, T., *The soul of the new machine* (New York: Avon Books, 1982).

37 Case based on an interview with Synthiea Kaldi, conducted by K.Goffin in March 2004.

38 Ellis, *op. cit.*

39 *Design Management Systems – Part 1: Guide to Managing Innovation. British Standard BS7000-1:1999*, British Standards Institution: London, 1999.

40 Wheelwright, S. C. and Clarke, K. B., *Revolutionizing Product Development* (New York: The Free Press, 1992. ISBN 0-02-905515-6).

41 Martin, M. J. C., *Managing Innovation and Entrepreneurship in Technology-Based Companies* (New York: John Wiley, 1994), ISBN 0-471-57219-5.

42 McGrath, M. E. (ed.), *Setting the PACE in product development* (Boston: Butterworth-Heinemann, 1996). ISBN 0-7506-9789-X.

43 Cooper, R. G., 'Third-Generation New Product Processes', *Journal of Product Innovation Management*, vol. 11, no.1, (1994), pp. 3–14.

44 Cooper, R. G., 'Stage Gate Systems for New Product Success', *Marketing Management*, vol. 1, no. 4 (1992), pp. 20–9.

45 O'Connor, P., 'From Experience: Implementing a Stage-Gate Process: A Multi Company Perspective'. *Journal of Prod. Innov. Management*, vol. 11, no. 3, 1994, pp. 183–200.

46 Cooper, R. G., *Winning at New Products* (Cambridge, Mass: Perseus 2001), 3rd edn ISBN 0738204633 and Cooper, 1992, *op. cit.*

47 Gobeli, D. H. and Brown, D. J., 'Improving the Process of Product Innovation' *Research-Technology Management* (March–April, 1993), pp. 38–44.

48 Cooper, R. G., 'Overhauling the New Product Introduction Process' *Industrial Marketing Management*, vol. 25, pp. 465–82 (1996).

49 Shapiro, A., 'Stages in the Evolution of the Product Development Process', in McGrath (1996) *op. cit.* p. 147.

50 Fraser, P., *Managing Product Development Collaborations* (Cambridge: University of Cambridge Institute for Manufacturing, 2003).

51 Adapted from Fraser, *op. cit.*

52 McGrath, 1996 *op. cit.* ch. 10, by Amram Shapiro.

53 See for example, 'A World of Work. A Survey of Outsourcing', in *The Economist* 13 November 2004.

54 Quoted in Jonash, R. S., 'Strategic Technology Leveraging: Making Outsourcing Work for You'. *Research-Technology Management*, vol. 39, no. 2 (1996), pp. 19–36.

55 Quoted in Chesborough, H. W. and Teece, D. J., 'When is Virtual Virtuous?' *Harvard Business Review* (1996), Jan.–Feb., pp. 65–73.

56 Doz, Y. and Hamel, G., 'Alliance Advantage: The Art of Creating Value through Partnerships' (Boston: Harvard Business School Press, 1998).

57 Chatterji, D., 'Accessing External Sources of Technology', *Research-Technology Management* (March–April, 1996), pp. 48–58.

58 Harris R. C., Insinga, R. C., Morone, J. and Werle, M. J., 'The Virtual R&D Laboratory'. *Research Technology Management*, vol. 39, no. 2 (1996), pp. 32–36.

59 Chesborough, H. W. and Teece, D. J., 'When is Virtual Virtuous?', *Harvard Business Review* (Jan.–Feb. 1996), pp. 65–73.

60 Fraser, P., Farrukh, C. and Gregory, M., 'Managing product development collaborations – a process maturity approach', *Proc. I. Mech. E.*, vol. 217, part B (2003) pp. 1499–519.

61 Harrigan, K., *Managing for Joint Venture Success* (Lexington, Mass: Lexington Books, 1986).

62 Fraser, *et al.*, 2003, *op. cit.*

63 Wheelwright and Clarke, *op. cit.* p. 91.

64 Adler, P. S., Mandelbaum, A., Nguen, V. and Schwerer, E., 'Getting the most out of your Product Development process', *Harvard Business Review* (March–April, 1996), pp. 4–15.

Chapter 8   People, Organization and Innovation

1   Bratton, J. and Gold, J., *Human Resource Management: Theory and Practice* (Basingstoke UK: Palgrave Macmillan, 2003), ISBN 0-333-99326-8, p. 485.

2   Beckhard, R. and Harris, R. T., *Organization Transitions: Managing Complex Change* (London: Addison Wesley, 1987), ISBN 0201108879.

3   Schein, E. H., 'Coming to a New Awareness of Organizational Culture', *Sloan Management Review*, vol. 25, no. 4 (1984), pp. 3–16.

4   Johnson, G. and Scholes, K., *Exploring Corporate Strategy* (Edinburgh, UK: Pearson Education Limited, 5th edn, 1999), ISBN 0-13-080739-7.

5   Balogun, J., Hope Hailey, V. with Johnson, G. and Scholes, K., *Exploring Strategic Change* (London: Prentice Hall, 1999), ISBN 0-13-263856-8, p. 229–34.

6   Schein, E. H., 'Organizational Socialization and the Profession of Management', *Sloan Management Review*, vol. 53, no. 3 (Fall 1988), pp. 53–65.

7   *Op. cit.* Balogun, J. and Hope Hailey, V. with Johnson, G. and Scholes, K.

8   Heracleous, L., 'Spinning a Brand New Cultural Web', *People Management*, vol. 1, no. 22, February 1995.

9   Adapted with permission from Schoeman, M., 'The Application of a Stage-Gate Process to Developing New Markets', *Confidential MBA Thesis, Cranfield School of Management* (2001).

10 Soupata, L., 'Managing Culture for Competitive Advantage at United Parcel Service', *Journal of Organizational Excellence* (Summer 2001), pp. 19–26.

11 *Ibid.*, p. 19.

12 Jelinek, M. and Schoonhoven, C. B., *The Innovation Marathon: Lessons from High Technology Firms* (Oxford, UK: Basil Blackwell, 1990), ISBN 0-631-15392-6.

13 *Ibid.*, p. 203.

14 O'Reilly, C. and Tushman, M., 'Using Culture for Strategic Advantage: Promoting Innovation Through Social Control', in Tushman, M. L. and Anderson, P. (eds), *Managing Strategic Innovation and Change: A Collection of Readings* (New York: Oxford University Press, 1997), pp. 200–16.

15 Zien, K. A. and Buckler, S. A., 'Dreams to Market: Crafting a Culture of Innovation', *Journal of Product Innovation Management*, vol. 14, no. 4 (1997), pp. 274–87.

16 Howard, R., 'The CEO as Organizational Architect', in Tushman, M. L. and Anderson, P. (eds), *Managing Strategic Innovation and Change: A Collection of Readings* (New York: Oxford University Press, 1997), pp. 631–41.

17 Sakkab, N. Y., 'Connect and Develop Complements Research and Develop at P&G', *Research-Technology Management*, vol. 45, no. 2 (March–April 2002), pp. 38–45.

18 Johne, F. A. and Snelson, P. A., 'Success Factors in Product Innovation: A Selective Review of the Literature', *Journal of Product Innovation Management*, vol. 5, no. 2 (June 1988), pp. 114–28.

19 Lim, B. C., 'Management of Technology and Innovation at ShinEtsu', Presentation to MBA students, UniversitiTeknologi Malaysia, Kuala Lumpur (November 1997).

20 Hargadon, A. and Sutton, R. I., 'Building an Innovation Factory', *Harvard Business Review*, vol. 78, no. 3 (May–June 2000), pp. 157–66.

21 Buckler, S. A. and Zien, K. A., 'The Spirituality of Innovation: Learning from Stories', *Journal of Product Innovation Management*, vol. 13, no.5 (September 1996), pp. 391–405.

22 Webber, A. M. and LaBarre, P., 'The Innovation Conversation', *Research-Technology Management*, vol. 44, no. 5 (September–October 2001), pp. 9–11.

23 Szwejczewski, M., Wheatley, M. and Goffin, K., *Process Innovation in UK Manufacturing: Best Practice Makes Perfect*, Department of Trade and Industry, DTI/Pub 5468/15k/06/01/NP (London, June 2001), p. 36.

24 *Ibid.*

25 Oke, A. and Goffin, K., 'Leading Edge Knowledge Management at Oxford Asymmetry', *Unpublished Teaching Case Study* (Cranfield School of Management, 2001).

26 Boxall, P. and Purcell, J., *Strategy and Human Resource Management* (Basingstoke, UK: Palgrave Macmillan, 2003), ISBN 0-333-77820-0.

27 House, C. H. and Price, R. L., 'The Return Map: Tracking Product Teams', *Harvard Business Review*, vol. 69, no. 1 (January–February 1991), pp. 92–101.

28 Houlder, V., 'Technology: Quiet Revolution', *Financial Times* (26 March 1996), p. 143.

29 Linganatham, T., 'Management of Technology and Innovation at Texas Instruments', Presentation to MBA students at Universiti Teknologi Malaysia, Kuala Lumpur (November 1997).

30 Drucker, P. F., *Innovation and Entrepreneurship* (Oxford, UK: Butterworth-Heinemann, 1985), ISBN 0-7506-4388-9.

31 Pavia, T. M., 'The Early Stages of New Product Development in Entrepreneurial High-Tech Firms', *Journal of Product Innovation Management*, vol. 8, no. 1 (March 1991), pp. 18–31.

32 Bhide, A., 'How Entrepreneurs Craft Strategies that Work', *Harvard Business Review*, vol. 72, no. 2 (March–April 1994), pp. 150–61.

33 Martin, M. J. C., *Managing Innovation and Entrepreneurship in Technology-Based Firms* (New York: John Wiley, 1994), ISBN 0-471-57219-5.

34 Drucker, *op. cit.*

35 Based on (supplemented by information from the internet) Hawe, J., 'A New Style', *The Wall Street Journal Europe* (Friday/Saturday/Sunday, 26–28 September 2003), p. R2.

36 Amabile, T., 'Minding the Muse', *Working Knowledge – A Quarterly Report on Research at Harvard Business School*, vol. IV, no. 1 (1999).

37 Staw, B., Sandelands, L. and Dutton, J., 'Threat-rigidity Effects in Organizational Behaviour: A Multi-level Analysis', *Administrative Science Quarterly*, vol. 26, no. 4, pp. 501–24.

38 Staber, U. and Sydow, J., 'Organizational Adaptive Capacity: A Structuration Perspective', *Journal of Management Inquiry*, vol. 11, no. 4, pp. 408–25.

39 Martin, M. J. C., *Managing Innovation and Entrepreneurship in Technology-Based Firms* (New York: John Wiley, 1994), ISBN 0-471-57219-5.

40 Wheelwright, S. C. and Clark, K., *Revolutionizing Product Development: Quantum Leaps in Speed, Efficiency, and Quality* (New York: The Free Press, 1992), ISBN 0-02-905515-6.

41 Anonymous, 'Face Value: The Mass Production of Ideas, and Other Possibilities', *The Economist*, vol. 334, no. 7906 (18 March 1995), p. 111.

42 von Hippel, E., Thomke, S. and Sonnack, M., 'Creating Breakthroughs at 3M', *Harvard Business Review*, vol. 77, no. 5 (September–October 1999), pp. 47–57.

43 Hershock, R. J., Cowman, C. D. and Peters, D., 'Action Teams That Work', *Journal of Product Innovation Management*, vol. 11, no. 2 (March 1992), pp. 95–104.

44 Nicholson, G. C., 'Keeping Innovation Alive', *Research-Technology Management*, vol. 41, no. 3 (May–June 1998), pp. 34–40.

45 Gwynne, P., 'Skunk Works, 1990s-Style', *Research-Technology Management*, vol. 40, no. 4 (July–August 1997), pp. 18–23.

46 *Ibid.*

47 Chesbrough, H. W. and Teece, D. J., 'When is Virtual Virtuous? Organizing for Innovation', *Harvard Business Review*, vol. 74, no. 1 (January–February 19969, pp. 65–73.

48 Galvin, D. and Sucher, S., 'WingspanBank.com', *Harvard Business School Case Study*, no. 9-600-035 (July 2002).

49 Henke, J. W., Krachenberg, A. R. and Lyons, T. F., 'Cross-Functional Teams: Good Concept, Poor Implementation', *Journal of Product Innovation Management*, vol. 10, no. 3 (June 1993), pp. 216–29.

50 *Ibid.*

51 *Ibid.*

52 Thomson. L. *Personality Type* (Boston: Shambhala Publications, 1998).

53 Belbin, R. M., *Management Teams* (London: Heineman, 1981).

54 Hayes, N., *Managing Teams: A Strategy for Success* (London: Thompson Learning, 2002), ISBN 1-86152-782-9.

55 Tuckman, B., 'Developmental Sequence in Small Groups', *Psychological Bulletin*, vol. 63, no. 6 (1965), pp. 384–99.

56 Tuckman himself did not draw a diagram of how teams develop. However, based on his work, various 'teamwork wheels' have been drawn over the years based. The version we show originates from Cranfield School of Management.

57 Souder, W. E., 'Managing Relations Between R&D and Marketing in New Product Development Projects', *Journal of Product Innovation Management*, vol. 5, no.1 (March 1988), pp. 6–19.

58 *Ibid.*, p. 10.

59 Nixon, B., 'Research and Development Performance Measurement: A Case Study', *Management Accounting Review*, vol. 9 (September 1998), pp. 329–55.

60 Schein, E. H., 'Three Cultures of Management: The Key to Organizational Learning', *Sloan Management Review*, vol. 71, no. 4 (Fall 1996), pp. 9–20.

61 McDonough, E. F., 'Faster New Product Development: Investigating the Effects of Technology and Characteristics of the Project Leader and Team', *Journal of Product Innovation Management*, vol. 10, no. 3 (June 1993), pp. 241–50.

62 Barczak, G. and Wilemon, D., 'Leadership Differences in New Product Development Teams', *Journal of Product Innovation Management*, vol. 6, no. 4 (December 1989), pp. 259–67.

63 Cooper, R. G. and Kleinschmidt, E. J., 'Stage Gate Systems for New Product Success', *Marketing Management*, vol. 1, no. 4 (1992), pp. 20–9.

64 Balachandra, R., Brockhoff, K. K. and Pearson, A. W., 'R&D Project Termination Decisions: Processes, Communication, and Personnel Changes', *Journal of Product Innovation Management*, vol. 13, no. 3 (May 1996), pp. 245–56.

65 Meyers, P. W. and Wilemon, D., 'Learning in New Technology Development Teams', *Journal of Product Innovation Management*, vol. 6, no. 2 (June 1989), pp. 79–88.

66 Balogun, *et al.*, *op. cit.*, p. 196.

67 www: opp.co.uk.

68 Bratton, J. and Gold, J., *op. cit.* (2003).

69 Katz, R., 'Managing Professional Careers: The Influence of Job Longevity and Group Age', in Tushman, M. L. and Anderson, P. (eds)., *Managing Strategic Innovation and Change: A Collection of Readings* (New York: Oxford University Press, 1997), pp. 193–9.

70 For a good explanation of all of the theories refer to Mullins, L. M. *Management and Organisational Behaviour* (London: Pitman Publishing, 4th edn 1996), ISBN 0-273-61598-X, pp. 497–517.

71 Bratton, J. and Gold, J., *op. cit.* (2003), p. 13.

72 Bratton, J. and Gold, J., *op. cit.* (2003), p. 485.

73 Torrington, D. and Hall, L., *Personnel Management: HRM in Action* (London: Prentice Hall, 1995), ISBN 0-13-149543-7.

74 Goffin, K. and Pfeiffer, R., *Innovation Management in UK and German Manufacturing Companies* (London: Anglo-German Foundation Report Series, December 1999), ISBN 1-900834-17-0.

75 Daft, R. L., *Organization Theory and Design* (Cincinnati, USA: South-Western College Publishing, 1998), ISBN 0-538-87902-5, p. 350.

76 Boxall, P. and Purcell, J., *op. cit.*, (2003).

77 Ancona, D. G. and Caldwell, D. F., 'Making Teamwork Work: Boundary Management in Product Development Teams', in Tushman, M. L. and Anderson, P. (eds), *Managing Strategic Innovation and Change: A Collection of Readings* (New York: Oxford University Press, 1997), pp. 433–22.

78 Howard, R., 'The CEO as Organizational Architect', in Tushman, M. L. and Anderson, P. (eds), *Managing Strategic Innovation and Change: A Collection of Readings* (New York: Oxford University Press, 1997), pp. 631–41.

79 Pettigrew, A. and Fenton, E. M. (eds), *The Innovating Organization* (London: SAGE Publications, 2000), ISBN 0-7619-6434-7, p. 251.

80 Goffin, K., Lee-Mortimer, A. and New, C., *Managing Product Innovation for Competitive Advantage* (London: Haymarket Business Publications, November 1999), ISBN 1-902226-151.

81 Case based on: Szwejczewski, M., Wheatley, M., and Goffin, K., *Process Innovation in UK Manufacturing: Best Practice Makes Perfect* (London: Department

of Trade and Industry, dti/pub 5468/15k/06/01/np, June 2001). This report includes photographs of the Lever Fabergé factory.

Chapter 9   Boosting Innovation Performance

1   Kaplan, R. S. and Norton, D. P., *The Balanced Scorecard – Translating Strategy into Action* (Boston, MA.: Harvard Business School Press, 1996), ISBN 0-87584-651-3.

2   *Ibid.*, p. 97.

3   Goffin, K. and Pfeiffer, R., *Innovation Management in UK and German Manufacturing Companies* (London: Anglo-German Foundation Report Series, December 1999), ISBN 1-900834-17-0.

4   Holman, R., Kaas, H.-W. and Keeling, D., 'The Future of Product Development'. *The McKinsey Quarterly*, 2003 no. 3, pp. 28–39.

5   Slack, N., Chambers, S. and Johnston, B., *Operations Management*, 4th edn, (London: Pitman) ISBN 0273679066 (2003).

6   Neely, A., Richards, H., Mills, J., Platts, K. and Bourne, M., 'Designing Performance Measures: A Structured Approach', *International Journal of Operations and Production Management*, vol. 17, no. 11, (1997), pp. 1131–52.

7   Goffin, K., 'Enhancing Innovation Performance', *Management Quarterly*, Part 13, October 2001, pp. 18–26.

8   Voss, C. A., Chiesa, V. and Coughlan, P., *Innovation – Your Move, Self-Assessment Guide and Workbook* (London: Department of Trade and Industry (UK), 1993).

9   Johnston, R. and Clark, G., *Service Operations Management*, Financial Times – (London: Prentice Hall, 2001), ISBN 0-2736-39226.

10   *Ibid.*

11   Kleinknecht, A., 'Indicators of Manufacturing and Service Innovation: Their Strengths and Weaknesses', in Metcalf, J. S. and Miles, I., *Innovation Systems in the Service Economy* (Norwell, Massachusetts: Kluwer Academic Publishers, 2000), pp. 169–86.

12   Chiesa, V., Coughlan, P. and Voss, C. A., 'Development of a Technical Innovation Audit', *J. Prod. Innov. Manag.*, vol. 13, no. 2, March 1996, pp. 105–36.

13   Majaro, S., *The Creative Gap* (London: Longman, 1988), ISBN 0-85121-196-8.

14   Feige, A. and Crooker, R., 'Innovationen als Medizin gegen Arbeitslosigkeit und Mittelmass', *Frankfurter Allgemeine Zeitung*, 7 December 1998.

15   Duhamel, M., *Promoting Innovation Management Techniques in Europe* (Luxembourg: European Commission), December 1999.

16   British Standard, *Design Management Systems – Part 1: Guide to Managing Innovation*, British Standard BS7000-1:1999 (London: British Standards Institution, 1999).

17   Anonymous, 'Managing Change in Your Organization', *International Trade Forum*, Issue 2/2000, pp. 26–8.

18   Updated from Goffin, K. and Pfeiffer, R., *Innovation Management in UK and German Manufacturing Companies* (London: Anglo-German Foundation Report Series), December 1999, ISBN 1-900834-17-0.

19   Chiesa, V., Coughlan, P. and Voss, C. A., 'Development of a Technical Innovation Audit', *J. Prod. Innov. Manag.*, vol. 13, no. 2, March 1996, pp. 105–36.

20   Coughlan, P. and Brady, E., 'Evolution towards Integrated Product Development in Subsidiaries of Multinational Enterprises', *International Journal of Technology Management*, vol. 12, no. 7/8, 1996, pp. 733–47.

21 Golder, P., 'Insights from Senior Executives about Innovation in International Markets', *Journal of Product Innovation Management*, vol. 17, no. 5, 2000, pp. 326–40.

22 Borins, S., *The Challenge of Innovating in Government*, The Pricewaterhouse Coopers Endowment for The Business of Government, Innovations in Management Series (February 2001).

23 Calantone, R. J., Vickery, S. K. and Droege, C., 'Business Performance and Strategic New Product Development Activities: An Empirical Investigation', *Journal of Product Innovation Management*, vol. 12, no. 3, 1995, pp. 214–23.

24 McGourty, J., Tarshis, L. A. and Dominick, P., 'Managing Innovation: Lessons from World Class Organizations', *International Journal of Technology Management*, vol. 11, no. 3/4 (1996), pp. 354–68.

25 Thamhain, H. J., 'Managing Technologically Innovative Team Efforts Toward New Product Success', *J. Prod. Innov. Manag.*, vol. 7, no. 1, March 1990, pp. 5–18.

26 British Standard, *op. cit.* (1999).

27 Borins, *op. cit.* (2001).

28 British Standard, *op. cit.* (1999).

29 Day *et al.*, *op. cit.* (1998).

30 Linder, J. C., Jarvenpaa, S. and Davenport, T. H., 'Towards an Innovation Sourcing Strategy', *MIT Sloan Management Review*, vol. 44, no. 4, Summer 2003, pp. 43–9.

31 Webber and LaBarre, *op. cit.* (2001).

32 Chesbrough, H. W., 'The Era of Open Innovation', *MIT Sloan Management Review*, vol. 44, no. 3, Spring 2003, pp. 35–41.

33 Chambers and Boghani, *op. cit.* (1998).

34 Sakkab, N. Y., 'Connect and Develop Complements Research and Develop at P&G'. *Research-Technology Management*, vol. 45, no. 2, March–April 2002, pp. 38–45.

35 Anonymous, 'Managing Change in Your Organization', *International Trade Forum*, Issue 2/2000, pp. 26–8.

36 Karol *et al.*, *op. cit.* (2002).

37 Cooper, R. G. and Kleinschmidt, E. J., 'Stage Gate Systems for New Product Success', *Marketing Management*, vol. 1, no. 4, (1992), pp. 20–9.

38 Chambers, C. A. and Boghani, A. B., 'Knowledge Management: An Engine for Innovation', *Prism*, Second Quarter 1998, pp. 31–9.

39 Day, G. S., Gold, B. and Kuczmarski, T. D., 'Significant Issues for the Future of Product Innovation', *J. Prod. Innov. Manag.*, vol. 11, no. 1, January 1994, pp. 69–75.

40 Karol, R. A., Loeser, R. C. and Tait, R. H., 'Better New Business Development at Dupont-I', *Research-Technology Management*, vol. 45, no. 1, January–February 2002, pp. 24–30.

41 Smith, G. R., Herbein, W. C. and Morris, R. C., 'Front-End Innovation at AlliedSignal', *Research-Technology Management*, vol. 42, no. 6, November–December 1999, pp. 15–24.

42 Case based on company documentation, an interview and personal correspondence with Cobra managers in May 2004.

43 Thamheim, *op. cit.* (1990).

44 Webber, A. M. and LaBarre, P., 'The Innovation Conversation', *Research-Technology Management*, vol. 44, no. 5, September–October 2001, pp. 9–11.

45 Borins, *op. cit.* (2001).

46 McGourty, *op. cit.* (1996).

47 Case based on an interview with Massimo Fumarola, conducted by K. Goffin in May 2004.

48 Wheelwright, S. C. and Clark, K., *Revolutionizing Product Development: Quantum Leaps in Speed, Efficiency, and Quality* (New York: The Free Press, 1992), ISBN 0-02-905515-6.

49 Bowen, H. K., Clark, K. B., Hollaway, C. A. and Wheelwright, S. C., 'Development Projects: The Engine of Renewal', *Harvard Business Review*, vol. 72, no. 5 (Sept.–Oct. 1994), pp. 110–19.

50 Koners, U. and Goffin, K., 'From Tacit to Explicit? An Exploratory Study of Knowledge and Learning from R&D Projects?', *Proc. 9th International Product Development Conference*, Sophia Antipolis, France, 27–28 May 2002, pp. 469–84.

51 Schindler, M. and Gassmann, O., 'Projektabwicklung gewinnt durch wissenschaftsmanagement: Ergebnisse einer empirischen Studie die Konzernentwicklung der Schindler Aufzüge AG', *Wissenschaftsmanagement*, vol. 1, January–February 2000, pp. 38–45.

52 Tushman, M. L., Newman, W. H. and Romanelli, E., 'Convergence and Upheaval: Managing the Unsteady Pace of Organizational Evolution', in Tushman, M. L. and Anderson, P. (eds). *Managing Strategic Innovation and Change: A Collection of Readings* (New York: Oxford University Press, 1997), pp. 583–94.

53 *Ibid.*

54 Schein, E. H., 'Three Cultures of Management: The Key to Organizational Learning', *Sloan Management Review*, vol. 71, no. 3, Fall 1996, pp. 9–20.

55 O'Connor, P., 'From Experience: Implementing a Stage-Gate Process: A Multi-Company Perspective', *J. Prod. Innov. Mgmt.*, vol. 11, no. 3, 1994, pp. 183–200.

56 Beckhard, R. and Harris, R. T., *Organisation Transitions: Managing Complex Change* (London: Addison Wesley, 1987), ISBN 0201108879.

57 Tushman, M. L. and O'Reilly III, C. A., *Winning through Innovation: A Practical Guide to Leading Organizational Change and Renewal* (Boston: Harvard Business School Press, 2002), ISBN 1-57851-821-0, p. 49.

58 *Ibid.*

59 Pettigrew, A. and Fenton, E. M. (eds), *The Innovating Organization* (London: SAGE Publications, 2000), ISBN 0-7619-6434-7.

60 Balogun, J., Hope Hailey, V. with Johnson, G. and Scholes, K., *Exploring Strategic Change* (London: Prentice Hall, 1999), ISBN 0-13-263856-8.

61 Stalk, G. and Hout, T. M., *Competing Against Time: How Time-based Competition is Reshaping Global Markets* (New York: The Free Press, 1990), ISBN 0-02-915291-7.

62 Schein, E. H., 'Coming to a New Awareness of Organizational Culture', *Sloan Management Review*, vol. 25, no. 4, Winter 1984, pp. 3–16.

63 Case adapted with permission from Goffin, K., Lee-Mortimer, A. and New, C., *Managing Product Innovation for Competitive Advantage* (London: Haymarket Publications, 1999), ISBN 1-902226-15-1.

Chapter 10 The Fugure of Innovation Management

1 Quoted by Bernstein, P. L., *Against The Gods: the Remarkable Story of Risk* (New York: John Wiley 1998), p. 203.

2 'A brother for her', *The Economist*, 18 December 2004, p. 111.

3   Maslow, A. H., *Towards a Psychology of Being*, 3rd edn (Wiley 1998).

4   Thomke, S., 2001, 'Enlightened Experimentation: the new imperative for innovation.' *Harvard Business Review*, Feb 2001, pp. 67–75.

5   Mackintosh, J., 2004, 'The assembly line is bunk says former Ford executive', *Financial Times*, April 20, 2004, p. 22.

6   Kahn, H. and Wiener, A., *The Year 2000: a framework for speculation on the next thirty-three years* (New York: MacMillan 1967).

7   Albright, R. E., 'What can past technology forecasts tell us about the future?', *Technological Forecasting and Social Change*, June 2002 ,vol. 69, no. 5, pp. 443–64.

8   Moore, G., 'Cramming more components onto integrated circuits', *Electronics*, 38 (1965).

9   Asenov, A., 'Every atom counts', *IEE Electronic Systems and Software*, 2004, vol. 2, issue 6, pp. 26–32

10 Walko, J., 'Scaling is dead. Long live innovation!' *IEE Review*, vol. 23 (2005).

11 There is great scope for argument over when technologies were invented and when they can be said to be fully exploited. For one view see Dussauge, P., Hart, S. and Ramanantsoa, B., *Strategic Technology Management* (Chichester: John Wiley, 1987) ISBN 0-471-93418-6, p. 19.

12 www.smart.com.

13 Challenge forum: 2003, *'Weak signals, Harsh impacts'*, www.chforum.org.

14 'Innovative India', *The Economist*, April 3, 2004, pp. 67–8.

15 Minderhoud, S., 'Product innovation at an ever increasing pace: experiences at Philips Electronics', *9th Annual Cambridge Technology Management Symposium*, Oct. 2003.

16 Case based on 'Identifying and Tapping the Potentials of Possible Future Business via Structured Communication – Visions of Vodafone Pilotentwicklung' in Kohlgrüber, M., Schnauffer, H.-G. and Jaeger, D. (eds), *Das einzigartige Unternehmen* (Berlin: Springer, 2003), ISBN 3-540-00581-1, company documentation, and interviews with Dr Christiane Hipp, Torsten Herzberg and Eva Weber in December 2004.

17 A very complete account of the venture is given in Takahashi, D., *Opening the X Box* (Roseville, Ca: Prima Publishing, 2002).

18 Takahashi (2002), *op. cit.*

19 *Ibid.* p. 151.

20 'A Serious Contest', *The Economist*, 8 May 2004, p. 73.

21 'Battling for the palm of your hand', *The Economist*, 1 May 2004, pp. 79–81.

22 Golder, P., 'Insights from Senior Executives about Innovation in International Markets', *Journal of Product Innovation Management*, vol. 17, no. 5, 2000, pp. 326–40.

23 Peters, T., *The Circle of Innovation* (Hodder & Stoughton, 1997) ISBN 0-340-71720-3, p. 453.

24 Case based on interviews with Mike Northcott and William Pipkin, Hewlett-Packard internal documentation, and Zell, D. M., Glassman, A. and Duron, S. A., 'Accelerating the Strategy Process: One Industry Giant's Attempt', *Proceedings of the Academy of Management Annual Meeting*, August 2004.

# Index